The Bhagavad Gita
in the Light of Kriya Yoga

THAT IS THE PATH WHICH IS DIRECTED BY THE REALIZED

क्षणमिह सज्जन सङ्गतिरेका भवति भवार्णव तरणे नौका

The Bhagavad Gita
in the Light of Kriya Yoga

Book One

PARAMAHAMSA HARIHARANANDA

Based on Babaji's, Lahiri Mahasaya's, and Shriyukteshwarji's original and authentic teachings on Kriya Yoga

Compiled and organized by
Swami Prajñanananda Giri

KRIYA YOGA INSTITUTE
HOMESTEAD, FLORIDA

Published by the Kriya Yoga Institute
P.O. Box 924615
Homestead, FL 33092-4615 U.S.A.
E-mail: institute@kriya.org
Web Site: www.kriya.org

The cover illustration is a classical style of hand painting from Orissa, India. The scene from the Mahabharata depicts Lord Krishna addressing Arjuna regarding the entire realm of the manifestation of the human spirit. The dialogue between Arjuna and the Lord on the battlefield is the Bhagavad Gita.

Library of Congress Catalog Card Number: 93-61393
ISBN: 0-9639107-1-X

PRINTED IN THE UNITED STATES OF AMERICA

ENVIRONMENTAL NOTE:
ALL PRINTED MATERIALS USED IN THIS PAPERBACK HAVE BEEN PRODUCED WITH ENVIRONMENTAL CONSIDERATIONS IN MIND.

We would like to offer our deepest love and thanks for the many volunteers who have participated in the production of this book. Their love and service to God and gurus has been exemplary.

EDITING & TYPESETTING: Peter Bumpus
ASSISTANT EDITORS: Little Ma, Jim Barr, Margot Borden, Terri Wright
TYPING: Ana McGroarty
COVER DESIGN: Chip Weston
ART: Lloyd Abrams, Bob Carty, Laurie Stuart-Nelson

I dedicate this book to all true seekers.

– Paramahamsa Hariharananda

Table of Contents

Table of Contents

Volume Two

Table of Contents

Volume Three

List of Illustrations

I pray very deeply to God, saints and sages of all religions, Paramahamsa Yogananda, Shriyukteshwarji, Lahiri Mahasaya, and Babaji that they will write through me the correct scientific and metaphysical meaning of the Bhagavad Gita, so that everyone can perceive a new light and can follow the Bhagavad Gita. Everyone who meditates accordingly, within a very short period will experience the truth in human life and will achieve Self-realization.

– PARAMAHAMSA HARIHARANANDA

Foreword

by Swami Prajñanananda Giri

The Journey

Life is a journey. People travel through it carrying the baggage of their karma, the seed impressions of all their previous activity, the aggregate balance sheet of all their pleasure and pain, and the results of all their interactions with friend and foe—all confused with their likes and dislikes. Some may consider life a pilgrimage; to others it may be a vacation, but its true purpose is to fulfill the cherished goal. When this goal is achieved, one has returned to where the journey began. Like a circle, the journey of life is complete only when it reaches its starting point. We must return to our source to fulfill our lives—with love, joy, and bliss.

On the journey of life we gather many experiences—sweet, sour, bitter, or salty. To transcend all these burning experiences, we must manifest our hidden diversity and inner spirituality. Then, the journey of life can rise from the elemental to the supramental state of consciousness, and finally to complete emancipation, as with Buddha, Christ, Ramakrishna, Lahiri Mahasaya, and others.

To smooth the hazardous path of evolution, the journey requires a great deal of effort. Continuous effort and proper guidance make the journey more pleasurable and less tiring. An experienced guide and a guidebook will help the traveller overcome the obstacles on this greatest adventure. The guide is the expert, one who has successfully completed the journey. The guidebook is the holy scriptures, which inspire, encourage, discipline, and dictate rules for daily life until one has completed the journey.

The Guidebook

From time immemorial, human beings have been on the path, which is sometimes straight and undisturbed, but many times it twists and turns and causes us to forget our destination or lose our way in the thick forest of material splendor. The guide and the guidebook are vitally important: They constantly turn our tired legs (our outlook) in the right direction.

Krishna, Christ, Moses, and Mohammed all lived in body form, and many realized masters and saints have walked the earth. In no place or time has human civilization lacked the blessing of spiritual guides to illuminate the path to liberation. It is only the failure to search that prevents us from discovering them. In addition, every religion and human civilization has been blessed with scriptures unique in their approach. One of these is the Bhagavad Gita. Writing a foreword for the commentary of this holy book is like trying to shine light on the sun with a lamp.

From my early childhood I have been reading this holy scripture, listening to its interpretation, even from the mouth of my own Guruji. Everyday I read, wonder, and ponder, ever amazed to find the fathomless divine ocean in this text. The Bhagavad Gita is a religious classic, a philosophical treatise, an esoteric work, a popular poem, a book on metaphysics and ethics, and a handbook on yoga and wisdom for spiritual seekers. As a guidebook, the Bhagavad Gita is unique in its approach, content, theory, philosophy, practical implications, and deep spiritual truth.

The Holy Books

The Bhagavad Gita is the Bible of the Hindus, but this comparison does not demonstrate the importance of this beautiful work. In civilization today, both these holy books have been widely printed and circulated. The Bible has been published and popularized all over the world by the Christian church. The Bhagavad Gita, without the support of any religion, has been spread by the love of those who have found the value of its hidden treasure.

All holy books transform our lives with their lofty ideas and practical guidelines. The Bible, Torah, Koran, and Bhagavad Gita all share the purpose of making life holy through inner transformation. Every holy book is a treasure-house of spiritual knowledge, but sincere seekers need proper understanding and must apply the scriptural teachings without a dogmatic outlook or fanatical ideas. These books are holy because, when followed, they help us transcend all limitations and bring completeness to life. In order to perceive the importance of the Bhagavad Gita as a scripture, one must understand a little about the breadth and depth of India's scriptures as a whole.

India's Spiritual Wisdom

Every country and civilization is unique. India, the home of the most ancient living civilization, has brought many religions to the world, such as *sanatana dharma* (Hinduism), Buddhism, Judaism, Sikhism, and others, and has originated much profound spiritual wisdom through many scriptures.

In Sanskrit, these scriptures are called *shastras*, from the root verb *shas*, meaning to teach, to rule, to command, to inform, to advise, and to correct. *Shastras*, the scriptures, are the theoretical aspect. When put into practice, they become *sadhana*. One who follows the scriptures is called *shishya*, the disciple. A disciple follows the path of discipline and is instructed by the guide in accordance with the guidebook.

Knowledge is the truth revealed. It is not the monopoly of anyone. Spiritual knowledge is clearly distinct from material knowledge. The subject of most scriptures is spiritual experiences—the revelations gained through a life of self-discipline and meditation.

Age-old spiritual wisdom found in different scriptures are classified as:

Shrutis:	the Vedas
Smritis:	books on ethics and theology
Puranas:	ancient episodes on dynasties of royal or spiritual significance
Itihasas:	history books
Prakriyas:	supplementary spiritual texts.

The Vedas

According to Hindu belief, the Vedas are without beginning. They are thought to be the texts revealed to the *rishis* as a result of their pure and contemplative lives. The Vedas are *apurusheyam,* that is, not authored by *purusha* or man. The Vedas contain many *suktas* or words of wisdom and wise precepts attributed to several sages, but in general, the *rishis* were merely the seers of the mantras—they discovered the Vedas, but they did not compose them or create them. Man is only an instrument of God who can spread these divine words.

The name "Vedas" is derived from the root verb, *vid,* to know, so literally the Vedas means knowledge, the books of wisdom. The word *vidya,* which means practical knowledge, also comes from *vid.*

The Vedas are four in number: Rik, Yajur, Sama, and Atharva. They are written and divided into different *sakhas* (recensions). There are 21 in the Rik, 101 in the Yajur, 1,000 in the Sama, and 9 in the Atharva, a total of 1,131. Only 10 recensions are available today. The others have been lost over the course of time.

The Vedas are also known as *shruti,* which refers to knowledge that is to be heard, contemplated, and meditated upon. Each *sakha* or recension of the Vedas is again divided into four parts: *samhita, brahmana, aranyaka, and upanishad.*

Samhita means that which has been collected and arranged in the form of a mantra. *Sam* means complete; *hita* means goodness and auspiciousness. This section of a recension always concerns bringing good news to people through the proper use of mantras. The *brahmanas* contain the Vedic ritual practices. *Samhita* (mantra) puts *brahmanas* (the rituals) into practice. *Brahmanas* are the guidebook that explain the art of using mantras.

Aranyaka is derived from *aranya,* meaning forest. The first two parts of a recension describe family life, but the *aranyaka* deals with the art of mental purity, attained through constant discipline, by retreating into the forest and spending time in contemplation and meditation.

The *Upanishads,* the essence of the Vedas, are placed near the end of the *aranyakas.* The four divisions are described as a harvest: *samhita* is the tree, *brahmana* is the flower, *aranyaka* is the unripe fruit, and the *upanishad* is the ripe, sweet fruit.

Upa-ni-shada means to sit side by side. It signifies the life that the disciple leads while sitting by the side of the teacher. It also means "that which brings one to Brahman's side." On this path, one can quickly and completely remove all ignorance and reach the state of perfect knowledge. The Upanishads are instructions open to personal interpretation by fit and worthy disciples. The Upanishads are also known as the Vedanta. Vedanta in its derivation, is *veda* and *anta* (end). It has two meanings: one is the text found towards the end of the Vedas, and the other is the ultimate experience, the end of all efforts to know the truth.

Smritis: The Books of Law

To achieve the goals of life, every person must follow some moral and ethical principles, as a householder or as a renunciate, living in society or in seclusion. These ethical and moral principles are sometimes very intricate and subtle, and are therefore difficult to understand and practice. Very systematic, logical, and analytical recordings are found in the Smritis. They are attributed to many sages like Manu, Parashara, Vyasa, and others. At times of confusion or when we are caught in a moral dilemma, the Smritis indicate what action should be taken or avoided, and what is good or evil. These books guide us through difficult situations.

Puranas

The Puranas are the third set of scriptures. These eighteen major and minor verses are accompanied by some auxiliary ones. Most were written by Vyasa and other sages. The Puranas can be called the magnifying glass of the Vedas. The Vedic injunctions presented as short and subtle statements within the Vedas are elaborated in the form of stories and anecdotes in the Puranas. Stories that instruct and guide leave a permanent impression on the mind. The Vedic injunctions such as restraint, patience, compassion, chastity, and other values are nicely illustrated by events in the lives of men and women. The Puranas are a creative literary work, an allegorical narration of the spiritual journey filled with symbolic characters such as demons and gods that represent the weaknesses and strengths in a person. The literal actions of the *devas* (gods) who teach lessons and the demons who create disasters reflect the more subtle aspects of good and evil in the external world and within ourselves.

The Puranas, eighteen in number, are broadly classified into three categories: the Vaishnava, the Shaiva, and the Shakta, covering different paths of spiritual practice and worship. The eighteen Puranas are: (1) Brahma Purana; (2) Padma Purana; (3) Vishnu Purana; (4) Shiva Purana; (5) Shrimad Bhagavata; (6) Narada Purana; (7) Markandeya Purana; (8) Bhavishya Purana; (9) Brahma Vairvarta Purana; (10) Agni Purana; (11) Linga Purana; (12) Varaha Purana; (13) Skanda Purana; (14) Vamana Purana; (15) Kurma Purana; (16) Matsya Purana; (17) Garuda Purana; and (18) Brahmanda Purana.

In addition to the eighteen Puranas, there are officially eighteen Upapuranas, although there are actually many more. The Upapuranas (auxiliary Puranas) contain descriptions of the glories of each month, guidelines for what should be practiced and followed each month, and a narration regarding the significance of holy places.

The Itahasas

Itahasas literally means history books. In India, people did not write history as chronological records the way we do in the West today. The two great works of Indian history, according to the scholars of the scriptures (Shastras), are the epic stories of the Ramayana, written by Valmiki, and the Mahabharata, written by Vyasa.

The Ramayana and the Mahabharata are also considered great epics, mostly describing different aspects of human civilization, including the various branches of knowledge. The stories in the Ramayana and the Mahabharata are in the bloodstream of the people of India. The Ramayana is rich with the life and teachings of Rama. Along with the family stories of the solar dynasty, it contains episodes relating to the lives of saints and sages and even commoners. The Ramayana shows us how to live our daily lives, which are full of chaos and confusion, without being distracted from the goal and the principles of life.

The Mahabharata is called the *panchamaveda*, the fifth Veda. It is an important epic, the scripture of India's eternal spiritual heritage and a rare treasure-house of wisdom for all mankind. According to its author, "It unveils the secrets of the Vedas and contains the essence of the Upanishads. It elaborates on the Itihasas and the Puranas, astrology, morality and ethics, life, science, medicine, charity, and generosity; it also describes holy places of pilgrimage, rivers, forests, oceans, and mountains. It is the greatest epic of mankind, rich with knowledge and applied knowledge (*jñana* and *vijñana*). It is a book on theology, political philosophy, a scripture of devotion and action, and a synopsis of all Aryan scriptures."

In the available editions of the Mahabharata there are 100,217 verses. Maharshi Krishna Dvipayana Vyasa, also called Maharshi Vyasa, authored this beautiful epic. His name comes from the following sources: Maharshi meaning great sage, Krishna for his black complexion, Dvipayana after the island on which he was born, and finally, his given name, Vyasa.

Maharshi Vyasa's Birth and Childhood

A spiritual master named Parashara had marvelous spiritual power due to his deep meditation and self-discipline. In a vision he was instructed to have a child who could inherit all of his spiritual treasure and be the mouthpiece of all spiritual wisdom.

After searching far and wide, Parashara finally met a young maiden by the name of Satyvati. Although Satyvati was very beautiful, her body emanated a natural bad odor that caused others to avoid her. Because of this odor, she was also known as Matsyagandha, the lady with the smell of fish. Despite this condition, Parashara chose her to be the mother of his child. By using his yogic powers he transformed Matsyagandha into Padmagandha, the lady with lotus smell. This young beautiful maiden gave birth to Parashara's cherished child on the small island of Dvipayana. This divine child was born on the full moon day in the month of July, which, to this day, is celebrated as Gurupurnima, the full moon of the gurus. On this day, the Master's Day, every spiritual student offers homage and devotion to his spiritual preceptor.

The divine child Vyasa became highly educated in morality, science, and spirituality as a result of diligent training by his father and mother. Therefore, he is also known as Vedavyasa, the great sage Vyasa or Shri Vyasa.

In Indian mythology Vyasa is considered immortal, and his name is synonymous with divine knowledge and wisdom. Vyasa, according to many scholars, is not a name, but a title endowed with supernatural power. The Vedas, as described earlier, are a vast treasure-house of spiritual wisdom and material knowledge. Prior to Vyasa, the Vedas were passed on primarily by memorization, chanting, and recitation from teacher to student. Vyasa compiled, arranged, and edited the scriptures of the Vedas and divided them into the four great books: Rik, Yajur, Sama, and Atharva. Thus, he was called Vedavyasa.

Since Vedavyasa was the source of divine wisdom and the author of many of the greatest scriptures of mankind, he was considered to be the master of mankind. Vyasa had many successful disciples who followed in his footsteps and carried out his work. He educated and trained his own son, Suka, who became the foremost of the seers and a *paramahamsa.* Vyasa, through his tremendous power of meditation, could see the past, present, and future at will. He could foresee the state of disaster that was going to befall mankind in the battle of Mahabharata.

He authored, as described earlier, the eighteen Puranas, the Brahmasutras, Vyasasmriti, and even the commentary on the Yoga Sutras of Patañjali known as Vyasa Bhasya. Along with these works, he also edited the Vedas. A scholar, a yogi, a great spiritual personality, Vyasa was revered by people of all classes and all stature. He was loved by royal dynasties and by saints and sages.

Wisdom is beyond the reach of the senses and the conception of the mind; it is realized through *prasthana trayi,* the tranquil mind, which is the result of deep meditation and study of the scriptures. India's spiritual wisdom is contained in many scriptures, thus allowing each person to interpret and receive them at their own level of consciousness and understanding. The scriptures give discipline to our lives and enlighten us if we follow them in the right spirit under the direct guidance of a qualified teacher.

Three major holy scriptures are highly recommended by all the masters for study and practice. Collectively, they are also known as *prasthana trayi. Prasthana* has several connotations, two of which are "departure" and "place of reality." *Trayi* means the number three.

Prasthana trayi is the set of three holy books that enables a person to go back to the source. As a river is born of a cloud and returns to the cloud through evaporation, similarly God is the source of creation, which is maintained and sustained through His love and power. God is all-pervading. The process of God-realization, or reaching reality, is accelerated through deep study of the scriptures, constant company of a true spiritual guide, and regular practice of self-discipline and meditation.

These three texts are:

- Shruti prasthana (*shruti* meaning the Vedas, the scriptures for realization from the Vedas), the Upanishads
- Smriti prasthana (the scripture based on the Smritis, the recorded spiritual treatise), the Bhagavad Gita
- Tarka prasthana (the scripture learned from logic, reasoning, and a system), the Brahmasutras

Along with the vast work of editing the Vedas, the vast treasurehouse of spiritual wisdom and material knowledge, Vyasa edited the Upanishads, the essence of the Vedas, the final and ultimate experience (*Vedanta*). *Vedanta* means the end of knowledge; knowledge ends in wisdom. Knowledge is the beginning, and wisdom is the end. From all the outstanding work of Vyasa, a small section of the Mahabharata was extracted, which is the Bhagavad Gita.

The third book, the Brahmasutras, contains aphorisms on the absolute, Brahman. These aphorisms expound subtle spiritual truths in a collection of phrases and sentences. Composed by the great sage Vyasa, this book is one of the most lovable books for seekers to this day.

The three royal descriptions of the eternal welfare of mankind are the collection of mantras (mystical, metaphysical statements) in the Upanishads, the aphorisms in the Brahmasutras, and the *shlokas* in the Bhagavad Gita.

The Bhagavad Gita

The Bhagavad Gita, popularly known as the Gita, is the Divine Song of the Lord. This small but beautiful scripture is found in the Mahabharata. The Mahabharata consists of eighteen volumes or *parvas* (literally meaning joints). The Gita is found in the sixth book called the Bhishma Parva, which contains the twenty-fifth to forty-second chapters.

Gitas are a spiritual tradition in India. Many holy books under the title of the Gita are still popular in Indian culture and spirituality. The estimates vary, but according to some, there are thirty-six books called Gita. Some of the Gitas are extremely important such as the Ashtavakra Gita, a discussion between the sage Ashtavakra and his student Janaka, a royal seer; the Uddhava Gita, a dialogue between Shri Krishna and Uddhava; the Guru Gita, a discussion between Siva and Parvati; and the Avadhuta Gita, the teachings of Avadhuta, a renowned, naked wandering saint, and so forth.

Although the Bhagavad Gita is only a small part of the great epic, the Mahabharata, it is the essence of the Upanishads. It contains the knowledge of the absolute, the Brahma Vidya, and it is a beautiful scripture on yoga. It consists of a discussion between Shri Krishna, the master, and Arjuna, the disciple, as recorded by Vyasa. It is also a conversation between the blind king, Dhritarashtra, and his knowledgeable minister, Samjaya. The Bhagavad Gita was delivered on the battlefield of Dharmakshetra Kurukshetra, before the battle commenced.

Krishna, the Teacher

Krishna is the teacher, the *acharya* or *gitcharya* of the Bhagavad Gita. Although people have many contradicting and controversial ideas about him, Krishna is nonetheless a divine personality. His life and teachings are elaborately described in three great epics, the Bhagavatam, the Mahabharata, and the Harivamsa, as well as in the Vedas and the Upanishads. His name is found in the Chhandogya Upanishad (3:17:6), where he is depicted as a historical and mystical character.

Krishna was born in the era of *dwapara* (about 5,000 years ago), in the prison of a tyrannical ruler, Kamsa, his maternal uncle. He was secretly transferred from the dark prison cell in Mathura on a rainy August night, at midnight. He spent his childhood in Vrindavan in the families of milkmen. As per tradition, he was initiated by his *kulaguru,* Acharya Garga, who gave him the divine name Krishna.

At the age of ten years and eight months, Krishna left Vrindavan. He went to the town of Mathura, where his presence brought an end to the tyranny of Kamsa. He freed his parents from the prison and was sent to the *gurukulam* (a hermitage for the education of sages) of Sandipani in Ujjaini. Together, Krishna and his elder brother, Balarama, attained complete knowledge of many subjects including politics, morality, warfare, and diplomacy. Then they moved to Dwaraka, a beautiful city on the west cost of Bharata (India), surrounded by water. Here he learned yoga from Ghora Angirosa, a great yogi.

During this period, there was a great dynasty of Kurus ruling the major part of the country from the capital, Hastinapura. In this dynasty of Kurus, a very critical situation occurred. The eldest son, Dhritarashtra, was not allowed to become king because he was blind. Instead, the younger brother, Pandu, was given the throne, and he ruled the kingdom with love and care. While Pandu was living in the forest, he met a tragic end to his life. His two wives Kunti and Madri and their five children, Yudhishthira, Bhima, Arjuna, Nakula, and Sahadeva (the Pandavas), were left behind. Madri sacrificed her life for her husband.

Pandu's older brother, Dhritarashtra, had 100 children with his wife Gandhari, who are collectively called the Kauravas. Duryodhana was the eldest. In their youth, the 105 cousins lived together. After the death of his brother, Dhritarashtra was crowned king, although unfit to rule due to his blindness. He received practical assistance from Bhishma, his uncle, who was a lifelong celibate, who promised not to take the throne.

Among the Pandavas and the Kauravas, Yudhishthira was the eldest. The Pandavas were of good nature, noble, honest, and generous, while all the Kauravas, including Duryodhana, were jealous, egotistical, and full of vanity and pride. All the Pandavas and the

Kauravas were taught and trained in their youth by Bhishma, their great uncle, as well as by Drona and Kripa (both happened to be in-laws). All were reputable teachers of the time.

The Pandavas, because of their self-control, discipline, service to the teacher, and devotion, excelled in every aspect of education, which inwardly incited jealousy in the minds of the Kauravas. Later on, as it was the law of the time, Yudhishthira, as the eldest, became the crown prince, which was unbearable for the Kauravas.

In light of the imminent inner rivalry and the family rift, and to bring peace to the kingdom, Duryodhana was enthroned and given part of the kingdom to rule. Being greedy and dishonest, he tried all evil means to bring an end to the Pandavas. He did not hesitate to poison them, and he secretly tried to burn them in fire. But the Pandavas escaped safely from all Duryodhana's evil tricks.

Finding no other way to reach his dishonest goal, Duryodhana decided to try to win the entire kingdom by using the evil means of playing dice. His maternal uncle, Shakuni, and his friend Karna assisted him in this heinous work. Duryodhana was successful. The Pandavas lost the kingdom, were humiliated, and were exiled for fourteen years, plus one year of living incognito. If they were traced or detected while living in disguise, they would have to serve another fourteen-year period of exile.

The Pandavas spent fourteen years in prayer and meditation in holy company and in holy places, while the Kauravas spent the same time in enjoyment, pleasure, and humiliating others.

When the Pandavas completed the period of exile, Duryodhana was supposed to return the kingdom to them. However, when the time came, he did not want to surrender his power. He even boastfully declared that he would not give them a piece of land the size of the point of a needle—without a battle. War was inevitable. Shri Krishna and other respected beings tried unsuccessfully to convince the evil-minded Duryodhana to change his mind, but the time for the battle at Kurukshetra arrived.

Both Duryodhana and Arjuna, the middle brother of the Pandavas, sought the help of Shri Krishna. Shri Krishna offered them two options: one could have all his military power, but Krishna would ride with the other as an unarmed chariot driver. Duryodhana eagerly preferred the first option, while Arjuna was delighted to have Shri Krishna as his chariot driver.

The Stages of Krishna's Life

The life of Shri Krishna, as described in different epics and scriptures, is full of fascinating episodes and marvelous teachings about his skill and talent, which we can learn from and apply in daily life.

As a boy in Vrindavan, Krishna was the epitome of divine love. His gait, look, talk, dance, and flute playing attracted the minds of everyone: humans, animals, and even plants and trees. During His childhood, which lasted ten years and eight months, while He was full of childlike athletic activity, Krishna became a center of reform in the inner and outer lives of people. In the second part of His life, Shri Krishna undertook his education and training. He lived at Dwaraka and led the life of a householder, while trying to bring peace and prosperity to people. During the third part of His life, Krishna was a teacher. He was a disciple of three great teachers of that time: Acharya Garga, Sage Sandipani, and Ghora Angirasa. He became the instrument for transmitting the essence of spiritual wisdom and a practical yogic lifestyle to His beloved disciples.

Mystical Krishna

Krishna's life was that of a great personality and a divine incarnation; his place and activities are called *lila* in classical language. Many people consider Shri Krishna to be more mystical than historical.

Although Krishna is a mythological and mystical figure, the yogis respect Krishna as the indwelling Self, the life principle in every living being. The body is regarded as a vehicle for reaching God-realization, for reaching the abode of the soul. Krishna literally means black, the absence of any color, namely, the formless state before creation. Krishna as the blue-colored boy, is the symbol of vastness. He is as infinite as the sky and the ocean are blue.

Krishna is a historical character as well as an *avatar*, the infinite God manifested in infinite existence. Krishna does not stand as a hero, rather as a secret center and a hidden guide in the life of every person.

In its etymological derivation, the name "Krishna" comes from *krish,* the land that can be cultivated, and *na,* the formless presence of the divine; therefore, Krishna is a name for the divinity manifested in the body land that needs to be trained and cultivated.

Flute and Conch

As a boy, Krishna always loved the flute, and from his youth onwards, he always had a conch. Both the conch and the flute are symbols of sound, *nadabrahma.* Sound is a divine aspect in meditation, through which one can reach higher levels of consciousness. These two instruments are the symbolic representation of meditation on the cosmic divine sound.

In yogic language, the flute is human life, the cerebrospinal system of humans. The traditional Indian bamboo flute has seven holes representing the seven centers in the spine and brain, of which six holes are played by the fingers and the seventh by the lips of the person who plays. In every human body, the mouth of the Lord, the indwelling soul, is breathing in and out, giving us the direct experience of the song of life.

Krishna's Disciples

Krishna is a universal teacher, beyond the limitations of time and place. Even in childhood, His life held a great message for all of mankind. While playing as a small child, He taught the art of selfless love for all. Over the course of time, His life and teachings, His dynamic leadership, and His knowledge and love touched the hearts of millions. Innumerable people all over the world love and follow His practices and teachings, worshipping Krishna as a divine incarnation.

Among His followers, two are considered to be his closest disciples, Arjuna and Uddhava, who was a Yadava. Coincidently, both of them were his cousins.

Arjuna, the son of Kunti (Krishna's aunt) and the middle brother of the Pandavas, was the most famous warrior. In the Bhagavad Gita (10), Krishna declared, "Among the Pandavas, I am Arjuna." Arjuna is a true seeker with a multifaceted personality. The name Arjuna means, *a - rajju – na,* one who is not tied. He is free from all bondage, but is considered to be in bondage. Another meaning of Arjuna is the art of earning real wealth. Arjuna, besides being the cousin of Krishna, was also his close friend (*sakta,* in Sanskrit). He eventually married Subhadra, Shri Krishna's sister. Arjuna followed Krishna's guidance, and their intricate spiritual conversation on the pain of Kurukshetra is the Bhagavad Gita.

The other close disciple of Shri Krishna was Uddhava, who was also his last disciple. This episode and the teaching and instructions of Shri Krishna to Uddhava are found in the Bhagavatam, which was compiled later as a separate book, sometimes called the Uddhava Gita.

Both these disciples followed their great teacher and His practical instructions with diligence and love. They excelled by practicing His teachings.

Arjuna Receives Initiation

When the battle of the Mahabharata was about to begin, a vast array of Kauravas were standing on the southwest part of the holy field of Kurukshetra. On the other side stood the Pandavas, enthusiastic and eager to jump into the fire of war. Arjuna was sitting in his chariot, which Krishna was driving. Arjuna directed Krishna to take the chariot into the middle of the battlefield so he could clearly see his opponent.

Shri Krishna followed Arjuna's instructions. He drove the chariot to where Arjuna could see the whole battlefield and all the warriors. Arjuna had a strange sensation. Looking at his friends and relatives assembled on the plain—Bhishma, the grand uncle, Drona and Kripa, the *acharyas*, the gurus, brothers, sons, nephews, and uncles, and so forth in both armies, Arjuna realized that his own kith and kin were ready to give up their lives for the sake of a kingdom.

Arjuna felt dejected, full of remorse and sorrow. "How can I be the cause of death for those whom I love, respect, and adore. It would be better for me to live and beg like a monk than to enjoy prosperity stained in blood."

When dejection is associated with the company of the master who is a holy saint and spiritual guide, it becomes a cause of spiritual evolution. Dejection is natural when someone apparently causes destruction or loss, but in this case, *vishada*, the dejected one, becomes a yogi. In fact, the first chapter of the Bhagavad Gita is called *Vishada Yoga*, "The Yoga of Dejection." In other situations dejection may lead to depression and other psychosomatic disorders in man.

In India's spiritual tradition, there are three beautiful episodes of dejection and sorrow that led to great spiritual philosophical treasure, rich with psychology, morality, and truth. Rama's dejection and the support and help given by his guru, the sage Vasishtha, is a masterpiece of yoga. Their dialogue became the great yogic treatise called Yoga Vasishtha. When King Suratha and a businessman named Samadhi, full of grief and remorse for loss of their kingdom, family, and business, approached the great sage Medha, the ensuing discussion gave birth to another scripture rising out of such state of delusion: the Shri Chandi, also known as the Durga Saptashati.

In the Gita, Arjuna's dejection, unwillingness to fight, wavering mind, and readiness to run away from the battlefield were ultimately good omens for him and for all. He expressed his despair to his beloved Krishna. Shri Krishna can be considered a great psychologist, as well as a practical and dynamic leader. He practiced what he thought. He patiently listened to all the complaints from His dear friend Arjuna. A true spiritual or social leader must be a good listener, who listens first, and then prescribes.

Arjuna's despair came from emotion. Emotional turmoil brings insanity and inconsistency. It affects our ability to judge good and bad. The irrational mind is far from the path of righteousness.

The Bhagavad Gita is the story of life, the life of a sincere seeker, as taught by Shri Krishna, initiating the true disciple into the path of Yoga.

The Battlefield of Life

The Bhagavad Gita is set on a battlefield. It describes a historical event, as well as mystical one, which actually took place at Kurukshetra, not too far away from present-day New Delhi. The battle is between cousins, relatives, and friends. In all of creative literature, it is rare for a practical philosophy of life to be taught and learned on a battlefield, but every human life is a battle to regain the lost kingdom of peace, joy, and happiness. The true life of a warrior is to conquer all the inner enemies. Our enemies are not outside, they are inside, in our minds. The two forces in the Mahabharata are the Pandavas, representing good qualities, morality, and values, and the Kauravas, symbolizing immorality, corruption, greed, and jealousy. This is the real mystical battle on Kurukshetra.

All the conflicts that arise in our social life, whether in the family, the workplace, society, or the world are due to inner conflicts and values, contradicting ideas and ideologies. The inner life of a person is a constant struggle between means and ends, values and ambitions, to do or not to do.

This story of battle is the story of life. In life, every person is a warrior who must fight, subdue, slay, and destroy the inner enemies that make us all weak and vulnerable to negativity. The enemies are anger, ego, jealousy, hypocrisy, greed, vanity, backbiting, treachery, and slander, to name a few.

Those people of self-control, disciplined in thought, word, and deed, who are directed and advised by a spiritual guide, will be victorious and successful. Moments of weakness or emotion, restlessness, and instability will disappear and they will regain the lost kingdom of peace within.

The Body Chariot

In ancient times, people used horses, elephants, chariots, and armies in battle. On the battlefield of life, the chariot is the human body. This analogy is found in the Upanishads. In the Katha Upanishad (1:3:4–5), it says that every human body is a chariot in which the soul sits. The senses are the horses. In order to be a successful warrior, the body chariot must be kept healthy and strong. The five horses (senses) yoked to the body chariot must be well trained and under control. If not, the horses may lead a life to disorder.

The soul is the charioteer. In the Bhagavad Gita, two people are sitting in the chariot, Krishna and Arjuna. Krishna, the true charioteer, is the soul (*atma*), and Arjuna is the individual self *(jiva)*. This describes the union of *jiva* and *atma*, individuality and soul. Every person must use their intellect and rationality to fight the battle of life, with the help of the body chariot and the charioteer.

Entrance to the Temple

The Bhagavad Gita can be compared to the temple. There are eighteen steps to enter into the *sanctum sanctotum*, the inner chamber of the temple. Each chapter reveals a different kind of yoga. This book of seven hundred verses, composed in *anushtup* and *trishtup* meter, is a beautiful poetic work, rich with philosophical ideas and spiritual truth.

The Bhagavad Gita is divided into eighteen chapters, the prominent Smritis are eighteen in number, there are eighteen Puranas and the total number of *shlokas* in the Bhagavatam is eighteen thousand. The Mahabharata consists of eighteen books, the total number of troops (*akshauhinis*, a special way of calculation) engaged in the battle of Mahabharata is eighteen, and the battle lasted for eighteen days.

The number nine is a complete number and is a symbol of divinity. The sum of numbers in any multiple of nine is also nine. For example, eighteen is one and eight, which when summed together equal nine. Each human being has three bodies: gross, astral, and causal. The gross, perishable body is merely the chariot. The causal body has seventeen aspects: five organs of action (hands, feet, arms, genitals, and mouth), five organs of perception (eyes, ear, nose, tongue, and skin), five types of vital breath (*prana, apana, samana, udana,* and *vyana*), the mind, and the intellect. The root of the body is ignorance, making a total of eighteen. To make progress on the path of realization is to keep the two bodies, the eighteen limbs, in complete control. According to yoga philosophy, there are eighteen steps to Self-realization, which correspond to the eighteen chapters in the Bhagavad Gita.

The Birthday of the Bhagavad Gita

As described earlier, the Bhagavad Gita is a discussion of a fundamental problem between two friends, Shri Krishna and Arjuna. Every fundamental problem needs a fundamental solution. They discuss the real problem of life and the means to overcome it.

The great warrior Arjuna was dejected, depressed, and reluctant to fight with the enemies. He was ready to leave without any further consideration. The beautiful and philosophical lesson taught by Shri Krishna at this critical moment was originally written as prose. Later, the sage Vyasa presented it in poetic form. This occurred on the day of the eleventh moon, *tithi,* in the lunar calendar, and at the time of the waxing moon, in the months called November and December in the West. To this day, this time of year is still considered the birthday of this scripture. The people in India celebrate the birthday of the Bhagavad Gita by praying, meditating upon it, and discussing its inner meaning.

Gita, the Mother

In the traditional way of reading the Bhagavad Gita, people learn rules and discipline. They say a beautiful prayer with verses of meditation. In one verse, the Gita is addressed *amba twan anusandadhami,* "O mother, I am following you." In this way, the scripture is personified, evoking the beautiful relationship of motherhood. Every seeker on the spiritual path is the child and the Gita is the mother.

Mahatma Gandhi said, "My physical body was nourished by the milk of my mother in childhood. My spiritual and intellectual bodies are nourished with the nectar-like truth contained in the Gita. When a critical situation arises in my life, I find a beautiful solution to this problem from the mother, the Gita."

The Three Methods of Teaching the Scriptures

The teachings in the Bhagavad Gita are revealed in three ways. The first way, the discussion between Krishna and Arjuna, which arose in the battlefield as a result of what was in the heart and mind of Arjuna, is the true teaching.

The second method derives from the lesson that occurred in the palace of the blind king, Dhritarashtra, the father of the Kauravas and the uncle of the Pandavas. Immediately before the battle, full of infatuation and attachment in the heart and worried about the future of his children, Dhritarashtra wanted to know what was happening on the battlefield of Kurukshetra. At that time, Maharishi Vyasa visited him.

Knowing the state of anxiety in the heart of Dhritarashtra, he wanted to use his yogic power to bless him with the power of vision, so that he could witness the events on the battlefield. Dhritarashtra refused to accept this gift because he could not bear to watch the destruction of his own family. Therefore, Vyasa gave a special blessing to Samjaya, one of Dhritarashtra's ministers, who was then able to see the happenings in the battlefield and narrate them to the blind king. Thus, the Gita begins with the conversation of the blind king and his minister.

The final approach explains how the Bhagavad Gita was written into book form. It is the discussion of Maharshi Vyasa and Lord Ganesha. When Vyasa wanted to write this great epic, the Mahabharata, he needed someone to act as his scribe. Lord Ganesha accepted this position, but with the condition that he would not stop writing until it was finished. Vyasa consented, but told Lord Ganesha that he would not write anything without understanding its inner meaning. This is how both the Mahabharata and the Bhagavad Gita came into the hands of mankind.

Just as the Bhagavad Gita was revealed in three steps, every scripture must be understood by three kinds of students: the ordinary student wanting to know the literal aspect; the mediocre student who wants to know the historical background; and the true student who wants to search deeply and discover the hidden and subtle truths.

The Four Main Characters in the Gita

In the seven hundred verses of the Bhagavad Gita, there are only four main characters: Dhritarashtra, Samjaya, Arjuna, and Shri Krishna. The dialogues of these four people comprise all eighteen chapters. If one studies the Bhagavad Gita systematically and analytically, the role of each of these characters can be understood.

First, Dhritarashtra asks Samjaya one question, which incited Samjaya to narrate the entire story of the Gita in detail. This is the only question from the blind king to his minister, the very first verse of the Gita. The inner meaning of the name, Dhritarashtra, is the mind, which is always behind, constantly confused and attached.

The second character, Samjaya, is a Brahmin and a minister of the blind king. He answered the king's question in nine steps, in forty-one *shlokas*. The name Samjaya is derived from *sam* (prefix) and *jaya* (verb). *Sam* means complete and thorough. *Jaya* means victory, complete success. An advanced yogi with inner tranquility is able to see things at any distance.

The third character is Arjuna, the hero, the warrior, the middle Pandava, who is the role model presented by the Bhagavad Gita. He asks twenty-one questions in eighty-four verses. His questions are practical, legitimate, philosophical, intricate, and deep.

The fourth character is the center of the Bhagavad Gita: the Lord, the blessed Shri Krishna. He is the center of life and the soul in every living being. He knew Arjuna's problem very well. He was close to Arjuna like a brother and was a friend, philosopher and guide to him in every step of his life. Arjuna opened his mind and heart, he accepted Shri Krishna as his teacher and guru, and he surrendered himself as his disciple (Bhagavad Gita 2:7).

Shri Krishna, out of His infinite compassion and boundless love, was ready to help Arjuna, at precisely the right moment. A friend in need is a friend indeed. He answered the questions of Arjuna in twenty-eight steps and 574 verses.

Shri Krishna is the central character, the *gitacharya* of the Gita. In one prayer, it is said that the Upanishads are the cows, Arjuna is the calf, and Krishna is the milkman who milks the nectar of the Gita so that wise people can enrich and nourish their minds and lives with these nectar-like teachings. This prayer shows that the purpose of Krishna's teaching was for a noble cause and for all of mankind.

Shri Bhagavan Uvacha

Although the Bhagavad Gita is a conversation between the two friends, Shri Krishna and Arjuna, all the replies of Shri Krishna are preceded by "*Shri Bhagavan uvacha*" (the blessed Lord said). The Bhagavad Gita literally translates into "The Divine Song" or "God speaks to Arjuna." The Bhagavad Gita says, "*Shri Bhagavan uvacha*" and not "*Shri Krishna uvacha*" (Krishna said), because all the discourse is actually God speaking to Arjuna through Shri Krishna.

Bhagavan in Sanskrit is from the root word *bhaga*, which means six glories: total affluence, strength, prosperity, glory, knowledge, and detachment. One who has all these glories is called Bhagavan. In the Gita, Shri Krishna is depicted as a divine personality, an incarnation Who is aware of the past, present, and future (Bhagavad Gita 4:5). Shri Krishna, with His boundless glories and yogic power, shows His cosmic, universal form to Arjuna in Chapter 13.

His superhuman and supernatural power, sharp intellect, foresight, and tremendous memory reveal the glory of the Lord. When Shri Krishna teaches the message in the Gita, He is not an ordinary person; He is completely absorbed in His divine nature. Krishna's message is not simply that of a human being with mere intelligence or understanding, but rather it is the divine message of the Lord sitting in the chariot in human form.

At first, Arjuna did not recognize the full manifest divinity in Shri Krishna. After his realization, he completely surrendered at the feet of the Lord and begged forgiveness. He followed Shri Krishna's instructions without question.

The Contents of the Bhagavad Gita

The content of the Bhagavad Gita is described in the concluding remark (colophon) at the end of every chapter, which in Sanskrit says, *iti shrimad bhagavadgitasu upanishadsu brahmavidyayam yogashastre*, which translates as, "The Bhagavad Gita is the essence of the Upanishads, the treasure-house of divine wisdom, the knowledge of Brahman, the absolute, and a scripture of yoga.

The Upanishads, as said earlier, are the mouthpiece of Self-knowledge. The Self is beyond the limits of the body, the play of the mind, and the reach of intellect. It must be known, experienced, and realized. One cannot reach this state by reading books or by intellectual cognition, but only through inner experience, by introverting the senses and the mind. This realization must be achieved through direct experience. Through this experience the play of the divine can be perceived—pure consciousness is experienced in every thought, word, and deed. In this way people can attain freedom from the karma (action) that binds them and achieve liberation.

A practical spiritual person, through meditation and self-inquiry, experiences continuous peace, which is godliness. In such a state, one is free from the tentacles of worry, anxiety, and fear, and discovers the bliss, joy, and serenity that is the inherent nature of the children of God.

Brahmavidya is knowledge of the Brahman, the absolute. The commandments of the Upanishads, the *mahavakyas*, the four great statements, contain this truth, *Aham brahmasmi*: "I am Brahman." In the Upanishads it says, *sarva khalvidam brahman*: "Everything is Brahman." There is no separation between the creator and creation.

The Upanishads and the *brahmavidya* are the theoretical aspects of spiritual truth. This theory must be put into practice. Through practice one gains experience and attains realization. Yoga is the practical aspect of spiritual truth. Theory and practice together bring beauty by expanding the arena of understanding, realization, and emancipation. Thus the Bhagavad Gita is not a dry book of philosophy or knowledge, it is a practical handbook on yoga and spirituality, ready to transform every human life into a beautiful paradise of peace and prosperity.

Yoga, the Pathway for Realization

As it is known to the modern world, yoga is an easy science for self-discovery and Self-realization. Yoga is one of the six branches of Indian philosophy, which was popularized in a very systematic way by the sage, Patañjali. In his book, the Yoga Sutras, the "aphorisms on yoga," the sage described the inner aspects of this subtle philosophy. Maharishi Vyasa wrote a commentary on the Yoga Sutras of Patañjali, now found under the name of Vyasa Bhasya. This text helps to make the scripture easier to understand and interpret.

Because Vyasa was the commentator on the Yoga Sutras as well as the author of the Bhagavad Gita, it is easy to find a similar approach in both. In the Bhagavad Gita, words such as yoga, yogi, *yogarudha,* and *yogeshwara* are used in various chapters as many as eighty-four times. Also, Shri Krishna is addressed as Yogeshwara, "the Lord of Yoga," three times.

Krishna, the Yogeshwara, taught the art of yoga to Arjuna, His beloved friend and disciple. This art brings self-control and self-discipline, which ultimately lead to Self-realization.

Every chapter in the Bhagavad Gita is named after a specific yoga. Yoga literally means union—the union of the body and the soul or the union of the individual self with the universal Self (the river merging with the ocean). All restlessness and effort disappear when one experiences this state of union. The eighteen chapters of the Bhagavad Gita clearly and lucidly reveal how a person can evolve from a human being to being God in a human being, starting with the "Yoga of Dejection," the first step, and culminating in the "Yoga of Emancipation and Liberation," the final step.

Yoga and the yogic lifestyle of moderation in food, sleep, and activity, combined with inner detachment lead to all-round development. Practicing yoga causes a complete transformation in a human being. Yoga is the active or dynamic aspect of the process of spiritual advancement.

As described by Patañjali (1:12) and the Bhagavad Gita (6:35), self-mastery through yoga is possible by using two techniques that work like the two wings of the bird: *abhyasa* (repeated practice) and *vairagya* (detachment). Practice brings perfection. An ounce of practice is better than tons of theories. Yoga is the practice of discipline in every step of life.

Action, Knowledge, and Devotion: The Yoga of Integration

The Bhagavad Gita illuminated the correct path for Arjuna. It did not allow him to retreat into idleness or to be overly attached. The path of yoga integrates life and creates harmony. The Lord says in the Gita, "One cannot remain idle for a single moment." Idleness is the path to self-destruction. One evolves through right action. Actions performed in the spirit of offering or sacrifice, without excessive attachment, lead one down the path of spirituality. Right action is directing the mind to work in the right spirit, using every moment and every breath in the pursuit of perceiving divinity. Through such action, one gathers experience, intuition, intelligence, and knowledge.

There is only one yoga, but it has three aspects that make it complete and beautiful: action, knowledge, and devotion. These are the three elements a person needs to mold their life into a life of God. Yoga is the path of love, resulting from knowledge, and it makes life more beautiful, harmonious, and divine. Although one will find different qualities praised in different parts of the Gita: action in one place, knowledge in another, and devotion in yet another part; in reality, these three must be integrated to bring about the quickest possible evolution.

Yoga as the path of integration makes a beautiful garland of action, knowledge, and devotion, harmonizing the hands, head, and heart of a person. The yoga described in the Gita, when followed systematically, step by step, by a sincere person, will allow the beauty of the soul to be manifest in its fullness.

Immortality of the Self

In its own beautiful way, the Bhagavad Gita clearly describes the true nature of the body and soul. The body is a garment that clothes the soul. It is limited and finite— but it is also a vehicle to lead the soul to its goal. The soul is pure, indestructible, immortal: No one can possess it, water cannot wet it, and fire cannot burn it. The soul sheds its garment, the body, and transmigrates from one body to the next carrying the impressions of past experiences. By explaining in detail the immortality of the soul, the Bhagavad Gita brings a new light to life and leads us to fearlessness. People are afraid of death, of losing someone or something, but this fear disappears when one realizes the immortal nature of the soul.

One who realizes this and leads life accordingly is *sthitaprajña*, established in wisdom. The concept of *sthitaprajña* is beautifully focused within the Bhagavad Gita. People seek knowledge, whether it is material knowledge, as with scientists, or the analytical and intellectual pursuits of philosophers. God has blessed man with the power to accept and understand different aspects of knowledge (*jñana*), but knowledge must always be applied to everyday life. *Vijña* is the practical application of knowledge. Through this one can experience and attain *prajñana,* and become *sthitaprajña*, established in wisdom. Such a person is free from all sorrow and suffering, and is constantly calm, blissful, fulfilled, joyful, and happy. This person is calmly active and actively calm, accomplishing all the duties of life with great discipline and detachment.

Reaching the Summit

There are many paths of self-unfoldment, but the destination is one. The Bhagavad Gita describes a river that reaches the ocean and merges into it. We can cast off finite names and forms and attain the infinite state, going from form to formless. To reach the summit, strong determination and persistent endeavor are necessary, but once the goal is achieved, all differences disappear. The view from the summit is identical to all.

This goal is found inside; we must apply the inward sense of religion. The Bhagavad Gita describes a spiritual happiness that is the culmination of sincere and sacred effort. To keep the mind always in the state of peace, bliss, and joy, one must practice regular *sadhana*, spiritual discipline. Without this, the mind cannot hold and behold the higher purpose of life. Give up the negative qualities of idleness and procrastination and strive sincerely. Temporary enthusiasm and emotion cannot be of real help.

The Essence of Scriptures

The Mahabharata glorifies the Bhagavad Gita, by saying, *sarva shastramayi gita:* "The Gita is the essence of all scriptures." The Gita is nonsectarian and universal; it is the spiritual handbook of sincere seekers. When you study the scripture of other religions, such as the Bible, you can find common spiritual threads between the two. Innumerable works compare the scriptures of different religions to the Gita.

In the Bible one reads: "So whatever you eat or drink, or whatever you do, do it all for the Glory of God." (1 Corinthians 10:31) The Bhagavad Gita (9:27) says the same thing. "I am in my Father; you are in me and I am in you." (John 14:20) "I and my Father are one." (John 10:30) The Bhagavad Gita (6:30 and 9:29) contains related teachings. Describing the immortality of the soul, the Bible says: "Don't be afraid of those who kill the body, but cannot kill the soul. Rather be afraid of one who can destroy both soul and body in hell." (Matthew 10:28) The Bhagavad Gita says the same in Chapter 2 and many other places. The Bhagavad Gita has been widely accepted by people all over the world. The Gita's universal outlook makes it complementary to many sacred texts of other religions.

The Gita's message is universal; it has become a light for mankind, surpassing the limitation of time. The Gita is a scripture for all humanity, not limited to the Hindus. The eternal wisdom it contains is written poetically and is presented very simply. According to some thinkers and spiritual personalities, one lifetime is not enough to study the Gita. It is useful until one attains liberation (*jivanmukta*). The Gita is a book of grace, a song book of divine love. The Gita brings unity to all of creation. Putting this wisdom into practice can bring it to life.

The Chief Commentators

The Gita has been recognized for centuries as an important scripture whose authority and status is equal to that of the Upanishads and the Brahmasutras. These three scriptures together are the *prasthana trayi.* Since ancient times the classical teachers of spirituality used these scriptures as a foundation for preaching their doctrines. They wrote commentaries on these scriptures. Neither the Upanishads, whose source is the Vedas, nor the Brahmasutras, presented in aphorisms, are easily understood, but the Bhagavad Gita is simple, and it is filled with hidden spiritual treasure to be discovered on many levels. Thus, numerous volumes of commentary have been written on the Bhagavad Gita. The Gita itself gives a more consistent view and pragmatic outlook than its commentaries because the commentators belong to different schools of thought, thus having different approaches to the text.

The best-known schools of thought are: *Advaita* (monism), *Vishisthadvaita* (qualified monism), *Dvaita* (dualism), and *Shuddhadvaita* (pure monism). Various commentaries on the Gita by *acharyas* aim at supporting their own traditions and refuting the others. These commentators, through their deep insight, each find their own system of thought and theology in this holy book. The best-known commentators are:

1. Shankara, whose most ancient commentary, the *Shankara Bhasya,* propounds monism, non-dualism, seeing Brahman as the only reality.

2. Ramajuna's *Shri Bhasya* is from the qualified dualism school of thought: In the beginning there is duality, but in the end it disappears.

3. Madhva wrote two works on the Gita: *Gitabhashya* and *Gitatatparya.* In his work he explains the dualistic approach, the distinction between creator and creation.

4. Ninbarka presents a doctrine of *Dvaitadvaita* (dual–non-dualism). According to him, *jiva* (the soul), *jagat* (the world), and God are different from each other. His commentary on the Gita is the *Tattvaprakashika.*

5. Ballava, a proponent of *Shuddhadvaita* (pure monism), teaches that purifying the ego through devotion leads to supreme unity.

Many different glosses have been applied to Shankara's interpretation by great spiritual personalities such as Anandagiri, Madhusudana Saraswati, and Siddharaswami. The Gita commentary of the saint of Maharashtra, Saint Jñaneshwar, popularly known as the *Jñaneshwari Gita,* is very popular among lovers of the Bhagavad Gita.

Modern Commentators

Through the ages the Bhagavad Gita has been loved, read, analyzed, interpreted, and explained in different ways, with many different meanings. One might wonder why there are so many different and sometimes conflicting interpretations of such a small book.

God is infinite. The Gita contains the direct message of the divine. God's instructions are infinite. Human consciousness is ever expanding and limitless because of its infinite possibility. Thus, there is no end to the possible interpretations of the Bhagavad Gita. Every single person can look at this scripture with a new outlook.

Among the modern commentators, a few names can be quoted such as B.G. Tilak (*Gita Rahasya*), Mahatma Gandhi (*Anasakta Yoga*), Vinova Bhave, Shri Aurovindo, Dr. S. Radhakrishnan, and Swami Chinmayananda. Every Hindu believes in differences and accepts them with love. The Vedas declare, "*ekam sad viprah vahudha vadanti.*" The truth is one, but people of knowledge speak in different ways. The truth is to manifest love within, through prayer and meditation, right action, and right living.

The Yogic Outlook

In Hinduism, there is a popular saying:

Yogi tahi janiye
Yo gita hi janiye

The above lines contain Sanskrit syllables that create a beautiful meaning: "The yogi (meditator) knows the Gita." The scriptures say that yogis enjoy the true beauty of the scriptures because they practice their meaning in daily life. The Bhagavad Gita is not a book to merely read and put aside, it must be put into practice. It is not for intellectual interpretation or arguments, it is a book of practical spirituality. One must live up to the canons of this beautiful scripture. It is loved, accepted, and adored equally by devotees who follow the paths of action and knowledge, by householders and renunciates, by *brahmacharis* and *swamis.*

Interpretation of the Bhagavad Gita took a new course with the commentary of Shri Lahiri Mahasaya. Many may know him as the fountainhead of Kriya Yoga and as a disciple of Shri Babaji Maharaj. This householder yogi led a life of inner detachment while living in the world. In spite of the natural difficulties of family life, the death of his dear ones, and other constraints, he set a practical example of yogic living before his disciples.

Lahiri Mahasaya encouraged everyone to read the Gita. His instructions were to read one verse daily; he even asked seekers to read it before taking initiation. He had it printed in the original text so this holy book could be distributed for free, to help people develop their natural love for the scripture.

Every evening, in the company of his disciples, Lahiri Mahasaya would explain a new metaphorical interpretation of the Bhagavad Gita or some other scripture. Some of the disciples took notes during these lessons, and these were printed later as the commentary of Lahiri Mahasaya (originally in Bengali).

Following in the footsteps of Lahiri Mahasaya, his able disciples such as Pandit Panchanan Bhattacharya, Swami Shriyukteshwarji, Sanyal Mahasaya, Suradhuni Devi, Swami Pravanananda, Pandayal Mazumdar, Prasad Das Goswami, and others wrote marvelous interpretations of the scriptures based on their meditative experiences. Most often these books were unique in their approach and were only available in Indian languages.

The yogic interpretation of the Bhagavad Gita ushered in a new era in the spiritual understanding of this book. Not only the teachings, but even the names of the characters reveal the nature of the human personality, the tendencies of good and bad. Every name has a beautiful correspondence with an aspect of human life. As a result, the whole significance of the Gita was revealed unto the human field of experience. For those who practice meditation and techniques such as Kriya Yoga, the Bhagavad Gita is an essential scripture to be studied and practiced. Kriya Yoga, the scientific meditation technique, helps us evolve from the lower propensities to the higher ones, transcend all weaknesses, and be merged in the state of cosmic consciousness and wisdom. Every human life is a battle that can be fought and won using the practical teachings from the Gita.

This commentary, a metaphorical interpretation of the Bhagavad Gita in the light of Kriya Yoga, as taught by Shri Babaji Maharaj, Lahiri Mahasaya, and Swami Shriyukteshwarji, is aimed at those with no knowledge of Sanskrit, who are trying to walk down the path of spirituality and Self-realization. My revered Gurudev, Paramahamsa Hariharanandaji, is a living, walking, talking, Bhagavad Gita. He reads, speaks, and practices the teachings of the Gita in his daily life. When I first came to him as a young college student, he was reading the Gita, a book of the Upanishads, and the Holy Bible.

Paramahamsa Hariharananda's commentary on the Bhagavad Gita extracts the philosophical essence from the different kinds of yoga.

He then distills this concentrated essence into a practical method of spiritual development. To Hariharanandaji, the Gita is a description of the long lost art Kriya Yoga, the scientific process of cultivating God consciousness, which was returned to the field of the world by Babaji Maharaj through the vehicle of Lahiri Mayasaya. Like the Bhagavad Gita, this Kriya Yoga is infused with passion and love for the Divine Being within us. With this simple technique, yogis of all kinds, as well as ordinary people, can magnify their daily practice.

Gurudev explains that we need not withdraw from the world to find God. Since God is everywhere and is everything, we can obtain Self-realization by perceiving God in everything we do and in everything around us. For example, we need not give up flavored food; rather, we should learn to perceive that the flavor of food comes from God, and that God creates the sensation of taste so that we can enjoy our food. We must realize that everything we do is done by the power of God, not by us.

The realization of this truth must be direct and personal. If we can perceive the presence of God in every word, thought, and deed, we can achieve liberation; we can attain the state of divine calm that is godliness. When all our worries, anxieties, and fears are offered to the divine, they no longer trouble us. Instead, we attain the bliss, joy, and serenity that is our inherent nature as the children of God.

The metaphorical meaning underlying the Gita as presented by Paramanhamsa Hariharananda offers a profound insight about how to achieve God-realization. A living master of Kriya Yoga for half a century, Hariharanandaji illuminates the common ground in the teachings of the Bhagavad Gita and Kriya Yoga. The teachings of the Bhagavad Gita and the practice of Kriya Yoga are particularly well suited to these times. Both are nonsectarian. People from any religious background, in any nation, in any stage of life can benefit from them. All that is required is a firm resolve and determination to experience the power of God within. The universality of the teachings are evident in Gurudev's commentary.

The Gita should be studied, understood, practiced, and realized. There is no end to the study of such a marvelous book. To those who tread the path of spirituality, the Bhagavad Gita is a beautiful guidebook that helps in every step of life. The sincere seeker, the serious student, should read one verse of the Gita daily and try to apply the lesson to daily life. Once the lesson is learned, it is wise to repeat it again. In this way, many beautiful, undiscovered, and unnoticed truths come to life. I remember the remark of a yogi to a young seeker. When this young man said that he had studied the Gita, the yogi corrected him by saying, "Never say 'I have studied the Gita'; instead say, 'I am studying the Gita,' for no one has completed the study of the Gita." Let this be your outlook. Study with love. This is the teaching of the Lord to a beloved friend, the disciple. It is up to us to let this marvelous book help us and guide us.

By studying and practicing the teachings of the Bhagavad Gita, you can transform yourself from *purusha* to Purushottama, from manhood to Godhood, in this life.

Interpretation and Meaning

Soul Culture in the Bhagavad Gita

The Yogic Theory of Evolution:
Heredity, Environment, and Culture

There is a famous proverb in Bengali:

gita khanda ikshudanda
gilile aswadan nei
guru pashey boshe boshe
sharoshey chibano chai

"If you swallow the raw stick of sugarcane, you will not taste the sweetness of the sugar."

In the same way, if you only read the words of the Bhagavad Gita, you won't learn the real meaning of these spiritual texts, which describe soul cultivation. On the other hand, if you sit by the side of the guru and read the Gita, learning its true meaning and meditating, then you will attain God-realization.

In the thirtheenth chapter of the Bhagavad Gita, a human being is described as twofold, consisting of a body, *kshetra,* and the soul, *kshetrajña,* the conductor of the body. The physical body consists of twenty-four gross elements, which are responsible for all the body functions such as sight, taste, touch, smell, and so forth. Ultimately, these twenty-four elements bind people to delusion, illusion, and error.

Since the soul is the conductor of the body and its twenty-four elements, the soul actually creates the delusion, illusion, and error. When a mother gives many dolls and toys to her child, the child becomes engrossed in playing with them and completely forgets about the mother. Similarly, human beings who remain in the extroverted state completely forget their own Mother Nature, the soul.

Realizing the presence of this forgotten soul is your birthright, your heredity. All beings are born of sexual pleasure, thereby receiving DNA from both parents. But this DNA cannot function if the soul doesn't activate the life force within it. Every human being is a living soul, and the soul nature is the true destiny. Your true heredity is your soul, created by the grace of God, not by parents.

In the thirteenth chapter, the soul, represented by Krishna, clearly teaches Arjuna, who symbolizes the condition of all human beings, that a good environment, which is a realized teacher, and following a teacher's instructions (such as the Kriya Yoga technique), allows a sincere seeker to perceive that the twenty-four gross elements are activated only by the soul. Furthermore, every person must also seek good culture, which is the constant search for the indwelling Self, both in meditation and in all aspects of practical life. Whatever aspect of culture you are involved in, whether you are an artist, scientist, factory worker, you must seek your true inner Self within that activity. Then you will automatically feel that your body is a precious body, a divine body, and not an evil body.

Your education in spiritual culture requires only that you merge into the formless state. This can be achieved through Kriya Yoga in a few minutes. The formless soul body will help you clear away awareness of your physical body. You will realize that your physical body is not yours—it belongs to the universe. Then you can go about your daily business with the awareness that you are the living power of God.

With soul culture, you realize that the entire human system is designed for God-realization. In the Bhagavad Gita (13:14), it clearly states: "Your hand is not your hand, it is the hand of God. Your eyes are not your eyes, they are the eyes of God. Your ears are not your ears, they are the ears of God. Your face is not your face, it is the face of God."

When you realize this, your whole body becomes the power of God. You can live in both the material and spiritual worlds, and you can experience liberation in every moment and every action. At this time the ignorance and evil in your body will disappear, and you will achieve knowledge, consciousness, superconsciousness, and godhood. You will understand that your body and soul are one, and have been one, always. In the Bible this is clearly stated in Luke (11:35–36): "If thine eye be single, thine whole body will be filled with light."

Our true heredity is the spiritual destiny of our soul. The best environment is the spiritual teacher. True culture is our spiritual homework, in meditation and daily life.

There is a deeper meaning to this. Every human being has three bodies. When you know yourself, you will know the essence of these three bodies—light, sound, and vibration. When you sit for meditation, you will lose all sense of the physical body— the *M* in *AUM* is erased. Only the *AU* remains, which is the soul and the superconscious state. This is the high-pitched ringing sound heard by your soul, the AUM sound:

A = Causal Body = Sound
U = Astral Body = Vibration
M = Physical Body = Light

The inner light seen when practicing Kriya Yoga is not the same light that falls upon the physical body. Kriya light is dark at the center with dazzling light around it. Ordinary sunlight is just the reverse; it is bright at the center, and dark all around it.

All knowledge comes from the soul—first as inner sound, then as inner vibration and light, finally as colors, thoughts, images, and words. So when you awake in the morning, and the first thing you listen to is the inner sound as taught by Kriya Yoga, you will have a higher response to your actions throughout the day. The inner sound constantly reminds you that your smallest, most ordinary actions are the actions of God.

In brief, the Bhagavad Gita teaches that there are three things in every human body. One is ignorance, the Kaurava army. Another is knowledge, the Pandava army. The third is the soul, Krishna, who conducts both the body and the soul, both ignorance and knowledge.

The extroverted state of awareness, the constant seeking of things outside yourself, can lead human beings to ignorance and evil. It is very easy to remain in this evil and ignorant state. Constant extroversion is a form of madness—the soul is split from the body. In general, most people are absorbed in this ignorance and evil, and therefore remain far from soul culture. The extroverted stage is easily obtainable and alluring, so people forget the truth; they forget to nourish the soul. Arjuna, however, chose the introverted state and achieved his true destiny, which was God-realization.

Only with the guidance of the realized master, Krishna, the soul, was Arjuna able to suppress evil and ignorance and remain in knowledge. Arjuna followed his master completely, so he was purified, his ignorance was dissolved, and he achieved God-realization. By accepting his teacher, Arjuna created a positive environment for himself. Arjuna also did his homework, cultivating awareness of his soul while on the battlefield of life. By choosing the higher culture of Kriya Yoga, Arjuna was able to gain control over the lower aspects of his biological force.

Anyone who remains in the introverted state using a technique such as Kriya Yoga, as taught by a realized master, can easily remove the evil and darkness within, and discover light, knowledge, cosmic consciousness, and God-realization. Living in the material world, these true seekers can remove their ignorance during every moment of their lives, and they can achieve constant liberation in every action. This is the yogic theory of evolution.

Summary of the Contents of the Bhagavad Gita

The Essence of the Bhagavad Gita is the Integration of all Yogas

1. *Arjuna Vishada Yoga* .... Yoga of Dejection
2. *Sankhya Yoga* .... Yoga of Inner Awareness
3. *Karma Yoga* .... Yoga of Action
4. *Jñana Yoga* .... Yoga of Knowledge
5. *Karma Sannyasa Yoga* .... Yoga of Renunciation of Action
6. *Atma Samyama Yoga* .... Yoga of Self-Mastery
7. *Jñana Vijñana Yoga* .... Yoga of Knowledge and Applied Knowledge
8. *Akshara-Brahma Yoga* .... Yoga of the Imperishable Brahman
9. *Raja Vidya Guhya Vidya Yoga* .... Yoga of the Secret Royal Science
10. *Vibhuti Yoga* .... Yoga of the Divine Glories
11. *Vishvarupa Darshana Yoga* .... Yoga of the Cosmic Form Revealed
12. *Bhakti Yoga* .... Yoga of Divine Love
13. *Prakriti Purusha Yoga* .... Yoga of the Body Field and Its Knower
14. *Gunatraya Vibhaga Yoga* .... Yoga of the Discrimination of the Triple Qualities of Nature
15. *Purushottama Yoga* .... Yoga of the Supreme Self
16. *Daivasura Sampad Vibhaga Yoga* .... Yoga of Discrimination Between Divine and Demonic Qualities
17. *Shraddhatraya Vibhaga Yoga* .... Yoga of Classification of the Threefold Faith
18. *Moksha Sannyasa Yoga* .... Yoga for Liberation Through Renunciation

Metaphorical Meaning of the Character Names

Pandava Family Members

DRAUPADI is the wife of the five Pandavas. Why are all five Pandava brothers married to one woman? Why is her name Draupadi? Read and contemplate deeply, and you will understand.

Wife means *shakti*, or power. Here, Draupadi is the *shakti* of the five gross elements. If you sow a seed, but do not use the five gross elements—earth, water, light, air, and space—the seed will not sprout; you cannot expect a plant to grow from the seed. So here, *shakti* is the life that comes from the five gross elements. Draupadi is the life and the wife of the five gross elements, symbolized by the five Pandava brothers. Draupadi means quickest action. When you sow a seed in the ground of the five gross elements, you will quickly produce life.

DRAUPADEYA The five children of Draupadi are called the Draupadeya; they are the atom power of the Pandavas. Thus, they are very powerful. The extract of these five powers exists inside the spinal canal. When spiritually adept people fix their attention in the coccygeal (first center) and in the nose, flowers and fruits can be smelled from a long distance, through the power of meditation. By fixing the attention in the second center and in the mouth, they will automatically experience taste without any object. When the attention is fixed in the third center and the eyes, they will develop the power, like Samjaya, to see what is happening in the distance. With the attention focused in the fourth center and on the skin, they will feel the divine vibration, which can be felt in every body part. When they concentrate and keep their attention in the fifth center and in the ears, they can hear from a long distance, and they can hear melodious sounds constantly, as described in the Bhagavad Gita (8:13). If we meditate deeply, we can surely remove all our evils. By coming up to the top center, we can perceive divineness.

DHRISHTADYUMNA is a great warrior on the side of Pandavas; he is the brother of Draupadi and the son of Drupada. *Dhrishta* means obstinacy and restlessness, and *dyumna* means the power to control the obstinance that comes from the external world. Every human being has obstinace and restlessness when the mind and thoughts remain in the lower centers inside the spinal canal. By practicing the Kriya Yoga technique however, we can withdraw our minds and thoughts up into the cranium. Then we see many divine lights in the pituitary, and our minds and thoughts become absorbed in that divine light. We become extremely calm, as described in the Bhagavad Gita (13:17).

DRUPADA is the king, as well as the father-in-law of the Pandavas, and the father of Draupadi, Dhrishtadyumna, and Shikhandin. He is the greatest warrior on the side of the Pandavas. Pandava means "knowledge body." Those who are on the side of the Pandavas are spiritual and divine. Drupada is short for *druta pada*, which means you must walk quickly and finish your duty. More specifically, you must meditate and completely realize the superconsciousness within you, without wasting time. Do not save anything for tomorrow. Since God is always with you, you should feel His presence right now. Unless you strive for this at once, you will not attain Self-realization. Those human beings who follow the warrior Drupada are the parties of the Pandava army, the *jñana paksha*, the knowledge party.

YUYUDHANA is a relative and disciple of Krishna, also known as Satyaki. He is the first warrior on the side of the Pandavas. *Yuyudhana* refers to someone who has the greatest desire for soul culture and the deepest regard for God and guru. If you have a profound desire for soul culture, but do not maintain implicit faith in God and guru, you do not have the foundation for spirituality. Every human being who wants God-realization must have unconditional love and loyalty to God and guru, and must question the guru about soul culture. Then, if you surrender, learn the technique, and practice daily, regularly, sincerely, and with deepest regard and desire, you will definitely be successful.

Suppose you want to learn how to drive a motor car. If you follow your instructor wholeheartedly and sincerely, and practice the technique with deep attention for a long period, you will become a good driver. You will be able to drive the car without the least danger, even on a crowded road. But if you do not maintain earnest desire and follow the directions of the instructor, you will never learn. Similarly, soul culture requires the deepest desire and obedience to the preceptor; then you can become a spiritual warrior like Yuyudhana.

VIRATA is a great warrior and king on the side of the Pandavas. The Pandavas lived incognito for one year in his palace. The metaphorical meaning of Virata is derived from *vigata* and *rata. Vigata* means that which is completely free, and *rata* refers to the body kingdom; therefore *virata* is one who is free from the mind, intellect, thought, and body sense—everything. By practicing Kriya Yoga inhalation, you will not feel anything in your body kingdom. You will only feel and perceive the king (soul) in the pituitary. By controlling the breath, people can attain Self-realization. With the help of breath mastery, spiritual people can withdraw from the worldly sense and achieve the superconscious state, which is the quality of the Pandavas. Thus, Virata helps the Pandavas.

DHRISHTAKETU is a great warrior on the side of Pandavas. The spiritual meaning of Dhrishtaketu comes from *dhrishtan ketava yah sah. Dhrishtan* means without a head, having only a body, while *ketu* is a dragon's tail. So Dhrishtaketu is always seeking his head. The true seekers of God will always keep their attention focused between the neck cervical junction and the fontanel, then all their sins, restlessness, attachments, and shortcomings will disappear. They can perceive the power of God within themselves. All spiritual power and the kingdom of heaven remain in the head and cranium.

All who want to achieve God-realization should forget their worldly senses and remain focused on their neck up to their head. When we feel as though our heads have been cut off, we will be beyond talk, sight, touch, and sound. If we cannot attain that stage, we cannot attain the formless stage, the ultimate goal of all religions. Kriya Yoga and the Bhagavad Gita teach nonsectarian views that lead to continuous liberation. We must always remain inside the head, and that is Dhrishtaketu.

CHEKITANA is a spiritual warrior on the side of Pandavas. The hidden meaning of Chekitana comes from *chekit*, which means within a short time, and is also the name of a small cricket-like insect, and *tan*, which means the divine sound and the various melodies that are the inaudible talk of God. When spiritual practitioners withdraw their senses from the gross body and enter the pituitary in the head, they hear a variety of melodious divine sounds in the ether. This enables them to attain extreme calmness, which is godliness. At that time nothing is perceived, only the formless state (*nirguna*).

KASHIRAJA is a great spiritual king as well as a great warrior. The meaning of Kashiraja is derived from *kashyate*, which means illuminated, and *rajyam*, which means divine light. When we meditate and withdraw our sensory awareness from the coccygeal to the medulla and keep pinpointed attention there, we will see divine light and will experience emancipation all the time.

PURUJIT is a great king. The inner, spiritual meaning of *purujit* is derived from *puran* and *jayati. Puran* means entire body and intellectual sense, and *jayati* means one who can conquer everything. Thus, Purujit is a powerful and spiritual man who has gone above his body, mind, intellect, and senses, and has merged in God.

KUNTIBHOJA This name comes from *kunti*, which means pinpointed attention on the soul, and *bhoj*, which means enjoying divine bliss. Kuntibhoja is constantly absorbed in God and in divine bliss.

SHAIBYA, a great spiritual warrior of the Pandava army, is very calm and divine. *Shaibya* refers to someone who is just like Shiva. Shiva is the formless god of the vacuum, the god of air and sound. Shaibya has attained that stage. Wisdom is Brahman. In that stage, people are pulseless, the ultimate goal of all religions. People who practice the shortcut technique of Kriya Yoga, the technique described in the Upanishads and the Bhagavad Gita, will attain this supreme stage.

YUDHAMANYU is a powerful spiritual warrior in the Pandava army. The true meaning of Yudhamanyu comes from *yudha*, which means to fight constantly and to subdue, and *manyu*, which means sin, evil, malice, and all other evil qualities that keep human beings far from God-realization. Yudhamanyu is a powerful, spiritual person. His meditation is deep and continuous, which enables him to withdraw his mind from all evils and negative qualities. If you follow the teachings of the Bhagavad Gita absolutely, you will overcome your biological forces and you will quickly proceed to the divine goal, like Yudhamanyu.

SAUBHADRA (ABHIMANYU) There are two names for the same person, the son of Arjuna and Subhadra (Krishna's sister). He is Krishna's nephew. Saubhadra penetrated a military formation of the Kaurava army and killed innumerable soldiers. In our spinal canal, there are millions of evil thoughts in each center. In the coccygeal center, there is a desire for money, and the more we have, the more we want. In the second center, there is endless desire for sexual pleasure. The more enjoyment we have, the more we seek. As a result, the mind is always extroverted. In the navel center, we can keep sound health with the simplest food, but we are not at all satisfied with this, so we seek more food. In the dorsal center, we experience endless desires. The more money we obtain, the more our evil desires increase, and we become full of vanity, pride, anger, and obstinacy. There are innumerable soldiers in the Kaurava army, and Abhimanyu is the cause of their destruction.

The word *abhimanyu* comes from *abhi*, which means to destroy, and *manyu*, which refers to all the evil and vicious qualities in human beings. Abhimanyu entered into the spinal canal, went straight to the heart center, and destroyed all the evil propensities inside the spinal canal.

If we penetrate from the bottom center to the heart center and destroy our evil qualities, we can free ourselves from viciousness, as stated in the Bhagavad Gita (6:25).

HRISHIKESHA is another name for Krishna. Krishna (the soul) was very powerful and full of divinity, but he was in human form. From his infancy, even before his birth, when he was in the womb of his mother, he materialized himself as Narayana and talked with his parents. On the day after his birth, Putana, the great demon woman, tried to poison Krishna by placing her poisoned nipple in His mouth. But Krishna not only succeeded in swallowing the poison, He also stopped her breath and chewed her ribs, killing her. From His very infancy, Krishna performed many miracles and exhibited many powers. Consequently, people gave Him 108 names, of which Hrishikesha is one. *Hrishikesha* is derived from *hrishika*, which means the senses in the body, and *Isha*, which means soul, Lord, master. So *Hrishikesha* means the one who is the conductor of our five sense telephones and of each of our body parts. Without the soul, we are nothing but lifeless bodies.

GOVINDA is another name of Krishna. Govinda is derived from *go, vin,* and *da. Go* means the whole world, *vin* means energy and pleasure, and *da* means to give to the entire universe. Govinda is the one who gives energy and pleasure to the entire universe.

GUDAKESHA is another name for Arjuna that is derived from *gudaka* and *Isha. Gudaka* means sloth, idleness, and sleep. *Isha* means the controller, the master. Arjuna never sleeps. When a human being sleeps, the power of God is not sleeping. Suppose you are sleeping on the left side, and your circulation is lessened. Immediately, the soul has you turn over. The soul is not sleeping. The soul has no idleness. Day and night, He conducts and guides every being. God has no sleep. The soul is the power of God, seen in those such as Jesus and Rama, and they do not sleep. This is why Arjuna is called Gudakesha: He is trying to achieve spiritual evolution by avoiding laziness and sloth. To realize your divinity you must always be alert of your inner Self, Krishna. Arjuna was the closest friend of Krishna, the soul. He was always wakeful to the presence of Krishna, the soul.

Rulers of the Kingdom

DHRITARASHTRA This name means one whose mind is always selfishly engrossed in the material world. The soul is always protecting, preserving, and conducting every human body, but everyone is blind like Dhritarashtra, who is not seeking God. If the father, the king, is blind, all of his sons will be obstinate, without control over their senses. So, whenever the worldly father and mother are blind to seeking God, their children will be turbulent, vicious, insolent, and proud. The children will not seek God and will be always absorbed in the material world.

DURYODHANA Because he is the eldest son of the blind king, Duryodhana is automatically evil-minded, malicious, silly, full of perversion, overly sensitive, and full of pride and anger. He does not seek the truth and is always misguided by evil ministers and bad company. Duryodhana is the king. Surely a king who does not possess divinity, affection, love, and balance of mind cannot rule well. The administration will not be in proper order, and the kingdom will be destroyed due to his ignorance. All human beings are like the insolent king Duryodhana: They fail to seek truth because they are filled with pride, vanity, anger, hypocrisy, and attachment. Lacking sense control, they will always remain in the extroverted state, ruled by the biological force.

SAMJAYA The Brahmin minister and messenger of the blind king Dhritarashtra describes the battle scene to the king. His name is short for *samyak jaya*, which means thorough control. Samjaya is one who has thorough control over his mind, thought, intellect, ego, and body sense, who has no worldly sense. He is always merged in God and remains in the pituitary. With his intuitive foresight, he can hear sounds from afar, as though he was watching television, sitting in a house. Samjaya can see everything happening on the far-off battlefield. Through the grace of the sage Vyasa, every realized person who remains in the pituitary near the soul is able to see or hear from long distances, judge right from wrong, shun all evil, and perceive the truth. That is Self-realization.

DRONACHARYA is the guru of both the Kauravas and the Pandavas. He is an excellent teacher who knows how to lead soldiers in battle. Dronacharya knew that Arjuna was the best fighter among the Kauravas and the Pandavas. Before the battle started, everyone stated their allegiance to either of the two parties. Krishna chose to stay with the greatest warrior, Arjuna. Dronacharya knew that if Krishna and Arjuna remained together, their party would surely win. Symbolically, Arjuna is knowledge and Krishna is the knower.

Dronacharya desired to be with the Pandavas and Krishna, and he expressed this desire to Duryodhana. Duryodhana was very proud and insolent however. He pointed out that his father had appointed Dronacharya as the teacher, and that his father had provided him with food and money. He told Dronacharya that he was ungrateful because he wanted to fight for the Pandavas, and he asked Dronacharya to fight with him. Dronacharya changed his mind immediately and joined the evil side. This was the habit of Dronacharya.

The word *dronacharya* comes from the word *druban*, which means something that rolls this way and that, like water on a lotus leaf or a *kana* leaf, which rolls from one side to another according to the wind. This is restlessness. Dronacharya is a person of vacillating temperament. He cannot judge what is right or wrong. All human beings are like Dronacharya, always vacillating. Dronacharya knew full well that the victory would be with Arjuna and Krishna. In spite of that, he accepted and embraced his death, joining the side of the losing company.

All human beings know that they have knowledge (Arjuna) and a soul (Krishna). Knowledge is light, and soul is the power of God. We all must seek that soul. Unfortunately, due to our vacillating temperaments, we do not seek the truth; we do not seek Self-realization.

Dronacharya received his greatest gift from his guru: He would not die until his seventh junction, his pituitary above the palate, was cut off by an arrow that passed through his fontanel. Symbolically, this means that people cannot remove their vacillating temperaments, restlessness, and fickle-mindedness until they cross the seventh junction and bring their awareness up to the pituitary. Those who practice the Kriya Yoga technique, which is the essence of the eighteen kinds of yoga described in the Bhagavad Gita, can control their senses, remove their vacillating temperaments, and know the true Self.

The death of Dronacharya symbolically means to remove all restlessness from the human body, to become free from mind, thought, intellect, ego, body sense, and worldly sense, and to remain above the pituitary, which will produce Self-realization.

Evil Warriors of the Kaurava Army

KAURAVAS These warriors are opposed to the Pandavas in battle. Kaurava comes from *kuru*, and *rava*. *Kuru* means to do work, and *rava* means the cry or disposition towards delusion in human beings. Kaurava refers to all the evil propensities that speak from within. When Jesus said that we must be born from above through water and spirit (John 3:5–7), he revealed that ordinary people allow their awareness to remain below in the lower centers. If you remain in the cranium, however, immersed in the soul, you can judge what is right and what is wrong.

Our biological force and our five sense telephones are always forcing us to do evil deeds, such as being a nuisance, eating what we cannot digest, or joining evil company and cooperating in evil activity. The Kaurava party represents the millions of cells, tissues, and atoms in our gross body that force us to commit evil, to be insolent, and to spoil ourselves. The whole Kaurava party, led by Duryodhana, inhabits our gross body and creates delusion and illusion. The general masses—those who are not seeking God and truth—are the Kauravas. Those who have immense wealth and prosperity, who want to spend it for unfair purposes and in evil action, have forgotten that they are born only for the purpose of Self-realization. This is why Jesus said it is easier to pass a camel through the eye of a needle than to lead a prosperous person to heaven.

In the Bhagavad Gita (7:16), it states that only four kinds of people can know God. Only those who are extremely aggrieved (heartbroken), who are poor, who are true seekers after real knowledge, or who are true seekers for salvation can know God.

BHISHMA The commander-in-chief of the Kauravas commands and directs the whole Kaurava army. Bhishma means firm determination of mind. He vowed not to marry and to never enjoy sexual pleasure. This is fine, but due to his extreme pride, he committed several mistakes. For instance, he promised not to look upon the face of Shikhandin, a pious girl, which was very dangerous for him. If Shikhandin appears before Bhishma on the battlefield, he must shut his eyes. What is the use of having a commander-in-chief such as Bhishma? When the battle was raging between Arjuna and Bhishma, Shikhandin was placed on Krishna's chariot at Arjuna's side. The moment Bhishma saw Shikhandin, he closed his eyes and stopped fighting. Arjuna shot a flurry of arrows that covered his whole body. After a long while, he expired.

Human beings are just like Bhishma, thinking they are very powerful, intelligent, scientifically advanced, and educated—full of ego. Engrossed in the material world, they do not keep their minds on spirituality. As a result, they do not have the peace, bliss, and joy that can be obtained through soul culture. They are constantly being hit by arrows, that is, tortured by worry, anxiety, and unpleasantness like Bhishma, because they have vowed, as did Bhishma, not to seek God. But joy, peace, and bliss can only be obtained from God-realization.

KARNA is also a son of Kunti, the most powerful warrior among all the soldiers of both the Kauravas and the Pandavas. Karna is misguided and overpowered by falsehood. When falsehood prevails, truth disappears. The metaphorical meaning of *karna* comes from its meaning in Sanskrit—ears. With our ears we hear good and bad talk, heart-touching and hateful talk, and sweet and unpleasant talk. For instance, suppose you are a very sweet, humble, well-behaved, polite, educated person, respected in society. If someone tells you that you are silly and talk like a madman, your mental state is upset the moment you hear these words, which go to your brain through your ears (*karna*). Or suppose you are extremely busy with some work, and then a very beautiful woman comes and says: You are very beautiful, I love you, I like you, I want to spend some time with you. When you hear these words through your ears, you are immediately transformed and you forget your work. Instead, you become busy with that person. Our ears want to hear melodious song, sweet words, praise, flattery, and soothing talk. The moment we become engrossed in it, we forget our actual work. This prevents us from gaining the truth.

Karna was such a skilled warrior that he could have killed any warrior he chose. He was not aware that he was a brother to the five Pandavas. On the morning of the day he was going to fight and kill the Pandavas, he was told that he was the eldest brother of the Pandavas. Immediately, his mind completely changed. He went to the battlefield determined to defeat them, but not to kill them. He wanted to go near them and love and kiss them, which he did.

Karna means that our ears are very strong. We can overcome all evil and remove our worries and anxieties, pitfalls, and shortcomings, but because of our *karna* (ears), we are completely distracted. We could prosper in our lives by gaining all-round development and Self-realization, but instead we are overpowered by bad company. However, if we can introvert our power of hearing toward the soul, we can achieve extreme self-control, education, peace, joy, bliss, and God-realization.

KRIPA is the brother-in-law of Drona, the guru of both the Pandavas and Kauravas. He is immortal and a ferocious warrior. "Do or die" is his sole motto. He is extremely brutal, very steady in animal habits, and not to be subdued by anything. Kripa means kindness and affection with attachment to something bad. Every person is Kripa.

At first, Kripa was firmly determined to be a highly qualified, prosperous, distinguished person in society, but he became attached to bad company out of compassion, then forgot his noble and high aspirations. He joined the Kaurava army as did Drona, but being immortal, he later took on the responsibility of training the Pandavas' grandchild after the Mahabharata war. Compassion, love, and a helpful nature are always immortal.

ASHVATTHAMA is an immortal soldier and the son of the fickle Dronacharya. Hence, the son of Dronacharya is fickle, but he always seeks glory and prominence. *Ashvatthama* means to have a disposition of being constantly on the go, of being relentless like a machine that is constantly running. Ashvatthama had many plans for destroying the Pandavas, but he never stuck to one plan, so none of them were successful. Similarly, every human being desires variety. Everyone is fickle. One desire after another arises in an endless chain, but real satisfaction is never obtained. Our endless desires prevent us from perceiving God. These desires hinder Self-realization. A person who cannot subdue desire cannot attain peace and Self-realization.

VIKARNA is a soldier of the Kaurava army, a dangerous warrior. His name describes one who is a strong believer, who is malicious, and who is addicted to improper works. He will do work that should not be done. This improper belief resulting from the biological force is the main obstacle to purity and truth. This is why Vikarna is with the Kauravas, and why all of us are in the Kaurava party. We don't believe in spiritual persons, or even in God. Although we are born for Self-realization, the first and foremost duty of every human being, it can be attained only by sincerely trying to know and perceive God. Unfortunately, our failure to believe in truth, God, and gurus keeps us from reaching the divine goal.

BHURISHRAVA is the son of Somadatta. *Bhurishrava* means hesitation and is derived from *bhuri* and *shrava. Bhuri* means many, and *shrava* means to hear. So *Bhurishrava* means one who is hearing many things about someone or something. If you hear or say many things, you will always be in the extroverted state, which is a characteristic of the Kauravas. Bhurishrava was a great warrior on the side of Kaurava, but he was fickle.

In Verse 58 of the Vivekachudamani of Shankaracharya, it says:

vagbaikharī śabdajharī śāstravyākhyānakauśalam
vaiduṣyam viduṣām tadvadbhuktaye na tu muktaye

"If we utter or chant mantras loudly to seek the almighty, it will produce nothing. If we cannot introvert our senses from the extroverted state, we cannot gain emancipation."

When we talk incessantly, shout irreverently, or sing loudly, it is like the talking and barking of a dog. Through talk, we cannot know God, we cannot receive liberation. When we remain in family life, constantly mixing and talking about worldly affairs, especially against spirituality, we are like the warriors of the Kaurava army.

JAYADRATHA is derived from *jaya*, which means win, and *drath*, which means to bluff with eloquent words. Jayadratha is the brother-in-law of Duryodhana. He was an uncultured person, always bluffing with falsehoods, and people were convinced by his exaggerations. In this world, there are many people who do not seek truth, and who, many times, speak against the truth.

This is another kind of person with little learning or knowledge about spirituality. A little learning is a dangerous thing. In the spiritual line, many cults have very little knowledge about spirituality. They exaggerate and speak highly of their own cult and try to convince many simple-minded people. They are misguided. The truth remains very far away, and we are all busy falsifying the truth. One ounce of practice of the Kriya Yoga technique is far better than tons of theories. Until you introvert your mind and go into the center where the soul is abiding, you will perceive nothing. Most people are like Jayadratha, in the party of Kaurava.

The Field of Battle

KURUKSHETRA contains *kuru* and *kshetra*. *Kuru* means to do—to do work. *Kshetra* means field. Every human being is a work field. But residing in the body field is the soul, Krishna. Kurukshetra is also a country where there was a vast land, which was the battlefield where the story in Bhagavad Gita took place. It is in the north of India near Delhi. The real battle occurs within the body of every human being.

DHARMAKSHETRA is another name for the battlefield of Kurukshetra. It comes from *dharma*, which means spirituality, and *kshetra*, field. In every human body, there are five qualities of divinity inside the spinal canal. At the top is Yudhishthira, the education minister. If we withdraw our power into the neck center, we will be wise. He is the eldest Pandava, abiding in every human body. The second is Bhima, the administrative minister of Krishna, controlling the air of each human body. Anybody who withdraws his air from the heart center to the pituitary will get divine power and can remain in the spiritual state.

We can achieve a third power by turning inward toward the navel center. This is where our food minister, Arjuna, resides. If you take spiritual food, you will get *dharma*, spirituality. If you attain *dharmakshetra,* then you are in the spiritual state. Arjuna was not conceived by sex pleasure. Kunti, his mother, inhaled from the navel center to the pituitary, so she conceived a divine child, Arjuna. Arjuna is the warrior who rides in the chariot near the pituitary, by Krishna's side. Food is of principal importance in every human body. Anyone who doesn't take food cannot develop energy, strength, or tremendous power.

Arjuna had tremendous power, which was recognized by Shri Krishna, so Krishna advised Arjuna to remain in the world and withdraw his senses from the lower centers to the upper center to acquire spirituality. In this sense, our navel center is our Dharmakshetra. Everyone in the universe is Arjuna. If we withdraw our power from the navel center to the pituitary, we will feel that the Kurukshetra, the human body, is also the Dharmakshetra, the spiritual body.

The fourth spiritual power is Nakula, which refers to endless desire for sex. This power is in the sacral center. From this power, people are conceived and evolve quickly toward spirituality. Through this power, the creation of God multiplies, and the human race can be transformed from ignorance to knowledge, from dishonesty to honesty, from unhappiness to happiness, and from bondage to liberation. Everyone who follows the soul will achieve liberation.

The last power of spirituality is in the coccygeal center, which is the fallow land, Kurukshetra. The owner of the land is Sahadeva. The entire power of the human being remains hidden in the coccygeal center. Those who can withdraw their senses by the power of Kriya Yoga will discover that the whole body is Dharmakshetra.

Dharmakshetra is the field of spirituality and morality. Every single human being is the field of activity and spirituality.

Illustrations

AUM activates the Triple Divine Powers: Divine Sound, Divine Vibration, and Divine Light

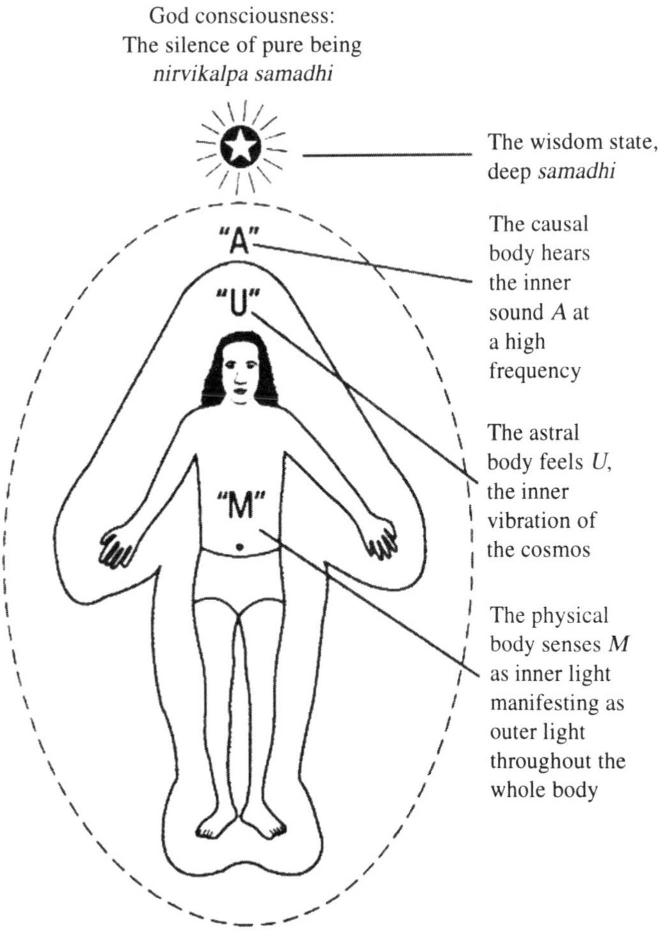
God consciousness:
The silence of pure being
nirvikalpa samadhi
The wisdom state, deep *samadhi*
"A"
"U"
"M"
The causal body hears the inner sound *A* at a high frequency
The astral body feels *U*, the inner vibration of the cosmos
The physical body senses *M* as inner light manifesting as outer light throughout the whole body

FIGURE 1: The causal body can hear the subtle voice of God; the soul is its inner ear. The astral body can feel the vibrating movement of cosmic consciousness near the pituitary as a spiraling sensation. The physical body can see the seven inner lights of the chakras in meditation as well as the visible light of the physical world. The physical world becomes *maya*, or illusion, when we forget that the soul is seeing through the physical body. Kriya Yoga activates the AUM power that creates continuous liberation.

The Human Brain—the Kingdom of God

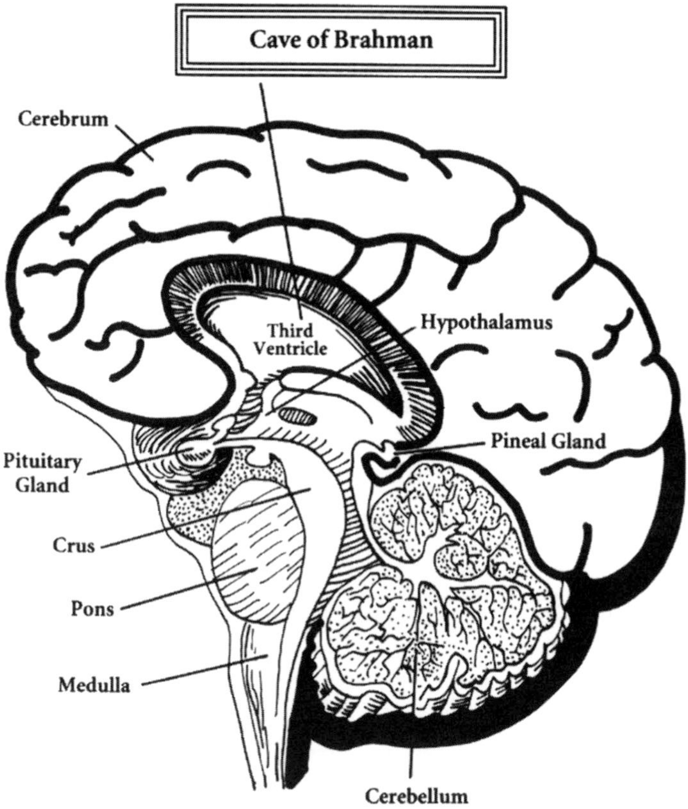

FIGURE 2: The living human brain is the mightiest power in creation. The life of every human being depends on it and is controlled by it. It has the power to reach beyond its own existence.

The "Cave of Brahman" is an etheric chamber where Brahman, the creative essence of the universal spirit manifests in mankind's fire altar of the individual soul (Krishna), where it burns and radiates pranic life force to the twenty-four gross body elements via the medulla, cerebellum, and so forth.

The pituitary and pineal glands, at opposite ends of the cave, are the positive and negative poles of Self-knowledge: solar–lunar, male–female, Krishna–Radha, and so on.

Seven Sacred Crossings: The Doorway between the Divine and Human Kingdoms

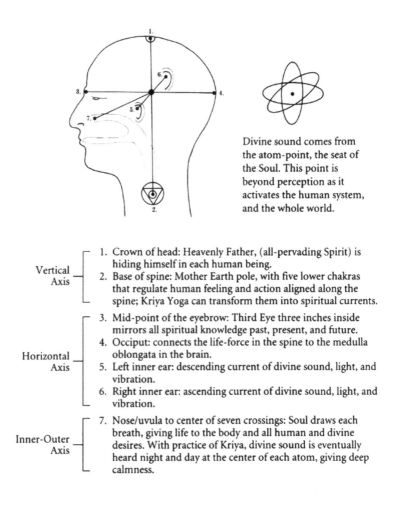

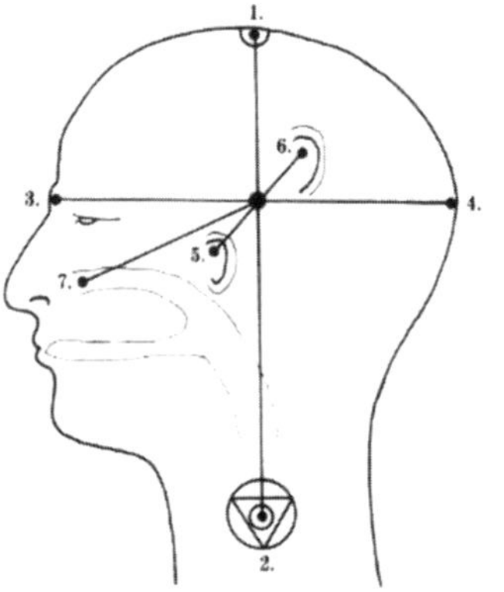

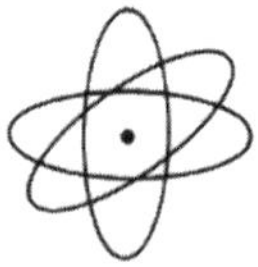

Divine sound comes from the atom-point, the seat of the Soul. This point is beyond perception as it activates the human system, and the whole world.

Vertical Axis

1. Crown of head: Heavenly Father, (all-pervading Spirit) is hiding himself in each human being.
2. Base of spine: Mother Earth pole, with five lower chakras that regulate human feeling and action aligned along the spine; Kriya Yoga can transform them into spiritual currents.

Horizontal Axis

3. Mid-point of the eyebrow: Third Eye three inches inside mirrors all spiritual knowledge past, present, and future.
4. Occiput: connects the life-force in the spine to the medulla oblongata in the brain.
5. Left inner ear: descending current of divine sound, light, and vibration.
6. Right inner ear: ascending current of divine sound, light, and vibration.

Inner-Outer Axis

7. Nose/uvula to center of seven crossings: Soul draws each breath, giving life to the body and all human and divine desires. With practice of Kriya, divine sound is eventually heard night and day at the center of each atom, giving deep calmness.

FIGURE 3: The seven sacred crossings enable beings to proceed towards godhood. Symbolized as Christ, and represented as a two-petalled lotus, this is the divine union of matter and spirit, *prakriti* and *purusha*. At this point, all duality dissolves into the eternal union of bliss and peace.

Some of the Organs and Glands Purified by Kriya Yoga.

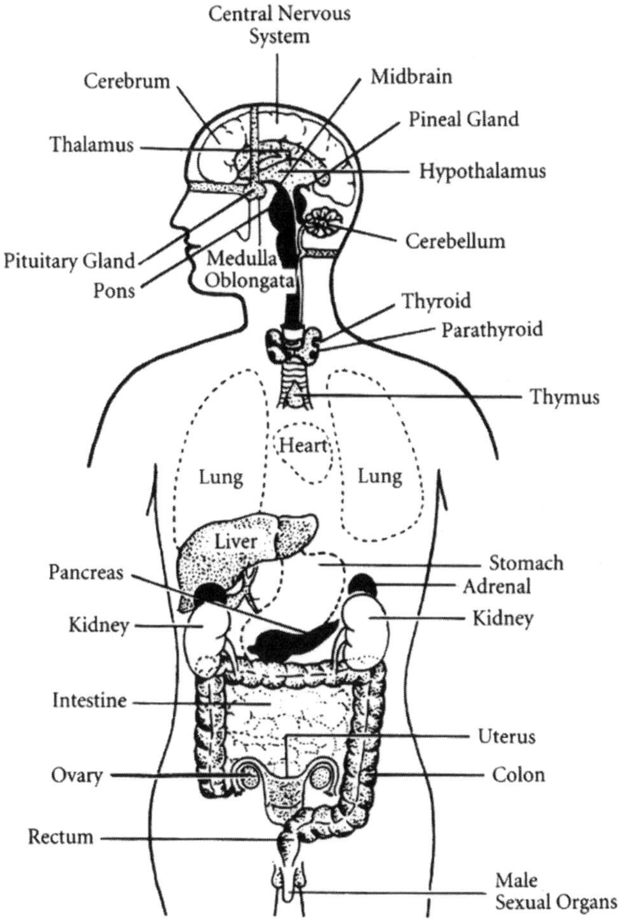

FIGURE 4: Organs and parts of the nervous system are affected positively by Kriya Yoga, building good health and preparing one for higher soul meditation.

The Effect of Kriya Yoga in the Spinal Cord

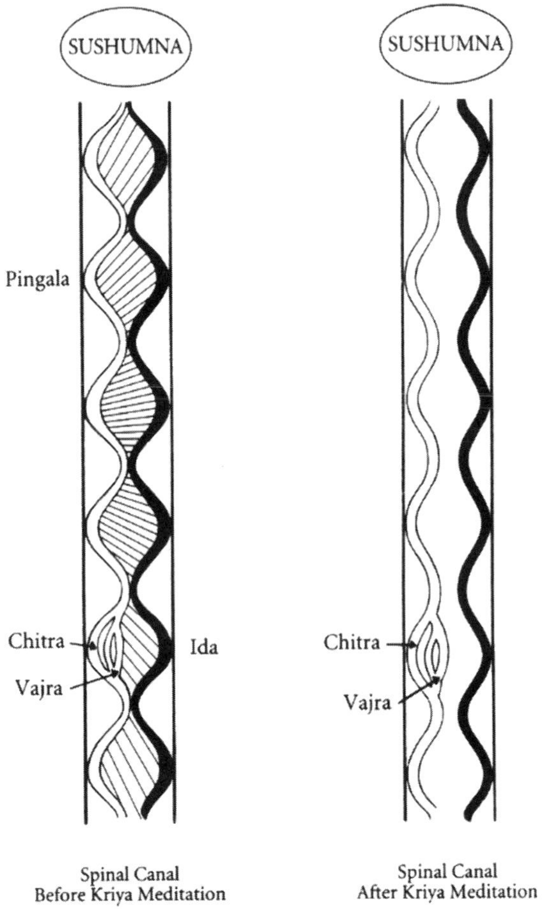

FIGURE 5: Kriya Yoga regulates the positive and negative fluctuations in the nervous system by magnetizing the spine. This opens the *sushumna* channel, which produces trmendous calm. The spinal column becomes an open channel for divine sound, light, and vibration.

The Kriya Method for Achieving the Stage Beyond Thought

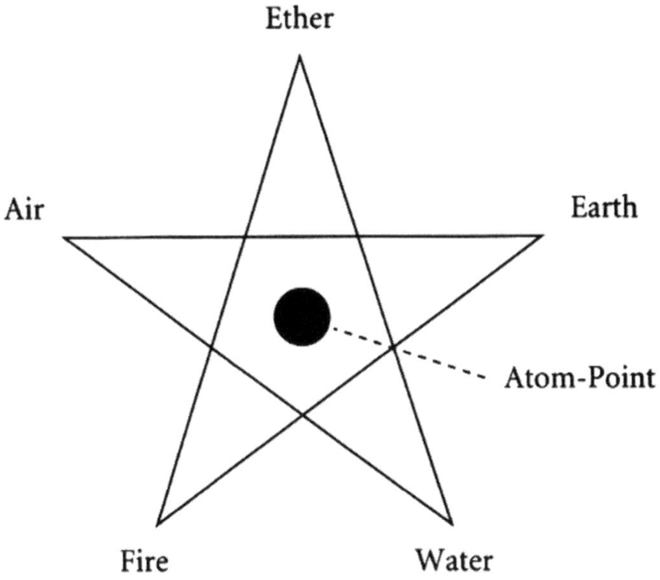

FIGURE 6: Focus your attention on the atom point in the anterior fontanel at the top of the head. If you stay focused in this empty inner space, then the distracting thoughts of the five elements (earth-money, water-sex, fire-food, air-emotion, and space-religion) cannot enter your mind. Your breath will grow very feeble, and you will enter *samadhi*, the thought-free stage. This is true single-minded meditation (Bhagavad Gita 5:27)

Every Human Body is a Bhagavad Gita

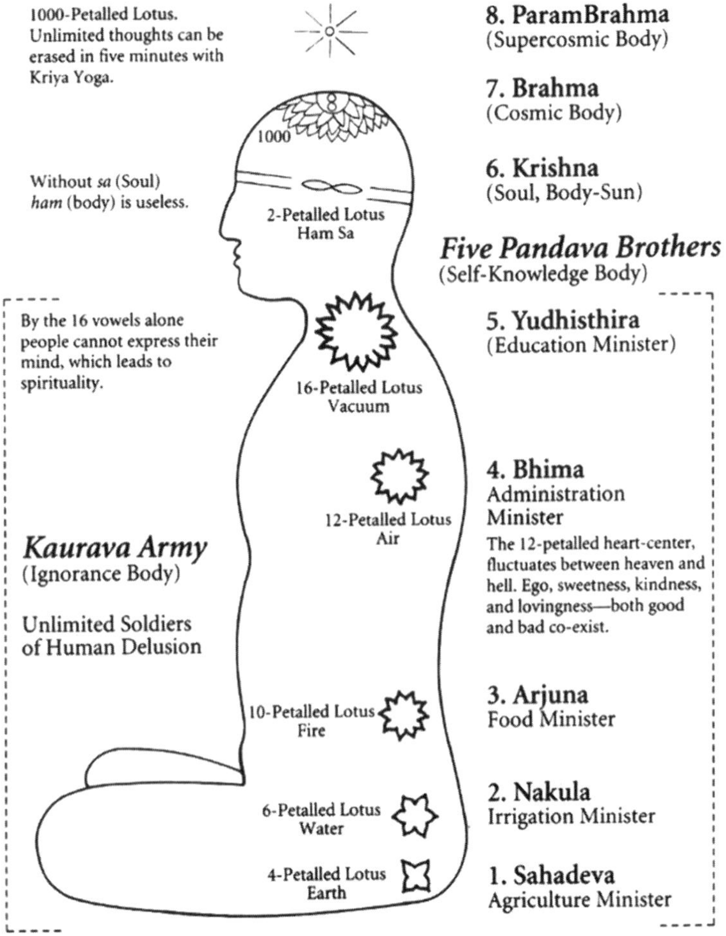

FIGURE 7: Human beings exchange feelings and thoughts through these fifty sacred letters, one for each lotus petal. When they cannot rise above their thoughts and worldly sense, their meditation is useless. With the first technique of Kriya Yoga, people can transcend mind, thought, intellect, and ego, and the body sense and worldly sense.

The Five Subtle Vital Airs in Every Human Body

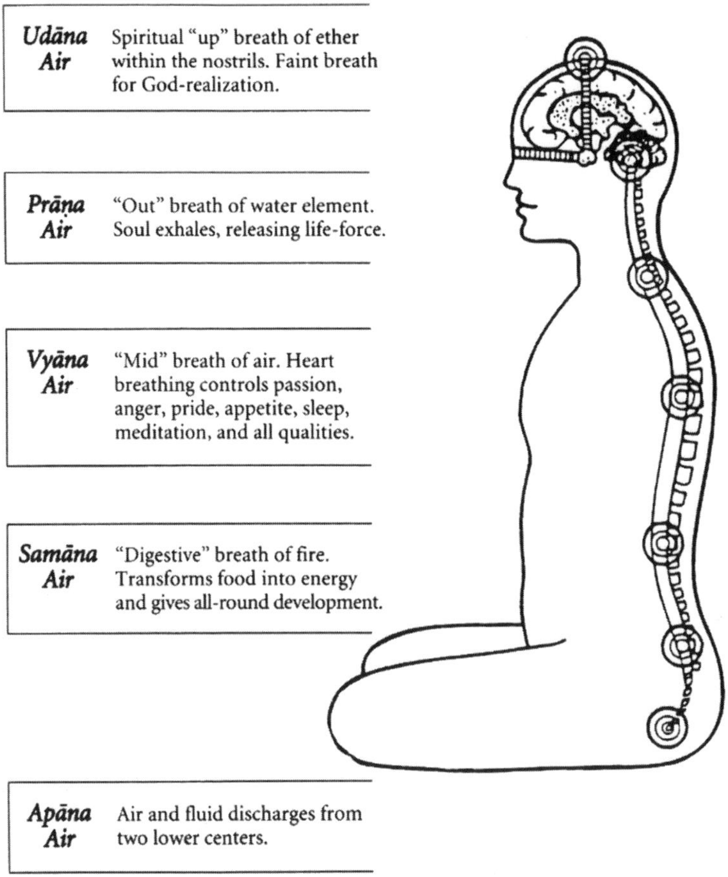
Udāna Air
Spiritual "up" breath of ether within the nostrils. Faint breath for God-realization.
Prāṇa Air
"Out" breath of water element. Soul exhales, releasing life-force.
Vyāna Air
"Mid" breath of air. Heart breathing controls passion, anger, pride, appetite, sleep, meditation, and all qualities.
Samāna Air
"Digestive" breath of fire. Transforms food into energy and gives all-round development.
Apāna Air
Air and fluid discharges from two lower centers.

FIGURE 8: Kriya Yoga meditation allows practitioners to become aware of their breath and regulate the five internal breaths.

The Seven Holy Fires in the Human System

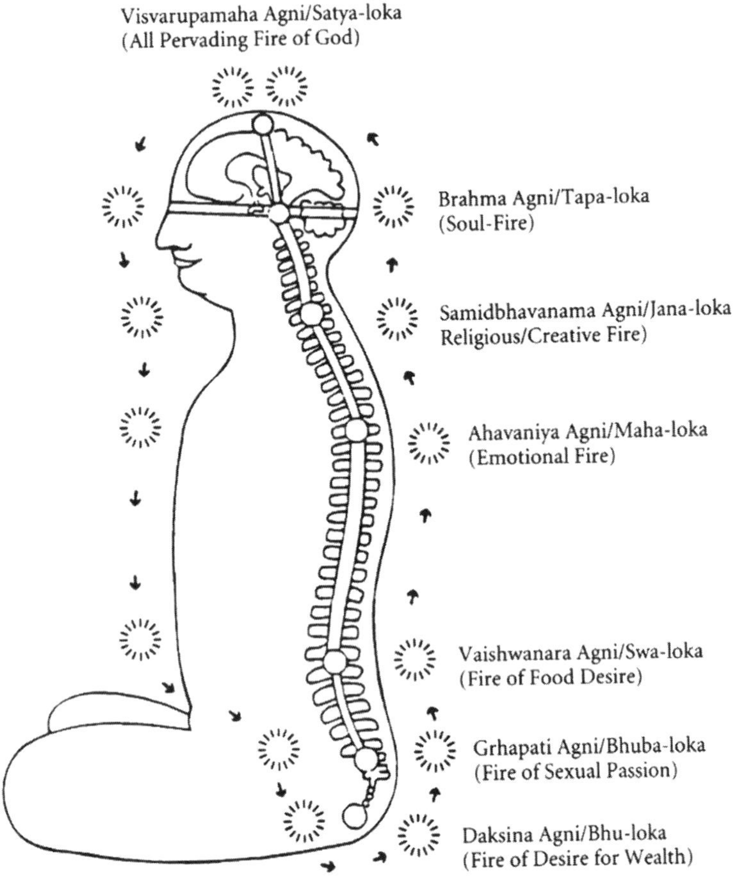

FIGURE 9: A Kriya yogi watches the seven "fires" circulating up the back of the spine and the seven "fires" moving down the front of the spine. These fires are the power of God. Outwardly, the fires manifest as seven types of desire; inwardly, they are perceived as lights that lead to knowledge, consciousness, superconsciousness, and cosmic consciousness. By watching this God fire in every action, you can perceive God as the sole doer in the body. This "solar" or divine fire grants constant alertness of the soul and liberation from karma.

One Cycle of Kriya Yoga
Completes a Solar Year of Spiritual Evolution

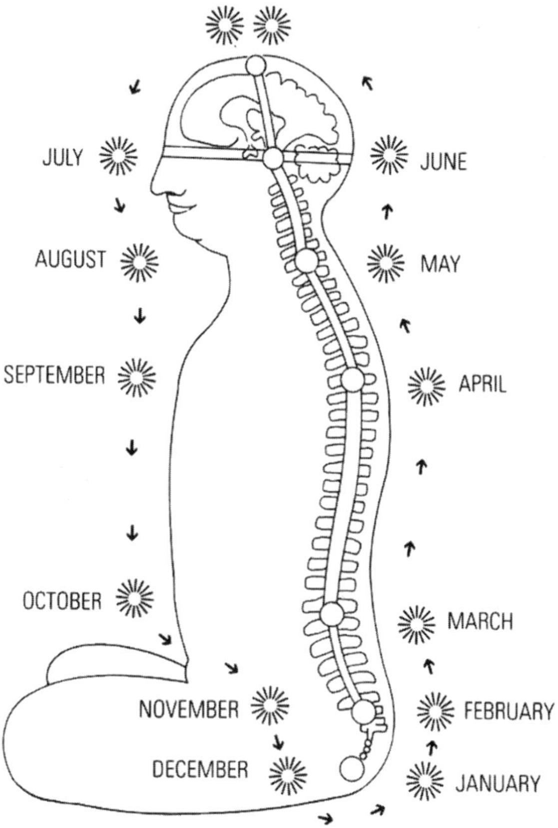

FIGURE 10: When the inner sound, light, or vibration is circulated in a microcosmic orbit up the spine and down the front of the body, this concentrated divine force acts like an internal sun that enables the Kriya meditator to complete an entire year's karma.

One Cycle of Kriya Yoga Includes the Phases of Every Lunar Month

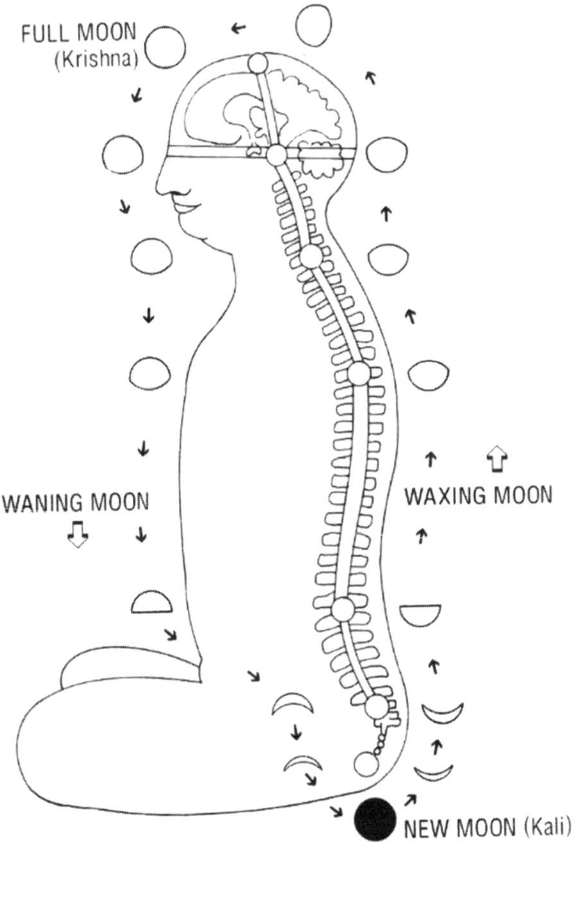

FIGURE 11: The moon cycle represents the changing desires of the human mind. Kriya Yoga balances the desire for money, sex, love, or food by drawing their elemental essences up the spine into the crown and back down into the coccyx. Kali, the dark goddess of the fifteenth, or new, moon symbolizes the *shakti* power coiled at the base of the spine. *Kala* is time, *i* is soul (Isha) who has mastered time, and therefore death. Krishna, who symbolizes the full light of soul consciousness, was born on the full moon.

The Correlations Between the Body Microcosm, Chakras, and AUM

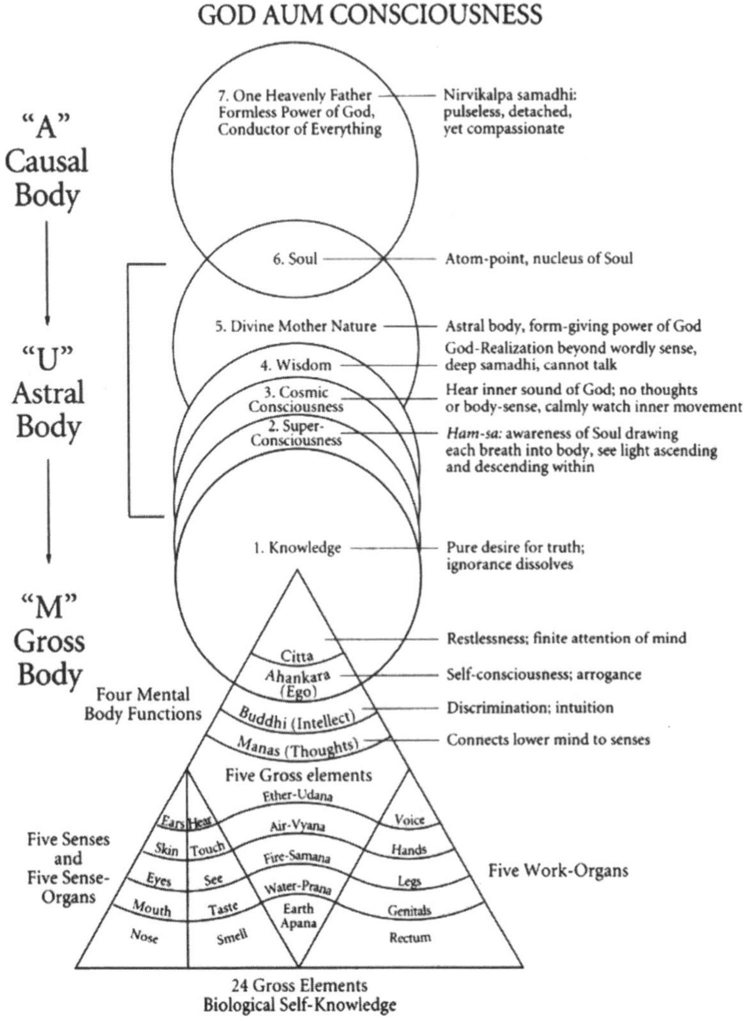

FIGURE 12: The human system, which includes the physical, astral, and causal bodies, is the prototype of the whole universe (creation) with the Creator (God) and various entities of human beings, spiritual and material.

Antasthavarna: The Seven Chakras

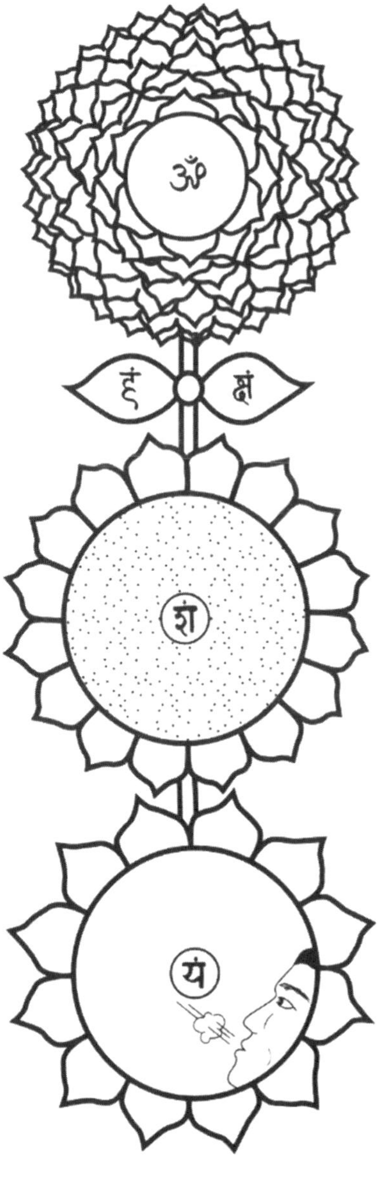

The Seat of the Creator, the One Formless Heavenly Father within every human being.

The image of heaven and earth in the human body. *Sa* is the image of heaven within the human body and indicates the Soul, the power of God that creates, activates, and conducts all the functions of the gross body. *Haṁ* indicates the earth and is the seed of the gross body.

In the beginning God created the Heaven and the Earth. (Genesis 1:1)

Vacuum/*Saṁ:* The first of the five primary gross elements of God's creation. It is formless, void, and dark.

And the Earth was without form, and void; and darkness was upon the face of the deep. (Genesis 1:2)

Air/*Yaṁ:* The second primary gross element of God's creation. The breath of God.

And the Spirit of God moved upon the face of the waters. (Genesis 1:2)

Fire/*Raṁ:* The third primary gross element of God's creation—solar light.

And God said, Let there be light: and there was light. (Genesis 1:3)

Water/*Vaṁ:* The fourth primary gross element of God's creation.

And God said, Let the waters under Heaven be gathered together unto one place. (Genesis 1:9)

Earth/*Laṁ:* The fifth primary gross element of God's creation.

And let the dry land appear: and it was so. And God called the dry land Earth. (Genesis 1:9-10)

FIGURE 13: Every human being is a microcosm of the universe. God creates human life according to the same fundamental procedures by which He created heaven and earth. The five root syllables, the sound vibrations in the five lower lotuses, are the first creations of God—space is *śam*, air is *yam*, fire is *ram*, water is *vam*, earth is *lam*—the primary gross elements from which all life grows. These seed syllables are *antasthavarna. Antasthavarna* means "life-giving sound, the generating life force that creates and establishes life."

The Placement of the Seed Syllables Within the Human Body

The Sanskrit language, from which all other languages have been derived, was formulated from the sounds of the 50 seed-syllables.

All the seed-syllables of the lotus petals are a manifestation, and an aggregation, of the seed-syllable Om, which is the power of God.

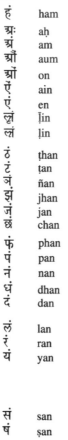

हं	ham
अः	aḥ
अं	am
औं	aum
ओं	on
ऐं	ain
एं	en
ॣं	ḹin
ॢं	ḷin
ठं	ṭhan
टं	ṭan
ञं	ñan
झं	jhan
जं	jan
छं	chan
फं	phan
पं	pan
नं	nan
धं	dhan
दं	dan
लं	lan
रं	ran
यं	yan
सं	san
षं	ṣan

क्षं	akṣam
अं	an
आं	ān
इं	in
ईं	īn
उं	un
ऊं	ūn
ऋं	ṛn
ॠं	ṝn
कं	kan
खं	khan
गं	gan
घं	ghan
ङं	ṅan
चं	can
डं	ḍan
ढं	ḍhan
णं	ṇan
तं	tan
थं	than
बं	ban
भं	bhan
मं	man
वं	van
शं	śan

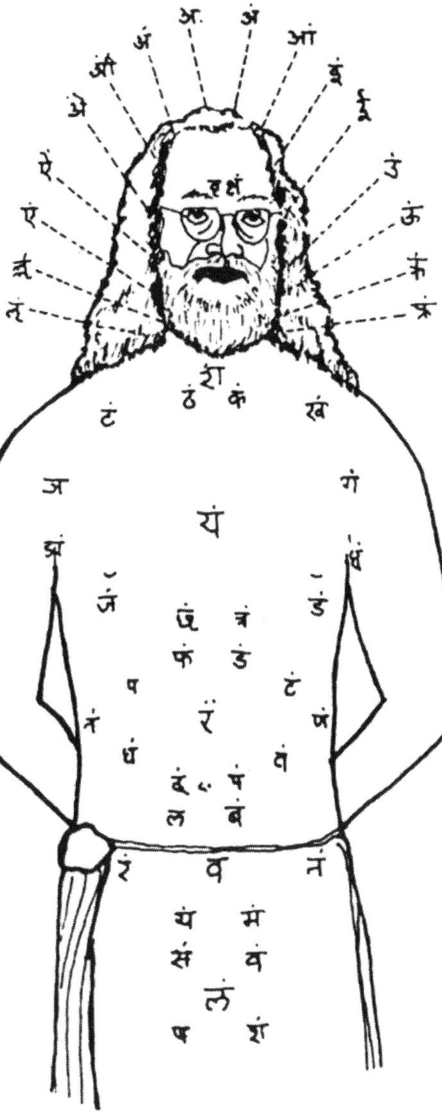

FIGURE 14: This is how all the seed syllables are positioned in the lotuses within the human body. Thoughts and propensities of the "I am," or ego, nature are produced by the forty-eight seed syllables that exist in the petals of the five lower lotuses. Kriya Yoga teaches how to remove them, whereby liberation and cosmic consciousness are attained.

The Sixth, Seventh, and Eighth Centers in the Human Being

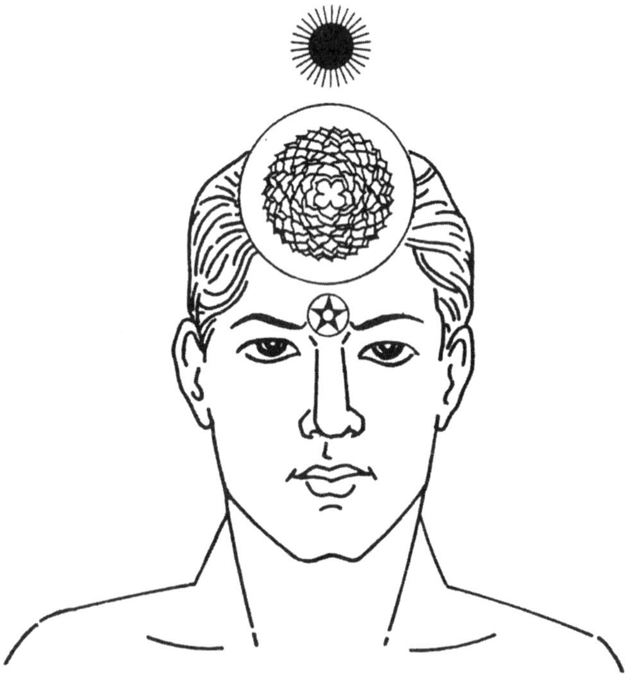

The Eighth Center: Eight-pointed Star *(Ishan)*. Above the body is the all-pervading power of God as it enters the human crown. It symbolizes infinity, the eighth divine fire, as it touches the finite. Whenever we move, we are always touching the power of God—the divine fire.

The Seventh Center: The 1000-petalled Lotus *(Mohadeva)*. The unmanifest infinity creates, energizes and pervades the manifest infinity (the universe, the creation), and remains compassionately detached.

The Sixth Center: Five-pointed Star Soul-center *(Pasu Pati)*. At the third eye, it is three inches deep at the mid-point of the eyebrows inside the brain. This atom-point symbolizes the Soul as Self-knowledge. It is beyond the fusion of the five elements (ether, air, fire, water, and earth). Your Soul manifests in the world as the five desires for money, sex, food, emotions, and religion.

FIGURE 15: The soul and the Supreme Soul.

The All-Pervading Fire of God

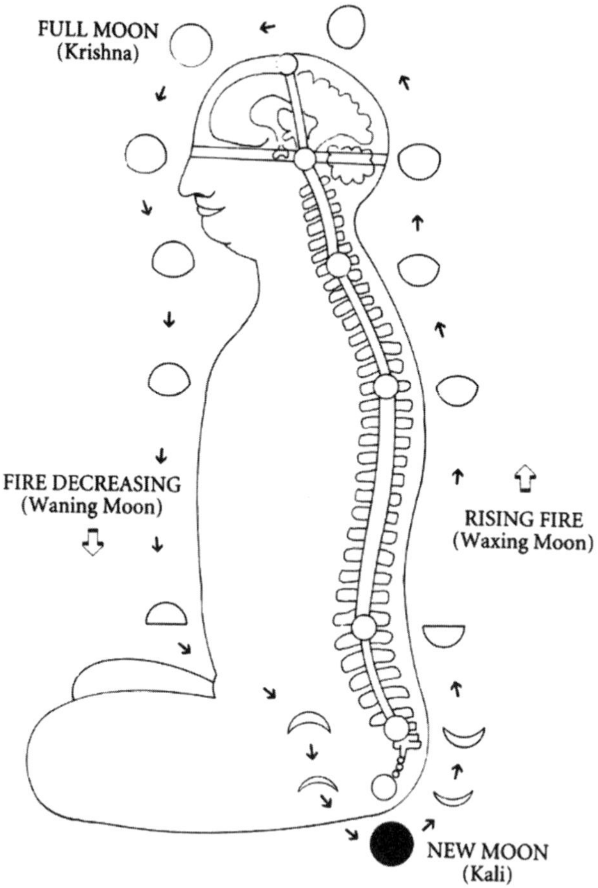

FIGURE 16: The moon cycle represents the changing desires of the human mind. Kriya Yoga spiritualizes the desire for money, sex, love, or food by drawing their elemental essence up the spine into the crown and back down into the coccyx. The fourteen phases or "lights" of the moon symbolize the life force in the fourteen centers (seven centers downward in front and seven centers upward in the back). The fifteenth, or new moon, recalls the spontaneous moment of creation by Mahakal. *Kala* is time, *i* is Isha, the great soul (Kali), who is the conductor of time.

The State of Cosmic Consciousness

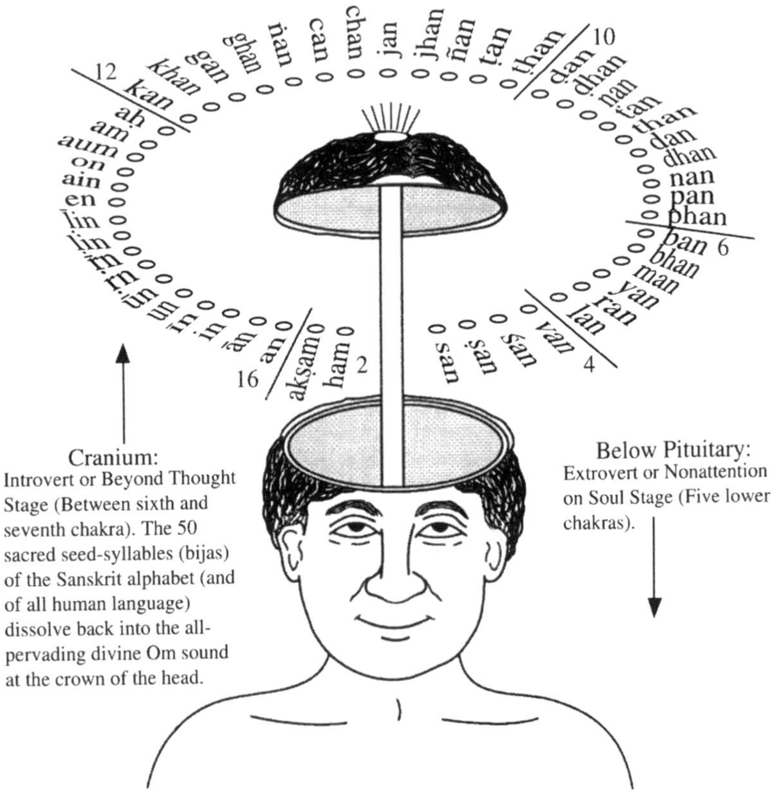
Cranium:
Introvert or Beyond Thought Stage (Between sixth and seventh chakra). The 50 sacred seed-syllables (bijas) of the Sanskrit alphabet (and of all human language) dissolve back into the all-pervading divine Om sound at the crown of the head.
Below Pituitary:
Extrovert or Nonattention on Soul Stage (Five lower chakras).

FIGURE 17: When, by the practice of Kriya Yoga, the fifty seed syllables, *ham-aksham*, are brought up from the lower centers and locked in the midbrain, they dissolve and become *ham-sa*. The two-petalled lotus has opened. At that time, the "I am," or ego, nature is completely deactivated. Liberation and spiritual illumination have been achieved, and the practitioner becomes an expression of cosmic consciousness in the world.

The Five Vacuums in the Cranium

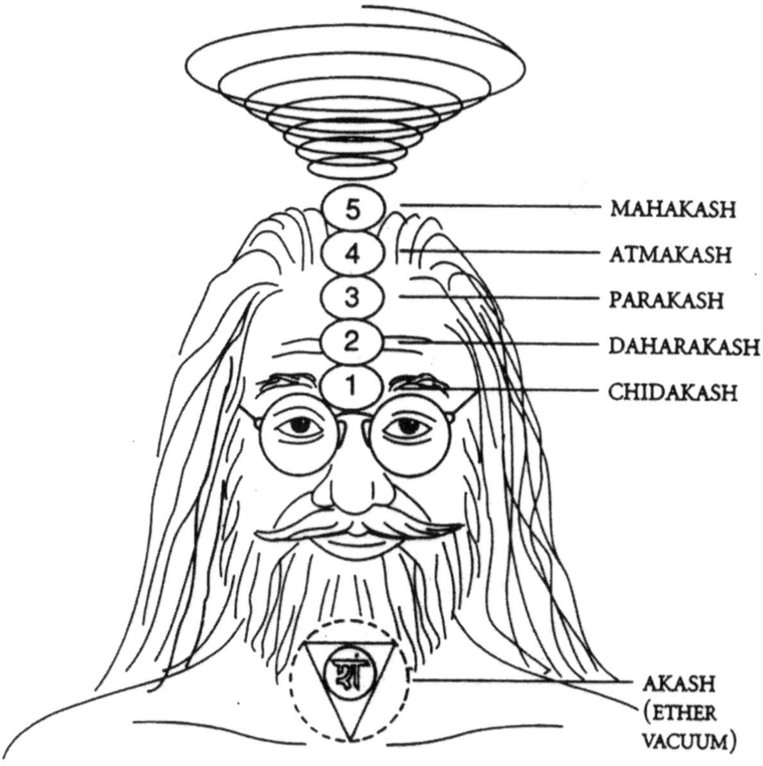

1. Chidakash: "life force" of human being in the pituitary.
2. Daharakash: "inner fire" born of meditation above the pituitary; no mind, body, ego, or intellect remains.
3. Parakash: "nothingness," superconscious state below fontanelle.
4. Atmakash: cosmic-conscious stage at the fontanelle.
5. Mahakash: "great emptiness," wisdom stage of nirvikalpa samadhi; merged in pulselessness above the fontanelle.

FIGURE 18: *Sunyam*, the five stages of meditative emptiness, have a common matrix of *akash*, which means "vacuum" or "empty space." *Akash* also means "sky," or "ether." The highest of the five primary gross elements occupies the space from the neck to the pituitary.

The Tree of Life

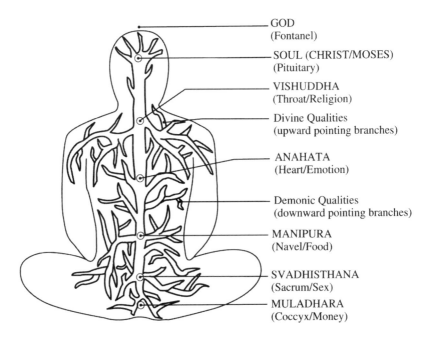

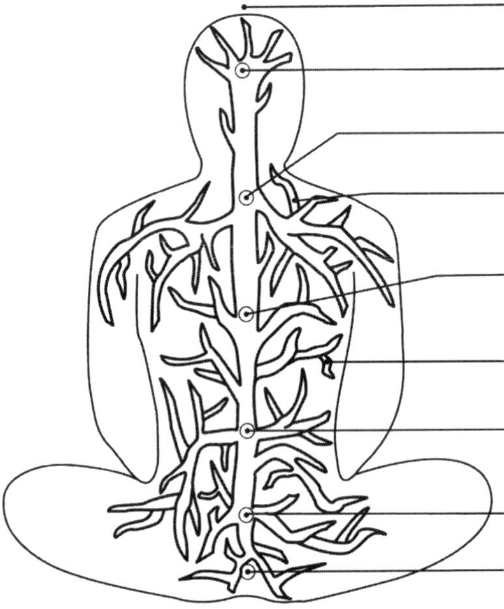

FIGURE 19: Every human body is an inverted tree (*See Chapter 15 of the Bhagavad Gita*). The root of the ordinary tree is below, but the root of the body tree is above. By Kriya Yoga meditation, one can go to the root of the body tree and destroy the ego, that is, achieve God-realization.

Chapter 1

Arjuna Vishada Yoga

The Yoga of Dejection

Introduction

Human life is a battlefield where we must fight the evil, weakness, and temptation inside us to reach a state of tranquility, peace, and emancipation. At first there is great deal of interest and enthusiasm for the fight, but after facing the practical problems of spiritual life, most become dejected, believing that there is no reason to lead a rigorous life of discipline and control.

In the Bhagavad Gita, Arjuna arrived at the battlefield prepared and ready to fight, but seeing the Kauravas before him, he felt his attachment to them, which led to infatuation. Since Arjuna was a hero and a very successful man, everyone was watching him at this critical juncture. Unfortunately, he fell prey to dejection and sorrow.

Metaphorically, Arjuna represents every spiritual seeker who is trying to reach the state of emancipation with the guidance of his divine preceptor, friend, and guide. But standing in the middle of the battlefield of life, overwhelmed by an inner struggle against all his negatives and weakness, Arjuna thought it would be better to avoid the battle, not because of his pure intellect or rational outlook, but due to his attachment to the world.

The Bhagavad Gita starts with an expression of anxiety from the blind king Dhritarashtra, who wishes to know what is currently happening on the battlefield of Kurukshetra. His minister, Samjaya, is sitting with him in the inner chamber of his palace in the capital city of Hastinapur. Samjaya will become the messenger.

The Bhagavad Gita is a poetic masterpiece, a beautiful composition of Maharshi Vyasa. It addresses all aspects of spiritual life in a very systematic way, step by step, as a discourse of questions and answers. The Bhagavad Gita is a complete spiritual text and gives all the answers to the inquisitive mind in a most logical and practical way.

Verse 1

dhṛtarāṣṭra uvāca
dharmakṣetre kurukṣetre
samavetā yuyutsavaḥ
māmakāḥ pāṇḍavāś cai'va
kim akurvata samjaya

Translation

Dhritarashtra said:
O Samjaya! When my children and the Pandavas assembled to fight on the sacred field of Kurukshetra, what did they do?

Metaphorical Interpretation

Dhritarashtra is the king, the elder brother of Pandu and the father of the Kauravas. His name has two meanings. First, it means one who is the protector, savior, and preserver of the body kingdom. But the question is: Who is really the savior of the body kingdom? The answer is: It is the soul, represented by Krishna, who continuously draws the breath in through the nose of every human being. In truth, Krishna is the savior, receiver, and protector of the body kingdom. But most ordinary human beings do not believe that their soul is the sole doer, responsible for all their actions. Rather, they attribute more importance to their own minds. So, in this sense, human beings are blind, not understanding that they must seek the soul to know themselves. Dhritarashtra is a blind king because he cares only for the material world. He has no clear judgment or knowledge. He could have easily prevented the battle, but due to his ignorance in darkness, he did not. The second meaning of Dhritarashtra is blind mind.

Our body is our Kurukshetra. *Kuru* means work. *Kshetra* means place or field. We constantly perform work and become consumed by it. Inside our spinal canal there are five work fields. The first four are the coccygeal, the money center; the sacral, the sex center; the lumbar (navel), the food center; and the dorsal (heart), the seat of emotions where many negative and positive thoughts such as anger, greed, suspicion, love, and compassion arise. These four centers are mostly biological centers. When consciousness is absorbed in these regions, people are engrossed in money, sex, food, pride, doubt, and friction. Human beings won't attain divinity engrossed in these activities and in the physical senses. The fifth center is the vacuum center, the religion and philosophy center. Together, these five centers are our Kurukshetra. People who cannot withdraw their minds from these lower centers cannot achieve the superconscious state.

Dharmakshetra is composed of two words, *dharma* and *kshetra*. *Dharma* comes from *dhri*, which means the power of receptivity, and *mana*, which means life. By the power of God and soul, we are all alive. *Dharmakshetra* is the place where our living soul remains.

In the Purusha Sukta of the Vedas, it says, *atra tiṣṭhaddaśa angulam*, which means: "The soul remains inside the cranium, ten fingers above our eyebrows." If you start at a level between your eyebrows and measure four finger widths of one hand up your forehead, then place your other hand above that to measure another four finger widths, and then again, two more finger widths, you are ten fingers above your eyebrows. At this point you will find a hole, the fontanel, which is the divine goal.

Most probably you have seen that every baby has a soft spot in the middle of its scalp. This is where the power of God enters into every human baby. It is called the *sahasra padma*, the thousand-petaled lotus. From here, God creates a thousand kinds of thought in every human being. If you penetrate down from the fontanel, you will find the anterior and posterior pituitary ten fingers directly below. This is the junction of our five sense telephones and the seven crossings of our life, which is the *dharmakshetra*. Our two vagus nerves and the other eleven pairs of cranial nerves start from this center, and our motor and sensory nerves also function from here.

If you can withdraw your senses from the five lower centers inside the spinal canal, which is *kurukshetra*, and focus your attention to penetrate above the cranium, which is *dharmakshetra*, you can withdraw knowledge from ignorance, honesty from dishonesty, immortality from mortality. Then, you can tap the spiritual force that remains inside the cranium.

The seven crossings is a junction that joins seven points. It is the intersection of lines between the fronts of our two ears, between the glabella and occipital, and between the fontanel and coccygeal centers. The seventh "point" is the path air travels when we inhale through our mouth and draw it up to the pituitary, with the breath making a cold sensation on our uvula. Jesus said you are to be born from above, that is, from the place of the seven sacred crossings, that is, the soul center. (*See Fig. 3, page 56*)

Dronacharya, the guru of the Pandavas and Kauravas, could not be killed unless somebody shot an arrow through his throat that crossed the place of the seven sacred crossings. *Dronacharya* is a fickle-minded person. So symbolically Dronacharya represents the fickleness in everybody. Until we raise our awareness above the junction of the seven crossings, our fickleness will not die or disappear. If our fickleness doesn't disappear, we cannot achieve God-realization. Until we cross this junction, we cannot transcend the human stage and we cannot attain godhood.

Although there was a historical battle on Kurukshetra between the Kauravas and Pandavas, metaphorically the fight is between ignorance and knowledge, between the evil and good in us all, not a fight between relatives or even human beings. The evil qualities of a human being are related to the body, as are the good qualities. But neither good or evil qualities can exist without the soul (Krishna), so Krishna is the mediator of the good and bad qualities in every human being.

Our ignorance is darkness, and our knowledge is light. *Kuru paksha* is our darkness and *pandava paksha* is our light. In a fight between light and darkness, who will win? When you enter a dark room and turn on the light switch, immediately the darkness disappears, converted into light. In this way, light (knowledge) defeats darkness (ignorance).

Inside every human body there is a mind, which is a blind king like Dhritarashtra. Thus, we live in darkness. Dhritarashtra knew that the people of Kaurava (ignorance) would surely be defeated by the Pandavas (knowledge). Yet, when the two parties assembled on the sacred field Kurukshetra, he asked Samjaya what they were doing.

All human beings are born for Self-realization. For this journey, a realized guru such as Shri Krishna will always guide, conduct, instruct, and lead us to the divine goal. Before we are realized however, we are engrossed and absorbed in the biological force, in a state of delusion, illusion, and error. We do not have the peace that comes from remaining absorbed in God. But the day will surely come when we will develop a virtuous inclination, and we will reach the divine goal; then our ignorance (darkness) will disappear in the light of the formless state, liberated and Self-realized. The whole creation is a manifestation of *prana,* the life force, the power of God. The higher aspect of this *prana* is Mother Nature, the spiritual energy or force. The lower aspect of *prana* is the biological force or energy, the lower nature.

When God first created human beings, they were savages and brutes. They did not know how to wear clothes, how to lie down on nice beds, how to eat food, or how to behave. Gradually, we have advanced and learned many things. Starting with little education, we are now extremely advanced scientifically; we can accomplish many things. Although we have no foresight like Samjaya, we scientifically see things from a long distance with inventions such as television. Samjaya was able to hear sounds or see sights over long distances with divine power. Through telephone and television, we can talk to friends and relatives around the world and see events happening in distant places. Scientifically, we are advancing toward the divine goal.

Those who practice the scientific technique of Kriya Yoga as described in the Bhagavad Gita (6:11 and 12) can perceive the Self in a very short time. Because we are the children of God, we have the potential for purity, love, and perfection. The purity and perfection of God always exists inside the cranium and the pituitary. When you meditate and move your awareness up into the pituitary, you can perceive God. Spirituality, divinity, and liberation are in your hands.

Verse 2

samjaya uvāca
dṛṣṭvā tu pāṇḍavāṇīkam
vyūḍham duryodhanas tadā
ācāryam upasamgamya
rājā vacanam abravīt

Translation

Samjaya said:
When King Duryodhana saw the regiment of the Pandavas arranged in the battlefield, he went to his teacher and spoke these words.

Metaphorical Interpretation

The word "meditation" comes from the word for "mind." When you can withdraw your mind from the body and material world, it is called meditation.

The Bhagavad Gita (4:29, 5:27, 6:11-15, 25, 26) describes some beautiful techniques for withdrawing your mind, thought, and intellect from the body and the world. These are the techniques practiced in Kriya Yoga, but they should be learned from a realized Kriya Yoga master. From the beginning, people practicing these techniques can withdraw their minds from the lower centers of the spinal canal, reach the pituitary, and see a dazzling golden light inside a blue island, like the tunnel between our two eyebrows. The light is the regiment of the Pandavas, and the tunnel between the two eyebrows is the battlefield. However, the longstanding influence of our biological force brings the mind down, and we must try again to bring it up. This is the real fight between the Kauravas (biological forces) and the Pandavas (spiritual forces).

Verse 3

paśyai 'tām pāṇḍuputrāṇām
ācārya mahatīm camūm
vyūḍhām drupadaputreṇa
tava śiṣyeṇa dhīmatā

Translation

O master of the Pandavas! Please see how your expert disciple (Dhristadyumna), son of Drupada, has made a worthy battle formation with the mighty armies of the Pandava.

Metaphorical Interpretation

Metaphorically, this verse gives a clear picture of the fight between the biological and spiritual bodies. Our biological body is full of ignorance, or darkness, and our spiritual body is full of knowledge, or light. Duryodhana is the mind, the king of every human being. He knew that in a fight between darkness and light, the darkness would surely disappear the moment the light switch was turned on. Having seen the regiment of the knowledge body, Duryodhana was so frightened that he addressed his own guru as "O master of Pandava," instead of, "O my revered master." This is not a battle between people; it is the spiritual battle between virtue and vice within every human being. The virtuous, the Pandavas and their party, remain above in the cranium. The "regiment" does not consist of people; it refers to many dazzling divine lights, like a rainbow in a circle. In the center, varieties of lights and stars are automatically perceived. Upon perceiving the divine light, divine vibration, and divine sound, the mind of a spiritual person is completely engrossed in this trinity, and that person feels love for God. Then our biological forces—our atoms, tissues, cells, diaphragm, and heart function—cool down. Automatically, the evil power, thoughts, and viciousness disappear, and the mind reaches the junction between the two regiments.

Verses 4–6

atra śūrā maheṣvāsā
bhīmārjunasamā yudhi
yuyudhāno virāṭaś ca
drupadaś ca mahārathaḥ

dhṛṣṭaketuś cekitānaḥ
kāśirājaś ca vīryavān
purujit kuntibhojaś ca
śaibyaś ca narapuṃgavaḥ

yudhamanyuś ca vikrānta
uttamaujāś ca vīryavān
saubhadro draupadeyāś ca
sarva eva mahārathāḥ

Translation

Here are heroes and great archers, equal in battle to Bhima and Arjuna: Yuyudhana, Virata, and the great chariot warrior Drupada,

Dhrishtaketu, Chekitana, the powerful king of Kashi, Purujit, Kuntibhoja, and Shaibya the foremost man,

Yudhamanyu the powerful, Uttamauja the brave, and the son of Subhadra (Abhimanyu), and the [five] sons of Draupadi. All of them are great heroes on the side of Pandava.

Metaphorical Interpretation

There was a historical war in Kurukshetra, a fight between the Kauravas and the Pandavas, but the real war is inside us. The Kaurava party is always busy with evil propensities, extroverted, full of ambition, living in darkness. Generally, every human being is in an extroverted state, in ignorance, darkness, and delusion. However, in every human there is also *dharmakshetra,* the Pandava army, the spiritual power that exists in the cranium and the spine. The Pandava party is the spiritual force: knowledge, consciousness, superconsciousness, and cosmic consciousness. For God-realization we require the powerful battalions of the Pandava party.

These verses list the names of the many soldiers on the side of the Pandavas. Each name has a metaphorical meaning. (*A more extensive discussion of the meaning of each warrior's name is given in "Metaphorical Meaning of Character Names."*) From the meaning of the names we can learn how human beings can remove their bad qualities and become one with the marvelous power of God. The fourth verse begins, *atra śurā maheṣvāsā. Maheshvasa* means they are extremely powerful. Knowledge is extremely powerful, more powerful than ignorance. Light dispels darkness. Knowledge liberates us from the clutch of ignorance.

Bhima means breath. The administrative minister, Bhima, gives us control over the five types of breath: *prana, apana, samana, udana,* and *vyana.* Bhima can transform evil tendencies into the divine by using the divine breath, a unique short, feeble breath. This special air, very slow and feeble, gives us control. When a devotee wants God-realization, he must have breath control. Breath control is self-control; breath mastery is self-mastery. This is Bhima.

Arjuna is food, which gives us our body and our strength. Arjuna is mastery over the desire for food. Food also provides us with the finest talent and intellect.

Next is Yuyudhana, one who is willing to fight the evil propensities connected with the body. Yuyudhana symbolizes a strong desire for purity, perfection, and love for gurus. When you always try to fight your evil propensities, you will reach God-realization.

Virata means *vigata rat,* literally, without kingdom, having no sense of the body. When you sit for meditation you cannot meditate if you have a body sense, a sense of the world, or many thoughts. Our body sense is an awareness of the physical body, its existence in time and space, including thoughts, ideas, visualization, and imagination. Within a short meditation period, you must go beyond mind, thought, intellect, ego, body sense, and worldly sense. This is Virata, the freedom from body sense. Using the Kriya Yoga technique, you can magnetize your spine by bowing and touching your head on the ground seven times; then you will automatically be free from any body sense and worldly sense. You can then withdraw your mind, thought, and intellect from the body sense, from the coccygeal to the pituitary, and enter the state without thought, the formless state, and ultimately the conscious *samadhi* state. This is Virata, a commander for God-realization.

Drupada means you are to go quickly. You should not wait; don't keep it for tomorrow. *Drupada* is *druta pada*: *Pada* means steps and *druta* means quick. Go quickly from the lower centers to the upper center in the pituitary and fix your attention in the atom point. Then immediately, within a minute's time, you will feel a sensation that is the movement of your soul. Also you will hear the talk of God, the *mantra* of God, and you will see divine illumination. We should not sit for meditation for a long period: When we do, we come back down to the biological state, the human state. An idle brain is the devil's workshop. If we can complete our meditation within a short period, we will become extremely alert and will perceive God.

Dhrishtaketu is also a spiritual warrior: *dhrishtan ketu. Ketu* is the south pole of the body. Ketu, a character in Indian mythology and a planet in Indian astrology, has a body up to the neck, but no head. Ketu's ambition is to get a head, so he is always looking to the north, where the power of God, the soul, Krishna, dwells. Similarly, if you have the desire to remain in the highest center, in between your eyebrows, inside the cranium, then you will attain self-control.

Chekitana is derived from *chekit*, which means immediately, and *tan*, sound. When you sit for meditation, you must keep your attention in the vacuum and fix your attention in the atom point, in the divine kingdom. Then you will immediately hear divine sound of many varieties, which will make you extremely calm. Also, your memory will be sharpened. *Kashiraja* means you are experiencing brilliant, dazzling, divine illumination of many colors. If you raise your eyebrows and remain inside the atom point, in the cranium, you will immediately see the divine light. Through this your thoughts will be transformed into cosmic consciousness, which will give you continuous liberation.

Purujit is another soldier for soul culture. *Puru* (from *pauran*) means body, and *jit* (from *jayati*) means to conquer, to go beyond your body sense. One who has gone beyond the body sense is a soldier on the side of the Pandavas. You must go beyond your body sense, hear the divine sound, and feel that you have no body. Until you physically die, you cannot receive the spiritual energy, so your body sense must disappear. For God-realization you require this formless state, which is *purujit.*

Ashtanga Yoga consists of eight limbs, eight groups of techniques, which are *yama, niyama, asana, pranayama, pratyahara, dharana, dhyana*, and *samadhi*. But Kriya Yoga is not Ashtanga Yoga. It is the last four parts of Ashtanga Yoga, which are *pratyahara, dharana, dhyana*, and *samadhi*. Purujit means *pratyahara*, complete freedom from the body sense. When we are completely free from the body sense, we experience *dharana*, the divine conception of God. *Dhyana* means being very near the door of God. This is the state of superconsciousness and cosmic consciousness. After *dhyana* comes *samadhi*, the state of wisdom. Wisdom is *prajña.* In the great commandments of the Vedas it is said, *prajñanam brahman*: "Wisdom is God." The highest stage of *samadhi* is *nirvikalpa samadhi*, the pulseless stage. In this stage, the devotee plunges into the infinite and experiences love for God and emancipation.

The next soldier is Kuntibhoja. The power inside the pituitary is called *kun (dhatu) ti. Kun* means atom – the finest atom point in the soul. Kuntibhoja refers to a monk who holds his attention like the needle of a compass in the pituitary. He also rolls up his tongue to the uvula, the soft palate. When this is achieved the divine nectar rolls down slowly, drop by drop, from the pituitary. As the practitioner drinks it, he is filled with bliss and transcendental joy, which is very helpful for attaining God-realization and achieving superhuman power. He can foresee the future and can hear sound from long distances, and he has many other miraculous powers. When you remain constantly in the atom point, you will realize that the power of God is doing everything: You talk from the atom point; you hear from there; you do your work from there; your five sense organs are activated there; your nine doors work from there; your twenty-four gross elements are working from that place. If you remain there, you will be free. You will perceive that you are completely saturated with God.

Shaibya means to be calm, to be still. In the Bible it says, "Be still and know that I am God." This is *shaibya*—one who has attained the vacuum (calm) stage of meditation, one who has extreme peace of mind. He is completely free from all worldly sense and perceives only the triple divine qualities in his whole body. He has attained the stage of Brahman and has merged with Brahman in the pituitary. He is extremely divine. He is God in every human being.

Yudhamanyu is a great warrior. *Yudha* means to fight; *manyu* means sin; therefore *yudhamanyu* is to fight with sin. If you open your eyes, you'll find the world is full of allure, full of temptation, full of evil, and full of the tendency to be extroverted. Your whole system is extroverted. This is why we require the soldier Yudhamanyu. He sits in the pituitary and does not allow any sin or evil impurity to rise up into the cranium from the biological force. If you keep your attention in the pituitary and search for the living power of God, which is your soul, Krishna, then you are Yudhamanyu. Then, when you meditate, you will not be distracted by desire for money, sex, or food, or by anger, pride, or cruelty. You also will not have a lower grade of meditation, such as *puja* (ritualistic worship), *tantra* (a special technique of rituals and meditation), or *japa* (chanting). These are spiritual practices, but of a lower grade. Yudhamanyu will give you the top grade of meditation: Kriya Yoga.

The next powerful warrior for the Pandavas is Uttamauja. *Uttama* means extremely beautiful, and *ojas* means strength. When a devotee nears this powerful state, he forgets his physical senses and merges with Mother Nature, which is supreme consciousness. He is free, filled with extreme divine sensation and divine power. Entering the *samadhi* state, the *sadhaka* perceives the eternal purity, experiences the omnipresent witness, and enjoys heavenly peace.

The great warrior Saubhadra is the son of Arjuna and Subhadra. Abhimanyu (another name for Saubhadra) entered the spine through the bottom center and proceeded north towards the fifth center and then reached the sixth center. After that, he did not come back; he remained there. Saubhadra knows how to remove evil, sin, and restlessness from the four lower centers. The devotee, when meditating deeply, remains steadfastly determined to withdraw his senses from coccygeal to sacral, sacral to lumbar, and lumbar to dorsal. The dorsal is the most vicious of the biological centers. Human madness, the desire for strong drugs and intoxicants, and viciousness have their seat there. With deep meditation you can ascend from the lower centers to the upper center. After that, you can feel the living power of God doing all the work you do; this is Saubhadra.

You are born of the flesh, so you desire things of the flesh. But Jesus said that the divine kingdom and heaven are within you. If you are born from above, through water and spirit, then you will desire Him. You do not have to wait for death to seek liberation; instead, you should find it right now. If you meditate, you will get liberation immediately. The Bhagavad Gita (15) says that the body is perishable, but the root of the body tree remains above in the soul. All the imperishable qualities are stored in your astral body, in the soul

(**Krishna**). When you meditate, you can perceive and realize *purushottama*, the almighty father of the universe.

The Draupadeya are the five sons of Draupadi, who was the wife of all five Pandava brothers. Her sons are the essence, or the atom power, of the five Pandavas. They are in the lower five centers of the spine. Draupadi means the quickest progress. Her sons are in the body to help you quickly reach the divine goal. Their power can immediately destroy the biological forces of any human being. They can draw their power up above the pituitary to the fontanel, and they can transmute that power. Negative tendencies will still surface, but you can immediately transform them into the positive by the power of the five sons who fight for your God-realization.

In everyday life, the five sons of Draupadi are particularly helpful and powerful allies. You work to earn income, and you require money for your livelihood, but you do not earn the money. Keep ninety percent of your attention in the fontanel while you are working, and you will quickly understand that money comes from the soul. Soul and money are one. This understanding comes from the power of the five sons of Draupadi who abide in the five lower centers. In the same way, in the second center you will feel that without soul you cannot experience sexual joy. You will enjoy sex, but you will remain mostly in the soul and feel that the joy is coming from God. Many foods will give you strength and energy, but when you go to the top, you will see that food really comes from God. Similarly, in the heart center, many negative emotions—anger, pride, envy, and so forth—will arise, but you can immediately remove them. Everything can be removed. The fifth center gives you the power to achieve top-grade meditation, which also comes from the soul, Krishna. With the help of the five atom powers of the Pandavas, we can easily eliminate evil and sinful thoughts and constantly enjoy God-realization and liberation.

The five sons of Draupadi are five powerful warriors who live in everybody. They are the greatest warriors for God-realization. After practicing Kriya Yoga, you will grasp the true meaning of all the names, and then you can apply that understanding in your practical life for the quickest spiritual development. All of these warriors are in Arjuna's knowledge party, the party of the Pandavas. They are the soldiers on the side of God-realization. The Bhagavad Gita exists only for God-realization.

In India, they say, *prasthana trayi:* "There are three books." One is the Bhagavad Gita, the second is the Upanishads, and the third is the Brahmasutras. Each verse in these three books guides us toward God-realization, liberation, and entry into the formless state. If you read one verse and apply it to your life, you will attain the divine goal, God-realization. One verse is enough. The same is also true for other scriptures such as the Bible, the Torah, and the Koran.

Verse 7–8

asmākam tu viśiṣṭā ye
tān nibodha dvijottama
nāyakā mama sainyasya
samjñārtham tān bravīmi te

bhavān bhīṣmaś ca karṇaś ca
kṛpaś ca samitimjayaḥ
aśvatthāmā vikarṇaś ca
saumadattis tathai 'va ca

Translation

O chief of (twice-born) Brahmins, guru Dronacharya, principal warrior, the leader of my army, please now know that I shall tell you about those who are the most distinguished commanders among us.

Besides your invincible self, there are Bhishma, Karna, Kripa the ever victorious in battle, Ashvatthama, Vikarna, Saumadatti (Bhurishrava).

Metaphorical Interpretation

In every human body there are two qualities: the divine and the demonic. Verses 4 to 6 explained in detail all the good qualities in a human being. Now, in the seventh and eighth verses, the bad soldiers, the evil, devilish propensities of the human being, are named.

The bad qualities are *kuru paksha.* Generally, human beings remain absorbed in the material world: in memory, money, pleasures of the senses, concern with status, addiction, fear, weakness of mind, ambition, and ignorance. They think they are very rich and will be extremely happy with these qualities and propensities. But this is ignorance. These people cannot determine what is good and what is bad.

Duryodhana is the king. Upon seeing the powerful soldiers of the Pandava army, the spiritual party, he gets nervous and feels that his side might not win the battle. So he first flatters his guru, Dronacharya, by telling him that he is the most powerful soldier, *bhavan.* Dronacharya means *druban. Druban* means to immediately melt away. When we think of money, our mind quickly goes and remains upon money. Similarly with sex, immediately our mind is absorbed in sex. The same is true for food. This is *druban,* one whose mind quickly melts, distracted by anything the moment he sees it, becoming absorbed in it. So he is not the best warrior, but the king is addressing him as though he was.

Dronacharya is the family guru of the Pandavas and the Kauravas. He knows that the side with Krishna and Arjuna will be victorious. But the king Duryodhana flatters him and says, "My father is giving money to you, but your sympathy is on their side. You should be grateful. You should not side with Arjuna; you should come to me." So Dronacharya melts and immediately turns and goes to the evil Kaurava side. This is Dronacharya, a man of vacillating temperament who fluctuates between right and wrong. Another meaning of the name Drona is fickle and restless. If a person is always fickle, how can he win in the battle of human life? A fickle person cannot attain peace.

Although Dronacharya is a teacher, he does not meditate deeply. He does not go above the cervical center to the soul center and the fontanel on the top. He remains in the five lower centers—coccygeal, sacral, lumbar, dorsal, and cervical—and remains absorbed in the senses. However, Dronacharya does have one power: He can only be killed if someone pierces his throat with an arrow that goes straight up through the top of his head, crossing the soul center and passing out through the fontanel. Then he will die immediately, and automatically his evil disposition will die.

On the battlefield, Krishna tells Arjuna: "Look, your guru is deeply heartbroken because his son has died. His bow and an arrow are around his neck because he is grieving deeply." The end of the bow looked just like the face of a cobra, but Arjuna did not realize it, so Krishna told Arjuna that a cobra was just about to bite the throat of his guru, Arjuna shot an arrow that immediately crossed Dronacharya's neck center, entered into his royal canal, crossed his soul center, crossed his fontanel, and came out of the top of his head. Dronacharya was freed from body consciousness. At that moment, Dhristadyumna cut off his head with his sword, which killed him.

Therefore, metaphorically, we understand that anyone who wishes to destroy all his evil propensities must bring his consciousness above the neck center to the soul center and the fontanel. Then, automatically, all the evil propensities dwelling in the five lower centers will die. If you can remain absorbed in the soul, you can easily destroy your bad mental habits and your fluctuation between right and wrong. By meditating deeply, you can overcome all your negativity and become God-realized.

Bhishma is the commander-in-chief of the Kauravas. His name means firm determination of mind, but he also has a false sense of prestige and a strong ego, and he cannot make correct decisions. Although Bhishma meditates and has love for Krishna, he is nonetheless stubborn. Shikhandi, a beautiful woman in her previous birth, was not able to marry Bhishma. She was reborn as Shikhandi, a great warrior who vowed to cause Bhishma's downfall. Bhishma's firm determination of mind, his obstinacy, and his ego cause him trouble. Even though he is the commander-in-chief, if he sees Shikhandi, now transformed into a warrior, standing before him in the battlefield, he will refuse to fight since he has vowed to turn away from all females. If Bhishma had been God-realized, he would have remained detached when he saw a beautiful woman. A beautiful woman would have been nothing special because he would have seen the power of God in everyone and in everything, even in beautiful ladies. The physical beauty would not have been real to him; true beauty is the power of God within a woman.

In the Bhagavad Gita (2:59), it says, "The worldly attachment of a person who practices austerity is suppressed, but his desire for enjoyment does not disappear when he meditates deeply and attains Self-realization. Even a person who is extremely unwell still desires sexual enjoyment and good food; he cannot avoid these desires. Even though the desires are always there, a God-realized person remains detached from the pleasures of food and sex—from any enjoyment. But Bhishma was not able to do this; he was stubborn and this caused his downfall. When he saw Shikandi, a lady, on the battlefield, he closed his eyes and was disarmed; he caused his own suffering. He was mortally wounded but died much later, after the battle. Metaphorically, his death means that he remained in his throat center and lower centers. In this material world, people are born for God-realization, but like Bhishma they remain attached to their ego and whims, their lives are not complete, and they do not achieve God-realization.

The third warrior is Karna, who is dangerous and very powerful. Karna means ears. When we hear something, we become absorbed in it and attached to it. Our ears are always willing to hear melodious songs. We are always busy with TV or radio. We set our radios to turn on early in the morning to wake us from sleeping. As soon as we hear the sound, we are enticed, engrossed in it. As a result, we forget to make a morning sacrifice to God. We do not pray; we do not meditate—we do not even say to God, "O Lord! I was extremely tired last night, but you gave me rest, and I am indebted to you. This morning, I have fresh energy and agility, so I offer my gross, astral, and causal bodies to Thee. If You do not inhale through my nose, I am nothing but a dead body; You are the sole doer in me; You inhale through me." We do not praise Him; instead, we are absorbed in melodious songs, gossip, scandalmongering, finding fault and weakness in others, and other bad habits. Karna means ears. By hearing, we become educated and become doctors, engineers, and so on, but if the *karna* is misguided, we become bewildered and can't do anything. When we speak ill of someone or say something that is not true, our ears hear it and believe it, then we cherish the misconception and impression.

The fourth great warrior is Kripa, who represents many things. Kripa can mean attachment and attraction. For example, suppose you see some beautiful flowers or an attractive human being with your eyes: Your heart and mind will be immediately absorbed. Attached and absorbed in beauty, you forget that you can never be truly absorbed without the soul. So we do not perceive the soul; instead, we are absorbed in matter and memory. We are fickle and restless in our hearts. As a result, we get heart trouble and many diseases. Thus, we do not have peace, which is our birthright. Another meaning of Kripa is graceful and sympathetic. Out of compassion and sympathy, Kripa became the commander of the Kauravas, even though he had been the guru of both sides.

The fifth great warrior of the *kuru paksha*, the Kaurava party, which represents our biological force or energy, is Ashvatthama, the son of Dronacharya. Dronacharya is fickle, so his son symbolizes the desire for name, glory, and fame. The metaphorical meaning of Ashvatthama is derived from *a*, no; *shva*, up to tomorrow; *tha*, existence; and *ma*, not: that which has existence until tomorrow. Ashvatthama has strong, endless desires. When one desire is fulfilled, another desire immediately arises. These desires are the biggest obstacle to soul culture in every human being. Until a devotee can remove ambition and transcend the extroverted state, the truth of life cannot be perceived, and peace of mind cannot be achieved.

The sixth warrior is Vikarna. Metaphorically, Vikarna symbolizes the situation where we hear something, then without determining whether it is right or wrong, we take drastic action. In this and other ways, most people remain very far from the truth. People say that Self-realization is very difficult, and we believe it, not remembering that the Self is always with us. Without the Self, we would not have sight, sound, touch, passion, or anger; we would not have any life in our body. The Self is everything. If we follow the teachings of the Bhagavad Gita and practice Kriya Yoga, we can perceive, conceive, and realize the Self during every action. We don't do it, however, because we are Vikarna. Having heard many things that turn us against the desire to realize the Self, we become convinced they are true, and this prevents us from correctly judging what is right and what is wrong.

Saumadatti is the seventh great warrior of the Kauravas. Saumadatti is the son of Somadatta; he is also called Bhurishrava. *Bhuri* means many and *shrava* means to hear; Bhurishrava is one who hears a lot of things; therefore, his mind is bewildered. Suppose someone hears about Hinduism, Islam, or Judaism and leaves his own religion to follow another. He is bewildered and perceives nothing. In the Bhagavad Gita (3:35 and 18:47), it says that everyone should follow their own religion. It is wise to die still adhering to your own religion; you should not follow the religion of others. In this world, we find many people like Bhurishrava. They hear many things and talk about many religions, but they accept neither their own religion nor those of others. This kind of person cannot perceive the truth and achieve the ultimate goal in life.

All human beings have many ambitions, many attachments, and little knowledge, which prevents them from prospering. Our five sense organs are our enemies when they are absorbed in the material world and attached to these extroverted perceptions. These propensities are within us; when we don't control them, we cannot become qualified, cannot become educated, and cannot become divine. The bad qualities in each human being are *kuru paksha.* Along with these bad propensities, we have ego, ambition, desire for enjoyment, extreme attachment, and only a little knowledge. Thus, we have no desire for God-consciousness, and we are not willing to work diligently to strengthen our character. Having no strong desire to shun our bad qualities, we retain our animal qualities.

In Patañjali's Yoga Sutra (2:3), the five kinds of sinful dispositions, the *pancha klesha,* are described: ignorance, ego, likes, dislikes, and attachment. They prevent human beings from proceeding forward toward the divine goal. Many soldiers in your body pull you toward the bad qualities. They are the forces of ignorance and darkness. Many soldiers also fight for the good qualities—knowledge, consciousness, superconsciousness, and cosmic consciousness. In every human being there is a struggle between the soldiers of darkness and those of light and wisdom.

Verse 9

anye ca bahavaḥ śurā
madarthe tyktajīvitāḥ

nānāśastrapraharaṇāḥ
sarve yuddhaviśāradāḥ

Translation

And many other heroes extremely expert in fighting and well equipped with missiles and weapons are here, willing to give up their lives for my sake.

Metaphorical Interpretation

After narrating the names of some great heroes, Duryodhana boasts with pride that there are numerous warriors on his side. The biological forces are full of delusion, pride, attachment, the constant desire for enjoyment, and narrow-mindedness. This is the sinful state of *kaurava,* our human body. The biological forces, the Kaurava soldiers, are addicted to evil work. They do not like spirituality. When anybody mentions spirituality, they quarrel unnecessarily to avoid the real truth.

In the Mahabharata (Adiparva 1:110–111), this is explained very well. It is as if in our body there are two trees, our body tree and our soul tree. The verses say:

om duryodhana manyumayo maha-drumaḥ
skandhaḥ karṇaḥ śakuni tasya sakha
duḥśāsanaḥ puṣpa-phale samṛdhe
mulam rāja dhṛtarāṣṭra maniśi
om yudhiṣṭhiro dharmamayo mahadrumaḥ
skandha 'ṛjuno bhīmasenaḥ sakha,
mādrīsutau puśpa-phale samṛdhe
mulam kṛṣno brahma ca brahmanaś ca.

Our body tree is a sinful tree, full of delusion; this tree is the body of the Kauravas, with its branches growing upward. In the evil body tree, Duryodhana is the leader, filled with sin, wickedness, and ignorance. Symbolically, Duryodhana is a very corrupt tree. Karna, a great warrior, is the trunk of that tree, which gives it support;

Shakuni, the advisor, is the branches of the tree, and Duhshasana, the administration minister, is the air of the tree. Air is the life of the tree. The leaves of the tree breathe air, which supports the life and growth of the sinful tree. Duhshasana is the brother of Duryodhana, and he is very vulgar, obstinate, and vicious. Since the Duryodhana tree is evil, the seed, flower, and fruit are automatically poisonous and sinful. The root of the poisonous tree is the blind king, Dhritarashtra. So, the root of our biological body is full of sin. And from the roots come the trunks, branches, leaves, flowers, and fruits, which are full of sin and crime and are seeking negativity. This is our sinful physical body tree.

The divine soul abides inside every human body tree. Without the soul, we cannot do anything; we can't even make a mistake. A mistake is not for the sake of error, but is for correction. Delusion is for dis-illusion, that is, illumination. In our body tree, there is also a virtuous body tree—our knowledge. When we can introvert our senses instead of remaining in the extroverted state, we will attain real knowledge.

In the second tree, Yudhishthira is the education minister of the soul (Krishna). It is said that Yudhishthira of the Pandavas is a virtuous, lofty tree. The trunk of the tree is Arjuna, who is the main protector of the tree. Bhima is the air of the tree. Air is the savior of the human body and of trees as well. The leaves of the spiritual tree gradually grow and bring spirituality up the body tree. Our breath control is gradually brought up to divinity. *Madrisutau* refers to the children of Madri, Nakula and Sahadeva (water and earth), who will produce divine fruit and flowers. *Mulam krishno* means Krishna is the root of all the spiritual trees. Human beings who follow the virtuous, spiritual tree will surely realize Brahman, attain the formless state, and receive joy and bliss, the ultimate goal of life.

Verse 10

aparyāptam tad asmākam
balam bhīṣmābhirakṣitam

paryāptam tv idam eteṣām
balam bhīmābhirakṣitam

Translation

Our army is meager and easy to conquer because it is guarded by Bhishma. But their army, guarded by Bhima, is unconquerable.

Metaphorical Interpretation

In this verse, King Duryodhana compares the relative strength of the armies before the battle begins.

From head to toe our biological forces or energies have unlimited evil soldiers that are vicious, worldly, and full of ordinary human propensities. These qualities are constantly imprisoning us in the family and increasing our needs and desires more and more. Millions of cells, atoms, and tissues and the five sense telephones are extroverted, so they drag us away from the truth.

In our body, the soldiers of the virtuous tree are very limited in number. There are only five ministers, one in each of the five gross elements, but they are very loyal to the soul. This is a pure monarchy. These ministers are pure knowledge, consciousness, and superconsciousness. Their soldiers are few and remain inside the cranium, near the soul, where they are well protected.

Verse 11

ayaneṣu ca sarveṣu
yathābhāgam avasthitāḥ
bhīṣmam evā 'bhirakṣantu
bhavantaḥ sarva eva hi

Translation

Therefore, protect Bhishma in particular, by all means, and stand firmly in front of your respective squads.

Metaphorical Interpretation

Bhishma is the commander-in-chief of the Kauravas. But why must all the ranks and regiments protect Bhishma so carefully? The real meaning of Bhishma is whims and fear, false and unnecessary oaths. Bhishma had vowed, as was known to everybody, that he would never look at the face of Shikhandi on the battlefield. So Duryodhana was thinking, if Shikhandi stands on the chariot of Krishna, Bhishma surely will not fight in the battle. Truly speaking, we are all Bhishma. We are whimsical; we do not fight against evil. We have time for the cinema, but less time or no time to seek God or soul culture, the ultimate goal of a human being.

Verse 12

tasya samjanayan harṣam
kuruvṛddhaḥ pitāmahaḥ
simhanādam vinayo 'ccaiḥ
śankham dadhmau pratāpavān

Translation

In order to cheer up Duryodhana, the aged grandfather of the Kurus, the very powerful and highly dignified granduncle, Bhishma, blew his conch shell with a loud war cry, like a lion.

Metaphorical Interpretation

When Duryodhana was explaining the strategy to Drona, Bhishma could see Duryodhana's state of mind. To remove fear and to make him happy, Bhishma blew his conch.

When you want to sit for meditation, many sinful and extroverted people will shout loudly to prevent you from meditating. Each one wants to promote his or her own philosophy or ideology and encourage others to follow. You will hear much negative talk, just as a tailless dog will always tell other dogs and jackals to cut their tails. Seeing the regiments of the knowledge body, Duryodhana was afraid and heartbroken. To cheer him up, Bhishma blew his virulent conch shell, which sounded like the roar of a lion.

Verse 13

tataḥ śankhāś ca bheryaś ca
paṇavānakagomukhāḥ
sahasai 'vā 'bhyahanyanta
sa śabdas tumulo 'bhavat

Translation

Then, many others blew a variety of conch shells, trumpets, and tabors, beat on kettle drums and large military drums, and blared forth on cow horns, which gave rise to a tremendous sound.

Metaphorical Interpretation

When a devotee sits for meditation and tries to control his mind, many of his friends will shout, speak ill of him, disturb him, and say there is nothing in meditation. They will say that many troubles will come to you when you meditate. You will not earn money and will not be able to get an education. So, the devotee becomes bewildered and cannot meditate due to the turmoil in the biological force. This state of confusion distracts the devotee from the spiritual path.

Verse 14

tataḥ śvetair hayair yukte
mahati syandane sthitau
mādhavaḥ pāṇdavaś cai 'va
divyau śankhau pradadhmatuḥ

Translation

Then Shri Krishna and Arjuna, seated on their excellent decorated chariot drawn by white horses, blew their divine conch shells.

Metaphorical Interpretation

Arjuna and Shri Krishna and the Pandava party now blow their conchs, which causes terror on the side of the Kauravas. When a person is truly sitting for soul culture, he withdraws his biological senses from the lower centers to the top center. But without the power of soul (Krishna), who remains in the pituitary, no one can meditate. The sincerely meditating devotee hears the vibrant divine sound of *Panchajanya* (Krishna's conch shell). The sound is very melodious. Hearing the sound of the conch, the mind, thought, and intellect of the devotee move up inside the cranium, and the devotee becomes extremely calm. In addition, the devotee observes a brilliant white circular light between the two eyebrows, symbolized by the white horses of the chariot. Inside the white circular light a dark blue island is seen, which is the power of Krishna. In the center, a white star is seen, which is Arjuna. The knowledge body, the third Pandava brother, Arjuna, who sits near the pituitary, is the fittest fighter in the Pandava army. The more a devotee meditates with his spine, neck, and head straight—seeking the soul—the more he will forget his body sense and hear the *om* sound.

The word *aum* consists of *A*, *U*, and *M*. *A* is our causal body. *U*, our astral body, gives us the divine vibration (life force) and is cosmic-consciousness. *M* is our gross biological body, which is the principal body. Without this body, we cannot experience all the varieties of pleasure; also, we cannot win Self-realization. By the practice of Kriya Yoga meditation, the devotee hears divine sound, perceives vibration, and merges with the astral body. At that time, he does not have any sense of the gross body, which is the *M* body. At that time, *M* is completely erased, and only *A* and *U* remain. The sound of *A* and *U* is *auuuuuu*, just like the sound of a conch blowing from a long distance. This is the real *om* sound. Having heard the divine sound and having seen the white light, the devotee realizes extreme calm, which is godliness. Real spirituality begins.

Verse 15–16

pāñcajanyam hṛṣīkeśo
devadattam dhanamjayaḥ
pauṇḍram dadhmau mahāśankham
bhīmakarmā vṛkodaraḥ

anantavijayam rājā
kuntīputro yudhiṣṭhiraḥ
nakulaḥ sahadevaś ca
sughoṣamaṇipuṣpakau

Translation

Hrishikesha (Shri Krishna) blew the conch *Panchajanya*; Dhanamjaya (Arjuna) blew his conch called *Devadatta*; Vrikodara (Bhima) of terrific deeds blew the conch called *Paundra*,

King Yudhishthira, the son of Kunti, blew the conch named *Anantavijaya*; Nakula blew the conch *Sughosa*; and Sahadeva blew the conch *Manipushpaka*.

Metaphorical Interpretation

All the Pandava warriors abide inside the spinal canal. When devotees withdraw their extroverted minds from the lower centers and focus their concentration on the upper center, they hear many divine sounds and remain absorbed in the soul. They hear the sounds of various bugles and other instruments. They experience peace, bliss, and joy.

Inside the spine, the five gross elements are associated with the five Pandava brothers. Earth is the element in the bottom center where all the wealth is; Sahadeva resides in the wealth center. The second center is water, and Nakula abides there. Nakula represents the endless desire for sexual play. We are conceived as the result of sexual pleasure, but we really live in the soul.

The third center is our food center. Arjuna and the fire *vaishvanara* reside there; this fire digests food to give us energy, power, and life. Arjuna remains near Krishna and fights. Why? Because, we need food to develop biological and spiritual force. When Arjuna's biological force was transformed into spiritual force by his guru (Krishna), he sat in the chariot with Him and fought the biological force.

Bhima, conductor of the air, is in our heart center, the fourth center. He guides human beings from the wrong path to the right one by controlling the air, (the breath). Yudhishthira is in fifth center, the vacuum center, and he leads persons up to the pituitary, where Krishna, the soul, resides, in the sixth center.

The spiritual meaning is that the *sushumna nadi* or *prana* channel in the center of the spine goes from the bottom to the top of the spine. When a devotee can control his breath and magnetize his spine, the air is transformed. Then the devotee can go from the lower centers to the upper ones, and in that time, the whole spine of the devotee is magnetized. By magnetizing his spine, a person can change his life force into radiant, all-accomplishing divine force, which in turn, hastens his physical, mental, intellectual, and spiritual regeneration and rejuvenation.

The more a devotee withdraws his power into the pituitary and keeps his attention in that point, the more he sees many divine lights and enjoys extreme calm. At that time he hears the bumble bee sound, buzzing sound, and humming sound in the coccygeal center. In the second center, there is a bugle sound; in the third center, a violin sound; in the fourth center, the sound of a church bell and deep gong bell; in the fifth center, a roaring sound and sea wave sound; in the pituitary, the sixth center, there are many sounds at once because the soul (Krishna) is there. As the devotee proceeds on towards the goal, he will feel extremely calm, and the sound will become more distinct and louder. Eventually, the sound becomes permanent and is called *anahata dhwani*, which means the never stopping divine sound.

Verse 17–18

kāśyaś ca parameṣvāsaḥ
śikhaṇḍī ca mahārathaḥ
dhṛṣṭadyumno virāṭaś ca
sātyakiś cā 'parājitaḥ

drupado draupadeyāś ca
sarvaśaḥ pṛthivīpate
saubhadraś ca mahābāhuḥ
śankhān dadhmuḥ pṛthak-pṛthak

Translation

The King of Kashi the excellent archer and Shikhandi the great chariot warrior, Dhristadyumna and Virata, the invincible Satyaki,

King Drupada, as well as the five sons of Draupadi, and the mighty-armed son of Subhadra (Abhimanyu) all blew their conchs.

Metaphorical Interpretation

There are many other warriors on the side of the Pandavas. Kashiraja is *prajña,* which means divine illumination, and Shikhandi is the power of concentration. Dhristadyumna, the commander in chief, is strong willpower. Abhimanyu is sense control. Through these, people unite with the divine and attain conscious *samadhi* (Subhadra is the blissful Mother Nature whose son is Abhimanyu). Draupadi draws divine energy from the coccygeal center up to the pituitary. The five sons of Draupadi have constant self-awareness in the five centers. Virata, which means no sense of body, represents the *samadhi* state.

Drupada is the strong desire to withdraw the senses from the bottom centers to the top center, which will quickly take one to the state of cosmic consciousness. In between our medulla oblongata and glabella, very near the pituitary, the soul (Krishna) is conducting our five sense telephones. The Pandavas remain there. They are staunch followers of Krishna, so surely they will achieve victory.

Verse 19–20

sa ghoṣo dhārtarāṣṭrāṇām
hṛdayāni vyadārayat
nabhaś ca pṛthivīm cai 'va
tumulo vyanunādayan

atha vyavasthitān dṛṣṭvā
dhārtarāṣṭrān kapidhvajaḥ
pravṛtte śatrasampāte
dhanur udyamya pāṇḍavaḥ

Translation

Thunderous sound from these conch shells resounded over the earth and in the sky and began to break the hearts of the sons of Dhritarashtra.

Then, Pandava (Arjuna), seated in his monkey-bannered chariot and beholding the warriors on the side of the sons of Dhritarashtra, lifted his bow.

Metaphorical Interpretation

Looking at the prosperity and happiness of the person, the enemies are jealous and heartbroken. In these verses, the preparedness of the Pandavas and miseries of the Kauravas are explained.

When a person sits for meditation with the deepest desire for realization and hears the mighty, vibrant divine sounds from the bottom center of the spine to the pituitary, the biological forces and viciousness of that devotee automatically become tremendously fearful. Mind, thought, and intellect are transformed into knowledge and consciousness, and therefore the devotee is completely self-restrained and calm, bringing the awareness above the heart center. However, the devotee cannot remain above the heart center for long, because all his passions and attachments pull him down below the heart center. When this happens, the devotee must keep his spine straight, as explained in the Bhagavad Gita (6:13), control his breath, and meditate deeply. Then he can cross the *vishnu granthi* (the vital knot of the heart center) and slowly rise up into the pituitary and ultimately the fontanel. Arjuna straightened his spine and took up his bow to fight the opponent. If a devotee does not sit with his spine, neck, and head straight and does not practice Kriya Yoga according to the guidance of the master, he cannot overcome his biological force.

When a person sits for meditation and rolls up the tongue, it will gradually go beyond the uvula and penetrate upward towards the pituitary. This is called *khechari mudra* (*kapidhwaja* stage). *Kapidhwaja* comes from *kapi*, which means son of air, who is Hanuman, and *dhwaja*, which means banner. On the chariot of Krishna, there is a banner with the monkey emblem of Hanuman. Why is the emblem of *kapidhwaja* shown on the flag of Krishna? The principal meaning is that Krishna (soul) is the life of every human being.

In the Jñana Shankalani Tantra. it says:

ayur vāyuḥ, balam vāyuḥ, vāyu dhātā śarīrinaḥ,
vāyu sarvam idam viśwa, vāyu pratyakṣa devata

Ayur vayu balam vayu means, "The soul (Krishna) continuously pulls the inhalations into our nose; this is why we are alive." The soul is the strength of every human being. If the soul (Krishna) does not inhale, we cannot digest the food that gives us power, energy, and agility, and then we cannot fight against evil. This is why Arjuna is in the navel. Without food, we cannot acquire the strength and energy to fight evil. Arjuna rides in the chariot of Krishna and fights evil, so he is called Kapidhwaja Pandava. Arjuna could not fight in the battle until the soul (Krishna) inhaled through his nose.

Vayur dhata sharirina means that in this world, human beings, animals, trees, plants, weeds, and creatures are alive because the soul (Krishna) draws every single breath into their bodies. *Vayu sarvam idam vishvam vayuh pratyaksha devata*: "The whole of creation, even the vacuum, is filled with air (soul)." There is no space where there is no air (soul). So, the soul (air) is all-pervading; the air (soul) is the living power of God. So, Krishna (soul) is the living power of God. This is why the symbol of the son of air (Hanuman) appears on the banner of the chariot.

Verse 21–23

hṛṣīkeśam tadā vākyam
idam āha mahīpate
[arjuna uvāca]
senayor ubhayor madhey
ratham sthāpaya me 'cyuta

yāvad etān nirīkṣe 'ham
yoddhukāmān avasthitān
kair mayā saha yoddhavyam
asmin raṇasamudyame

yotsyamānān avakṣe 'ham
ya ete 'tra samāgatāḥ
dhārtarāṣṭrasya durbuddher
yuddhe priyacikīrṣavaḥ

Translation

Now, O Lord of the earth (Dhritarashtra), (Arjuna) spoke the following words to Hrishikesha (Krishna).
[Arjuna said:]
O Achyuta (one who does not deviate from his divine glory), place my chariot between the armies,

so that I can see the parties assembled here with whom I will have to fight in the battle.

I want to observe those warriors who are here ready to fight that which is pleasant to the evil-minded Duryodhana.

Metaphorical Interpretation

Arjuna refers to Krishna as "Achyuta." *Achyuta* is one who does not deviate from his divine state. Arjuna was bewildered and desired to eliminate the negative qualities, the Kaurava army. He asked Krishna to place their chariot between the soldiers of the two parties, so that he could observe those he would have to fight.

Here, *arjuna* refers to the knowledge body that remains in the navel center. He asks his soul (Krishna): "Am I to fight with my evil propensities, anger, greed, suspicion, cruelty, and my animal nature, which are related to my body and which I do not want to remove? Are you telling me to fight against all evil propensities and to remain fixed in the soul?" When a person wants soul culture and sits for meditation, he asks himself: "Am I to avoid gossip, friends, pleasures of the senses, temptation, avarice, bad company, playing cards, cinema, and addictions? Should I remove them?" Having thought about this question deeply, Arjuna could not decide, so he asked his reverend guru (soul, Krishna): "O, my preceptor, I cannot judge what to do." Then his guru told him: "You were born for Self-culture. You require good company. I am your intimate friend. I am always merged in your body, and I am the one inhaling through your nose; you are not inhaling. You must meditate."

This is the first stage of the devotee. He learns a meditation technique such as the Kriya Yoga technique described in the Bhagavad Gita, and he practices it. In the beginning, he has some doubts, and he also has doubts in the second stage. The more he meditates, the more the biological force diminishes. Gradually he can withdraw his senses above the heart center. He hears divine sound, perceives divine vibration, and sees divine light, and gradually he becomes extremely calm. He attains peace, bliss, and love for God. This is the ultimate goal of every human being. Once a seeker is aware of his negative qualities, he tries to eliminate them intelligently.

Verse 24–25

saṁjaya uvāca
evaṁ ukto hṛṣīkeśo

guḍākeśena bhārata
senayor ubhayor madhey
sthāpayitvā rathottamam

bhīṣmadroṇapramukhataḥ
sarveṣām ca mahīkṣitām
uvāca pārtha paśyai 'tān
samavetān kurūn iti

Translation

Samjaya said:
O Bharata (born in Bharata family), as requested by Gudakesha (Arjuna), Hrishikesha (Shri Krishna) placed the beautifully decorated chariot in the middle of the two armies.

In front of Bhishma, Drona, and other great kings, he said: "Here it is. Look, O Partha, the Kurus are assembled here to fight."

Metaphorical Interpretation

The devotee willing to sit for meditation thinks about his good and bad qualities, and his compassionately detached and adverse sides. On one hand, he is gaining superconsciousness, knowledge, love for God, detachment, control of the five senses, control of the heart, and a strong desire for God-realization. He struggles for existence with soul awareness and for divine perception. He always keeps his attention focused in the pituitary, and he wants to merge in God. These are the positive spiritual soldiers of every human being.

On the other hand there is a strong desire for constant passion, anger, greed, avarice, delusion, ego, pride, vanity, unnecessary sleep, drowsiness, doubt, idleness, procrastination, madness, fear, whims, malice, and suspicion in every human being. These are the negative Kaurava soldiers that exist in every human being.

So, in truth, this epic is not a battle between people; it is a battle between knowledge and ignorance. Undoubtedly, the guru (the soul) will point out the ignorance of your life, which is darkness and causes suffering. The knowledge of your life will give you light, which will bring peace, joy, and bliss. Krishna (the soul) places the divine chariot (body) between the good and evil sides of every human being.

The upper portion of each human being is the spiritual knowledge body and the lower portion is the biological body. This is why Jesus and the spiritual masters of all religions advise you to keep your divine energy from flowing out of the lower centers by withdrawing it from them and raising it above, near the soul. Then you can perceive reality and truth. In this verse the first teaching of the Lord is revealed in a subtle way: "Arjuna! Behold and see the negative qualities in your life that must be eliminated."

Verse 26

tatrā 'paśyat sthitān pārthaḥ
pitṝn atha pitāmahān
ācāryān mātulān bhrātṝn
putrān pautrān sakhīms tathā

Translation

Standing there, Arjuna scrutinized the armies of both parties and observed his paternal uncles, granduncles, preceptors, maternal uncles, brothers, cousins, grandfather, sons, grandsons, and friends.

Metaphorical Interpretation

This verse describes Arjuna's perception of the Kauravas and his own army on the battlefield of life, represented as relatives.

Our thoughts, ambitions, and passions are related to our bodies. They always cause us to direct our awareness outward, which prevents intellectual and spiritual development. When we teach children, we try to withdraw their minds from tempting things so they can sit for their education and spiritual training. We do not like to forbid relationships among the students, but their minds always wander off to their affectionate relatives and intimates. When a student is educated, however, he can read novels, histories, or amusing books.

Similarly, in the beginning of God-realization, students require guidance from a teacher such as Krishna in order to successfully control their senses. A spiritual person seeking Self-realization need not avoid his relatives, shun his family life, or leave his service; instead, for spiritual study, as with secular education, the seeker should follow a good teacher who will help him introvert his mind. The mind must not constantly remain in the extroverted state.

Verse 27

śvaśurān suhṛdaś cai 'va
senayor ubhayor api
tān samīkṣya sa kaunteyaḥ
sarvān bandhūn avasthitān

Translation

Then Arjuna, son of Kunti, having seen his friends, fathers-in-law, and relatives ready to fight in the battle,

Metaphorical Interpretation

Arjuna saw all his relatives present on the battlefield of life.

It is the natural instinct of children to move constantly hither and thither, to play, and to enjoy themselves, instead of concentrating their minds in study. Even if you say, "Please come, read your books," the children will remain attached to their playmates and will begin to cry. In a similar way, Arjuna was extremely melancholy and became dejected. The first chapter of the Bhagavad Gita is the chapter about dejection. So Arjuna went to Krishna to express his state of his mind.

Verse 28–30

kṛpayā parayā 'viṣṭo
viṣīdann idam abravīt
[arjuna uvāca]
dṛṣṭve 'mam svajanam kṛṣṇa
yuyutsum samupasthitam

sīdanti mama gātrāṇi
mukham ca pariśuṣyati
vepathuś ca śarīre me
romaharṣaś ca jāyate

gāṇḍīvam sramsate hastāt
tvak cai 'va paridahyate
na ca śaknomy avasthātum
bhramatī 'va ca manaḥ

Translation

Overcome with great pity and sadness, he said:
[Arjuna said:]
O Krishna, having seen my relatives in front of me who are very eager to fight,

my limbs are weak, and my throat and mouth have become dry. My whole body is trembling; my hair is standing on end,

I am losing my grip on the bow; my skin is burning. My mind is reeling and I am not even able to stand.

Metaphorical Interpretation

These verses narrate very intelligently the condition of an ordinary person at the time of a crisis. Their minds are depressed, and they will drown in grief and disaster if they are not able to overcome their emotions.

When students appear for a final examination, they become nervous. Their throats become dry; they feel feverish; they have to urinate often; sometimes they feel dizzy. Negative thoughts and fears of failure enter their brains. When they receive the examination sheet however, their minds become extremely agile. Similarly, a human being seeking soul culture must struggle hard to come up to the pituitary when he is attempting to withdraw his awareness from his worldly senses according to the directions of his master. Many thoughts, anxieties, and physical uneasiness keep him from entering the cranium. At this time he requires the constant guidance of the master. This is why Arjuna calls his master "Keshava," which comes from *ke*, meaning who is functioning, and *shava*, meaning dead body. Arjuna is saying, "My reverend friend, I cannot withdraw my senses from the biological force or from the psychological force. Will You kindly help me? I want to stay always by Your side, because You are the sole doer. I want nothing else; please allow me to stay with You always. My current condition is miserable."

Verse 31

nimittāni ca paśyāmi
viparītāni keśava
na ca śreyo 'nupaśyāmi
hatvā svajanam āhave

Translation

O Keshava (Krishna), I find the omens inauspicious, and I do not see any good coming from killing my friends and relatives in the battle.

Metaphorical Interpretation

Here Arjuna tells Krishna about the condition of his mind and his way of thinking at this point in his struggle for evolution.

All human beings have desires for money, sexual pleasure, food, status, gossip, and they wish to eat, drink, and to be merry; they do not want purity, perfection, and God-realization. Even though Arjuna has a strong desire to fight this apathy and wants to stay with Krishna all the time, he has some of the delusions of ordinary people and does not want to go up to the pituitary, to leave his biological force. Thus, he feels dejected, but this feeling will surely lead him to the divine in the future. Here, he expresses his unwillingness to destroy his own kith and kin, his own biological force.

Verse 32–35

na kānkṣe vijayam kṛṣṇa
na ca rājyam sukhāni ca
kim no rājyena govinda
kim bhogair jīvitena vā

yeṣām arthe kānkṣitam no
rājyam bhogāḥ sukhāni ca
ta ime 'vasthitā yuddhe
prāṇāms tyaktvā dhanāni ca

ācāryāḥ pitaraḥ putrās
tathai 'va ca pitāmahāḥ
mātulāḥ śvaśurāḥ pautrāḥ
śyālāḥ sambandhinas tathā

etān na hantum icchāmi
ghnato 'pi madhusūdana
api trailokyarājyasya
hetoḥ kim nu mahīkṛte

Translation

O Krishna! I covet not victory or kingdom or pleasure. O Govinda, what is the use of kingdom or luxury in life?

Those for whose sake we seek kingdom, enjoyment, and pleasure are arranged on this battlefield, staking their lives and property.

Teachers, uncles, fathers, sons as well as granduncles, maternal uncles, fathers in law, grandsons, brothers-in-law, and other relatives are here.

Though they may kill me, O Madhusudana, I am not willing to kill them, not even for the sovereignty of the three worlds, so why for this world?

Metaphorical Interpretation

To be successful in life, one must control the mind and suppress its restlessness. Unfortunately, many people stop their struggle for success in the middle, confused about the goal and the way.

Human beings are so attached to everything in the material world that they cannot withdraw their minds into spirituality for Self-realization. Even when they know that meditation will bring them balance of mind, amity, affection, and pleasure, they remain attached.

In this world, all human beings, however rich or poor, are engrossed in mundane matters. They all have many shortcomings, worries, anxieties, want of money, excess of money, diseases, and frictions. They do not like soul culture.

At this point, Arjuna's consciousness is stuck in the bottom three centers, just like people of ordinary consciousness. Therefore, his mind is completely absorbed in the material world, and he does not want to bring his awareness above the navel center to enter the divine kingdom. Fortunately, his guru (Krishna, also called Govinda and Madhusudana) is so intelligent that he persuades him to fight against the violators of truth (his relatives) so he can discover the real truth of life, where he will find a far greater peace than material fulfillment could ever bring him.

Verse 36

nihatya dhārtarāṣṭrān naḥ
kā prītiḥ syāj janārdana
pāpam evā 'śrayed asmān
hatvai 'tān ātatāyinaḥ

Translation

O Janardana (the name of Krishna, who removes people's worries), although the sons of Dhritarashtra (Kauravas) are extremely wicked, insolent, sinful, and malicious, I think we should not kill them, because we will be even more sinful than them if we do.

Metaphorical Interpretation

In the entire Bhagavad Gita, there is no description of a battle, even at the end. The Bhagavad Gita is purely allegorical, but it is also a conversation between Arjuna and Krishna that takes place before the epic battle of the Mahabharata. Arjuna is the spiritual student of Krishna. Arjuna is seeking soul culture, but he does not wish to suppress all the biological forces in himself and transcend them; he even thinks that destroying sinful thoughts is sinful, which is not correct. We are attached to delusion and the virulent biological force, which is very tempting.

All human beings are just like Arjuna; every person's soul (Krishna) wishes him well. Krishna is an efficient teacher who intelligently leads us towards knowledge, education, and Self-realization. He is our lover and savior who helps us evolve quickly by causing us to have many negative thoughts. These mistakes are not for the sake of error, but for correction. All human beings have delusions, but they are not for delusion itself, but for dis-illusion, the end of delusion.

Verse 37–39

tasmān nā 'rhā vayam hantum
dhārtarāṣṭrān svabāndhavān
svajanam hi katham hatvā
sukhinaḥ syāma mādhava

yady apy ete na paśyanti
lobhopahatacetasaḥ

kulakṣayakṛtam doṣam
mitradrohe ca pātakam

katham na jñeyam asmābhiḥ
pāpād asmān nivartitum
kulakṣayakṛtam doṣam
prapaśyadbhir janārdana

Translation

O Madhava! We should not slay the sons of Dhritarashtra, our own relatives, for how can we be happy by killing our own kinsmen?

Although these people through blindness and clouded greediness do not perceive the evil of destruction of their own race and the sin accruing from eternity to their friends,

Still, O Janardana (Krishna), why should we, who clearly see the sin involved in destruction of the family, not think of turning away from such sin?

Metaphorical Interpretation

Arjuna argues logically that he should not eliminate negative forces—not out of compassion, but out of inner confusion, which leads him to grief and dejection. He believes that destroying the relatives will make it difficult to maintain the regular activities of life.

When a human being does not seek Self-realization, his mind remains absorbed in the animal qualities. We are all rational beings, but the power of our mind remains trapped in the spinal canal, making us nothing but rational animals. In truth, however, we are the children of God; we have God-like purity and perfection; we require Self-realization. To acquire a spiritual education, people must practice extreme self-restraint; unfortunately, the minds of students always run back to matter and memory. In the night when they sit for study, they feel drowsy. To gain a higher education (Self-realization), these students should fight against their extroverted tendencies and their sloth, withdrawing their minds from drowsiness. By doing so, they can become spiritually educated. The Latin word for education is *educare*, which means to seek the soul dwelling within—which is Self-realization.

Verse 40

kulakṣaye praṇaśyanti
kuladharmāḥ sanātanāḥ
dharme naṣṭe kulam kṛtsnam
adharmo 'bhibhavaty uta

Translation

With the destruction of the family, the age-old spiritual tradition of the family is lost. Upon the destruction of spirituality, impurity gradually grows in the whole family.

Metaphorical Interpretation

The word *kula* in these verses refers to not only the family, but to all the activities in life that are manifested through the spine and the chakras. The word *kulakshaye* is composed of *kula* and *kshaye*. *Akuler kul* means helper of the helpless. In this sense, God is the only helper of every helpless person. *Kshaye* means destruction of spirituality. *Kulakshaye* means that those who do not seek God will find spiritual destruction and will be deprived of joy, peace, and bliss. People who do not seek God will seek only evil and will be separate from the truth.

When a true seeker sits for soul culture, he hears divine sound and the evils of his biological body are suppressed; he proceeds toward God and finds peace. When a human being remains in the mundane world, he is separate from God and cannot experience peace, joy, and bliss. This is the loss of *kula dharma*, which makes one far from Self-realization. When a human being deviates from the spiritual path, he seeks only sin and commits much mischief. Everyone should follow a technique such as

Kriya Yoga, which is described in the Bhagavad Gita (4:29, 5:27, and 6:12, 13, 25, and 26). Learning Kriya Yoga is like learning to drive a car. If you do not learn to drive safely, you cannot reach your destination; you will get into extreme trouble, and you may even meet your death.

Verse 41–43

adharmābhibhavāt kṛṣṇa
praduṣyanti kulastriyaḥ
strīṣu duṣṭāsu vārṣṇeya
jāyate varṇasamkaraḥ

samkaro narakāyai 'va
kulaghnānām kulasya ca
patanti pitaro hy eṣām
luptapiṇḍodakakriyāḥ

doṣair etaiḥ kulaghnānām
varṇasamkarakārakaiḥ
utsādyante jātidharmāḥ
kuladharmāś ca śāśvatāḥ

Translation

With the growth of impiety, O Krishna, the members (women) of the family become corrupt, and with their corruption, O Varshneya (descendent of Vrishni, i.e., Krishna), there is intermixture of culture.

Intermixture of culture leads the race and the destroyers of the race to hell. Deprived of offering of rice balls and water, the ancestors of the race have a downfall.

The age-old traditions and family customs of the destroyers of the race get ruined because of this intermixture created by the deeds of these destroyers.

Metaphorical Interpretation

Varnashankara refers to the mixture of biological and spiritual force. When a devotee sits for meditation, he can easily withdraw his senses, come to the pituitary, and experience divine light, divine vibration, and divine sound. With the help of *jyoti mudra*, a Kriya Yoga technique for purifying the senses (which one should learn directly from a teacher), the devotee will perceive a brilliant, charming, and dazzling light and will reach the state of *paravastha*, which means Mother Nature. Mother Nature is the real female, who leads us to merge with God. But if the devotee gets mentally upset as a result of disease or death in the family or some other calamity, he cannot stay in the supra-mental or formless state, and his mind falls back down to the biological nature. This is *varnashankara*, which means the admixture of opposites. Only continuous absorption in the transcendental state can produce liberation. When people let their awareness slip down below the cranium, they experience unpleasantness, restlessness, and endless desire; there is no peace, joy, and bliss.

Verse 44–45

utsannakuladharmāṇām
manuṣyāṇām janārdana
narake niyatam vāso
bhavatī 'ty anuśuśruma

aho bata mahat pāpam
kartum vyavasitā vayam
yad rājyasukhalobhena
hantum svajanam udyatāḥ

Translation

O Janardana (Krishna)! We have heard that those who have lost their family tradition always remain in hell for an indefinite period.

Alas! Guided by lust for throne and enjoyment, we are bent on committing great sin and killing our relatives.

Metaphorical Interpretation

Due to his delusion, Arjuna tells Krishna that he doesn't want to suppress his worldly ambition and that he will not kill anybody. Arjuna is thinking that this battle only for his own liberation is unworthy. Krishna, however, will teach him that the soul is immortal. Arjuna is not fighting; he is just an instrument, a mere body chariot. Krishna is the real driver of life and all human beings. The seeker should not merely ponder what He says, but follow His teachings and act accordingly.

Verse 46

yadi mām apratīkāram
aśastram śastrapāṇayaḥ
dhārtarāṣṭrā raṇe hanyus
tan me kṣemataram bhavet

Translation

To me, it would be far better if the sons of Dhritarashtra, with weapons in hand, killed me in battle, while I remained unarmed and unresisting.

Metaphorical Interpretation

Here, Arjuna shows his outward compassion, because he prefers to be killed rather than to kill.

Generally, sadness comes from sloth and idleness, which grows from delusion. In that stage, people do not like to proceed onward, either in education or in spirituality. We always say that we are suffering, but at the same time it is very easy to keep eating, drinking, and making merry. We want the pleasures of the senses, amusement, play, gossip, and addiction, but we do not want higher education or spiritual development. We feel it is far better if we die as we are; we do not care for intellectual and spiritual growth.

Verse 47

saṃjaya uvāca
evam uktvā 'rjunaḥ saṃkhye
rathopastha upāviśat
visṛjya saśaram cāpam
śokasaṃvignamānasaḥ

Translation

Samjaya said:
Having said this, Arjuna cast away his bow and arrows and sat down on the chariot in the battlefield, his mind agitated by grief.

Metaphorical Interpretation

This is Samjaya's concluding statement describing the condition of Arjuna's mind in the battlefield of life. Instead of fighting, he sat down dejected and sorrowful in the chariot.

To succeed in a university examination or in the spiritual life is difficult. Every day you must struggle, go to the teacher regularly, fight with the downward-pulling biological energy, study steadily, and overcome sloth and drowsiness. Success requires struggle for either scholastic or spiritual students. Even though they know full well that they will be extremely happy at the end of their life despite difficulties in the beginning, they still become disheartened and sit down idly.

The essence of the first chapter is dejection. If a human being does not experience dejection, he cannot prosper in his life. The astonishing thing about this chapter is that nothing is said about a battle between the warriors. It does not say that one person is killing another; it gives no results of the battle and does not say when the battle ends. Furthermore, nothing is said about the battle in the remaining chapters. Rather, the remaining chapters explain how a human being can achieve sense control, biological control, food control, and habit control. Through this control, one can gradually master the divine technique. These chapters relate how the guru leads devotees gradually to liberation and balance of mind, amity, love, compassion, humbleness, and sweetness. Through balance of mind, even in family life devotees will constantly feel that God is the sole doer.

Although the first chapter appears to be about a battle between two armies, it has a much deeper meaning. It describes the fight between the biological and spiritual forces. The soul (Krishna) is the conductor of both these forces, so, when there is a fight between ignorance and knowledge, knowledge will surely win, and all human beings will attain Self-realization.

This is the scientific and metaphorical interpretation of the Upanishads and yoga in the first chapter of the Bhagavad Gita.

Summary

The first chapter of the Bhagavad Gita is called *Arjuna Vishada Yoga,* which means "The Yoga of Dejection of the Great Hero Arjuna." It is natural for dejection and sorrow to crop up in the beginning stage of spiritual life and inner transformation.

This chapter contains forty-seven verses. The chapter starts with the one and only question from the blind king Dhritarashtra, which is followed by Samjaya's narration and Arjuna's own descriptions. This chapter contains also the words of the king, his eldest son Duryodhana, as well as the Lord, Shri Krishna, but they are placed in such a way that it is not easy to see this. From the following arrangement of the verses and their contents, it can be well seen:

Verse 1: The question from the blind king (which represents the human mind) to Samjaya.

Verse 2: Samjaya begins to reply by talking about Duryodhana, the eldest son of the blind king, who is approaching his master, Drona. In the subsequent verses Duryodhana speaks to Drona in an egotistical manner.

Verse 3: Duryodhana tries to irritate Drona by mentioning the name of "Drupadaputra," the son of Drona's sworn enemy, Drupada.

Verse 4–6: The important great heroes of the Pandava army are described by Duryodhana.

Verse 7–9: Duryodhana assesses the military power of his own army.

Verse 10–11: The inferiority complex in the mind of Duryodhana is revealed.

Verse 12: Bhishma blows his conch.

Verse 13: The Kaurava army sounds war trumpets, kettle drums, conchs, and so forth.

Verse 13–18: Krishna and the Pandavas blow their conchs.

Verse 19: A description of the Kauravas' jealousy.

Verse 20–21: Arjuna asks Shri Krishna to place the chariot in the middle of the field, so he can see with whom he must fight.

Verse 24–25: Shri Krishna places the chariot in front of Bhishma and Drona. Verse 25 contains the only dialogue of the Lord to Arjuna, requesting him to examine the Kauravas carefully.

Verse 26–28: Arjuna's sorrowful state.

Verse 29–30: The eight qualities of timidity and depression are described.

Verse 31-46: Arjuna describes the futility of the battle, giving the impression that he is speaking like a wise man.

Verse 47: The concluding remark from Samjaya about Arjuna's sorrowful state.

The first chapter of the Bhagavad Gita is the opening of the treasure of this holy scripture. Most commentators neglect this chapter, because they believe it does not contain the teachings of the Lord. But Shri Lahiri Mahasaya, with his unique outlook as a realized yogi, revealed the beautiful, practical, and metaphorical meaning of this chapter and the symbolic names of the characters, which are really the inner negative and positive qualities that everyone possesses.

Dejection or depression is a medium for spiritual transformation when one approaches and follows the inner guide and preceptor.

Chapter 2

Samkhya Yoga

The Yoga of Inner Awareness

Introduction

The spiritual teacher is a true guide who helps the student at the critical time of dejection. Arjuna's sorrow was caused by his emotional attachment to the Kauravas, who represent the negative qualities in a person, even though they had caused much harm. Arjuna preferred the path of renunciation to the path of action, but his attitude toward renunciation was not based on knowledge and understanding; it was the result of his temporary dejection.

Arjuna can mean "straight and clean." He expressed his feelings to Shri Krishna directly, without any second thoughts. Shri Krishna's teaching about the ultimate reality starts in this chapter, aimed at dispelling Arjuna's state of grief and sorrow.

Both Duryodhana and Arjuna surveyed the battlefield scene and the assemblage of kith and kin, relatives, and teachers. Duryodhana was filled with ego and anger, whereas Arjuna had sympathy and sorrow. This depicts the contrast in their characters and the differences in their personalities. Arjuna's *vishada* (dejection) was a *yoga* (opportunity), because he accepted the help of his true guide, Shri Krishna, who showed Arjuna the correct path at this critical juncture.

A confused and dejected person cannot take a rational step. When a person knows this and approaches a true teacher to seek his guidance with faith, his mind settles in truth. This is what Arjuna did. The soul is the true guide. When the mind has sorrow, one should retreat to the cave of the cranium, become absorbed in soul consciousness, and receive inner strength and reality. This second chapter is called the Aphorisms of the Gita, which are elaborated in later chapters. The second chapter highlights the truths of life and wisdom.

Verse 1

samjaya uvāca
tam tathā kṛpayā 'viṣṭam
aśrupūrṇākulekṣaṇam
viṣīdantam idam vākyam
uvāca madhusūdanaḥ

Translation

Samjaya said:
Madhusudana (Krishna) then said the following words to Arjuna, who was extremely moved with pity, drowned in distress, full of sorrow; his eyes were filled with tears and agitation.

Metaphorical Interpretation

Samjaya vividly describes Arjuna's mental condition. Arjuna was overpowered with grief and dejection.

When people experience delusion it brings dejection, the cause of tears. Delusion is the biggest hindrance to Self-realization. To become established in the divine kingdom, we must thoroughly control our illusions, because the ensuing dejection creates bondage. Then we fail to proceed towards spirituality. Anyone who wants constant liberation must thoroughly control dejection and error.

Sorrow is the symbol of weakness and should be overcome intelligently.

Verse 2

śrībhagavān uvāca
kutas tvā kaśmalam idam
viṣame samupasthitam
anāryajuṣṭam asvargyam
akīrtikaram arjuna

Translation

The blessed Lord said:
Arjuna, in this very critical moment, why has this weakness overtaken you? This is not noble, not heavenly of you.

Metaphorical Interpretation

This is the first verse of the Lord's teaching that is preceded by *sri bhagavan uvaca. Sri* consists of three letters in Sanskrit: *sa*, *ra* and *i*. *Sa* means head as well as breath; *ra* is the root word symbolizing fire or illumination; *i* is the energy. Therefore, *sri* means one who remains in the head, in the sense of someone who can hold their awareness between the pituitary and the fontanel through breath control, while experiencing illumination and divine energy. In this divine state, divine guidance is forthcoming.

When a devotee meditates, he sometimes goes to a higher state of spirituality, sometimes he comes down to a lower level. Arjuna was an intimate friend of Krishna; he could constantly maintain his awareness in the cranium, near the soul (Krishna). But even a ready spiritual aspirant such as Arjuna sometimes becomes deluded. Arjuna's consciousness was in the navel center, and he became dejected.

But Arjuna was a true seeker. When he meditated, he would transcend the biological level, which is below the eyebrows, and enter the spiritual center, which is inside the cranium. He practiced *yoni mudra*, also called *jyoti mudra*, and saw the intense, heart-touching, brilliant, divine light that is called Mother Nature. But when Krishna brought Arjuna face to face with natural phenomena, his awareness descended back down into the gross body, and immediately he became dejected and attached to the material world. Krishna brought him down for one reason only. God does not want human beings to be dejected. He desires that everybody should know the soul. When human beings are dejected and deluded, they will achieve Self-realization through it. Heaven is in the cave of cranium, and hell is keeping your awareness on the thoughts generated down in the spine, which is filled with emotion and desires that will bring disgrace and dejection.

Verse 3

klaibyam mā sma gamaḥ pārtha
nai 'tat tvayy upapadyate
kṣudram hṛdayadaurbalyam
tyaktvo 'ttiṣṭha paramtapa

Translation

O Partha! (Son of Pritha, Arjuna) Do not give way to such impotent unmanliness. It does not befit you as a warrior. Please shake off this feeble-hearted worry and wake up, O scorcher of enemies (Arjuna)!

Metaphorical Interpretation

This verse contains a mild rebuke from the teacher to the disciple, encouraging him to overcome the weakness and emotion of the heart. Shri Krishna is exhorting Arjuna to strive, trying to help him reach the superconscious state. Krishna teaches Arjuna breath control, by which Arjuna can overcome worldly restlessness, bringing his concentration up to the pituitary and going beyond mind, thought, and intellect to where the superconscious state exists.

The word *uttistha* comes from *urdhey tistha. Urdhey* means at the north of the body, meaning inside of the head, and *tistha* means to stay and to be firmly established. Krishna is instructing Arjuna to keep his awareness up in the top of the head, where Krishna, the guru and the soul, resides.

Anyone who controls his breath and brings his *prana* into the pituitary achieves *shambhavi mudra*, which destroys delusion. At that time he acquires extreme power; his biological lower self dies and his divine Self awakens.

Verse 4

arjuna uvāca
katham bhīṣmam aham samkhye

droṇam ca madhusūdana
iṣubhiḥ pratiyotsyāmi
pūjārhāv arisūdana

Translation

Arjuna replied:
O, Madhusudana (Krishna, the killer of evil propensities), how shall I aim arrows in the battle at Bhishma and Drona? Both of them are worthy of worship.

Metaphorical Interpretation

Arjuna uses apparently intelligent conversation to sum up his worries and make a sorrowful statement about his unwillingness to fight. He says he does not wish to kill respectable people such as Bhishma and Drona.

Bhishma means fear and *drona* means fickle-mindedness. If a devotee such as Arjuna does not control his fear and fickle-mindedness, he cannot overcome the forces of the biological nature, which remain in the body below the eyebrows. Fortunately, Arjuna had his guru to lead him above delusion. This is why he addresses Krishna as Madhusudana in this verse. *Madhu* means delusion and error, and *sudana* means destroyer. So Arjuna is saying, "O destroyer of my delusion, how can I remove the fear and fickleness from my mind and sit near You in the pituitary?"

In the Mundaka Upanishad (2:2–4) it says, *praṇavo dhanuḥ, śaro hy ātmā, brahma tal lakṣyam ucyate, apramattena veddhavyam, śaravat tanmayo bhavet. Pranava dhanu* is *omkardhwani*, which means "just like a bow." *Sharo hy atma* means that one's inhalation and exhalation are like arrows. *Sharavat tanmayo bhavet* means that when a person is shot with an arrow, his attention becomes pinpointed, absorbed in that particular place. If we can pierce the soul with an arrow of inhalation, we will have pinpointed concentration on the soul as Brahman, the infinite joy that we are ultimately seeking. *Apramattena veddhavyam* means that a devotee should keep his attention one hundred percent on the soul without letting the attention wander elsewhere. With every breath, air touches the soul; therefore, breath mastery is self-mastery.

Until devotees suppress their fear and fickleness and follow the Kriya Yoga inhalation technique, they cannot fix their attention on the soul. The moment they ascend to the soul they will perceive intense divine sound, divine vibration, and divine light, and will feel love for God. At that time, fear (Bhishma) and fickleness (Drona) will automatically be vanquished.

Verse 5

gurūn ahatvā hi mahānubhāvān
śreyo bhoktum bhaikṣyam apī 'ha loke
hatvā 'rthakāmāms tu gurūn ihai 'va
bhuñjīya bhogān rudhirapradigdhān

Translation

In this world, it is better to live on alms than to kill reverend gurus (elders). If we kill them, we will have to enjoy wealth and pleasure in the form of sense enjoyments stained with blood.

Metaphorical Interpretation

Arjuna says he would prefer to follow the path of beggar, satisfied with whatever is given to him or whatever is available in the lower centers, than to fight and gain the divine kingdom in the cave of the cranium. When many people think about seeking Self-realization, their awareness descends down into the biological force, which makes these people think it is wise to remain in the material world. This ignorance is widespread.

Verse 6

na cai 'tad vidmaḥ kataran no garīyo
yad vā jayema yadi vā no jayeyuḥ

yān eva hatvā na jijīviṣāmas
te 'vasthitāḥ pramukhe dhārtarāṣṭrāḥ

Translation

We cannot understand whether it is better to fight or not to fight, nor do we know whether it is better to win or be defeated. If we kill the sons of Dhritarashtra who are standing before us, we will not wish to survive.

Metaphorical Interpretation

Arjuna is clearly and completely confused; he cannot decide what is good. He is baffled because he cannot choose between pleasure and peace. Like Arjuna, when devotees want to sit for soul culture, they feel bewildered and think: "What should I do? Should I remain under the control of body nature ignorance, or should I submit to the control of Mother Nature? If I remain under the control of the body nature, I will be busy with eating, drinking, and merrymaking. If I allow Mother Nature to rule me, it will undoubtedly be strenuous, but the ultimate result is pleasant, giving peace, joy, and bliss. The temptation of the mundane theater is so tempting. I cannot decide what to do."

Verse 7

kārpaṇyadoṣopahatasvabhāvaḥ
pṛcchāmi tvām dharmasammūḍhacetāḥ
yac chreyaḥ syān niścitam brūhi tan me
śiṣyas te 'ham śādhi mām tvām prapannam

Translation

Unable to judge what is right or wrong and deprived of my heroic nature, I am now a victim of the strain of cowardliness. I therefore ask You, please let me know, what is suitable for me? I am Your disciple, I surrender myself, please teach me.

Metaphorical Interpretation

This is one of the most beautiful verses in the Bhagavad Gita, the surrender of Arjuna at the feet of Krishna (the master): "O Krishna! My mind is bewildered, and I am unable to decide what is right. Please teach and guide me. I am your student."

If you want to meditate, you must shun ego identification absolutely. Yield to the teachings of a master. It is essential to accept only one spiritual teacher. Disciples should maintain implicit faith in and loyalty to the spiritual master, following his or her teachings completely. If you don't, you cannot proceed quickly to the divine goal. You must say to your preceptor: "Please lead me to the royal door."

Verse 8

na hi prapaśyāmi mamā 'panudyād
yac chokam ucchoṣaṇam indriyāṇām
avāpya bhumāv asapatnam ṛddham
rājyam surāṇām api cā 'dhipatyam

Translation

Even if I obtain forever an undisputed, abundantly wealthy kingdom on this earth and lordship over the gods, I do not see any way to remove my sorrow, which gives me constant pain (dries up the senses).

Metaphorical Interpretation

This is the last verse where Arjuna prays to Shri Krishna, entreating him to show him the correct path to freedom from sorrow and pain. Nowhere in the Bhagavad Gita will you find a battle between two armies and bloodshed. The Bhagavad Gita is only describing the battle between ignorance and knowledge. Arjuna, representing the ordinary person, wants to completely suppress the biological force by practicing a technique such as Kriya Yoga (*described in the fourth to the tenth chapters of the Bhagavad Gita*). By the practice of *asana* (postures) and *pranayama* (breath control), a devotee can achieve thorough control over the body kingdom. The more he practices, the more he will attain supreme power and divine glory. Inhalation is our life, the power of God within us. When the breath energy or *prana* enters the fontanel, we experience many miracles and peace of mind, which is more valuable than the worldly kingdom. If you do not meditate deeply, you cannot attain *nirvikalpa samadhi* or go beyond human destiny (*karma*) and the latent tendencies (*samskaras*). Human destiny, the latent tendencies, and attachment to the material world are the enemies of spiritual life.

Verse 9

samjaya uvāca
evam uktvā hṛṣīkeśam
guḍākeśaḥ paramtapaḥ
na yotsya iti govindam
uktvā tūṣṇīm babhūva ha

Translation

Samjaya says:
Having thus spoken to Hrishikesha (Krishna), the great warrior Gudakesha (Arjuna) told Govinda, "I will not fight," and became silent.

Metaphorical Interpretation

When the mind is silent, truth is revealed. A restless mind distracts you from the presence of the Self within.

Gudakesha is someone who constantly maintains alert awareness in the soul. Hrishikesha comes from *hrishi kanam isha*, which means the conductor of the five sense telephones. Another name for Krishna is Govinda, from *go, vin,* and *da*; *go* means worldwide, *vin* means to all human beings, and *da* means giving pleasure. The complete meaning of Govinda is that the indwelling soul gives extreme pleasure to our five sense telephones throughout our body. After expressing all his emotion and sorrow in the previous verses, Arjuna now tries to be alert—Gudakesha. He is finally able to control his senses (Hrishikesha) and talk like Gudakesha.

Verse 10

tam uvāca hṛṣīkeśaḥ
prahasann iva bhārata
senayor ubhayor madhye
viṣīdantam idam vacaḥ

Translation

O Dhritarashtra, when Hrishikesha (Krishna) saw Arjuna extremely aggrieved in the midst of the two armies, he smiled and spoke to him.

Metaphorical Interpretation

A truly self-disciplined person will smile when he sees an ordinary person dejected in the battle of life. He knows that when a human being desires soul culture, two powerful soldiers, one from the army of ignorance and one from the army of knowledge, will appear in the mind of the devotee. One party prevents the seeker from fighting ignorance and prevents meditation, the other party urges the person to victory over the body nature.

Without the soul, represented by Krishna, Arjuna or any human being won't have any biological and spiritual force. Without the soul, human beings have no existence. Krishna smiled because Arjuna was His intimate friend. If Arjuna does not take food or drink for some days, life (the soul, Krishna) cannot stay in his body. Without food, a seeker lacks strength and agility. Fighting is not possible without food. Without food, Arjuna will not have biological and spiritual force. Metaphorically, Arjuna is the food minister, the awareness that remains in the navel center.

The soul is the real guru of every human being, so there is a strong relationship between Krishna and Arjuna. This is why Krishna was smiling, lovingly and intelligently teaching Arjuna (the knowledge body) how to meditate and attain Self-realization. The smile of the teacher brings solace to the heart of the student.

Verse 11

srībhagavān uvāca
aśocyān anvaśocas tvam
prajñāvādāmś ca bhāṣase
gatāsūn agatāsūmś ca
nā 'nuśocanti paṇḍitāḥ

Translation

The blessed Lord said:
Arjuna! you are lamenting over those who should not be lamented for. Yet, you also speak words of wisdom. The wise grieve neither for the living, nor for the dead.

Metaphorical Interpretation

Arjuna speaks like a very educated person who is not truly wise. To become truly wise is very difficult. Without soul culture, one cannot maintain balance of mind. By the practice of Kriya Yoga, the *ida* and the *pingala* inside the spinal canal are separated and the *sushumna* opens. Then the real power of God comes up from the coccygeal center to the pituitary and the fontanel, which gradually removes the human madness and restlessness that reside in the body. The *ida, pingala,* and *sushumna* are three channels of *prana* or life force that determine the natural tendencies of people. Depending on a person's stage of evolution, the *prana,* or life force, flows differently through these channels in the astral body.

In the Gheranda Samitha (5:84) it says, *hamkāreṇa bahiryāti saḥkāreṇa viśeta punaḥ*: "When we exhale, the *prana*, the life force or vital air, exits the body (*ham*)." This is an extroverted state of awareness. If the soul does not pull the inhalation *sa*, then the body is dead. Remembrance of *sa* is the introverted state.

Ham also denotes the physical, which cannot survive without *sa*. *Ham* is absorbed in the biological body, but it can gradually be raised up into the pituitary where *sa* abides. This is *hamsa sadhana*. When a devotee maintains attention at the top, he perceives that everyone is an immortal soul and that no one dies. In this state, the devotee is truly wise; he will not grieve over the possible death of a living person, or even for someone who has died.

Some people may speak as though they have profound intellects, but their behavior is ordinary. A wise person lives in the present, without being affected by the past or the future.

Verse 12

na tv evā 'ham jātu nā 'sam
na tvam ne 'me janādhipāḥ
na cai 'va na bhaviṣyāmaḥ
sarve vayam ataḥ param

Translation

In fact, there was never a time when I, you, or these kings didn't exist. Neither shall we cease to be in the future.

Metaphorical Interpretation

The Lord explains that He is imperishable, that He existed even before His birth. As a body, everyone is mortal; as a soul, everyone is immortal. Arjuna believes that he is a perishable body, but it is not so—he existed before his birth. All the kings are also immortal. Before their births, they were immortal souls. At present, we are on the earth. We will leave our perishable bodies, but our imperishable body will remain in the vacuum forever.

Without the sea there are no waves. Without waves, the sea still exists. When the wave of an individual body and personality perishes, the soul remains. The soul is immortal; the wise do not lament for the dead. Seek your immortality.

Verse 13

dehino 'smin yathā dehe
kaumāram yauvanam jarā
tathā dehāntaraprāptir
dhīras tatra na muhyati

Translation

After childhood, youth, and old age take place in one body, the soul incarnates in another. The wise person does not have any illusions about this.

Metaphorical Interpretation

The Lord is describing the immortality of the soul and the mortality of the body. Imagine you are eighty years old. First you were a baby, but your babyhood expired; then you became a youth and your youthful stage expired. Then you reached middle age, but that age expired when you reached eighty. These are the various stages of the life cycle. Old age will also end; then, only the all-pervading spirit will remain. People of soul culture always say that the soul is immortal. The appearance of birth and death is a drama that deludes us.

You should not lament over death. Please meditate and achieve Self-realization.

Verse 14

mātrāsparśās tu kaunteya
śītoṣṇasukhaduḥkhadāḥ
āgamāpāyino 'nityās
tāms titikṣasva bhārata

Translation

O son of Kunti (Arjuna)! The contact between the senses and their objects gives rise to the feelings of heat and cold, and pleasure and pain. They are transient and fleeting; therefore, O Bharata (Arjuna), endure them with patience.

Metaphorical Interpretation

We enjoy the world with our five senses, which are our enemies because they pull us down to the material world with the experience of duality. When we enjoy the material world, we remain in the body kingdom. During that time, our awareness is trapped below the pituitary. But without the soul, we could not see the beauty of the world; we could not experience taste, smell, sound, or touch; we could not perceive anything.

By the practice of Kriya Yoga, we can learn how to introvert our senses and keep our awareness above, near the soul. Then all the worldly forces, the body sense, thoughts, and intellect are completely transformed into superconsciousness and cosmic consciousness. Then we do not feel pleasure and pain, or heat and cold; instead, we will enjoy an extreme calm called conscious *samadhi.* When duality disappears, spiritual experience begins, and with more meditation, the devotee will attain *nirvikalpa samadhi*, the formless state. In this stage, the devotee experiences real peace.

Verse 15

yam hi na vyathayanty ete
puruṣam puruṣarṣabha
samaduḥkhasukham dhīram
so 'mṛtatvāya kalpate

Translation

O best of men! Only one who is not moved by sense perceptions or by pleasure or pain, and who is filled with calm, can attain blissful immortality.

Metaphorical Interpretation

During sleep you are extremely calm and do not experience pleasure and pain, passion and anger, or even a sense of the world. But you are asleep. In Kriya Yoga, a simple, scientific technique of breath control is taught that allows this to be achieved while awake. Any human being who comes to a true master and receives good guidance in Kriya Yoga will attain the calmness of a sleeping person within a short period. This is called *yoga nidra.* The first word, *yoga*, means oneness of body and soul; the other, *nidra*, means sleep. But *yoga nidra* does not refer to sleep; it is constant awareness of the inner Self. In this state, one does not have a body sense, or even a sense of the world; pleasure and pain are nothing and the practitioner is merged with infinity, the almighty father. This is the formless state, the ultimate goal of all religions. The divine nectar gradually flows down from the fontanel of the devotee, who then attains the blissful, immortal stage of being.

Verse 16

nā 'sato vidyate bhāvo
nā 'bhāvo vidyate sataḥ
ubhayor api dṛṣṭo 'ntas tv
anayos tattvadarśibhiḥ

Translation

There is no eternal existence of changeable things, and there is no destruction of eternal things. The reality of both is discerned by the seer of the truth.

Metaphorical Interpretation

Any perishable thing in the universe, even a human body, is changing and undergoing modification. The human body is made of twenty-four gross elements and is undoubtedly composed of matter; the soul abides inside this body. Without the soul, every human body is lifeless, since the soul is the motive power of the body. Thus, every human body is a form of God. God is truth. Without the power of God, there is no truth. But people are absorbed in matter and memory instead of God, so they cannot perceive the truth.

The thirteenth chapter of the Bhagavad Gita discusses in detail the difference between the body field and the knower of the body field. According to the Bhagavad Gita, if all human beings practiced the Kriya Yoga technique, they would all feel the power of God, even in the body field. During every action and and thought, they would perceive God.

Even when a light bulb is off, the electricity is constantly there, right up to the bulb. The moment you turn on the switch, the bulb lights and the darkness disappears. Similarly, our body bulb is full of darkness (ignorance), and you don't see the divine light of God consciousness, even though the divine current (soul) is always there.

Flip the switch and turn on the body bulb by the practice of Kriya Yoga; then you can constantly feel that every body part and the soul are one. Bodies are the power of God, as are matter and memories. As the Chhandogya Upanishad (3:14:1) says, *sarvam khalvidam brahma:* "You can feel the presence of the divine everywhere. Truth is everywhere."

Verse 17

avināśi tu tad viddhi
yena sarvam idam tatam
vināśam avyayasyā 'sya
na kaścit kartum arhati

Translation

In the visible world, all that you see is the imperishable, indestructible soul. No one can destroy the indestructible

Metaphorical Interpretation

Names and forms change by the power lent them by the soul. The soul is in everything: changeless, imperishable, beyond all these forms.

The twenty-four gross elements, all living beings, the entire manifest world—everything you feel and perceive is the living presence of God. He abides in all matter, even in food, which is transformed into energy and then into life. If you meditate, your life will be divine. Before creation, God was one; after creation, although He is yet one, He abides in many. In the Holy Bible (Genesis 2:7), it says, "And the Lord God formed man of the dust of the ground and breathed into his nostrils the breath of life, and man became a living soul." God made every human being and breathed through the nostrils of every human being. He abides everywhere. In the Shvetashvatara Upanishad (6:11) it says, "The only one God remains hidden in the formless state in every human being."

If you meditate, you will perceive the imperishable soul in every human being. Human beings and the soul are inseparable, but the human being is engrossed in delusion, and the soul is beyond delusion. You should not lament.

Verse 18

antavanta ime dehā
nityasyo 'ktāḥ śarīriṇaḥ
anāśino 'prameyasya
tasmād yudhyasva bhārata

Translation

Undoubtedly, the indwelling soul is imperishable and indefinable, but the body is perishable. O Arjuna! Defend and fight.

Metaphorical Interpretation

We are born for soul culture. Everything in creation is also in our bodies. Every human body is a miniature form of the universe. Any person may die at any moment, so you should sit for meditation right now. Fight. When you meditate, you will automatically feel that you have no sense of your biological body; you will only perceive the soul pervading your whole body. You will feel one with God, and then you will feel deep love for God.

The body you live in dies every moment, but inside the perishable body temple, the imperishable one loves. Realize it. It is possible, but you must kill all the negative qualities in the inner battle between the introverted and extroverted states.

Verse 19

ya enam vetti hantāram
yaś cai 'nam manyate hatam
ubhau tau na vijānīto
nā 'yam hanti na hanyate

Translation

Both are foolish who think the soul is capable of killing and who think the soul could be killed, because the soul does not kill and no one can kill the soul.

Metaphorical Interpretation

The soul remains compassionately detached in the body, formless and free. No one can cut or touch the soul. It has no physical form and is imperishable. The formless soul cannot be destroyed. Although the body is born and the body dies, the soul is beyond birth and death. A gold ornament is born and over time is destroyed, but the gold is changeless and formless.

The soul is the image of God, Who is love. So the soul is the source of all love, peace, and joy, which is experienced in deep meditation.

Verse 20

na jāyate mriyate vā kadācin
nā 'yam bhūtvā bhavitā vā na bhūyaḥ
ajo nityaḥ śāśvato 'yam purāṇo
na hanyate hanyamāne śarīre

Translation

For the soul there is never birth or death. Having once been, never does it cease to be. It is unborn, everlasting, eternal, and ancient. It is not destroyed, even when the body is slain.

Metaphorical Interpretation

The Lord consoles Arjuna by telling him that the soul is everlasting and eternal. No one can kill, touch, burn, or drench it; it never changes. Suppose you have a five-dollar bill, which you use to make a purchase. The five dollars are not lost. You have given the bill to the shopkeeper. The shopkeeper is not going to burn it; he gives it to someone else. So it is changing and changing. Eventually, the five-dollar bill is torn and tattered; still, it is not destroyed. If you give it to the bank, they will exchange it for a fresh one. The old note will go to the government, which will store it and issue a fresh note for it. We change as we age and grow older; after that, we go to God. We change our bodies and nothing dies.

When you meditate, you are not killing your parents, relatives, friends, or intimates. You are suppressing your worldly restlessness. By a scientific technique you are going from a lower to a higher stage.

Verse 21

vedā 'vināśinam nityam
ya enam ajam avyayam
katham sa puruṣaḥ pārtha
kam ghātayati hanti kam

Translation

O Partha, how can a person who knows that the soul is imperishable, unborn, eternal, and unchangeable kill anyone or cause anyone to kill?

Metaphorical Interpretation

Arjuna knows that without the soul he is nothing but a lifeless body that won't be able to find peace. His mind is absorbed in the material world, but he knows there is no permanent peace there. Arjuna is a sincere seeker, but he is not Self-realized. He wants Self-realization.

Arjuna's condition is like that of a fish. A fish sees the bait and is very attracted to it. The fish knows that there is an iron hook inside the bait, which is very painful and deadly. In the same way, Arjuna is attracted to the material world, but knows there is a hook in it. Unlike the fish, Arjuna wants to be free of this attraction. For this reason, he is willing to learn the details of freedom from his guru (Krishna). His guru tells him to suppress his biological forces and meditate, so he will be able to rise up to the soul and feel like a deathless child, so he will merge in divine joy. Then, when he returns to his biological force and participates in family life, he can avoid evil in every moment; in every action he will perceive that only God is working. He will have constant liberation. The advice in the Bhagavad Gita improves both family life and divine life.

Through meditation you can realize that you are the imperishable soul—then you can live a life of love and joy with every breath.

Verse 22

vāsāmsi jīrṇāni yathā vihāya
navāni gṛhṇāti naro 'parāṇi
tathā śarīrāṇi vihāya jīrṇāny
anyāni samyāti navāni dehī

Translation

Just as a man puts on new garments, leaving old ones; similarly, the embodied soul takes on new physical bodies, giving up old useless ones.

Metaphorical Interpretation

Birth and death are nothing but changes of state. When you rise up from body consciousness and experience the formless state, you are truly born. When you go from the body-conscious state to the formless state, that is called death, but if you have been truly born, you know that you are not dying, because you perceive the immortality of the soul. So Arjuna and all seekers can reach the vacuum stage if they meditate. Everyone can continuously fix their awareness in the soul and reach the deathless state. When you can earn this through meditation, you will be free from pleasure and pain even while you participate in everyday life.

The person who uses the body garment to realize God becomes the deathless soul.

Verse 23

nai 'nam chindanti śastrāṇi
nai 'nam dahati pāvakaḥ
na cai 'nam kledayanty āpo
na śoṣayati mārutaḥ

Translation

Weapons cannot cut the soul; it can neither be burned by the fire, nor drenched by the water, nor dried by the wind.

Metaphorical Interpretation

The soul, the invisible formless, is Self-born. It is its own source. From the formless, invisible soul without attributes, the five great elements are born: earth, water, fire, air, and ether. Hence the five great elements, also know as *pancha mahabhuta,* cannot affect the soul. Their individual, natural power cannot change the formless, attributeless soul. They are powerless against it. Fire cannot burn it; air cannot dry it; water cannot drench it; weapons cannot cut or damage the formless, all-pervading soul. The soul is even subtler than the sky. No one can destroy the sky, even less the soul, which is beyond all means of destruction.

Verse 24

acchedyo 'yam adāhyo 'yam
akledyo 'śoṣya eva ca
nityaḥ sarvagataḥ sthāṇur
acalo 'yam sanātanaḥ

Translation

The individual soul is unbreakable and insoluble and cannot be burned or dried. It is immovable, omnipresent, unchangeable, and everlasting.

Metaphorical Interpretation

Before creation, God is formless. After creation, God transforms Himself into five gross elements and the universe. He nevertheless remains formless. Since the God Self is fire, how can fire burn Him?

How can a sword cut the formless vacuum? By the practice of Kriya Yoga, we can raise our awareness above the coccygeal (base of spine) center, and rise above the earth sense; above the sacral (sexual) center, the water sense; above the lumbar (navel) center, the fire sense; and above the dorsal (heart) center, the sense of air. When, by using a technique such as Kriya Yoga, we withdraw our senses above the cervical (throat) center, we reach the formless state. The cervical center is the vacuum, which means there is nothing; the gross existence ends and only the subtle remains. No one can touch the vacuum.

Just above our neck, there are five vacuums: *chidakasha, dharakasha, parakasha, mahakasha,* and *atmakasha.* When devotees withdraw their senses into the pituitary, they experience the formless state, beyond the awareness of the five sense telephones. This is the basis of godhood, the ultimate goal of all religions. The formless state is only perceptible in deepest meditation. To convince Arjuna to fight for this, the Lord constantly repeats the same ideas in several verses. To correct Arjuna's imperfect understanding of spirituality, Krishna is constantly repeating, "You cannot lament, you cannot lament, you cannot lament." Then after many verses, He repeats the same thing again.

Chidakasha is the human life force in the pituitary, the inner sky. *Dharakasha* is the etheric fire just above the pituitary where there is no mind, body, ego, or intellect. Here, everything is born by meditation. *Parakasha* is the superconscious state of nothingness just below the fontanel. *Atmakasha* is the state of cosmic consciousness at the fontanel. *Mahakasha,* also called *paramatmakasha,* is the wisdom above the fontanel, where the soul is merged with God in the pulseless state of *nirvikalpa samadhi.*

Verse 25

avyakto 'yam acintyo 'yam
avikāryo 'yam ucyate
tasmād evam viditvai 'nam
nā 'nuśocitum arhasi

Translation

This soul is unmanifest, unthinkable, and immutable. Therefore, knowing it as such, you should not grieve.

Metaphorical Interpretation

When we bring our awareness above the pituitary, we can attain the state beyond thought, and we can perceive the soul, which is beyond conception. We can see the bulb of the soul and the light emanating from it, but the electricity in it is beyond all perception. The soul is beyond all thought. The Kena Upanishad (1:5) says, "What thoughts cannot perceive, but who reveals the thoughts, know that alone to be the soul."

The soul is changeless. When you experience it, you are free from grief and absorbed in eternal peace and love.

Verse 26

atha cai 'nam nityajātam
nityam vā manyase mṛtam
tathā 'pi tvam mahābāho
nai 'nam śocitum arhasi

Translation

O Mighty-armed (Arjuna)! Even if you think the soul will constantly have birth and death, you still should not lament.

Metaphorical Interpretation

Every moment we inhale, and then we exhale our life. After the breath goes out through our nostrils, and before we inhale again, it is like death. When we inhale, it is a new birth. Thus, with every inhalation and exhalation we experience birth and death. But practically speaking, who is inhaling and exhaling? The answer is, only the soul.

Count how many times we are born and die in one day. When you realize that the soul experiences birth and death with every breath, then you cannot lament.

The Lord addresses Arjuna as "Mighty-armed" because a person who is strong in mind and free from fear is worthy of experiencing this truth of life.

Verse 27

jātasya hi dhruvo mṛtyur
dhruvam janma mṛtasya ca
tasmād aparihārye 'rthe
na tvam śocitum arhasi

Translation

It is certain that after birth, death is inevitable, and after death, birth is bound to occur. You should not lament over the inevitable.

Metaphorical Interpretation

As long as you have body consciousness, you cannot forget about death. Try your utmost to forget your body sense and worldly sense so you can merge with God. By practicing Kriya Yoga, according to the Bhagavad Gita, you can withdraw your awareness to the pituitary, and all your thoughts and human madness will completely disappear. If your awareness stays in the lower level of the cranium, you will remain in delusion. Do not lament—follow the soul and understand the real truth of human existence. Birth and death are two banks of the river of life; life flows eternally past them, unaffected by their passing.

Verse 28

avyaktādīni bhūtāni
vyaktamadhyāni bhārata

avyaktanidhanāny eva
tatra kā paridevanā

Translation

O Bharata (Arjuna)! Before birth, all beings are unmanifest. They will become unmanifest again when they are dead. They are manifest only in the intermediate stage. What then is the point of lamentation?

Metaphorical Interpretation

When the baby is in the womb in an early fetal stage, it is very difficult to know whether it is male or female. But the living soul is already there. Before birth, the baby is formless, unseen, unmanifest. When the baby is born, we see the form of the baby; then the baby abides in the universe. The baby is full of life and is constantly restless. But that restlessness is not the restlessness of the baby. If the formless soul did not inhabit the baby, the baby would have no restlessness. After the baby has gradually grown to old age and died, we can no longer see the form of the baby, its body.

By practicing Kriya Yoga, people can feel the existence of the formless. Then, in every activity, the existence of God can be felt. In this way, every human being can feel calm during restlessness, and restlessness during calm, from birth to death.

"O humanity! Why do you lament for the expiration of the body?"

Verse 29

āścaryavat paśyati kaścid enam
āścaryavad vadati tathai 'va cā 'nyaḥ
āścaryavac cai 'nam anyaḥ śṛṇoti
śrutvā 'py enam veda na cai 'va kaścit

Translation

Many think the soul is something extraordinary; others think the soul is something marvelous; some hear that the soul is astonishing, but having only heard about the soul, no one truly knows it.

Metaphorical Interpretation

Undoubtedly, God-realization is amazing and very surprising. The scriptures say, *koṭi-suryaḥ pratikaṣam candra-koṭi suśitalam*: "The soul is like the illumination of ten million suns, but there are no scorching rays. It is cool like the rays of ten million moons." No one can express the power of God in words or with the five senses. It is only perceived in deepest meditation. This perception requires the deepest desire and the guidance of a realized master. The closer the devotee comes to the divine goal, the more he perceives supernal light, super-divine vibration, and various kinds of divine sound. But so long as he does not achieve the pulseless state, and the *nirguna*, *nirvikalpa,* and *turiya* stage, he cannot perceive and merge into God. When he returns to the lower centers, he can only perceive some idea of what God is like. This is only a perception, not realization. Spiritual experience is beyond all description because it is transcendental.

Verse 30

dehī nityam avadhyo 'yam
dehe sarvasya bhārata
tasmāt sarvāṇi bhūtāni
na tvam śocitum arhasi

Translation

O Bharata! The embodied soul is always imperishable in all living bodies; therefore, you should not lament for any being.

Metaphorical Interpretation

The soul is alive in every thing and every place. It abides in inanimate and immovable objects, in forest, stone, and sand. The one living soul abides everywhere. In every human being, the power of the soul sees, hears, laughs, and plays. Without the soul, nothing is possible. Since it is imperishable in everything, why do you lament? You should seek the soul through all the diverse aspects of your being. If you do not meditate, you cannot perceive unity in diversity and diversity in unity. You are born only for this, your Self-realization. Since the soul is imperishable, do not grieve. Every moment, time passes away. Don't waste time; try to experience the truth.

Verse 31

svadharmam api cā 'vekṣya
na vikampitum arhasi
dharmyād dhi yuddhāc chreyo 'nyat
kṣatriyasya na vidyate

Translation

Seeing your duty, you should not be afraid and your body should not tremble. You are *kshatriya* (born in the family of warriors). For a warrior, there is nothing superior to spiritual battle.

Metaphorical Interpretation

Although *svadharma* is usually translated as duty, it also has a deep spiritual meaning. *Svadharma* is composed of *sva* and *dharma*. *Sva* means soul, and *dharma* means virtue, so *svadharma* means soul culture.

Breath is our life; without breath, we have no life. By controlling the breath, we can control the mind. In every mood, our breath varies. When you are passionate, your respiration rate is very high. When you are angry, your rate is even higher. At these times, you are extremely restless and your heartbeat is rapid. With this stress, your motor and sensory nerves become extremely tired. Your arteries become stiff. Your arterial age is your real age. For instance, suppose you have sufficient money, but you do not know where to keep it. Because of your fear and anxiety, you heartbeat is constantly rapid, you experience sleeplessness and heart pain. You may even die early.

When you go to sleep, your inspiration and expiration slow within a minute; you enter deep sleep and find peace. During this time, all your nerves, tissues, and atoms are resting. In the morning, when you awake, you feel rejuvenated. You have fresh energy.

By practicing Kriya Yoga, as described in the Bhagavad Gita, you will become extremely calm—taking slow, even, and deep inhalations. Through this, your brainpower becomes fertile, free from the biological and body sense. This is *svadharma*—soul culture through breath control.

The soul (Krishna) always wants to take you from evil to good, from restlessness to calm. This is the quality of your soul. Krishna is saying, "Look at the condition of your breath and do not be afraid. You have been born into a family of warriors. You should be a strong and able ruler who can kill the negative qualities within you. By controlling your breath, you can come up to Me in the pituitary. Why are you perplexed and nervous?"

In the Puranas, it says that the technique for finding the Self is called *dharma*, or spirituality. In the dictionary, it says that *dharma* (religion) means an association with a good spiritual master. Withdraw your power inside the cranium and perceive the Self—that is *dharma*, that is spirituality.

Verse 32

yadṛcchayā co 'papannam
svargadvāram apāvṛtam
sukhinaḥ kṣatriyāḥ pārtha
labhante yuddham īdṛśam

Translation

O Partha! Happy are the warriors who get such an unsolicited opportunity for war, which is an open gateway to heaven.

Metaphorical Interpretation

The fortunate warrior has the opportunity to fight the inner enemies. This opportunity is rare. In such a war one can easily enter the cave of cranium, which is heaven, opened for the victorious. It is possible to win the battle with breath control.

If the power of God does not draw breath into us, we are dead. When we constantly feel the power of God inhaling through our nose, that is heaven. The door to heaven is the nose. When we control our breath and calmly watch Him, realizing that we enjoy the sense pleasures because He is inhaling for us, we will surely achieve continuous liberation.

This is why the Lord tells Partha (Arjuna, the food minister), "I inhale through your nose and through the nose of every human being. If I don't, neither you nor anyone can digest food to have energy, agility, and strength, and you therefore cannot fight against evil. As long as I am pulling the inhalations from the top of your head, please love Me. Follow Me. Raise your consciousness to the top of your head, to the fontanel, where I abide within you. Feel My importance and your door to heaven will constantly be open. You will have continuous peace, joy, and bliss."

Verse 33

atha cet tvam imam dharmyam
samgrāmam na kariṣyasi
tataḥ svadharmam kīrtim ca
hitvā pāpam avāpsyasi

Translation

You will surely lose your prestige as a warrior and incur sin if you neglect your duties and do not fight this spiritual battle.

Metaphorical Interpretation

The Lord describes the defamation that will come to Arjuna if he does not fight.

Arjuna is the food minister. We are all Arjuna. From food we get knowledge, consciousness, mind, thought, and intellect; we also get money, sexual desire, anger, and suspicion. In the scriptures it says, *mana eva manuṣyāṇām, kārana vandha mokṣayoḥ,* which means, "The mind is the cause of human bondage and also the source of our liberation."

Krishna is saying, "Because I inhale for you, you can digest food and get strength and energy to struggle for existence. If your mind is focused below the navel, you will remain in the biological force, which will keep you in the bondage of extreme worldly desire. But if you withdraw your senses above your navel center and up to the pituitary, you will automatically perceive Me and you will be liberated.

"Passion, anger, wealth, and sense pleasures are all related to the body; they are like family relations. They are the Kaurava party, evil and vicious. If you don't fight them, you will lose your reputation as a good warrior. It will be heinous and sinful for you to neglect your sacred duty. Once the dark propensities of your mind know of your weakness, they will be more powerful and will trouble you.

"You are not in the party of ignorance (Kauravas); you are in the party of knowledge (Pandavas). I, your friend and guru and the life inside your pituitary, advise you to practice soul culture because you are a *kshatriya*, a warrior of the spiritual party."

Verse 34

akīrtim cā 'pi bhūtāni
kathayiṣyanti te 'vyayām
sambhāvitasya cā 'kīrtir
maraṇād atiricyate

Translation

All beings will always talk of your undying infamy; for a man of proper stature, loss of prestige is worse than death.

Metaphorical Interpretation

Arjuna (the seeker) has not yet started to meditate, but he is willing to start, he has the power to meditate, and he can succeed in meditation. The Lord is saying, "I am the source of every human being, as well as the sole doer. When I cannot convince human beings that I am doing all the work, they live just like animals. When humans do not seek the imperishable soul, people think ill of them."

The soul is imperishable and abides in the pituitary of every human being. When you constantly fix your attention there, and even up to the fontanel, you will have eternal fame. If you do not seek the soul and are nothing but a rational animal, you will never truly be respected.

Verse 35

bhayād raṇād uparatam
mamsyante tvām mahārathāḥ
yeṣām ca tvam bahumato
bhūtvā yāsyasi lāghavam

Translation

The great chariot warriors, who previously appreciated your valor,

may not consider this a kindness; they will consider you a coward, who left the battlefield out of fear.

Metaphorical Interpretation

Every human being must strive for self-evolution by controlling the senses. The Lord teaches, "Your five sense organs are your enemies, the mighty soldiers of the Kaurava army. Your eyes pull you out into the external world, and you become absorbed in it. Your ears wish to hear melodious talk, so they also pull you outward. Similarly, your skin, nose, and mouth pull you into heinous activity. If you do not fight against your evil tendencies and do not rise above your two eyebrows, near the soul, the evil forces will destroy your reputation, saying that you are a coward and a warrior unfit to conquer them."

Verse 36

avācyavādāṁś ca bahūn
vadiṣyanti tavā 'hitāḥ
nindantas tava sāmarthyam
tato duḥkhataram nu kim

Translation

What could be more distressing than having your enemies calling you ill names and underestimating your ability?

Metaphorical Interpretation

Arjuna is in the battlefield in the middle of two parties: his spiritual battlefield. He must draw his sensory awareness up above the five sense telephones, then overcome them, so he can enter the realm of the soul. Unfortunately, like a coward, he refuses to fight; therefore, he is hated, laughed at, and scorned by the Kaurava party. Once the army of the mind knows that the strength of wisdom is weak, they will create trouble in everyday life with ever-increasing temptation, ambition, and distraction.

Verse 37

hato vā prāpsyasi svargam
jitvā vā bhokṣyase mahīm
tasmād uttiṣṭha kaunteya
yuddhāya kṛtaniścayaḥ

Translation

O son of Kunti (Arjuna)! If you are killed in battle, you will go to heaven; if you win, the entire world will be yours. Therefore, cheerfully get up and fight with strong determination.

Metaphorical Interpretation

In a friendly way, Krishna, representing the soul, tells Arjuna, who represents every human being, that he must fight against his evil propensities, suppress his biological wickedness, and bring his awareness up into the pituitary to discover the finest conception of God. In the phrase *uttishtha kaunteya, kaunteya* means "O son of Kunti." *Kunti* means the finest conception. Arjuna received that finest conception from his mother. The word *uttishtha*, or *urdhey tishtha*, means to remain inside the cranium. At this point in the dialogue, Arjuna is resolved to meditate.

The Lord is saying, "I will guide you slowly, and slowly you will achieve divine meditation. If you die before you reach the divine goal, you will attain divinity nonetheless. If you are completely successful in meditation in this lifetime—namely, if you attain *nirvikalpa samadhi*, the formless and pulseless stage—you will perceive that I abide in everything in the material world. You will be continuously liberated. Everyone must reach that stage so they can experience liberation, even if they are householders and even if they are prosperous. So, Arjuna, constantly practice Kriya Yoga. Don't stop."

In the Bhagavad Gita, (6:40 onward), Krishna states that the more you meditate, the more you will feel God in the mundane world.

Verse 38

sukhaduḥkhe same kṛtvā
lābhālābhau jayājayau
tato yuddhāya yujyasva
nai 'vam pāpam avāpsyasi

Translation

You do not sin if you fight for the sake of the battle while performing your duty, and without preferring pleasure or pain, gain or loss, victory or defeat.

Metaphorical Interpretation

This verse explains the outlook of an efficient yogi, a true warrior. The Lord is saying, "You must maintain implicit faith and loyalty in Me." *Atmavai gurur ekam*: "Your soul, Krishna, is your only guru."

"Don't look for pleasure and pain, proceed onward according to My instructions. O Arjuna! If you do not remain in Brahman (the soul), in Me, that will be a sin. No person in the universe can exist without the soul. By meditating, you will achieve a balance of mind that is not possible without it."

The Lord's request of Arjuna is this: "Please meditate and fight your evil propensities. Transcend your five sense telephones and perceive that I am doing everything. By practicing meditation, balance of mind and calm are achieved; then you can rise above the play of duality, and you will be unaffected by opposites such as pleasure and pain, success and failure, and the others. In happiness and unhappiness, in loss and gain, in everything—realize that I am conducting all and everything."

Verse 39

eṣā te 'bhihitā sāmkhye
buddhir yoge tv imām śṛṇu
buddhyā yukto yayā pārtha
karmabandham prahāsyasi

Translation

O Partha (Arjuna)! This attitude has been presented to you from the point of view of Samkhya (philosophy). Now hear the same from the point of view of self-discipline (practice). Equipped with this state of mind, you will be able to free yourself completely from the shackles of karma.

Metaphorical Interpretation

The first chapter described the coming battle between two cousin–brothers, who are really the biological and spiritual forces in every human being. Now, the Lord is explaining, "I have told you in detail about Self consciousness (superconsciousness) in terms of the Samkhya philosophy. Self consciousness is the way to know your Self, your soul. This is called *samkhya yoga.* In Verses 2 through 38, Krishna gave Arjuna instructions about how to obtain Self consciousness through Kriya Yoga. Now in Verse 39, He says, "O Arjuna! I have told you about soul consciousness. Now I will teach you the practical technique of *karma yoga.* Please listen with full attention. If you practice it carefully, you will be free from worldly bondage.

"A dead man cannot act. Spiritual action comes from Brahman (the soul, Krishna), and Brahman comes from imperishable God. Withdraw your sensory awareness from the lowest centers and raise it up into the pituitary; then, when you perform work in the world, you will feel that God is doing the work through you. You must become His instrument. When you constantly experience the soul doing the work; then, having done the biological work, you will experience constant liberation.

Verse 40

ne 'hā 'bhikramanāśo 'sti
pratyavāyo na vidyate
svalpam apy asya dharmasya
trāyate mahato bhayāt

Translation

In the beginning of this selfless effort, no effort is wasted, nor is there any adverse result. A little progress on this path can save you from perilous danger.

Metaphorical Interpretation

Regardless of its intensity, self-effort for spiritual evolution is glorious.

The practice of soul culture is selfless work. This selfless work leads a seeker towards God. In the beginning, as with Arjuna, many people get a little dejected, but the strongest desire and a strict master can redirect the seeker towards the divine path. Every work incurs some result, so selfless soul culture will surely lead the devotee to success. Even if it is only a little practice, it doesn't matter. As little drops of water make a mighty ocean, selfless soul culture enables a person to perceive God, even in the mundane world. A little spiritual practice makes one free from the fear of loss, pain, and death.

Verse 41

vyavasāyātmikā buddhir
eke 'ha kurunandana
bahuśākhā hy anantāś ca
buddhayo 'vyavasāyinām

Translation

Those who stick to this path with determination have but one aspiration, O dearest child of the Kurus (Arjuna); however, the minds of those who are fickle go in various directions.

Metaphorical Interpretation

Arjuna is very active in his selfless spiritual work, so the Lord addresses him as "Kurunandana," one who is very active in selfless soul culture. The Lord is teaching Arjuna how he must proceed diligently with selfless work. As a result, Arjuna can see the tremendous effulgence that is the first manifestation of the formless father before creation. Arjuna's fixes his mind completely on God and becomes absorbed in divinity. But those who do not practice this spiritual *karma yoga*, which is Kriya Yoga, are always restless and do not have peace of mind. Their minds constantly run from one thought to another. This vacillation brings about suffering and human madness.

Verses 42–44

yām imām puṣpitām vācam
pravadanty avipaścitaḥ
vedavādaratāḥ pārtha
nā 'nyad astī 'ti vādinaḥ

kāmātmānaḥ svargaparā
janmakarmaphalapradām
kriyāviśeṣabahulām
bhogaiśvaryagatim prati

bhogaiśvaryaprasaktānām
tayā 'pahṛtacetasām
vyavasāyātmikā buddhiḥ
samādhau na vidhīyate

Translation

O Partha (Arjuna)! Those who have extreme desire, who look upon heaven as the supreme goal and argue that there is nothing beyond heaven and pleasures, and who are devoted to ritual practice to the letter of the scriptures, are unwise. They utter flowery speech recommending various acts for acquiring pleasure and prosperity through fortunate birth and the fruit of their actions.

Those whose minds are carried away by such flowery speech cannot attain *samadhi*, because they are attached to pleasure and prosperity.

Metaphorical Interpretation

"O Partha (Arjuna)! The ignorant, restless, and self-interested cannot merge with God and attain *samadhi*. Those who read endless spiritual books containing interpretations of the scriptures written by ordinary people, who think the heavenly pleasures within them are the ultimate goal of life, say there is no truth in the *shrutis* (revealed scriptures). They cherish their strong desire for the fruit of their own actions. They are undoubtedly silly.

Many tempt the minds of people with sweet words about God-realization, but advise them to remain busy with many rituals and formal religious play. If you listen to these people, your mind will always remain absorbed in worldly pleasures, and consequently, your struggle for religious devotion will be slow. You will constantly be restless, and you will never be able to attain *samadhi*.

In the Bhagavad Gita, the Lord explains how people can attain the formless stage, which is the ultimate goal of human life. In India today, especially for those practicing Hinduism, there are many rituals to perform, from many scriptures. Back in the Vedic era, people only practiced *ashtanga yoga*, without worshipping any deity. By these means, even children older than twelve years attained God-realization. They had intuitive power, and could foretell, curse, and bless; they could even give divine power to others.

After the Vedic period came the Aryan period. During that time they had even more divine power, because they practiced *ashtanga yoga*. After the end of the Aryan period and the *dwapara yuga*, the *kali yuga* began. During this period, people were extremely busy worshipping an unlimited number of deities in the hope of material gain.

Today, even with the spread of education and scientific research, people are busy with religious practices and dogmatic and fanatical ideas. Truth remains very far away. The more people achieve material gain, the more restless they become. Material gain, pleasure of the senses, and status are undoubtedly required in moderation. Along with these, however, people should meditate very deeply. Krishna tells Arjuna that until you meditate very deeply, you cannot perceive the real truth, you cannot attain *samadhi*, the divine goal.

Verse 45

traiguṇyaviṣayā vedā
nistraiguṇyo bhavā 'rjuna
nirdvandvo nityasattvastho
niryogakṣema ātmavān

Translation

O Arjuna, the Vedas describe three qualities. Be free from these three qualities, rise above the pairs of opposites, remain balanced, and be unconcerned about the supply of wants and the preservation of what has been already attained. Be established in the Self.

Metaphorical Interpretation

The Lord is saying, "O Arjuna, in the Vedas many things are written about religion. If you follow these prescriptions, you will have wealth, prosperity, and also fluctuations of mind. But if you follow the Bhagavad Gita, you will go beyond the triple qualities of delusion and discover peace, godliness, and the formless state. When you do so, you will be beyond duality, firmly fixed in purity. Then I will supply you with everything according to your need. I therefore request that you always remain in the pituitary with Me."

The Lord is teaching Arjuna the supreme technique for Self-realization. He explains that inside the spinal canal there are many channels: *ida*, *pingala*, *vajra*, *chitra*, and *sushumna*. The *sushumna* is the divine channel, usually covered by the other ones, which is why people are caught in the material world. The *ida* channel gives extreme idleness, sloth, procrastination, recklessness, inconsideration, and imprudence. These are the obstacles to spirituality. The *pingala* channel gives extreme agility, ambition, selfishness, pride, vanity, arrogance, hypocrisy, impurity, violence, insolence, lack of sense control, attachment, extroverted awareness, and ignorance. All these qualities belong to the Kaurava party, as do the *chitra* and *vajra* paths, which create extreme attachment and delusion at the navel and heart centers. All these channels suppress passage of *prana* (life force) through the *sushumna* channel, which flows from the coccygeal to the fontanel.

Krishna is urging Arjuna to practice Kriya Yoga (*as explained later, Bhagavad Gita, 4:1–3*), so he will see all the Kaurava qualities that block the seeker from achieving spirituality. As these obstacles are gradually overcome, the entire *sushumna*, the royal, divine channel of God, will be completely open. When this occurs, the seeker is free from duality and is pure. Without the hindrance of the Kauravas, a devotee can easily rise up to God. This is the battle of the Kauravas and the Pandavas. Since God is the conductor of both parties, a sincere student can easily draw his awareness up and sit near the Lord, even while living in the body chariot, where the soul is the driver.

Verse 46

yāvān artha udapāne
sarvataḥ samplutodake
tāvān sarveṣu vedeṣu
brāhmaṇasya vijānataḥ

Translation

When there is a flood covering the land on all sides, one does not need a little pond or well. Similarly, those who are Self-realized (*brahmanas*) do not need to read religious books.

Metaphorical Interpretation

The Lord is telling Arjuna that when you realize God, you will *be* God; you will perceive that your skin, bone, and marrow—everything—are the power of God. Even if you are a householder, you will feel the power in every thought and action and in whomever you see. You will feel the soul working through you. Then no evil, animal tendencies, pitfalls, shortcomings, and viciousness can enter you. You will be pure and perfect. You will have continuous liberation, the ultimate goal of every human being.

When the flood comes, it covers everything; there is only water. Through practice of spirituality, when the flood of love comes, you are free from all limitations, you are Self-realized. Your life becomes a holy scripture.

Verse 47

karmaṇy evā 'dhikāras te
mā phaleṣu kadācana
mā karmaphalahetur bhūr
mā te sango 'stv akarmaṇi

Translation

You have every right to do selfless work, but you should not cherish any desire for the fruits of your work. Do not let the fruit of your action be your object, or attachment to inaction.

Metaphorical Interpretation

Krishna is saying, "O Arjuna! Follow Me and practice Kriya constantly. Watch your slow, long, spontaneous inhalation, which will surely give you peace. If I do not inhale, you cannot survive. Without Me, you are merely a dead body. Your only duty is to work and maintain implicit faith and loyalty in Me. So do your spiritual work and be constantly vigilant from the coccygeal center to the fontanel, and again from top to bottom."

Ma phaleshu kadachana means that you should not expect any fruit as a result of your actions. Certainly, when you work at your job, you expect a salary or wages as the fruit. If you work a whole month and do not get paid (receive the fruit), you will not continue to work. The real spiritual meaning of *ma phaleshu kadachana* is that you realize that you are not really working—the soul is working. If soul does not inhale, Arjuna cannot expect any fruit. The soul is working through Arjuna, so the soul will receive the fruit of his work. In the Bhagavad Gita (11:33) it says, *nimittamātram bhava savyasācin*: "O Arjuna, you are merely an instrument; I am the operator of the instrument."

The reward of any activity does not go to the instrument, it goes to the operator of the instrument. The Lord is explaining that you cannot stop your spiritual work: When you become a humble instrument, everything you do is spiritual work. Furthermore, continue to meditate, and when you become realized, you will constantly feel that the operator and instrument are the one soul, who is enjoying the fruit of the work.

Verse 48

yogasthaḥ kuru karmāṇi
sangam tyaktvā dhanamjaya
siddhyasiddhyoḥ samo bhūtvā
samatvam yoga ucyate

Translation

O Dhanamjaya (Arjuna), remain in yoga, perform your duties, give up your attachments, and don't let your mind dwell on success or failure; balance of mind (equanimity, equilibrium, harmony) is yoga.

Metaphorical Interpretation

This verse is a beautiful definition of yoga and describes the results of yoga. When a person fixes his attention in the pituitary and is absorbed in the soul, he has balance of mind. This kind of mind cannot be concerned about the fruits of action. When you can penetrate into the cranium, your mind will become calm and you will reach the formless stage. The formless stage is the godly stage. When you attain this, you will perceive everything with equanimity. The state of equanimity and balance is the state of yoga, free from all distractions.

Verse 49

dūreṇa hy avaram karma
buddhiyogād dhanamjaya
buddhau śaraṇam anviccha
kṛpaṇāḥ phalahetavaḥ

Translation

Selfish work is far inferior to this yoga of equanimity. O Dhanamjaya (Arjuna), seek refuge in this evenness of mind. Meditate selflessly; wretched are those who crave the fruit of action.

Metaphorical Interpretation

The Lord highlights the beauty of yoga and teaches Arjuna the relationship between knowledge and activity: "O Arjuna! If your mind becomes restless and is engrossed in the material world while practicing Kriya Yoga, everything will be baffling. If you selflessly fix your attention in the fontanel and practice Kriya Yoga meditation, you will achieve the formless stage and divine bliss. Until you have pinpointed attention, you will not succeed."

Verse 50

buddhiyukto jahātī 'ha
ubhe sukṛtaduṣkṛte
tasmād yogāya yujyasva
yogaḥ karmasu kauśalam

Translation

Endowed with equanimity, one frees oneself in this life from virtue and vice. Devote yourself to this yoga of equanimity. Skill in action is yoga.

Metaphorical Interpretation

The Lord tells Arjuna, "If you want superconsciousness, you must follow the Bhagavad Gita and its techniques for Self-realization. When you attain Self-realization, you cannot perceive your gross body, your biological body, or even your selfishness. Upon reaching partial *samadhi*, devotees feel the superconscious state and the supreme state. They completely forget their preordained force (*samskaras, karma*). The technique of Self-realization is called yoga. You can learn the technique from a realized yogi who can lead you to the divine goal."

"Skill in action is yoga," this verse states: It is a beautiful definition of yoga. Work with divine consciousness and experience Who is doing the work from within.

Verse 51

karmajam buddhiyuktā hi
phalam tyaktvā manīṣiṇaḥ
janmabandhavinirmuktāḥ
padam gacchanty anāmayam

Translation

The wise human being remains in equanimity, renounces the fruits of actions, becomes free from the bondage of birth and death, and reaches the blissful divine stage.

Metaphorical Interpretation

The blissful state of liberation proceeds from the hard work of mediation and a balanced lifestyle. These are the qualities of a wise person. Learned true seekers of God always fix their attention on the soul and perceive the soul everywhere they look. They do not cherish any fruits of their work, nor do they feel any worldly ambition. Thus, they reach the superconscious state, becoming free from birth and death, and during every action, they feel liberated.

Verse 52

yadā te mohakalilam
buddhir vyatitariṣyati
tadā gantāsi nirvedam
śrotavyasya śrutasya ca

Translation

When your sense of selfless devotional service enables you to cross beyond the depths of delusion, you will become indifferent about what is yet to be heard and what has already been heard.

Metaphorical Interpretation

Without the soul, you cannot feel pleasure and pain. Hence, even the perception of pain is the perception of God. When you get a gold coin, you feel happy about it. If you then receive a copper coin, you do not pay it any heed. When you reach the superconscious state and get a taste of God, where the whole treasure of the universe is contained, you are no longer tempted by any shiny material object. When a human being becomes free from delusion by practicing Kriya Yoga, melancholy disappears.

Verse 53

śrutivipratipannā te
yadā sthāsyati niścalā
samādhāv acalā buddhis
tadā yogam avāpsyasi

Translation

When your mind is bewildered by conflicting statements in various spiritual books, remain steady in pinpointed meditation on God. You will feel the oneness of God (Self-realization) within you.

Metaphorical Interpretation

The real spiritual book is the book of one's own life, which can be free from all the conflicting outlooks of the lower centers. The farther you proceed in your spiritual development, the more you will feel the divine illumination of the entire world. In meditation, varieties of color will entice your mind, and you will hear various melodious sounds. You will be charmed with divine melody and vibration from the heaven down to the ground, which will absorb your mind and give you the highest consciousness. Afterwards, when you come back down to your everyday life, you will always feel that whatever you see or touch is really seen or touched only by the soul. You will have union with God.

Krishna teaches Arjuna, the food minister, that since you must take food, your mind will succumb to the biological force, which is ignorance. You should overcome that ignorance, however, because you are the third Pandava (Arjuna, the knowledge body). With the help of your knowledge body, you should convert your ignorance into knowledge. In the second chapter, Krishna constantly teaches Arjuna how to change his ignorance into knowledge and how to transform his delusion into illumination. Krishna explains that, although Arjuna is the food minister, he is still Krishna's minister; Krishna is the king of the body. You should gradually bring your awareness up from the navel center to the heart center, heart to cervical, and cervical to pituitary (*as explained in Bhagavad Gita 6:25*). Having heard all this, Arjuna is convinced because Krishna is his friend and intimate and divine relative. Arjuna agrees to follow Krishna (the soul). Therefore, Arjuna now begins to ask Krishna many questions about spirituality.

Verse 54

arjuna uvāca
sthitaprajñasya kā bhāṣā
samādhisthasya keśava
sthitadhīḥ kim prabhāṣeta
kim āsīta vrajeta kim

Translation

Arjuna asks:
O Keshava (Krishna)! What are the characteristics of those established in wisdom who have attained *samadhi* (whose minds remain in God consciousness)? How do those constantly merged in God speak? How do they sit? How do they walk?

Metaphorical Interpretation

Arjuna asks about the qualities of a spiritually advanced person: What are the traits of those who have attained wisdom and *samadhi?* Krishna explains that there are seven stages of *samadhi*: (1) *subhechha*; (2) *vicharani*; (3) *tonumanasa*; (4) *sattapatti*; (5) *asamshakti*; (6) *padartha bhabini*; and (7) *turiya samadhi*. Those who attain *samadhi* develop one of these seven spiritual dispositions. From Arjuna's many questions, Keshava is completely certain that his delusions have completely disappeared.

A person who attains the first stage of *samadhi* has a strong urge to seek God in the material world. In food, in drink, and in every action he perceives God and finds that God is kind to him. The second stage is about the same: The person achieves liberation, constant perception of the Self, and love for God. A person in the third stage always remains in the soul, in an introverted state, perceiving the soul as the sole doer. In the fourth stage, some superhuman power is obtained, and divine sound, divine light, divine vibration are felt.

The Lord is telling Arjuna and all true seekers of God in the universe about the greatest stage of God-realization. Since Arjuna is somewhat attracted to soul culture, he is curious about spiritual people: how they move, how they talk, and the results of their meditation. He asks Lord Krishna these questions because he wants to attain the highest stage. The symbolic meaning is that a person who desires God-realization will ask his indwelling Self, his soul, his superconscious awareness, how far he has proceeded towards purity, perfection, and love for God.

Verse 55

śrībhagavān uvāca
prajahāti yadā kāmān
sarvān pārtha manogatān
ātmany evā 'tmanā tuṣṭaḥ
sthitaprajñas tado 'cyate

Translation

The blessed Lord said:
O Partha (Arjuna), when a person thoroughly gives up all the cravings of his mind and is satisfied in the Self by the Self, he is said to be well established in wisdom.

Metaphorical Interpretation

When devotees fix their attention in the pituitary and remain in the fontanel, they can relinquish all their worldly thoughts and ambitions and stabilize their mind in the supreme power. When mind, thought, intellect, ego, body sense, and worldly sense appear in that stage, *samadhi* is attained. In *samadhi*, everything merges, and afterwards when the devotee comes back to the mundane worldly theater, he feels *sarvam khalvidam brahma* (Chhandogya Upanishad 3:14:1), that is, he feels that in the whole world, whatever he sees, thinks, or experiences, is the power of God. Any person who attains this stage is called *sthitaprajña*.

The spiritual person who is unperturbed in misery and free from attachment, fear, and anger is called *muni* (a spiritual person). A *muni*'s mind is engrossed in meditation. In Sanskrit, *muni* means *manah samlina manasa*, a person whose mind is completely merged in knowledge. Those who can transmute their minds into the superconscious state are in meditation. So meditation does not mean to pray or chant mantras loudly, mentally, or slowly, or to move beads with the hands, or to sing spiritual hymns.

The Kena Upanishad (1:2–9) states that when our five senses are busy with chanting, hearing, seeing, and imagining, we cannot know God. In the beginning, to withdraw our minds, we should chant only for a short period, just like Chaitanya Mahaprabhu, Ratnakar, Tulsidas, Rama, and Krishna did. After that, until we can introvert our minds and go into the center where our five senses originate and remain there constantly, it is not meditation.

When people can withdraw their senses from the world and remain in the soul, they feel the extreme calm that is godliness. In that stage, devotees cannot feel whether they are inhaling. In the Yoga Sutras of Patañjali (2:49), it says, *tasmin sati svāsa-praśvāsayor-gati vichhedaḥ prāṇāyāmaḥ*, which means, "Devotees are merged in the soul and spiritual miracles, so they cannot watch their incoming or outgoing breath." In this state, their breathing rate is very slow and they cannot feel sadness, attachment, fear, or anger; furthermore, worldly pleasure means very little compared to divine pleasure. A devotee reaching that stage is a *muni*.

Verses 56–57

duḥkheṣv anudvignamanāḥ
sukheṣu vigataspṛhaḥ
vītarāgabhayakrodhaḥ
sthitadhīr munir ucyate

yaḥ sarvatrā 'nabhisnehas
tat-tat prāpya śubhāśubham
nā 'bhinandati na dveṣṭi
tasya prajñā pratiṣṭhitā

Translation

He whose mind remains undisturbed in sorrow, who does not seek pleasure, and who is free from passion, fear, and anger is called a sage, established in wisdom.

The mind of a person who is free from affection, attachment, fondness, love, and tenderness, who is not affected by pleasure and pain, and who is above these qualities is established in wisdom.

Metaphorical Interpretation

The Lord advises Arjuna not to crush his biological or psychological force. Instead, a seeker must learn to feel unity in diversity. Whenever you have a body, you will surely feel pleasure and pain, but without a soul, you could not feel pleasure, affection, attachment, fondness, love, or even pain. The true devotee must develop equanimity during both pleasure and pain. Whenever you remain in the soul, you will realize that the soul cannot die or be killed. Hence, your relations cannot die or be killed. You will always feel your immortality. Then you are *sthitaprajña*, in the wisdom stage, living as a liberated soul free from the turbulent play of the mind.

Verse 58

yadā samharate cā 'yam
kūrmo 'ngānī 'va sarvaśaḥ
indriyāṇī 'ndriyārthebhyas
tasya prajñā pratiṣṭhitā

Translation

When devotees fully withdraw their senses from sense objects, as the tortoise withdraws its limbs from all directions, they are established in wisdom.

Metaphorical Interpretation

Through self-restraint, the tortoise can withdraw its limbs and head inside its shell for self-protection at the time of trouble, remaining as still as a piece of rock. Similarly, when human beings meditate and withdraw their five senses into the center where the soul abides, they are detached from the dualities of the world. The senses remain in the soul. The devotees perceive divine bliss. Afterwards, when they come back down to the material world, they feel, hear, and see from the soul; all their limbs now function from the soul. They know that the mundane worldly play is carried out by Him, and they attain the God stage, the wisdom stage.

Verse 59

viṣayā vinivartante
nirāhārasya dehinaḥ
rasavarjam raso 'py asya
param dṛṣṭvā nivartate

Translation

The sense objects recede from an abstinent man, with the exception of taste. Even taste falls away after the absolute is realized.

Metaphorical Interpretation

Attachment is bondage and the cause of all troubles. Although the worldly attachment of those practicing austerity is suppressed, their desire for enjoyment does not disappear. If they meditate deeply, however, and achieve Self-realization, their attachments will totally depart. Someone truly detached from the distracting play of the senses is free. For Arjuna to succeed, the Lord must teach Arjuna about deep meditation. He says, "As the son of a warrior, you will not find peace if you do not fight with your biological forces." For example: A tuberculosis patient must be isolated and restrained from sexual enjoyment and physical exertion. If you only advise the patient to restrain himself, he will eventually lose control. Even with full knowledge about his disease and his need for rest, his mind will remain focused on sex pleasure and he will be restless. On the other hand, if a tuberculosis patient meditates and, by remaining in the center of his soul, perceives the true controller of his five senses, all his worldly desires will be given up to the soul and God; then he can easily control his senses.

Verse 60

yatato hy api kaunteya
puruṣasya vipaścitaḥ
indriyāṇi pramāthīni
haranti prasabham manaḥ

Translation

O son of Kunti (Arjuna)! Even for true seekers of liberation, the sense organs and work organs are so turbulent and powerful that they forcibly try to take over and control the mind, intellect, and ego.

Metaphorical Interpretation

You cannot forcibly withdraw your awareness from the five sense organs until you have an intense desire for soul culture. Those who verbally express desire for liberation, who chant and pray and look at deities and the crosses of Jesus, but shed crocodile tears for worldly interests, cannot perceive God. Until a devotee introverts his mind and goes into the center, controlling the breath skillfully, spiritual attempts will be useless, a waste of energy and time. Yoga and meditation are skill in action. Lead a spiritual life intelligently with self-control and emancipation.

Verse 61

tāni sarvāṇi samyamya
yukta āsīta matparaḥ
vaśe hi yasye 'ndriyāṇi
tasya prajñā pratiṣṭhitā

Translation

Having controlled the senses, true seekers should sit for meditation, remaining firm, and devoting the heart and the soul to Me. These seekers will be established in wisdom, which means that their senses are under control.

Metaphorical Interpretation

The five sense telephones are powerful warriors of the Kaurava party with virulent strength. If you do not introvert your sensory awareness, seek the soul, and remain there firmly and constantly, you may deviate from the truth. This is the real battlefield: fighting with the lower biological force. If you can fight, win, and constantly fix your mind on the soul, you will always attain wisdom. A person of wisdom is free from the play of the senses and the displays of the mind because he is self-disciplined.

Verses 62–63

dhyāyato viṣayān pumsaḥ
sangas teṣū 'pajāyate

sangāt samjāyate kāmaḥ
kāmāt krodho 'bhijāyate

krodhād bhavati sammohaḥ
sammohāt smṛtivibhramaḥ
smṛtibhramśād buddhināśo
buddhināśāt praṇaśyati

Translation

Thinking of the sense objects repeatedly, a person will develop attachment for them. From attachment springs desire, from unfulfilled desire comes anger.

From anger arises delusion; from delusion, confusion of memory and loss of reason. Without discrimination, the person goes to complete destruction.

Metaphorical Interpretation

The Lord describes the danger of downfall in spiritual life and indirectly cautions that one should be absorbed in the soul, not in sense objects.Krishna has said, " If you remain with me, you will get wisdom." Now he cautions, "If you don't fight the biological force, your life will be spoiled, you will be ruined, and you will be nothing but a rational animal."

Verse 64

rāgadveṣaviyuktais tu
viṣayān indriyaiś caran
ātmavaśyair vidheyātmā
prasādam adhigacchati

Translation

The person (self-controlled yogi) who withdraws his senses completely and overcomes his attraction and aversion finds peace of mind, even if he still enjoys some objects with his five senses.

Metaphorical Interpretation

In this verse, the Lord gives instructions to Arjuna that are completely opposite to the teachings of the preceding two verses. In those two he instructed Arjuna: "If you remain engrossed in material objects, you will find delusion and destruction; so you must fight (meditate)." In this verse, however, he tells Arjuna: "Fight and meditate and keep your mind one hundred percent in the soul and know that it is the sole doer of everything. Without the soul, your five sense telephones cannot function. If you believe this firmly, when your sense telephones are immersed in sense objects, you will be free from attachment and will discover peace of mind and joy."

Suppose a person has just learned the technique for driving a motor car, has successfully passed the examination, and has obtained a license to drive. In the morning, she drives to the office on a crowded road. Her five sense telephones, hands, and legs are extremely busy driving the car speedily and using the steering wheel, gears, and brake, and watching the mirror and crossroads. When the light is red, she brakes and stops the car. When the traffic is free, she drives the car very fast and reaches the office just in time. That was her goal.

Similarly, if you fight your biological force, suppress your worldly and physical senses with the help of Kriya Yoga inhalation, magnetize your spine, and follow the teacher wholeheartedly, surely you can discover the Self in the pituitary. You will recognize that the soul is the conductor, fighter, savior, and doer of everything. If you meditate in this way for a long period, when you come back to the material world, you will see that your gross body is like the car and that your soul is the expert driver. Your five sense telephones are always functioning, and the soul will guide you through the dangers on the streets. The soul is not attached to anything. Automatically, the soul orchestrates the use of the gears and brakes by using the limbs of the body, quickly taking you to your destination. You get to your office on time, and you are peaceful and joyful. A dead person cannot have peace. Peace, bliss, and joy only come from absorption in God. A person established in wisdom enjoys real peace and the bliss of the Self.

Verse 65

prasāde sarvaduḥkhānām
hānir asyo 'pajāyate
prasannacetaso hy āśu
buddhiḥ paryavatiṣṭhate

Translation

When you gain self-control by meditation, you will feel divine bliss, and all your sorrows will perish. The minds and intellects of contented people are firmly established in the Self.

Metaphorical Interpretation

All human beings who practice Kriya Yoga with the deepest desire and pinpointed attention can merge into God in a short period. They can perceive supernal divine light in the pituitary and in the fontanel. At that time, ignorance disappears, the mind transforms into superconsciousness, and the blissful stage is obtained. Without this, you cannot proceed towards the divine goal where guru, God, and you sit together, where all danger disappears, and your love for God and your belief in God increase.

There are some misconceptions about the meaning of guru. *Gu* means your invisible body (soul), and *ru* means your beautiful gross body (*rupa*). But guru also means an educated, realized teacher. Without a teacher for doctors, no one can become a doctor. Without engineering teachers, no one can become an engineer. Similarly, without a realized teacher, no one can learn how to become realized.

A person is known by the company he keeps. If you stay in the company of bad people, surely you will be bad and you will be dishonored. If you remain in the company of good people, you will be highly respected. Arjuna was engrossed in delusion, but by being in the company of his real master, Krishna, and following his advice one hundred percent, his evil, sorrow, and negative qualities were suppressed. Although his whole system was functioning in the biological force, he remained detached, feeling his guru (soul) functioning through him.

Verse 66

nā 'sti buddhir ayuktasya
na cā 'yuktasya bhāvanā
na cā 'bhāvayataḥ śāntir
aśāntasya kutaḥ sukham

Translation

The person who has not controlled his mind and senses cannot have a discriminating intellect. Nor can such a person have sense of duty, and thus has no peace. How can there be happiness for someone lacking peace?

Metaphorical Interpretation

A person without discrimination is miserable. The person whose mind is not engrossed in the soul is not intelligent and has no firmness of mind. The person who does not seek the soul through the technique of soul culture cannot get peace. The person who has no peace cannot perceive divine bliss. The Lord tells Arjuna firmly, "If you do not fight your biological force, you are not an intelligent person. You will not be respected by anyone, and you will be dishonored."

Students who do not withdraw their senses from the material world cannot give full attention to their studies. They cannot become educated, wise, and respected; educated people will ignore them. Similarly, if you do not practice and withdraw your senses from the lower to the higher level of soul culture, you cannot remove your ignorance and cannot get peace of mind. So, practice Kriya very diligently. Otherwise, your mind will slip back down occasionally, and you will not retain liberation and bliss. A person should stay in the state of *yukta*, united with the soul.

Verse 67

indriyāṇām hi caratām
yan mano 'nuvidhīyate
tad asya harati prajñām
vāyur nāvam ivā 'mbhasi

Translation

Just as a storm overpowers a boat at sea, the mind engrossed in the biological force and the sense organs leads a person away from discrimination.

Metaphorical Interpretation

The senses are restless. They go in different directions, creating a storm in life. When you do not control your senses, your extreme enemies, you will be overcome by them and will not be able to judge right and wrong. You will be bewildered. You have the high valor needed to overcome your biological force, so fight it. Otherwise, you will be dishonored.

In the Yogic texts it says, *indriyāṇām manoratha mananātha uṣṭha marutaḥ*: "The mind is the king of the five senses, but the breath is the king of the mind." By controlling the breath, you control your wild mind. During sleep, your breath is nicely controlled by the soul; therefore, you are calm; in fact, your mind is overpowered by the calm. By magnetizing your spine and regulating your breath, you can subdue evil and your mind, thought, intellect, ego, and body sense. Then, your wisdom will stay with you. If you don't do so, you cannot use your intellect and you will be dishonored.

Verse 68

tasmād yasya mahābāho
nigṛhītāni sarvaśaḥ
indriyāṇī 'ndriyārthebhyas
tasya prajñā pratiṣṭhitā

Translation

Therefore, O Mighty-armed (Arjuna), people who can thoroughly control the power of the virulent five senses are established in wisdom in every subject.

Metaphorical Interpretation

What is the sign of a true devotee? True devotion is attaining Self-realization and merging with God. Without self-control, sense control, heart control, and withdrawing the senses, you cannot conceive God, meditate upon God, and realize Him. Human beings with these skills reach cosmic consciousness and know that the soul is driving the body car.

Verse 69

yā niśā sarvabhūtānām
tasyām jāgarti samyamī
yasyām jāgrati bhūtāni
sā niśā paśyato muneḥ

Translation

During the time that is night to all beings, the God-realized person remains awake; when all beings are awake, it is night to the sages.

Metaphorical Interpretation

Most human beings are far from soul culture in spiritual darkness. During the day they are engrossed in the five senses and the material world, so they are constantly in delusion, which is spiritual darkness. Although they are in daylight, due to their spiritual ignorance, it is truly night. This is the darkness of spiritual blindness. They lead a miserable life in spiritual darkness, restless and devoid of peace. *Munis*, people of meditation, have no delusion like ordinary human beings. They are constantly engrossed in the soul. In the daytime, in whatever they see, *munis* perceive the soul everywhere, pervading everything. They have no illusions, only illumination. There is no night (darkness) for them; everything is light (knowledge). That which is night to the ignorant is day to soul-cultured people. Devotees must fight against the worldly propensities and find knowledge, which is light. This is the nature of delusion and illumination.

When knowledge is merged in the light of the soul, the five sense telephones sleep, which is night for the senses. When human beings are far from the soul, their five sense telephones are functioning in the material world, which is day for the senses, but covers the soul in darkness.

Verse 70

āpūryamāṇam acalapratiṣṭham
samudram āpaḥ praviśanti yadvat
tadvat kāmā yam praviśanti sarve
sa śāntim āpnoti na kāmakāmī

Translation

Those persons attain peace whose desires enter into them like the waters flow into a changeless sea being filled up from all sides. Such people do not desire objects.

Metaphorical Interpretation

As the waters of many rivers enter the ocean, which remains unruffled though filled from many sides, so do Self-realized devotees merge the many aspects of their lives into the soul and find peace. But not so for one who is a slave to desires, ambitions, and passions.

A person with spiritual awakening shuns all negative qualities. The life of such a person is full and complete, even when living in the material world of sense objects. Such a person is always the same, even as many turbulent rivers of life flow into his changeless consciousness.

Consider an example. When little children go to the market and find a large variety of dolls and toys, they want to take all the things from the market. But when elderly persons see dolls and toys, they do not pay any attention to them. They are not charmed by these things and they do not look at them. Similarly, realized yogis, those who have attained *shambhavi mudra*, a higher stage of Kriya, are always engrossed in soul, even when they come from the meditation stage. They have self-control, self-reliance, self-possession, and self-knowledge. In this stage, the devotees find soul everywhere and remain detached from negative things, whereas the minds of those who do not meditate are like children. Whatever they see in the world, they want to take into their own possession. So they are constantly restless, unpleasant, unhealthy, and sleepless.

The Lord is telling Arjuna to remove his childishness and sorrow, to stand up to the negative propensities within, and joyfully rise and be ready. "Fight your biological force!" He says. "Withdraw your sensory awareness from the lower centers into the higher center, to the north, inside the cranium where I reside. I am like an ocean—you can enter into Me and merge in Me. I care for all people. Anyone who meditates will not be absorbed in delusion; even while living in the world they will have no illusions."

Verse 71

vihāya kāmān yaḥ sarvān
pumāṁś carati niḥspṛhaḥ
nirmamo nirahaṁkāraḥ
sa śāntim adhigacchati

Translation

One who gives up desire and roams the world, free from attachment, free from the idea of me and mine, and devoid of pride, finds peace.

Metaphorical Interpretation

A truly spiritual person is free from ambition and attachment, free from ego, vanity, and exhibitionism.

Metaphorically, the Lord is telling Arjuna that many devotees attain a little knowledge about spirituality, they can perform many types of miracles. When they get these powers, they immediately go to the public to exhibit them. Many people run to them and are charmed by these miracles. By doing so they deviate from the real path of God-realization and remain busy with religious play and dogmatic views, which cannot help them reach the formless stage. Moreover, the ones who exhibit miracles and earn a lot of money have vanity, self-praise, hypocrisy, pride, and impurity; they cannot proceed to the divine goal either. On the other hand, those who meditate very deeply and always feel that He is the doer will never experience delusion or attachment; instead, they will perceive God.

Verse 72

eṣā brāhmī sthitiḥ pārtha
nai 'nām prāpya vimuhyati
sthitvā 'syām antakāle 'pi
brahmanirvāṇam ṛcchati

Translation

O Partha (Arjuna), such is the state of the God-realized person. In this state, he overcomes delusion. When established in this state at the last moment of the life, he attains complete emancipation and bliss.

Metaphorical Interpretation

"O Partha (Arjuna), I have described in detail the God-realized person, free from delusion, illusion, and error and established in the Brahman. Such a devotee is liberated during life, and at the last moment of his life he acquires eternal emancipation. A life of meditation is a life of bliss, in every step."

The Lord is guiding Arjuna from ignorance to knowledge in order to show all human beings how to rise from ignorance to knowledge. People require enthusiastic, expert, tenacious, and alert teachers and parents. The general tendency of young students is to remain in worldly play. To turn them from the extrovert stage, they should be given work to study in both spiritual and mundane matters. The teacher should constantly devote his energy to the students. Then students, both worldly and spiritual, will proceed towards knowledge. Knowledge will lead them to the ultimate goal.

The Lord (soul) is undoubtedly an enthusiastic, tenacious, alert, and fit teacher for Arjuna, who was overwhelmed with sorrow and was unwilling to fight against his biological force. In various ways, the Lord taught Arjuna the duty of the *kshatriyas* (warriors). Then He gradually taught him how to withdraw all human madness up into the pituitary, where it is absorbed into the ocean of God. When the waters in the river of biological force merge with the ocean of God in the pituitary, the ultimate goal of life is achieved. The water in the ocean can never flow back up the rivers again. There may be waves in the ocean, but the waves are nothing but ocean. This is *brahmisthiti*, the perception of Brahman.

In the last verse, the Lord is saying, "O Arjuna! If you always remain in the ocean of God, you will never believe that a wave on that ocean, created by the flow of a river, is a wave of biological force; rather, you will perceive that it is nothing but God in wave form. If you are established in this perception at death, you will permanently merge with God."

Arjuna was a great warrior. He followed his master through and through. During his life, while riding in his body chariot, he always sat by the side of his divine guru, Krishna, in the cave of the cranium. He knew that the Lord alone, his indwelling soul, was doing the driving.

This is the scientific and metaphorical interpretation of the Upanishads and yoga in the second chapter of the Bhagavad Gita.

Summary

In life the hero is free from fear and is established in faith. Faith in scriptures, faith in the spiritual instruction of the teacher, faith in oneself, and ultimately faith in God are the requirements for each traveler on the path of spirituality.

Arjuna had reverence for Shri Krishna. After revealing his state of mind in detail, and then achieving understanding at a critical moment of his life, he surrendered at the feet of the Lord: "I am Thy student, disciple; make me disciplined in my life. I completely surrender at Thy feet" (2:7).

At this juncture, the divine gospel of the Lord starts teaching practical spirituality. Theory and words are not knowledge; for true knowledge, one must experience the essence of spiritual life. Each verse of this chapter depicts the truth of life.

Verse 1: Samjaya explains Arjuna's condition in a heart-touching way.

Verse 2–3: The Lord not only disapproves of Arjuna's reasons for not fighting with evil, but also reprimands them as cowardly.

Verse 4–6: Arjuna attempts to justify his stance by any means.

Verse 7–8: Arjuna surrenders to the Lord as a disciple ready to accept instruction.

Verse 9–10: Samjaya describes Arjuna's silence and his keen attitude to listen and to learn.

Verse 11–30: The Lord teaches the immortality of the Self, and the impermanence of the body and the so-called pleasures.

Verse 31–37: Using reason, the Lord justifies the inner battle of killing the negative propensities.

Verse 38–39: Conclusion of the discussion of *samkhya yoga* and an introduction to *karma yoga*.

Verse 40–53: *Karma yoga* is further elaborated. The Lord gives two beautiful definitions of yoga: "Equanimity is yoga" (*samatvam yogam ucyate*, 2:48) and "Perfection in action is yoga" (*yogah karmasu kaushalam*, 2:50).

Verse 54: Arjuna asks the Lord four questions about *sthitaprajña*, the one who is established in wisdom.

Verse 55–70: The qualities of *sthitaprajña* (the man of wisdom); the necessity of having control over the senses.

Verse 71–72: Passionate wishes, indomitable desires, and ego are the obstacles in the path of eternal peace.

The essence of the second chapter can be summarized in three steps:

1. Immortality of the soul
2. The limit of the body
3. The practice of yoga leads to wisdom through thorough control of life. Yoga is possible through regulation of the body as it functions through the chakras, by means of breath control.

Chapter 3

Karma Yoga

The Yoga of Action

Introduction

Having explained the philosophy of life completely, the Lord spoke highly of the man of wisdom, *sthitaprajña*. But how does one reach such a state? Is it necessary to renounce the world or is it better to follow the path of action? Naturally, Arjuna's mind was filled with doubt. He was confused.

At first, Arjuna thought that the path of renunciation was best. However, real spiritual life starts with the perception that the indwelling Self is the essential nature of the living being. Perceiving the soul (*ya*) in both physical and mental activities (*kri*) is the foundation of spiritual life. Worldly people are spiritually asleep, but spiritual seekers awaken to discover their spiritual nature hidden in the cave of the cranium.

Human life is *yajña* (a sacrifice, fire ceremony). In every breath one must perceive this inner *yajña*, that is *nitya yajña*, the continuous offering. In this chapter, the Lord elaborately explains the principle of *karma* (action).

Verse 1

arjuna uvāca
jyāyasī cet karmaṇas te
matā buddhir janārdana
tat kim karmaṇi ghore mām
niyojayasi keśava

Translation

Arjuna asked:
O Janardana (Krishna)! If You think consciousness and wisdom are far better than action, why do You force me to be entangled in dreadful actions (*karma yoga*), O Keshava (Krishna)?

Metaphorical Interpretation

From Arjuna's question it is clear that the battle of the Bhagavad Gita is not between relatives, but between the evil and divine qualities within every human being. In this verse, Arjuna addresses Krishna by two different names, Janardana and Keshava. Let us think deeply about why Arjuna addresses Krishna as Janardana. Janardana has two different meanings: First, Janardana is derived from *janman* and *ardana. Janman* means a birth. *Ardana* means to crush or to destroy. One who frees a person from birth and death, bringing liberation, is Janardana. Second, consider that only a human being can achieve Self-realization, not an animal being. Krishna is the soul, the conductor of the biological and spiritual forces. The soul is constantly moving us from ignorance to knowledge, from illusion to illumination, and from darkness to light. Thus, Janardana also means, *jananam arci ardanam karoti*: "One who destroys all one's enemies," which are all our negative qualities. The negative power of every human being is the demonic power. The soul (Krishna) helps transform that negative power into divine power. Thus, Arjuna addresses Krishna as Janardana.

Arjuna also addresses Krishna as Keshava. Keshi is a demon who likes to disturb and kill spiritual people. When Krishna was born and people realized that he had incarnated, Krishna's enemies sent the demon Keshi to kill Him. But Keshi was killed by the child Krishna. *Shava* is the dead body of a human being. A human body is in delusion and does not like to seek God. Keshava (the soul) abides in the body and removes the demonic power from it, bringing a human being from impurity to purity, from imperfection to perfection, and from ignorance to God-realization. *Keshava* also refers to the triple aspects of nature: creation (*ka*), destruction (*isha*), and maintenance (*va*).

In the second chapter, Krishna told Arjuna in detail how he could suppress his demonic power (ignorance) and transform it into knowledge, consciousness, cosmic consciousness, and wisdom. At this point, Arjuna thought that theoretical knowledge alone was enough. He was not ready to work and practice in order to achieve real knowledge. Furthermore, even while one is practicing, the knowledge acquired is not perfect. Therefore, Arjuna was confused and asked Krishna why he should allow himself to be engrossed in *karma* (action).

Krishna knew that cosmic consciousness and wisdom could not be reached without work. No one can discover cosmic consciousness merely by hearing about it. Everyone must work to earn it. One ounce of practice is better than tons of theory. Krishna extolled the value of practicing *karma yoga*, which is Kriya Yoga, through which Arjuna could earn the true experience of what human life is.

Verse 2

vyāmiśreṇe 'va vākyena
buddhim mohayasī 'va me
tad ekam vada niścitya
yena śreyo 'ham āpnuyām

Translation

With apparently confused statements, you bewilder my mind. Please tell me definitely the one principle by which I will attain the highest good.

Metaphorical Interpretation

In the first chapter, Arjuna was not willing to fight. In the second chapter, Krishna tried his utmost to convince Arjuna to eliminate his evil tendencies and achieve the superconscious state. Now, Arjuna asserts that he thinks Krishna is talking ambiguously. Arjuna is very happy, and if Krishna says that Arjuna shouldn't fight with his biological forces, Arjuna will be even happier, because he wants to avoid the fight. This is why Arjuna says that Krishna speaks highly of both knowledge and action, which Arjuna thinks are contradictory.

People think that the path of knowledge is very easy. They do not understand that to be established in knowledge, they must work hard. The apparent contradiction between work and knowledge confused Arjuna, and he said, "Please tell me decisively, between the two paths, which will be better for me?"

Verse 3

śrībhagavān uvāca
loke 'smin dvividhā niṣṭhā
purā proktā mayā 'nagha
jñānayogena sāmkhyānām
karmayogena yoginām

Translation

The blessed Lord answered:
O sinless Arjuna! In this world, there are twofold paths, about which I told you previously. Those who practice the yoga of wisdom get supreme consciousness, and those who want to know Me through work should follow the yoga of action.

Metaphorical Interpretation

The Lord replies: "If you follow the yoga of wisdom, you will surely reach Me without fail. In addition, if you follow Me in the yoga of action (Kriya Yoga), you will reach the same goal. But, as I told you, if you do not withdraw your sensory awareness up into the pituitary and then to the fontanel, and if you do not continuously know that all the work you are doing is really done by the soul, it is all useless. These two paths appear to be different, but in reality, they are one. Only by practicing the yoga of action can you perceive Me always. Through this, you are practicing the yoga of wisdom. The two paths are correlated and causally connected.

Verse 4

na karmaṇām anārambhān
naiṣkarmyam puruṣo 'śnute
na ca samnyasanād eva
siddhim samadhigacchati

Translation

A human being cannot attain the state of non-action (the formless stage) by avoiding action; not even by *sannyasa* (renunciation) does one attain perfection.

Metaphorical Interpretation

Knowledge is the fruit of action. Without action, one cannot rise to non-action. External renunciation also will not lead to the state of perfect happiness.

Here, the Lord is explaining that you must open your spinal canal (the *sushumna*) by practicing the yoga of action (as described herein); then uplift your consciousness to the soul. The soul (the power of God) is the *purusha*, the male element, and every gross body is the female element, *nari*. At every moment, we must feel the union of the power of God with the gross body. This union is continuous; we cannot separate the two. The union is maintained through the breath. If the breath stops, the body is a dead body, not a divine body. So long as the breath continues, you are constantly in touch with the indwelling Self.

Everyone should practice the Kriya Yoga technique of simple breath control. The breath is not held. The breath simply enters and flows out. The indwelling Self is so kind to us. He is constantly inhaling and giving us material joy. In reality, this material joy is not material joy, it is divine joy.

If you practice a technique of self-control, such as the Kriya Yoga technique taught by Babaji, Lahiri Mahasaya, and Shriyukteshwarji, you can find calm and divinity in a short while. To enjoy calm at the center of every action is true *sannyasa*, that is, watching (*sann*) the *ya*, the power of God, in every action and at the center of every action. Until you withdraw from your senses (female), you cannot bring your female body, your nature body, to merge with the male body, the soul. You cannot find peace until your male and female bodies merge.

In the Tantra Shastra it says that you can merge with the divine through sexual pleasure, but this cannot happen through ordinary sensual sexual pleasure. The Kularnava Tantra (5:112) says, *paraśakti ātma mithuna samyogānanda iśvare muktāste maithunam tat syāt ītare strinişevakaḥ*, which means: "Those who withdraw from their natural body and mind (the female body), and merge into the soul at the pituitary (the male aspect of a human being) experience real sexual pleasure." They experience extreme peace, bliss, and joy. Those who only enjoy sensual sexuality are not experiencing true spirituality; they only enjoy the male and female physical bodies.

Krishna is saying, "If you truly withdraw and merge into Me, you will attain spirituality and God-realization." He also says, "If you avoid the biological fight and dress like a renunciate monk, you cannot find success in life. You must perform the duty of meditation and right action."

Verse 5

na hi kaścit kṣaṇam api
jātu tiṣṭhaty akarmakṛt
kāryate hy avaśaḥ karma
sarvaḥ prakṛtijair guṇaiḥ

Translation

Human beings cannot exist without work, even for a moment. Everyone is mechanically forced to do work according to the qualities born of nature.

Metaphorical Interpretation

From infancy until death, in every moment, all human beings are engrossed in activity according to their stage of life. In addition, the three qualities of nature remain in the *ida*, *pingala*, and *sushumna*. Depending upon a person's stage of evolution, the *prana*, or life force, will flow differently through these channels in the astral body. The force flowing in the *ida* leads people to idleness and gossip; the *pingala* leads to extreme activity, prosperity, worldly involvement, and restlessness; the *sushumna* leads people to Self-realization, the ultimate goal of every human being. The breath and *prana* are connected, so the nature you exhibit depends upon whether your breath passes mainly through the left nostril, the right nostril, or equally in both. Through practice of meditation, the energy path in the *sushumna* is cleared, so the *prana* can flow there.

The Lord says that human beings need a good guide and master to lead them from the coccygeal center to the pituitary. Therefore, He suggests that Arjuna should suppress his biological force and practice a technique such as Kriya Yoga. Then Arjuna can constantly be united with God. Because he is the son of a warrior, Arjuna should not rebel against his duty, but should fight his biological force. The Lord is strongly emphasizing the necessity of the yoga of action.

Verse 6

karmendriyāṇi samyamya
ya āste manasā smaran
indriyārthān vimūḍhātmā
mithyācāraḥ sa ucyate

Translation

The person who outwardly controls the five organs of action, but mentally recalls the objects of the senses, is a person of delusion, a hypocrite.

Metaphorical Interpretation

The five organs of action are the mouth, for speaking; the hands, to give and take; the legs, for movement; the genitals for pleasure and procreation; and the anus, for excretion.

Every individual receives a mind as a gift. The mind needs work. It wants to roam from one place to another. Ordinary people may externally appear to withdraw the mind from sense objects, but will go on thinking about them mentally. The Lord is saying, "Arjuna, you are the son of a warrior, but you are withdrawing from the duties of your five organs of action in spite of your destiny, which is not good. Moreover, your mind remains absorbed in the five sense telephones, and you are lamenting over what you have forsaken. This is delusion and does not reflect your true identity."

Many people pretend to be spiritual, thinking of themselves as spiritually advanced, but they do not practice meditation, so they cannot advance. Instead, their minds remain absorbed in the objects of the senses. They cannot attain Self-realization. Cleaning the mind is more important than controlling the organs of action.

Ostentation is not spirituality; it is rather ridiculous. Krishna is instructing Arjuna to meditate according to the technique he taught him so that his mind will be free and he can achieve Self-realization.

Verse 7

yas tv indriyāṇi manasā
niyamyā 'rabhate 'rjuna
karmendriyaiḥ karmayogam
asaktaḥ sa viśiṣyate

Translation

The person who controls his sense organs with his intellect while using his organs of action, who remains detached, is a superior person.

Metaphorical Interpretation

The Katha Upanishad (1:3:3–4) offers the parable of the chariot, in which the senses are the horses, and the intellect is the reins that must control the restless and turbulent beasts. The senses are easy to control when the mind is tranquil and free due to Self-inquiry and striving toward a higher purpose in life. Ordinary people are enslaved to their senses, but a superior person uses the senses and mind intelligently.

Sit by the side of the guru, lock the nine doors of your senses and organs of action, follow the guru's technique absolutely, and act according to his advice; then you can introvert your awareness, raise it to the pituitary, then to the fontanel, and attain the formless stage. By this, you will attain Self-realization. You will be a supremely intelligent person.

Verse 8

niyatam kuru karma tvam
karma jyāyo hy akarmaṇaḥ
śarīrayātrā 'pi ca te
na prasidhyed akarmaṇaḥ

Translation

It is wiser to work than not to work. Perform your allotted duty. If you do not work, it is very difficult to maintain your livelihood, or even to survive.

Metaphorical Interpretation

Karma (action) is *dharma* (duty). No one can be idle. Nobody can give up the work of life except when they are absorbed in deep meditation. Through proper work, in God consciousness, the mind is cleansed. Even from the practical viewpoint, to maintain the family and to maintain the body, one must work. Work is the foundation for healthy living. If you give up working and pretend that you are a good devotee, you will not have peace of mind. Your mind will always fluctuate, and you will be unhappy.

There are two types of work: one for the body, mind, family, and society, and the other is the work of the breath (*pranakarma*). Your breath constantly goes in and out; without this work, your body cannot survive. If you control your breath according to the instructions of the Bhagavad Gita (4:29–30, 6:25, and 18:42), you will automatically receive more oxygen, which is nutrition for your brain. The oxygen will purify your blood and give you more vitality, through which you will get sound health. By magnetizing your spine, your brainpower will increase. It will impart skill, prompt understanding, sound mental health, freedom from disease, and long life. With this advantage you can earn your livelihood, and you will achieve Self-realization and happiness too.

Verse 9

yajñārthāt karmaṇo 'nyatra
loko 'yam karmabandhanaḥ
tadartham karma kaunteya
muktasangaḥ samācara

Translation

The world is bound by action. The one who is engrossed in the material world is in bondage. O son of Kunti (Arjuna)! Please do selfless work to become free from attachment.

Metaphorical Interpretation

Actions are the cause of bondage as well as liberation. Working with attachment brings pleasure and pain, but working with God consciousness brings liberation. In every work, one must go to the root of all action. Breath is the way. Work as an oblation is like a *yajña* (sacrifice).

The Lord is explaining that the power of God is the divine fire. Oxygen preserves and protects this divine fire (the soul). The soul (fire) is the life of oxygen, and oxygen is the life of the soul. The soul is constantly inhaling. Without oxygen, human beings cannot survive. By the practice of meditation and the control of breath, you can constantly watch your soul; that is real and constant liberation, the real *yajña* (fire ceremony).

"O son of Kunti (Kunti means "the finest conception of God"), Arjuna, you are of the finest conception. You can constantly watch Me by watching your incoming and outgoing breaths, because I am constantly inhaling and exhaling. If you do, you will know Me. If you don't realize that I am the sole doer, you will be only a rational animal, in bondage, mechanically performing actions. If you constantly watch Me during every action, you will enjoy constant emancipation.

Verse 10

sahayajñāḥ prajāḥ sṛṣṭvā
puro 'vāca prajāpatiḥ
anena prasaviṣyadhvam
eṣa vo 'stv iṣṭakāmadhuk

Translation

In the beginning of creation the Creator, having created everything including sacrifice, said, "By this you shall propagate. Let your desires be fulfilled simply by milking the divine wish-fulfilling cow within."

Metaphorical Interpretation

Ishta kamadhuk: Kamadhenu is not an ordinary cow. Anything you ask of her is immediately granted. God is compared with

Kamadhenu. If you meditate and achieve Self-realization, God will give you peace, bliss, joy—everything.

In ancient times, the Almighty Father, after having created everything, entered into His creation. Consequently, human beings have two bodies: the gross body and the soul. The gross body cannot do anything; the invisible body (the soul) is constantly activating and propagating the gross body with every breath. This breath maintains the divine fire in the gross body, where oxygen is offered to the soul as an oblation. Thus, human beings are alive. Ultimately, any output propagated through the five sense organs, is propagated by the power of God—not just in human beings, but in the whole world. Anyone who practices the original technique of Kriya Yoga (*kri,* work*; ya,* the soul) who watches the power of God in the seven centers inside the spine, can perceive how God is evolving them and propagating new thoughts and ideas, giving them divine joy, like Kamadhenu.

We are the living seed of God, and this seed has the power to pervade everything. Anything born from such a powerful seed is an expression of the indwelling soul. Everything created through the nine doors of our five sense organs is holy; it is God expressing, propagating, and evolving through us, twenty-four hours a day, without rest.

When we realize this during every breath, we can tap into the bliss of the continuous and divine creative act. God makes a sacrifice in every moment by offering Himself to us selflessly in each of the thousands of breaths we draw each day. The practical way to study this is with the Kriya Yoga techniques, which teach us how to make a breath offering to our own soul.

When we watch the power of God in all seven centers inside the spine, we can observe the process of God (in the form of the soul) giving birth to new thoughts, feelings, desires, and so on. To experience that inner stream of creative flow is to know the divine and boundless joy of Kamadhenu, the holy cow. Kamadhenu, practically speaking, is found in the bliss of meditation. She is our Mother Nature, our superconscious and cosmic-conscious states of awareness.

Verse 11

devān bhāvayatā 'nena
te devā bhāvayantu vaḥ
parasparam bhāvayantaḥ
śreyaḥ param avāpsyatha

Translation

By this you will foster the gods and let the gods foster you. Thus fostering each other, you shall achieve the highest state.

Metaphorical Interpretation

When your mind is merged in God consciousness, offering every work to God and offering every breath to the inner fire produces genuine spiritual progress. In every sense organ, there is the presence of God that can be worshipped with love and inner awareness. A sincere seeker leads this kind of life and attains the highest bliss, not wasting a moment of time in idleness and lethargy. All actions are accomplished through the spine.

The *ida, pingala,* and *sushumna* are three channels in the spine that determine the natural tendency of people, depending on where the *prana* (life force) flows. Your inhalation is the oblation, or offering to the divine fire (soul). In each of the seven centers in your spine, in different forms, there is a subtle fire, and oxygen is giving oblation to that fire. When you offer oblation to the soul in each center from the coccygeal to the fontanel, your consciousness can enter the sixth center and even the seventh center, the super-vacuum center.

This verse has the word *devan,* which means *div dhatu*, the sky, or ether. If you withdraw your mind from your neck center up to the fontanel, you will perceive five etheric levels: *chidakasha, daharakasha, parakasha, atmakasha,* and *mahakasha.* As you take your mind from the lower to the higher level of consciousness, you will automatically perceive different kinds of spirituality. Your silliness will disappear, and you will have more calm, which is godliness. When you perceive the love of God, which is all-pervading, the soul, the living power of God, will love and bless you. Then you will perceive that God is in the human being and the human being is in God. Waste time with none but God (the breath), and time will not be wasted.

Verse 12

iṣṭān bhogān hi vo devā
dāsyante yajñabhāvitāḥ
tair dattān apradāyai 'bhyo
yo bhunkte stena eva saḥ

Translation

The soul, being satisfied with your sacrifice, will satisfy you according to your requirements. But one who enjoys everything without offering it to God is like a thief.

Metaphorical Interpretation

Every *karma* (action) performed in soul consciousness is a sacrifice (*yajña*). There is no selfishness or attachment. It brings more joy and love. Not only that, but with inner peace and joy, one achieves more in the mundane world. People who undertake any action only for self-achievement and sense pleasure, without inwardly offering it to the Lord, is a thief who will find only constant fear and unhappiness.

The Lord is telling Arjuna, "I am inhaling through you; I am the life force in every human being. I am in matter, memory, and pleasure. I have given you the twenty-four gross elements, all the objects for the pleasure of your senses. You enjoy everything but you have totally forgotten Me. You feel no gratitude toward Me. You do not perceive Me as the sole doer. You do not think about all this, so you are like a thief. I have given you the qualities of a warrior, but you do not want to fight the war."

In this verse the Lord is also referring to the fight against the biological force. He is saying, "Control your breath and sit by My side in your body chariot. Then you will be grateful to Me, and you will not be treated like a thief. You will recognize that you are an instrument, and that I am the power behind every body instrument. Meditate and realize the truth; then you will be blessed."

Verse 13

yajñaśiṣṭāśinaḥ santo
mucyante sarvakilbiṣaiḥ
bhuñjate te tv agham pāpā
ye pacanty ātmakāraṇāt

Translation

Those who are Self-realized offer everything to God; afterwards, they enjoy what remains. They are free from sin and liberated. On the other hand, those who are not pious, who prepare food for themselves but do not offer it to God, are engrossed in sin.

Metaphorical Interpretation

Every work performed in God consciousness is a real offering, a sacrifice (*yajña*). The result of such work is joy and happiness. Every breath inhaled and exhaled in God consciousness is a sacrifice (*pranayajña*); the result of this breathing practice is inner calm, tranquility.

The Lord is teaching Arjuna about *prana* during inhalation and exhalation. In *pranayama,* or *prana karma*, without locking your nose, you must inhale, hold, and exhale according to the directions of the master. Then you will have rest and balanced *prana*, balanced life force. Every inhalation is food for the soul and should be offered consciously to it. *Pranayajña* is when your life force transforms into divine life force, and you merge in God. Then the devotee feels only liberation; that is, he has offered everything to God and is enjoying only what remains: peace, bliss, and joy. A devotee who attains this stage experiences constant liberation.

Locking the nose means pressing the nostrils closed with the thumb on one side, and the middle and ring fingers on the other side of the nose. Only the right hand is used. This is the traditional, ordinary method of locking the nose. This also means to seal off the nose, so that no air can enter in or come out.

Verse 14–16

annād bhavanti bhutāni
parjanyād annasambhavaḥ
yajñād bhavati parjanyo
yajñaḥ karmasamudbhavaḥ

karma brahmodbhavam viddhi
brahmā 'kṣarasamudbhavam
tasmāt sarvagatam brahma
nityam yajñe pratiṣṭhitam

evam pravartitam cakram
nā 'nuvartayatī 'ha yaḥ
aghāyur indriyārāmo
mogham pārtha sa jīvati

Translation

All beings have evolved from food, which grows by the power of rain. Rain is formed from vapor, as a result of the oblation that has been offered. Oblation is the path of *karma* (action). Offering human inhalation is oblation to the soul fire. Likewise, it nourishes the human life force.

Work is originated by the indwelling Self in every being. The indwelling soul is derived from the indestructible Brahman. Therefore, the all-pervading infinite God is present in every action (which is *yajña*).

O Partha (Arjuna), those who live full of sensual and sinful passion, who do not follow this cycle of creation in the world, live in vain.

Metaphorical Interpretation

Desire and ambition are the sins. Free from the clutch of desire, one can unite with God. Ordinary people try to fulfill their desires in many ways, but this is the eating of sinful food.

After creating the universe, the Creator entered into His creation. Every human body is a miniature universe; the five gross elements are present throughout. The lowest center in the spine manifests the gross element of earth, but all five gross elements are there. Earth, water, fire, air, and ether are all present. The seed of God (the soul) is also there. When we cultivate the earth, sow seeds, and water them, food grains are produced—grown by the soul (human beings). We eat food and drink water, from which we get energy. This energy is transformed into life and divine light. Without fire (sunlight), we cannot expect any crops; even vapor requires sunlight to form. The sun is the fire, the light, and the soul. Without Him, no one can survive. Without vapor, which is formed by sunlight or by even a little fire ceremony (*yajña*), there will be no clouds, no rain, no life in plants and human beings. We all are working and growing crops with the help of the soul, and that multiplicity of soul comes from the unity of soul, which is infinite. This constant transformation of God into different forms, on many levels at once, is the living power in everything. Whoever does not realize that everything is done by the power of God is merely a rational being whose life is in vain.

The essence of these three verses is that inside our spinal canal there are six centers: coccygeal, sacral, lumbar, dorsal, and cervical centers, and the medulla. Above these, there is another center, the fontanel. During meditation, devotees rotate their awareness from the lower to the upper centers, and then from the upper to the lower centers, as they inhale and exhale, according to the instructions of the guru preceptor.

The lowest center, the coccygeal, is the earth center, which is the prosperity center because the earth contains diamonds, gold, iron, petroleum, coal, manganese, potassium, sodium, magnesium, and so on. Rice, wheat, other grains, and vegetables are also grown in the earth. From all these, people have prosperity. The second center, sacral, is the water center, where attachment, affection, bondage, germination, and sexual desire reside. We are all conceived through the sacral center because we are human beings, but we are also divine.

The third center is the lumbar center, which is the fire center, the food center. This fire is called *vaishwanara*. The fire in the soul center is called *brahma agni* and is the multiplicity of the divine being. The soul pulls inhalation from that center, and the food eaten by the human being is digested by God with that air. From that food grows energy, strength, life, and all kinds of positive and negative dispositions.

In the scriptures it is says, *mana eva manuṣyāṇām, kārana vandha mokṣayoḥ*: "The mind, thoughts, and ego in every human being cause bondage and liberation. If we keep our mind in the lower three centers, we will experience delusion, illusion, and error. These are the main causes of bondage and the animal nature. These centers constantly pull us towards the animal qualities, making us restless and separate from the truth. Until devotees climb above the lower three centers, they will not be able to perceive truth, and they will remain in bondage.

We must bring our awareness into the next three centers, the dorsal, the cervical, and the medulla by the practice of Kriya Yoga. This will give us emancipation.

In the food (navel) center, various "airs" are generated that lead human beings toward bondage, including fear, anger, pride, hypocrisy, impurity, lack of self-control, ego, the extroverted state, love, and various dispositions towards objects of the senses. According to yogic science, fifty moods can be experienced by every human being. Each of these moods depends on a specific breathing pattern; therefore, there are fifty breathing patterns (fifty types of air) in every human being. The moods are states of mind. Each air depends predominately on the kind of food and drink consumed, even on intoxicants (drugs). The navel center determines the breathing pattern and the state of mind.

The devotee must also be very careful of the dispositions created in the heart (dorsal) center. These can lead people towards pomp and grandeur, which also hinder Self-realization. The dorsal center is our air center. In our every disposition—in passion, anger, avarice, and even in sleep—the patterns of inhalation and exhalation vary. When we sleep, our inhalation is less, and we experience extreme calm. In the same way, when our breath is well controlled by the practice of a meditation technique such as Kriya Yoga, we move towards godhood.

If we can remain in the pituitary (medulla) and ultimately in the fontanel by the practice of Kriya Yoga, we can attain the formless stage where we continuously hear divine sound, perceive divine vibration, and see divine light. A devotee, with the help of an expert guru (the soul), can rotate her sensory awareness from the lower centers to the higher ones, and from the higher to the lower centers in cyclical order. The more the devotee practices this, the more she will feel divinity in each center and will be free from sin and viciousness.

When you feel that all actions come from the soul and that the results of these go to the soul, you will not be entangled in delusion and will be merged in God-realization.

Verse 17

yas tv ātmaratir eva syād
ātmatṛptaś ca mānavaḥ
ātmany eva ca samtuṣṭas
tasya kāryam na vidyate

Translation

Self-realized people, who are delighted in the Self, gratified by the Self, and contented in the Self, are free from all bondage; for them, no work needs to be done.

Metaphorical Interpretation

The Lord is telling Arjuna, "Without spiritual work you cannot perceive the living presence of God within you. Wherever the living presence of God is experienced, there is spiritual work. Human beings think that according to their own flow of thoughts, action automatically ensues. This is not true. Thought and action depend on the soul. Thought originates in the soul and work is done by the power of the soul. You may think that you will fight a battle, but without the soul, you cannot. Understand that the soul is the cause of all works done through you and through every human being."

There are two currents in every human being. One is introverted and the other is extroverted. When you think that you will fight on the battlefield, that is the extroverted current. The extroverted current flows downward, which bewilders you.

Let's consider the introverted current. The yoga of action means that each of us must work. When the flow of your life and your work goes towards the pituitary, that is the introverted current. In this state you will feel that you are not doing the fighting; rather, you will feel that the soul is conducting the fight with the biological object.

Once you have practiced yoga according to the teachings of the Bhagavad Gita and have come up into the pituitary, you will realize that you are not doing the work; rather, it is your soul, Krishna, working. When you have realized this, you will feel only divine bliss and joy. Though you live and work in the world, you will not experience bondage. You will have divine freedom. You can experience freedom even while living in the world.

Verse 18

nai 'va tasya kṛtenā 'rtho
nā 'kṛtene 'ha kaścana
na cā 'sya sarvabhūteṣu
kaścid arthavyapāśrayaḥ

Translation

The Self-realized person is not interested whatsoever in either performing action or not performing action; this person does not depend on anyone for any self-interest.

Metaphorical Interpretation

The Self-realized person is called the incarnation of God. He is detached from action and inaction. He does not require any ritual.

He works only to uplift human beings, praying for diseased or frustrated people and protecting them from difficulties and danger. When ambition disappears, then action leads to a state of non-action.

"O Arjuna! I have explained the technique of Kriya Yoga (the yoga of action). Those who practice it daily, regularly, and sincerely, with love and devotion, will have success in their meditation and will become Self-realized." Although these devotees live in the universe, they will continuously feel God functioning through them. These superhuman beings infuse their power into the general populace. While working for the good of humanity, they feel that God is doing everything. Constantly absorbed in God during every action, they feel no want; God fulfills their every need.

Verse 19

tasmād asaktaḥ satatam
kāryam karma samācara
asakto hy ācaran karma
apram āpnoti pūruṣaḥ

Translation

Being detached, constantly perform your duties efficiently. The person who does so attains the supreme state.

Metaphorical Interpretation

Life is activity. Activity can lead one to bondage or liberation. Perfection in action is the real freedom.

Once again, the Lord states that attachment is the source of all evil. Detachment is the source of emancipation. When you feel that you are working, it is bondage; when you feel the soul (Krishna) working through you, it leads to liberation.

The Lord also stresses a teaching similar to one found in the Katha Upanishad (2:1:10), which states, *mṛtyos sa mṛtyum āpnoti ya iha nāneva paśyati:* "If you do not feel the soul working during every thought and action, you will constantly be bound to sense objects, which is death."

Meditate very deeply, live in the world, and constantly feel the soul working through you. You will find liberation. All multiplicity is delusion, but the unity of experiencing the soul in everything is liberation.

Verse 20

karmaṇai 'va hi samsiddhim
āsthitā janakādayaḥ
lokasamgraham evā 'pi
sampaśyan kartum arhasi

Translation

It was by action alone that Janaka and others attained perfection. You should undertake all selfless action with the intention to do good as well.

Metaphorical Interpretation

Perform all action without a sense of doership and enjoy liberation as did great personalities such as Janaka, the king and seer who was the best example of combining meditation and right action well. To achieve this state, one must be conscious of the seven *lokas* associated with the seven centers. From lowest to highest, they are: (1) *bhu-loka*, (2) *bhuva-loka*, (3) *sva-loka*, (4) *maha-loka*, (5) *jana-loka*, (6) *tapa-loka*, and (7) *satya-loka*. These seven *lokas* are the seven steps of meditation.

A *loka* is a place or central space where the activity of any of the seven chakras takes place. The *bhu-loka* is where the first chakra (literally "wheel") of money and earthly treasure is offered as oblation to the soul. *Bhuva-loka* is where the sexual pleasure of the second chakra and the resulting newborn child are offered as oblation to the soul. In *sva-loka*, food and the third chakra's fire of human biological life force are offered to the soul as oblation. *Maha-loka* is the space at the heart—the fourth chakra—where one's feelings, such as the love for one's wife, husband, or children, are offered to the soul as oblation. *Jana-loka*, in the throat, is the fifth chakra center where mantras, spiritual thoughts, and religious feelings are offered to the soul as oblation.

Tapa-loka is the sixth chakra, in the midbrain, where every breath of oxygen is offered to the fire of consciousness, to the light and life of the soul. *Satya-loka*, at the fontanel, is the crown chakra where the soul, in its pulseless state, merges with the wisdom of God. This is the place where the river Ganga enters the ocean and forgets its name. This place is beyond sound, beyond light, beyond vibration; it is a multi-dimensional realm beyond human consciousness.

Devotees practicing higher Kriya must calmly watch the divine vibration, sound, and light from the bottom to the top center. In each center, they must practice Kriya very deeply. By practicing the yoga of action—by carefully watching the power of God in each center—all evil, viciousness, and restlessness is transformed into purity and perfection. In ancient times, the realized *rishis* (those of right vision) and the *munis* (those of meditation) practiced Kriya and meditated deeply. Through this work, pitfalls and shortcomings disappear. To reach this stage, you must work hard for spirituality, as described in this chapter. Through your work, you will achieve purity of mind and success in life. You will be calmly active and actively calm.

Verse 21

yad-yad ācarati śreṣṭhas
tad-tad eve 'taro janaḥ
sa yat pramāṇam kurute
lokas tad anuvartate

Translation

Generally, people follow the great ones, imitating their exemplary standard of action.

Metaphorical Interpretation

Example is better than precept. In general, people try to lead their lives like great people such as Janaka and others.

Most people's natural instinct is to keep their minds absorbed in sense objects, which leads to illusion and error, and they do not have peace of mind. On the other hand, those who are Self-realized always control their breathing from the lower to the upper centers. This breath control is self-control. These devotees proceed towards the soul and calmness, which is godliness. They also have balance of mind, amity, affection, and other good and positive qualities, which lead to peace, joy, and bliss. Every human being should seek the path of peace, their birthright.

Verse 22

na me pārthā 'sti kartavyam
triṣu lokeṣu kimcana
nā 'navāptam avāptavyam
varta eva ca karmaṇi

Translation

O Partha (Arjuna), I have no need to perform routine work in the three worlds (the universe); I have no desire for anything. In spite of that, I engage in action.

Metaphorical Interpretation

People with higher spiritual consciousness, realizing the presence of God in everything, are free from ambition. Still, they engage in action to teach others.

The Lord is telling Arjuna, "O Arjuna, your soul is compassionately detached from your body, which is three bodies—the gross, astral, and causal. I pervade all three. I constantly inhale for every human being, for their physical, mental, intellectual, and spiritual growth. I calmly exist in every body in a formless state. I give all people the chance to discover their divine Self, by giving them pleasure and pain, prosperity and adversity, gain and loss. I am constantly doing work. Why shouldn't you work? Follow My path and see Me."

Verse 23

yadi hy aham na varteyam
jātu karmaṇy atandritaḥ
mama vartmā 'nuvartante
manuṣyāḥ pārtha sarvaśaḥ

Translation

O Partha (Arjuna)! If I was lazy and did not work, everyone would follow Me.

Metaphorical Interpretation

The Lord is saying, "Arjuna, you are a *kshatriya* and the son of a warrior, but you lament; you throw down your bow and arrow like a lazy person. Consider My behavior: I have no routine work and no ambition for anything, but I am at your side on the battlefield. I don't have to do anything; still, I am working for you, for your progress and evolution. I am not required to do this, but if I don't work and teach you, you cannot learn the truth that I am doing work through you. I am constantly working to lead every human being from darkness to light."

"You are a food minister. If you descend from the food center to the two lower centers, you will feel affection for your biological force. Because of this, I am sitting by your side to instruct you, to lead you upward from the navel center to the fontanel.

Every spiritual person must be a hard worker to overcome his or her negatives, to become absorbed in the divine.

Verse 24

utsīdeyur ime lokā
na kuryām karma ced aham
samkarasya ca kartā syām
upahanyām imāḥ prajāḥ

Translation

If I do not work, this world will perish; people will remain in the biological force and will deviate from religion and spirituality. If that were the case, I would be the main cause of the adulteration of spirituality. The ensuing confusion would hamper evolution.

Metaphorical Interpretation

The Lord is telling Arjuna that He is constantly trying to help everyone evolve, helping all human beings rise from the irrational stage to rationality, and then to the divine.

If the soul does not lift your attention up from the lower centers to the fourth center, that is, to the heart center where all your evil, emotion, animal tendencies, delusion, anger, avarice, pride, and self-arrogance reside, you won't evolve to the rational stage. The lower part of the heart center is full of evil; divinity begins in the upper part of the heart center up to the cervical center. The more you advance toward the pituitary, the more you will unite with the divine.

If Krishna was not Arjuna's master and spiritual guide, Arjuna could not proceed with his spiritual evolution. Evolution theory submits that our disposition is based on heredity, environment, and culture. All human beings are born as a result of sex pleasure, but we are living souls, which is our heredity. Heredity is spirit. We arrive on the earth of twenty-four gross elements, having totally forgotten that we are living souls.

The teacher, the spiritual preceptor, is part of the environment. If the environment does not caution you and teach you, you cannot evolve and realize that you are a powerful living soul. If you forget this and live submerged in the animal qualities, it is called *varnashankara,* the mixing of opposites. Descending to falsehood is degeneration. It is the soul's, the preceptor's duty to lead you towards truth; this attunement with the divine guidance comes with regular meditation.

Meditation awakens the divine power and raises it from the lower centers to the upper centers. When you can perceive that the spirit, represented by Krishna, conducts both your heredity (soul) and your worldly activities, you are His instrument. By following your spiritual guide, you will constantly be in the spirit (Krishna). Then your divine evolution will proceed, and you will never sink back into the *varnashankara* stage. Rather, you will feel that you derive from joy (Krishna), and in joy you are working and evolving.

While in your body chariot, remain in divine joy in the pituitary.

Verse 25

saktāḥ karmaṇy avidvāṁso
yathā kurvanti bhārata
kuryād vidvāṁs tathā 'saktaś
cikīrṣur lokasaṁgraham

Translation

O Bharata (Arjuna)! A person of delusion acts with attachment to action, but the wise person acts with detachment for the evolution (welfare) of the world.

Metaphorical Interpretation

Work should be done with love, not with attachment. Right action leads to detachment. Attachment is the cause of all troubles. Attachment is bondage. If you want freedom, remain compassionately detached.

Deluded people are busy with objects and matter. Their life's purpose is to eat, drink, and be merry. They do not feel the soul working through the body; they think the gross body is working by itself. People of illumination attain Self-realization and know that no one can eat, drink, or be merry without the soul. Realized people know that all thoughts come from God. They try to teach others how to go from delusion to illumination.

Verse 26

na buddhibhedam janayed
ajñānām karmasanginām
joṣayet sarvakarmāṇi
vidvān yuktaḥ samācaran

Translation

A wise man will not disrupt the minds of ignorant people who are attached to material objects. Understanding them fully, the wise will instead perform work of devotion and engage them in that work.

Metaphorical Interpretation

Through their lives and actions, exemplary personalities always show people the way to perfection. They set an example for others, making them free from all chaos and confusion.

The Lord is telling Arjuna: "See My example? I am being tactful. You were deeply depressed when you saw the warriors of both parties on the battlefield. At that time, I could have forced you to fight. But I did not. Instead, I have explained that even though I need not work, I remain in every human being, working all day and all night. Now, you are convinced that you must work and fight with your biological force to see that there is no separate identity between you and Me. You feel that whatever you are doing has already done by Me. Your delusions have disappeared. Therefore, please meditate deeply and be Self-realized. Teach others how to remain detached during every action."

Verse 27

prakṛteḥ kriyamāṇāni
guṇaiḥ karmāṇi sarvaśaḥ
ahamkāravimūḍhātmā
kartā 'ham iti manyate

Translation

All good and evil works are done by the qualities of nature, but the egotistical person thinks, "I am the doer."

Metaphorical Interpretation

Work reveals a person's nature. Depending on their nature, people pursue different activities. Spiritual people are free from ego and the sense of doership. Attachment to work and the attitude of doership is the cause of all bondage.

The Lord is telling Arjuna to meditate very deeply until he reaches *samadhi.* Even then he must meditate daily. Through every action he must perceive that the soul is the doer.

A little learning is a dangerous thing. Many devotees are very shallow in meditation. Consequently, they remain absorbed in the material world with its pomp and grandeur, and they maintain the philosophy of eating, drinking, and being merry. Absorbed on the worldly stage, they always feel pride, vanity, and self-interest. They think that they are very intelligent and are doing everything tactfully.

Verse 28

tattvavit tu mahābāho
guṇakarmavibhāgayoḥ
guṇā guṇeṣu vartanta
iti matvā na sajjate

Translation

O mighty-armed (Arjuna)! Realized people who perceive the three qualities (*gunas*) never indulge in sin and sense gratification. They have a thorough knowledge of devotional work and its result.

Metaphorical Interpretation

The Lord is telling Arjuna that he laments because he is absorbed in the triple qualities of nature.[1] Arjuna was deluded to think that he would be doing the work on the battlefield, killing many people. When he realized that he would not be fighting, that instead, the soul would be fighting through him, then he was free from bewilderment and sorrow.

Consider an example. One person has died in a family. The other family members are heartbroken, crying, and bewildered. Someone passing by their house can hear the heartrending sorrow of the family, but does not cry. In the same way, your soul is detached from the body nature and *maya* (delusion).

Your actions do not taint the soul. By detachment, the soul is separate from work and the triple qualities of delusion, and therefore free from sorrow. A person who practices Kriya deeply can remove the power that causes delusion, illusion, and error from the *ida*, *pingala*, and other *prana* channels, thereby becoming free from the obstructions of the triple qualities. Meditating deeply, their power will rise up and stay in the atom point in the fontanel. At that time, these devotees become free from the worldly sense. They are in *samprajñata samadhi*, which means they do not go into the pulseless state, but remain in the state of cosmic consciousness very near to the door of God.

Verse 29

prakṛter guṇasammūḍhāḥ
sajjante guṇakarmasu
tān akṛtsnavido mandān
kṛtsnavin na vicālayet

Translation

Some remain completely attached to action and deluded by the triple qualities, the three *gunas*, according to their intelligence. The person of perfect knowledge should not disturb the minds of the ignorant who know only a little.

Metaphorical Interpretation

In this universe many people are absorbed in the triple qualities of nature. *Tamasa guna* is sloth, idleness, and procrastination. It is in the *ida* channel inside the spine. *Rajasa guna* is extreme activity, desire for prosperity, sense pleasures, eating, drinking, and merry-making. It also manifests as extreme forms of religion full of dogmatic views, fanatic ideas, and religious rituals. *Rajasa guna* is in the *pingala* channel inside the spine. The third quality is *sattva guna*, which is both religion and spirituality. Religion is religious ritual, and spirituality is characteristic of a true seeker of God—one who achieves calm in the formless stage. *Sattva guna* remains in the *sushumna* channel inside the spinal canal.

There are four kinds of spirituality. *Uttama brahma satbhaba* is the state of those who withdraw their divine power through the spinal canal from the lower centers to the upper center and remain free from intellect, body, mind, ego, and worldly sense, merging with God and attaining the formless. They perceive that the soul is the conductor, even in everyday life. They are the most advanced spiritual people.

Dhyana bhavastu madhyama is the second level of spirituality. It is achieved by those who withdraw their senses above the cervical region and perceive some truth and peace and can experience the triple divine sensations—vibration, light, and sound. Unfortunately, they come down again, below the heart center, and experience restlessness. They can then return to the pituitary.

The third level of meditation or spirituality is *stutir japa adhama bhava*. People at this level pray, read books, chant hymns and mantras, and move *mala* beads, but they remain engrossed in the body and its worldly senses. They are religious but not spiritual. They do not experience the triple divine qualities like those at the second level.

Now the fourth grade of meditation or spirituality *is bajhya puja adhama dhama*. People in this stage are restless, always extroverted, and body-conscious. They worship idols with flowers, fruits, and sandal paste and chant mantras, imagine crosses, and worship stones. They are engrossed in emotions, suggestions, speculation, dogmatic views, and fanatical ideas, and they are very happy with this.

"O Arjuna! I will say some more about those people who are rational animals, such as Dhritarashtra, Duryodhana, and the rest of the Kaurava party. Wise and spiritual people will not speak to them or attempt to guide them because they have no spiritual qualities. I told them to be divine and to compromise with the Pandavas, but I failed to convince them. When there is no belief in God and guru, there is no spirituality. They will remain absorbed only in pleasures of the senses, wealth, and property. But I know you have implicit faith, loyalty, and love for Me. This is why I have told you in detail about the three qualities."

Verse 30

mayi sarvāṇi karmāṇi
samnyasyā 'dhyātmacetasā
nirāśir nirmamo bhūtvā
yudhyasva vigatajvaraḥ

Translation

Fix your mind on Me. Dedicate all your actions, desire, ego, and mental effort to Me; completely surrender yourself; being free from expectation and egoism, fight.

Metaphorical Interpretation

The Lord is explaining the hidden mystery of the yoga of action. The aim and object of the yoga of action is to combine knowledge, action, and the completion of work with love, bliss, and peace. The sign of selfless work is dedication—knowing that you are not the doer (God is the doer), and that nothing belongs to you. When devotees are willing to meditate, they must completely surrender to God, surrender all the fruits of action to God, perform selfless work, and eschew lamentation. These four qualities make life more peaceful, free from stress and strain. Expectation brings anxiety that spoils the joy in life.

Inhaling and exhaling are work that comes from God. Without God, no one can do either. By breath mastery, devotees can develop self-mastery. When we sleep, we have breath mastery. At that time, we can control all our propensities; we have only peace. In the same way, with the control obtained from breath mastery, we can draw all our propensities in the lower centers up the *sushumna* channel to the soul, removing all ambition and automatically producing the divine calm that is godliness.

Follow the Kriya Yoga technique and you will feel that God alone conducts everything. You will not lament and will fight only mechanically.

Verse 31

ye me matam idam nityam
anutiṣṭhanti mānavāḥ
śraddhāvanto 'nasūyanto
mucyante te 'pi karmabhiḥ

Translation

Any person who performs his duties according to My instructions with faith, without any malice or self-interest, will be free from all bondage and will find liberation.

Metaphorical Interpretation

Devotees who maintain firm faith in and deepest love for the guru and his teachings, who do not find fault with others, who practice Kriya Yoga with intense desire, daily and sincerely, who feel that God is practicing Kriya through their body, will be free from the bondage of work. Thus, performing your duties purifies your life. It brings inner satisfaction.

Verse 32

ye tv etad abhyasūyanto
nā 'nutiṣṭhanti me matam
sarvajñānavimūḍhāṃs tān
viddhi naṣṭān acetasaḥ

Translation

Those who find fault in others, who do not perform works according to My instructions, who are devoid of conscience (discrimination), who are ignorant and have deviated from the truth, will be ruined.

Metaphorical Interpretation

"Arjuna! Follow Me absolutely and fight your ignorance; you will evolve and achieve liberation. If you do not follow Me and do not fight the forces of your biological nature, you will never evolve spiritually. This will be death to you. The rational animal is ignorant, filled with lament, lazy, always finding fault in everything, and unable to attain spiritual evolution. When you examine the faults of others, your life is miserable. Instead of looking at the faults of others, look into your own mistakes."

Verse 33

sadṛśam ceṣṭate svasyāḥ
prakṛter jñānavān api
prakṛtim yānti bhūtāni
nigrahaḥ kim kariṣyati

Translation

Wise men work according to their conscience, which is their highly evolved destiny (their nature), whereas in general, human beings follow their lower preordained qualities. What can self-restraint do!

Metaphorical Interpretation

Human beings are under the control of eight aspects of the body nature: ether, air, light, water, earth, mind, intellect, and ego. By the law of nature, human beings are always absorbed in body consciousness and guided by their instincts. They do not see that the indwelling Self is working through them, because the soul nature has been absorbed into the body nature. Hence, they are not willing to fight. But Arjuna is the son of a warrior, so he must fight his body nature.

Mother Nature is *paravastha*, the state of cosmic consciousness, perceiving that the soul (Krishna) is doing everything through the body. If you meditate and withdraw your sense awareness from your body nature and raise it up to Mother Nature, your body nature will automatically be conquered. This is the real fight for spirituality. The battle depends upon your effort and its intensity.

Verse 34

indriyasye 'ndriyasyā 'rthe
rāgadveṣau vyavasthitau
tayor na vaśam āgacchet
tau hy asya paripanthinau

Translation

Attachment and aversion for objects of the senses abide in the senses. To clear the path to Self-realization, these are the main obstacles to conquer.

Metaphorical Interpretation

Our senses are gifts from God and should be properly used. Those who do not control them are ultimately their victims. They bring disaster into life.

The Lord is explaining that when you associate with worldly people, you become like them and forget the truth. However, if you respond to His touch, the touch of your guru and soul, and if you follow His instructions, you will surely attain divinity. You need thorough control of the senses to rise from the lower centers to the higher ones. Then you will be free from attachment, the main hindrance to soul culture. If you feel that God is the sole doer in you, pleasure and pain will not cause you any trouble.

Verse 35

śreyān svadharmo viguṇaḥ
paradharmāt svanuṣṭhitāt
svadharme nidhanam śreyaḥ
paradharmo bhayāvahaḥ

Translation

One should follow one's own religion (duty) even if it is devoid of merit, rather than follow the religion (duty) of others. It is better to die while following your own religion (duty) than to follow that of another, which would be dreadful.

Metaphorical Interpretation

In Sanskrit, *dharma* has many meanings, such as duty, religion, property, responsibility, and more. People whose religion is very ornate with pomp and grandeur, filled with shouting, chanting, and dancing, are unwisely engrossed in religious ritual. It is wise to accept death, if necessary, in order to remain in your own religion, but the dogmatic views and fanatical ideas of other religions should not entice you.

"O Arjuna, you are a Pandava! Your religion is to fight with evil, but you are not following your religion—this means death to you."

In this verse, *sva* means soul, *svadharma* means to seek the soul, and *para* means nature. To become absorbed in nature and its sense objects, although they are beautiful, charming, and attractive, leads to delusion and error. Do not become absorbed in nature. Control your senses and come up to the medulla and the pituitary, even though you will undoubtedly have some trouble doing so in the beginning. You will find divinity, peace, and bliss. If you don't introvert the awareness attached to your five sense telephones, it will be dreadful; your whole life will pass in melancholy.

Verse 36

arjuna uvāca
atha kena prayukto 'yam
pāpam carati pūruṣaḥ
anicchann api vārṣṇeya
balād iva niyojitaḥ

Translation

Arjuna asked:
O Varshneya (Krishna)! Why do people commit sinful acts, even against their own will or as if by force?

Metaphorical Interpretation

Arjuna said to the Lord: "O all-pervading Soul! I know that I am the son of a warrior, and I should fight with the evil persons provoked by You. I also know that You are an immortal soul, forever within me. In spite of this, by the force of some power, my mind keeps going down the wrong path toward the biological nature. I cannot understand who is forcing me to do so, or why."

Metaphorically, this verse means that all human beings realize they are rational beings who should strive for Self-realization.

Nevertheless, their minds become engrossed in matter and memories, the main obstacles to soul culture. When they try to sit for meditation according to their gurus' direction, they proceed upward only a little. Their previously generated karma and their attachment to sense objects causes them to fall down to the lower three centers and deviate from the truth. Their destiny, the aggregate balance sheet of their prior births, is so great that they cannot proceed upward.

Verse 37

śrībhagavān uvāca
kāma eṣa krodha eṣa
rajoguṇasamudbhavaḥ
mahāśano mahāpāpmā
viddhy enam iha vairiṇam

Translation

The blessed Lord said:
Passionate desire and anger are the vital enemies of the God-realized person. Passion and anger originate from rajas (actions with attachment to wealth, sensual pleasure, pomp, and grandeur). Passion remains always unfulfilled, and anger is a vicious enemy; these are the vital, sinful enemies in this world.

Metaphorical Interpretation

Arjuna has asked: "How are most people's minds forcibly taken from spiritual concerns to worldly affairs? What causes it? Who is the conductor?" The Lord answers that sexual and carnal desire and anger exist in every human being (*explained in 2:62–67*). These are the principal reasons why human beings don't attain God-realization. Those engrossed in these passions are the most sinful persons. *Kama*, desire, and *krodha*, anger, which both arise out of rajasic nature, are like clouds that cover the soul sun, making people commit mistakes and fall from spirituality in the darkness.

Symbolically this verse means that if you practice Kriya according to the directions of the Bhagavad Gita, without expecting any results, you can come up to the pituitary and achieve God-realization. However, if your mind runs after worldly objects during meditation, your desires will gradually increase. Then when these desires are not fulfilled, your mind will gradually descend into the lower centers; automatically, you will feel more anger and ambition, and you will deviate from the truth. This is the biggest obstacle to a successful life. At this point, the Lord is asking Arjuna to maintain implicit faith in Him.

If you maintain implicit faith in the Lord, you will feel your life filled with spirituality. Even when you come down to worldly duties, you will never feel anger. You will realize the incarnation of love, as Babaji Maharaj and Jesus did.

Verse 38

dhūmenā 'vriyate vahnir
yathā 'darśo malena ca
yatho 'lbenā 'vṛto garbhas
tathā tene 'dam āvṛtam

Translation

As fire is obscured by smoke, as dust covers a mirror, or a child remains hidden in the womb of the mother, so the strongest desire and passion (illusion, delusion, and error) surround and obscure Self consciousness and spiritual knowledge.

Metaphorical Interpretation

Without a soul, you have no face. So, in every human body, there are two faces: One is form and the other is formless. If you don't meditate, you will feel that God is very far from you; you'll be absorbed in delusion, illusion, and error. If you live in delusion, you cannot see your real face. Delusion, illusion, error, and strong ambition for worldly objects cover the human mind with darkness, just as a mirror is covered by dust. On the other hand, when you meditate, you will rise from the lower centers to the top and realize that you and He are one, and have always been one. With this illumination, you see that your own face, which you do not possess, belongs to the soul. You no longer see your face in the mirror—you see the face of God. If you take the advice of your guru preceptor and practice yoga, it is like cleaning the surface of a mirror. Automatically, your real face becomes visible.

Until you meditate deeply, you cannot see the fire that is covered by smoke, or you cannot see the divine living baby covered by the womb of the mother. Spiritual practice removes the veiling power of delusion and brings enlightenment.

With spiritual knowledge, human ignorance, which is like a covering of dust on a mirror, is cleansed. The more you live a spiritual life, the more your power rises into your higher centers. Then you can comprehend God. Your third (spiritual) eye will be opened. Jesus said (Matthew 6:22), "If thine eye be single, thy whole body shall be full of light." In the Bhagavad Gita (13:17), it says, *jyotiṣām api taj jyotis tamasaḥ param ucyate*, which means, "The ignorance of every human being disappears when spiritual knowledge, the light of God, flashes."

There are three steps of meditation for God-realization: *karma*, work; *jñana*, spiritual knowledge; and *prema*, love for God. The more your delusion disappears and you come up nearer the soul, the more you will perceive the divine movement sensation and hear the divine sound within you. Through this, you will feel *prema*, love for God, and divine ecstasy.

Verse 39

āvṛtam jñānam etena
jñānino nityavairiṇā
kāmarūpeṇa kaunteya
duṣpūreṇā 'nalena ca

Translation

O son of Kunti (Arjuna)! Superconsciousness (knowledge) is completely burned out of the spiritual person by insatiable fire in the shape of desire, the constant enemy of the wise.

Metaphorical Interpretation

Even knowledgeable people seem to be deluded with ambition and passion. Ambition comes from the mind. Mind is the fountain of all ambition and sense pleasure. These desires remain in the body, and after satisfaction, they will saturate the mind again, through memory. The Lord warns, "O son of Kunti! As long as devotees remain below the cranium, they cannot uncover their spiritual energy." The mind is either the main hindrance to soul culture or the positive energy behind it. When devotees bring their awareness above the pituitary and the fontanel, their ambition and worldly thoughts disappear. At that moment, these devotees have the finest conception of God, perceiving that the knower and its object are one.

Krishna always emphasizes that if you do not follow His teachings, you will always be burned by your worldly desires. Desires are the main hindrance to God-realization. You must fight with these biological forces.

Verse 40

indriyāṇi mano buddhir
asyā 'dhiṣṭhānam ucyate
etair vimohayaty eṣa
jñānam āvṛtya dehinam

Translation

The mind, intellect, and the five senses are the receptacles of human perception. Knowledge is covered with these three qualities. Human beings absorbed in desire have only delusion.

Metaphorical Interpretation

In ordinary human endeavor, there is the vital play of senses, mind, and intellect. These aspects of life are positive when directed towards to the soul and divine experience. They can be negative, however, when one is deluded, always chasing the pleasures of sense objects.

The abode of ambition is in the region above the coccygeal center and below the pituitary. Worldly people remain in these centers. Although they may engage in religious ritual, their minds and thoughts are still absorbed in worldly affairs. This prevents soul culture. To succeed, meditate deeply and follow the yoga of action. Come up to the pituitary and attain Self-realization.

Verse 41

tasmāt tvam indriyāṇy ādau
niyamya bharatarṣabha
pāpmānam prajahi hy enam
jñānavijñānanāśanam

Translation

O best of Bharatas (Arjuna)! Turn your awareness within, away from the five senses, then subdue your ambition, which is full of sin. Ambition destroys knowledge, consciousness, and wisdom.

Metaphorical Interpretation

Worldly ambition, preordained qualities, and destiny are hidden in all human beings. This is why Lord Krishna is forcing Arjuna to follow the yoga of action. Arjuna and all sincere seekers must work and struggle to control the five sense telephones. Those who follow the Kriya Yoga technique described throughout the Bhagavad Gita can learn to introvert their five sense telephones and free themselves from ups and downs, pitfalls, worries, anxieties, and sins.

Then, through meditation, they will perceive that God and three-fourths of the world are formless; they will feel His presence in every manifested thing.

During deepest meditation, the superconscious stage is reached. In that stage, one has the conception and perception of God, knowing His thoughts and wishes, desiring union with Him extremely, ultimately merging in *savikalpa samadhi*, conscious *samadhi*, and even in *nirvikalpa samadhi.* A successful person constantly keeps the mind and senses under control.

Verse 42

indriyāṇi parāṇy āhur
indriyebhyaḥ param manaḥ
manasas tu parā buddhir
yo buddheḥ paratas tu saḥ

Translation

The five sense organs are more powerful than the gross body; the mind is more powerful than the sense organs; the intellect is more powerful than the mind; the soul (Self) is greater than the intellect.

Metaphorical Interpretation

You can control the senses, mind, and intellect only by leading a soul-conscious life, because the soul is the supreme. Until you introvert your five sense telephones, you cannot attain Self-realization. This is the essence of this verse.

Lord Krishna also provides some details about the human system in this verse. The human body is made of twenty-four gross elements and the soul. These gross elements always keep human beings in an extroverted state. Undoubtedly, the five sense organs are powerful, and are attracted to and absorbed in material objects (matter and memories), but without a soul, all human beings would be dead bodies. The five sense telephones would exist, but they could not act.

The Lord is pointing out that Arjuna is absorbed in the material world. Arjuna said he would not fight with the sense objects. But without the soul (Krishna), there would be no sense objects, and Arjuna would not be able to fight or refuse to fight. In the yoga of action, you must work, that is, you must fight your sense organs. The Lord is fighting through you. He is the sole doer in every organ of the human being and in the whole of creation.

The mind may be more powerful than the five sense organs, but without the soul, the body is dead. By practicing meditation, you can transform your body into soul. Intellect may be more powerful than mind, but without the soul and its breath, everything is inactive. If you do not maintain implicit faith, love, and loyalty in the soul (Krishna) and do not act according to His instructions, you cannot perceive the Creator and cannot have peace, bliss, and joy. Therefore, every human being should seek the soul, the power of God that is always within them.

Verse 43

evam buddheḥ param buddhvā
samstabhyā 'tmānam ātmanā
jahi śatrum mahābāho
kāmarūpam durāsadam

Translation

O Mighty-armed (Arjuna)! Having discovered the Self, the supreme power over the intellect, overcome your imperishable and insatiable desire with firm determination. Desire is the principal enemy, hard to conquer and an obstacle to soul culture.

Metaphorical Interpretation

Passion and ambition are the great obstacles. Fortunately, a seeker with keen interest and sincere self-effort can destroy them completely. In the previous verse, Krishna told Arjuna how the yoga of action (Kriya Yoga), implicit faith in guru and God, and constant awareness of the inner Self can lead to continuous liberation. Now, He calls Arjuna "Mahabahu," which means a great warrior. The Lord is assuring Arjuna, "If you introvert your mind, thought, intellect, and ego, you will be able to rise from the lower centers up to the pituitary; then you will perceive only My presence within you."

Elsewhere in the Bhagavad Gita the Lord says, "Slowly inhale, withdraw your senses from the lower center, magnetize your spine, and constantly fix your attention on Me, inside the pituitary. Then you will achieve complete breath control, which is self-control. In that stage, you will discover that you and I are one." This is the *hamsa* stage, when *ham* and *sa* are one. Your material gross body—the perishable body—is *ham*. The power that draws the breath up into your nose is *sa*, your soul. When you experience the *hamsa* stage, you forget your worldly existence. You feel that *sa*, your inhalation, is the life in your gross body. This is cosmic consciousness: You are absorbed in the triple divine qualities: divine vibration, sound, and light; you love God; you are free from a sense of the world and desire.

This verse again makes it clear that the battle of the Bhagavad Gita is not between people—it is between the biological and spiritual forces. Both forces are conducted and guided by the soul (Krishna).

In order to instruct all people, everywhere, to guide them to the divine, the Lord tells Arjuna that work is the principal requirement for Self-realization, as explained in this chapter about the yoga of action. This is the scientific and metaphorical interpretation of the Upanishads and yoga in the third chapter of the Bhagavad Gita.

---

[1] The triple qualities of nature are: *sattva*—spiritual, good propensities; *rajas*—passionate, active and restless propensities; and *tamas*—dull, inertia and lethargic nature. For more details, please refer to the Bhagavad Gita, Vol. 3, Chapter 14.

Summary

This chapter deals with *karma* (action) more than any other. Action is both physical and volitional. It can bring bondage or it can cause liberation. Externally renouncing action is hypocrisy and leads to spiritual downfall; rather, one must control the mind through breath control while performing all works. When your works are performed as an offering to the supreme Self, they will be liberating.

Ordinary people become restless through their activity. Restlessness is demonic, but calmness during activity is divine. Through balance of mind, you can learn to be calmly active and actively calm. Then, work is worship.

This chapter can be summarized as follows:

Verse 1–2: Arjuna, bewildered, asks, "Which is superior: *karma* or *samkhya* (knowledge)?"

Verses 3–4: A description of two attitudes—*karma* and *samkhya*—and the importance of *karma.*

Verse 5: It is impossible to avoid action. It is natural in many activities, such as breathing.

Verse 6: Avoid a false external show of renunciation.

Verses 7–8: The definition of *karma yoga*, the yoga of action.

Verses 8–16: Action is *yajña* (sacrifice) An explanation of the state of detachment and the significance of *karma yajña* (offering all action to the soul, *kri* and *ya*).

Verses 17–19: A self-content man has no *karma.*

Verses 20–24: Janaka is cited as an example to show that all the activity undertaken by such free souls is for others; Krishna cites Himself as another example.

Verses 25–26: A man of knowledge acts with detachment and encourages others to follow that path.

Verses 27–29: The differences between people of knowledge and people of ignorance.

Verses 30–32: Offering every activity to the Lord, God.

Verses 33–35: The senses have great apparent strength. Do not try to kill or destroy the senses; rather, keep them skillfully under control.

Verse 36: Arjuna asks how he can know the cause of man's mistakes and sinful activities.

Verses 37–43: The Lord explains in detail that *kama* (passion or desire) is the root cause of all evil. He also explains how to use willpower, by controlling the senses and the mind.

In His concluding remark on *karma*, Lord Krishna strongly recommends overcoming *karma* and ruthlessly destroying it.

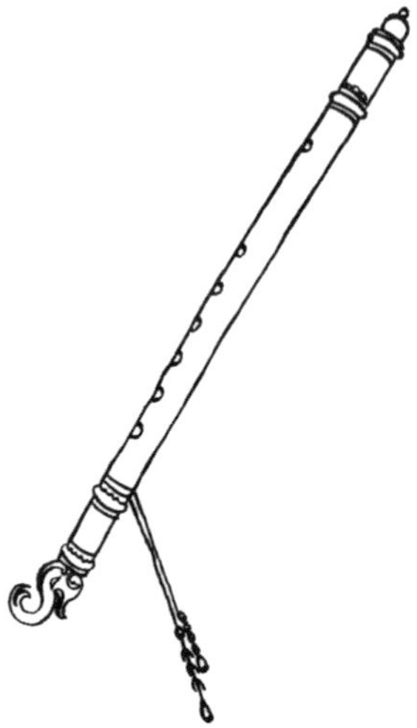

Chapter 4

Jñana Yoga

The Yoga of Knowledge

Introduction

Yoga is the path to the divine state where you are absolutely free from the tyranny of the mind. The tradition of yoga in general, and Kriya Yoga in particular, is ancient, starting with creation.

Before giving Arjuna the details of yoga philosophy and practice, the Lord must prepare Arjuna's body and mind for a life in yoga. A genuine teacher creates the proper environment for a disciple's Self-unfolding. After explaining in detail the principle of *karma*, the Lord emphasizes that disciples must practice the activities of daily life while immersed in the state of yoga, (*yogastha kuru karmani*, Verse 2:48). For this, one must have knowledge—knowledge of what is to be done and what is to be avoided. Yoga is the means of gaining self-control, discipline, knowledge, and liberation.

This chapter, "The Yoga of Knowledge," starts with the Lord's introduction to the heritage of yoga, then elaborates on different kinds of action, and ultimately describes the state of non-action.

Verse 1

śrībhagavān uvāca
imam vivasvate yogam
proktavān aham avyayam
vivasvān manave prāha
manur ikṣvākave 'bravīt

Translation

The Blessed Lord spoke:
I declared this indestructible science of yoga to Vivasvan. Vivasvan told it to Manu, and Manu taught it to Ikshwaku.

Metaphorical Interpretation

In this chapter the Lord addresses the union of knowledge and action, which produces superior results. Although the chapter is about the yoga of knowledge, it also considers the union of knowledge and action. In Chapter 2, Arjuna was unwilling to fight with his relatives (his biological nature), so in Chapter 3, the Lord described the yoga of action in detail. Now, while the Lord is explaining the yoga of knowledge, He is also stating that the union of knowledge and action and love is best. This is the union of *jñana*, *karma*, and *bhakti*, which will quickly lead human beings to the formless stage and liberation.

This first verse describes the lineage and tradition of yoga and meditation, which is passed on from generation to generation, with ups and downs in its popularity and practice. The metaphorical meaning of this verse is very intricate. Until a person meditates deeply, its real meaning cannot be understood. It is full of allegorical teachings.

The epic story of the Mahabharata declares that Vivasvan introduced this secret yoga to Manu; then Manu taught it to Ikshwaku. But Vivasvan actually refers to the solar dynasty. The Lord first taught Kriya Yoga to the first king of the solar dynasty, whose name was Vivasvan. Shri Ramachandra, a divine incarnation, was born into that solar dynasty, but the king, Vivasvan, was the fifty-eighth generation before the birth of King Shri Ramachandra, the son of King Dasaratha of Ayodhya, India. The son of Vivasvan was Manu, who was also a king. The Lord taught the Kriya Yoga technique to him.

After forty generations, Ikshwaku was born; the Lord then taught the same Kriya Yoga to him. About two centuries after Ikshwaku, Yudhisthira was born; his dynasty is called the lunar dynasty. The Lord taught him Kriya Yoga. This is the history recounted in the verse.

The metaphorical meaning of this verse is that there are four *nadis* (cords or channels) in the spinal canal of every human being. The first is the *pingala nadi*, the sun cord (also called *vivasvan).* It is on the right side of the spine and directs human beings toward the biological forces. On the opposite side is the *ida nadi*, called *manu*, which refers to the mind. It is the lunar dynasty, which causes worldly attachment and delusion.

A third small cord (*nadi*) near the neck center is called *vajra nadi* or *ikshwaku nadi*. The fourth cord is the *chitra nadi*, near the heart and solar plexus center. The *chitra nadi* causes extreme worldly attachment, desire for power and passion, and keeps us in a state of delusion. These four channels are the main obstructions of the *sushumna nadi,* which is the spiritual passage in the spinal canal. The Lord teaches us how to use yoga to purify these four cords, freeing space in the *sushumna nadi* in the spine, so we can become divine. When the *sushumna* is open, human beings can easily ascend to the upper center in the soul.

Ikshwaku was a king in the solar dynasty. Solar means the sun, but the soul is truly the sun. If you have no soul, you cannot see the sun. The sun gives light. Light is knowledge; ignorance is darkness. So *ikshu* refers to the spiritual eye that focuses alert attention in the soul. Through this, continuous emancipation is possible.

The symbolic meaning of this verse becomes clear. Having taught Arjuna the yoga of action, the Lord now tells him how to withdraw his divine power by using the yoga of knowledge, that is, by soft and feeble Kriya inhalation. This will free the *ida, pingala, vajra,* and *chitra nadis* so the devotee can easily ascend to the pituitary. Those who do so will be illuminated by divine light like the sun, *vivasvan*. These practitioners will feel soothed as their minds experience divine joy, which is *manu*. One who has thorough control of the five sense organs is also called *manu*.

By practicing Kriya Yoga you will hear the divine sound, *ikshu*, which is consciousness of the soul. You are not to chant. Remain calm and God will chant the divine sound, which you will hear.

In ancient times, in the *satya yuga* (*yuga* means era), there were no temples, churches, mosques, or synagogues. There was no worship of idols or images of deities. There were no mantras, no spiritual songs, and no hymns. Only *ashtanga yoga* and *chaturanga yoga* were taught, the latter being Kriya Yoga. Through practice of these yogas, all people were divine and powerful.

The more a devotee practices Kriya, the yoga of action, the more a devotee will rise toward the superconscious stage, the yoga of knowledge. He will then automatically have love for God, *bhakti*. This yoga of knowledge is the union of *karma*, *jñana*, and *bhakti*.

The wisdom eye is *ikshu;* it is the kingly eye that inspires constant love for the divine. The lower stage of thought is called mind. When the mind ascends into calmness, it becomes King Manu. At last the devotee feels that his soul is a real sun, *vivasvan*. Without a soul, human beings have nothing. The pure mind is the real king, *manu*, which fills us with attachment to the material world. Our third eye is the real eye, which leads us to truth.

When practicing Kriya Yoga, your attention is always dwelling simultaneously on the body material world and on the soul. You will sense the power of God in all matter. One eye will remain on the soul, and the other on money, sex, food, and the heart center, but you must always remain compassionately detached. Every spinal center functions from the soul. Without the soul, or inhalation, you have nothing—no money, no wife, no husband, no house—nothing. So practice perceiving the soul during every moment.

By practicing Kriya Yoga you can judge what is right and what is wrong. You can easily avoid wrong when your power of judgment remains in the *ikshu* eye, or third eye, which means the soul. Remember, one ounce of practice is far better than tons of theory.

Verse 2

evam paramparāprāptam
imam rājarṣayo viduḥ
sa kālene 'ha mahatā
yogo naṣṭaḥ paramtapa

Translation

All those kings who were highly realized generation after generation were aware of this yoga, O Paramtapa (slayer of enemies, Arjuna)! Over a long period of time this secret yoga technique has declined in the world.

Metaphorical Interpretation

The Lord calls Arjuna "Paramtapa." *Paramtapa* is composed of *param shatrun tapati. Param* means supreme, *shatrun* means enemy, and *tapati* means one who can burn. The real meaning of *paramtapa* is one who can easily burn that great enemy, the delusion and error hidden within us. Arjuna comes from a warrior family, so Paramtapa Arjuna can easily and quickly burn or kill the supreme enemies: delusion and error. Unfortunately, Paramtapa Arjuna was engrossed in the material world. He was not willing to fight or suppress his evil propensities. This is why the Lord gradually led him to the yoga of action. Now, in this chapter, He teaches Arjuna the synthesis of *karma, jñana,* and *bhakti* yogas as one yoga. Thus, the Lord explains the yoga of knowledge.

In this verse the word *rajarshi* appears, which comes from *raja* and *rishi. Raja* means king, and *rishi* means a person of right vision. Right vision comes from the spiritual force, which remains in the cranium. Hence, the Lord is telling Paramtapa that Kriya Yoga practice (*karma yoga*) will carry him up near the soul. Then you will be a *rajarshi*, a person of right vision. Until you practice yoga, you cannot be a *paramtapa,* a great warrior, and you cannot prevent your body nature from deviating from the right path.

The Lord, when he teaches Paramtapa Arjuna, is indirectly telling all human beings that everyone is *paramtapa*. Anyone who constantly practices the yoga of action, meaning *karma*, *jñana*, and *bhakti* yoga, will surely achieve Self-realization.

The divine power of a human being is in the soul, in the superconscious state. Every human being who so desires can easily withdraw the consciousness from the lower centers and raise it to the higher center. As a result, cosmic consciousness is attained, and the true nature of the soul is perceived.

The Lord is also telling people in general, who usually remain in the lower centers where the yoga of action is suppressed, where the truth is forgotten, that if they follow Him, they will surely be able to keep pinpointed attention on the soul. Then they will be *rajarshis*, people of right vision.

This verse describes the tradition of teaching meditation and spiritual life from generation to generation. Over time, both prosperity and adversity will come to pass.

Verse 3

sa evā 'yam mayā te 'dya
yogaḥ proktaḥ purātanaḥ
bhakto 'si me sakhā ce 'ti
rahasyam hy etad uttamam

Translation

O Arjuna, you are my intimate friend, and you are my devotee, so today I have told you the very old secret and best transcendental mystery of *brahma vidya*, the science of the yoga of knowledge, which is truly profound.

Metaphorical Interpretation

The name "Arjuna" means one who is not tied to anything by the biological forces. Although at this point Arjuna is engrossed in worldly affairs and biological forces, he is nonetheless the best of disciples and Krishna's intimate friend, so Arjuna will surely follow the soul (Krishna).

Until you develop deep faith, love, and loyalty, you cannot perceive the real truth. First you should understand that the soul and the body are one. Without the soul, you have no separate existence. With this knowledge, you can literally feel the power of God, which exists forever within every human being. Seek Him through the yoga of action (*karma*) and the yoga of knowledge (*jñana*); then you will develop a real love for God and feel the all-pervading power forever within you.

In this verse, the Lord teaches that a true devotee or disciple is like a friend who always remains very close to the preceptor. In this case, the preceptor will teach the devotee all the hidden spiritual wisdom without any reservations.

Verse 4

arjuna uvāca
aparam bhavato janma
param janma vivasvataḥ
katham etad vijānīyām
tvam ādau proktavān iti

Translation

Arjuna asked:
Vivasvan (the sun) was born long before your birth, whereas you have been born not so long ago, so how is it possible that you initiated Vivasvan into this yoga? I cannot understand it.

Metaphorical Interpretation

Arjuna questions Lord Krishna, who is supposed to be his contemporary, about his age: How could he have taught others who lived far before his present time?

Each human body is a microcosm. The "sun" refers to the *pingala nadi*, which is inside our spine on the right side. The *ida nadi* is the moon, or mind, inside our spine on the left. *Ikshu nadi*, the spiritual eye, is inside the upper part of our spinal canal. All these are created by the soul. Without the soul, the sun cord, moon cord, and *ikshu* cord could not be activating the body.

The Lord is the ancient soul in every human body. Without the soul there is nothing. You believe that you are a separate body, but that is wrong. Krishna is saying, "O Arjuna, you have the wrong impression of Me. I am the ancient agent of God. I am the living soul in every human being."

That soul is also called the sun. If the sun does not illuminate the world, everything is dark. Similarly, if the soul sun does not remain in the body, it is dead. This is proclaimed in the Isha Upanishad (17) as well.

Verse 5

śrībhagavān uvāca
bahūni me vyatītāni
janmāni tava cā 'rjuna
tāny aham veda sarvāṇi
na tvam vettha paramtapa

Translation

The Blessed Lord said:
Many births have passed for me, O Arjuna! I know them all, whereas you do not, O destroyer of enemies.

Metaphorical Interpretation

Our soul, the Lord, is an imperishable body. The body engrossed in delusion is our perishable body. The Lord knows all; our gross body and astral body are the sources of our delusion.

The gross body and the astral body are made of twenty-four material constituents: the five gross elements, the five sense organs, the five organs of action, the five sense vital breaths (*prana*), plus the mind, intellect, ego, and memory. The organs of action are the mouth, hands, legs, genital organs, and rectum. The sense organs experience sound, touch, sight, smell, and taste.

These twenty-four material constituents maintain human delusion, so our gross body is not aware of the all-pervading body within it. The Lord said to Arjuna: "You do not know your past history, but I am all-knowing, so I remember My past, present, and future, as well as the destiny of all things."

The soul is beyond delusion, illusion, and error, so the soul (the Lord) knows the beginning, middle, and end of life. Krishna is the agent of God, who was born with the creation, so everything is known to Him. On the other hand, the gross body, with its ego, is engrossed in the triple qualities of delusion, so it knows nothing about Him. Ordinary human beings, with their little egos, forget the happenings of the present life, so how can they remember those long past? God concludes, "O Arjuna, the difference between you and Me is the difference between worldly people and the soul-conscious spiritual being."

Verse 6

ajo 'pi sann avyayātmā
bhūtānām īśvaro 'pi san
prakṛtim svām adhiṣṭhāya
sambhavāmy ātmamāyayā

Translation

Even though I am unborn, with knowledge that does not wane, the Lord of beings — still I wield my own *prakriti* as though I came into being by my own creative power.

Metaphorical Interpretation

The Lord is saying that the soul is Brahman, all-pervading and omnipresent; therefore, this power of God is beyond birth and death, ever-present in every human being. The soul is the conductor and protector of all beings, through the help of Mother Nature (*yoga maya*). The soul abides in every human body. The soul appears in many forms with many names. The destiny of each particular person causes them to cherish various moods, but in reality, the soul is unchangeable.

Verse 7

yadā-yadā hi dharmasya
glānir bhavati bhārata
abhyutthānam adharmasya
tadā 'tmānam sṛjāmy aham

Translation

The Lord said:
O Arjuna! Whenever there is a decline in right living and an increase in wrong living, I assume a physical body.

Metaphorical Interpretation

When you practice breath control and self-control, divinity will manifest in your life. When people are engrossed in their worldly natures, feeling like their material bodies and material gain are the ultimate goals, they want nothing else. They only want to eat, drink, and be merry. In this state, they totally deviate from the truth. They are swept away, believing that they are scientists inventing many things, or doctors helping their patients, or they are rich, and so on. They do not want God. They do not realize that their breath is being constantly drawn into them by the soul, without which they are merely dead bodies. The indwelling soul alone is the cause of all they are doing.

When the general population becomes engrossed in the worldly nature, an agent of God descends into the world. According to the needs of that time, the agent teaches people scientifically that a body car is useless without the soul driver—without the soul, there can be no eating, drinking, and merrymaking. He also explains that the power of God abides in food. Without this power, human beings have nothing. An agent of God (son of God) is transformed spiritually into specific forms that allow scientific people to perceive the soul in understandable ways. People can follow this new agent of God; they can learn to feel the power of God in every inhalation. Because they believe He loves them very much, they love Him, seek Him, and feel deep gratitude towards Him. However, if they do not follow His instructions precisely and completely, they cannot find real peace, joy, and bliss.

Verse 8

paritrāṇāya sādhūnām
vināśāya ca duṣktām
dharmasamsthāpanārthāya
sambhavāmi yuge-yuge

Translation

The Lord continued:
For the protection of those who are committed to the Self and for the destruction (conversion) of those who follow *adharma*, I come into being in every age to establish *dharma*,

Metaphorical Interpretation

People remain absorbed in delusion and sin because they do not know how to withdraw their consciousness from the lower centers. Hence, they remain in the lower centers of the spine. This is why the Lord first teaches the yoga of action, and then the yoga of knowledge. Without action, people will never get knowledge. So the Lord constantly tells Arjuna and all worldly people to practice breath control, that is, self-control. Breath mastery is self-mastery.

When you sleep, you breathe with a unique inhalation. During this time, you do not have any thoughts, passion, anger, or sorrow. If you practice these deep inhalations, calm is automatically achieved.

That calmness is godliness, and in this state, all your power comes up into the pituitary, near the soul. As a result, all your evil propensities disappear, and you are free from the worldly senses and the body sense. You experience divine sound, divine vibration, and divine light. You can achieve constant liberation, peace, bliss, and joy. By magnetizing your spine, your life force changes into radiant, all-accomplishing divine force. This in turn gives you physical, mental, and intellectual regeneration and rejuvenation, and you will merge with the divine.

When you get up from the bed in the morning, your power has been regenerated and you are rejuvenated. By the same process, by practicing Kriya Yoga, a combination of *karma*, *jñana*, and *bhakti* yogas, you will always be alert. In every action, you will feel the power of God working through your soul, and all your viciousness and restlessness will disappear. Your human madness will disappear and you will experience continuous liberation, the ultimate goal of all religions.

Verse 9

janma karma ca me divyam
evam yo vetti tattvataḥ
tyaktvā deham punarjanma
nai 'ti mām eti so 'rjuna

Translation

The one who knows about My divine birth and action with clarity, O Arjuna, by giving up the body, is not born again. Instead, he attains Me.

Metaphorical Interpretation

The Lord of the universe, the Father of all religions, is one. He is beyond birth and death, therefore He has no father and mother. Before creation God was formless and all-pervading, according to

His own wish. When He first created the whole universe, He remained formless as a soul.

No one can touch Him, cut Him, or burn Him. Although He is everywhere, even in every single part of the human body, He is unknown and unseen. He is everywhere and He is nowhere. He is the ultimate resource of the universe, the knower and the knowable, the highest abode. He is in the vacuum and in the cervical center. He is in the air and in the dorsal center. He is in the fire and in the lumbar center, and in the eyes of every person. He is in the water, in the sacral center, and in the mouth. He is in the earth, in the coccygeal center, and in the nose. He is in the sun, moon, stars, and planets, but He remains compassionately detached. He is the greatest teacher in all moving and unmoving creation. He is worthy of adoration.

The agents of God sometimes appear on the earth in human form, but they have the same qualities as the Lord of the universe.

By practicing Kriya Yoga, you can withdraw the sensory awareness from the body, mind, thought, ego, and worldly experiences. Then you can ascend to the soul, knowing the formless qualities of God and perceiving the soul's indomitable power, the agent of God. Perceiving it, one merges with God. When people attain cosmic consciousness and wisdom, they enjoy constant liberation as long as they remain in the universe. After death, they merge with God and become one with God.

This is the wish of God; it is why He created this universe. The Lord, the creator, is the ancient one Who existed long before the creation.

Verse 10

vītarāgabhayakrodhā
manmayā mām upāśritāḥ
bahavo jñānatapasā
pūtā madbhāvam āgatāḥ

Translation

Free from craving, fear, and anger, totally resolved to be with Me, taking refuge in Me, purified by My discipline of knowledge, many have returned to My Nature.

Metaphorical Interpretation

Human beings engrossed in the lower centers of the body suffer from extreme attachment, fear, anger, sorrow, greed, pride, arrogance, suspicion, doubt, want of amity, want of peace, and want of balance of mind. They live lives of many troubles, with fear and anger making existence miserable. On the other hand, if they practice Kriya Yoga, the yoga of action, and become established in the yoga of knowledge, their divine power will rise up from the lower centers of the spine, and they can transcend the five sense organs. The true nature of the soul, the power of the Lord, is in the cranium. Those who keep their attention totally focused up in the pituitary and fontanel will surely experience extreme calm, which is godliness.

When people start to realize that what they do in the world is really done by the power of God, feeling like the human body is just a body car, and that the soul is the driver, gradually, they will become liberated.

Verse 11

ye yathā mam prapadyante
tāms tathai 'va bhajāmy aham
mama vartmā 'nuvartante
manuṣyāḥ pārtha sarvaśaḥ

Translation

O Partha (Arjuna), in whatever way a human being seeks Me and surrenders unto Me, I accept them and reward them accordingly; all human beings follow My path in different ways, but the goal is one.

Metaphorical Interpretation

Every action bears its fruit. No work is wasted. Time is the only factor. Eventually people who work with love for God receive the supreme state of divine calm.

God is one. That one God is the father of all religions. Different people of different religions seek Him and meditate on Him in different ways. The Christians contemplate Him according to their own system. The Muslims meditate on Him according to their own system. The Hindus worship Him according to their own system. This is all good, but the ultimate goal of all religions is the same.

God is beyond expression (*avyakta*), beyond the triple qualities of delusion (*maya*), always formless (*nirguna*). Before creation, He was formless, unknown, and unseen. After creation, He became seen and manifest, but His power as the soul in every human remains formless, unknown, and unseen. After death, all human beings merge back into the formless. In the Bhagavad Gita (2:28 and 10:20), it says that people of all religions will attain God-realization when they perceive the infinite formless.

The paths are many, but the goal is one. This verse declares the beauty of unity in spite of all diversity.

Verse 12

kāṅkṣantaḥ karmaṇām siddhim
yajanta iha devatāḥ
kṣipram hi mānuṣe loke
siddhir bhavati karmajā

Translation

Many seek material gain and worship many gods to acquire the fruits of their actions, for in the human world results born of action come very quickly.

Metaphorical Interpretation

There are six centers in our spine. In each center, there is a deity. For instance, in the coccyx, the deity is Ganesha, and the seed syllable is *lam*. Ganesha is the deity of wealth. People in India keep an image of Ganesha in their store or office, but they often want only money. Money can bring pleasure or pain, but not peace. If you have a lot of money, you may be anxious; you may develop heart pain and disease. People worship different gods in different ways, with many ends in view. Then they harvest the fruits of their actions.

It is not enough to worship the deity in each center. When you practice Kriya Yoga and gradually withdraw your mind, thought, and intellect from the lower centers, lifting your awareness and sitting near the soul up in the sixth center, God will respond. You will have everything; you will continuously experience a state of God consciousness. When you earn money, you will be deeply aware that you cannot earn money without God. Through this experience, you will gain liberation as well as material gain.

The power of God is in every inhalation. That is how you have sexual pleasure. Even while enjoying sex, you can perceive God remaining compassionately detached within you. In any center in which you have sensation, please say: "O God! I am indebted to You." Then, you will be successful in the material world, and you will have constant liberation.

Because of their narrow material goals, people cannot clearly foresee the real objective of life. Achieving this objective is a process of evolution.

Verse 13

cāturvarṇyam mayā sṛṣṭam
guṇakarmavibhāgaśaḥ
tasya kartāram api mām
viddhy akartāram avyayam

Translation

The system of four castes has been created by Me based on the differentiation of qualities and actions. Although I am the creator of all these, know Me as a non-agent and immutable.

Metaphorical Interpretation

The soul is always compassionately detached. The destinies of all human beings unfold according to their nature with the help of the soul. Without the soul and the triple qualities (*sattva, rajas,* and *tamas*) of delusion (*maya*) and destiny, no one can do anything. The soul is the sole doer, but the soul is also a non-doer. For example, a king does not personally do any of the work of the kingdom. The subordinate officers do the work, while the king gets all the credit.

A person's mentality determines his caste. Through changes in disposition, a person can belong to all four castes in one day. A person whose mind is on the soul, realizing God, is a *brahmin*—traditionally the priest caste. When that person's mind goes below the heart center, he or she becomes a *kshatriya*, of the warrior caste. When the mind remains in the region from the third center to the bottom center, this is a *vaishya*, the merchant and farmer caste. When the mind is in the thighs and lower legs, this same person becomes a *sudra*, of the laborer caste, someone who helps the other three castes.

In the Vedic hymn Purusha Sukta, it says: *Brahmana asya mukham asit*: "Those people whose minds dwell above the neck center are *brahmin* by caste, because they feel only Brahman in every step of their life." *Bahur rajan-nyah kritah*: "Those who keep their sense awareness between the heart and arms, who work and fight their evil propensities, are *kshatriya* by caste." They defend against the bad qualities in the lower centers. Arjuna was a *kshatriya*. The Lord forces Arjuna to fight his evil propensities and come up to the higher centers. *Uru-tadasya yad vaishya*: "Those who remain between the heart center and the lowest center are called *vaishya*." Their minds always remain on food, drink, sex, and animal qualities such as anger, pride, and suspicion. They don't want Self-realization; they are the third caste of people. The Lord exhorts every human being to rise up to the upper center from the lower ones. *Padbhyam sudrah ajyata*: "Those whose minds remain in the region from the coccygeal center to the legs are the fourth grade, or caste, of people." Our spinal canal is the fallow land that is covered with a jungle of matter; in other words, it is covered with vicious lower propensities.

The Lord encourages Arjuna (and everyone in the whole universe) to cultivate the fallow land and sow divine seeds. This means you should withdraw your consciousness from your lower centers to the upper center. This was said by Jesus, it is stated in the Mahabharata, and it is written in the Bhagavad Gita (4:42). Come to the upper center and achieve *laya yoga*, the formless stage!

In the Jñana Shankalini Tantra, it says, *urdhva shakti-bharet kantha*, which means: "If you withdraw your senses from the lower centers to the upper center (to the neck and even above), you will belong to a high caste of people." You will know Brahman, which makes you a *brahmin*. Being a *brahmin* is not a question of the caste you were born in, your creed, or your skin color; it is a matter of withdrawing your senses from the lower centers to the upper center.

The Lord helps every human being. Everyone who follows Him with the deepest faith can transform their destiny and achieve Self-realization. These faithful seekers will feel themselves sitting very near the soul, the Lord, or Allah, or Jesus, or Moses. They will achieve Self-realization, the ultimate goal of every human being and of all religions.

Verse 14

na mām karmāṇi limpanti
na me karmaphale spṛhā
iti mām yo 'bhijānāti
karmabhir na sa badhyate

Translation

Actions do not affect Me. Desire for the fruits of action does not exist in Me. One who knows My true nature is detached during every activity.

Metaphorical Interpretation

The Lord says that agents of God (sons of God) are not like worldly people. Their birth and life and death is quite different from that of ordinary human beings. They descend to earth only to teach human beings that all humans have the same soul qualities as the agents of God. Everyone who follows these agents of God and emulates their qualities will surely attain the superhuman divine stage of life.

The Lord is saying that the soul is not the body. In fact, the soul cannot be attached to anything. The soul is like a light in a room that allows people to see one another and talk, but the people's sight and speech do not affect the light. The Lord Jesus, Rama, and all the sons of God teach human beings that they should not feel like their actions are their own. The fruit of an action is not theirs, because a dead person cannot act, and a dead person cannot enjoy the fruits of action. All activity is done by the soul, so the fruit of all works goes to the soul. The Lord Jesus and Rama and many others lived this way. They descended into the world and taught us liberation. Follow their teachings and you will be free from all action and the fruits of your action.

The Lord had a deep friendship with Arjuna and the five Pandavas. When His mission was finished, He told them He was leaving them, that He was always free. Krishna left his friends and his body. Similarly, Jesus came and taught human beings how to be born from above and how to strive for liberation. After He was crucified, He proved that He was an immortal soul. He returned to his twelve advanced disciples, but He did not stay in the world. In the presence of all His disciples, He ascended, went back to God, telling His disciples to spread the message of God in the world.

In this verse, the Lord explains that He manifests on earth to teach us how to attain liberation. Throughout the Bhagavad Gita Krishna explains how to awaken the divine power and bring awareness into the pituitary by practicing of the yoga of action and the yoga of knowledge.

Verse 15

evam jñātvā kṛtam karma
pūrvair api mumukṣubhiḥ
kuru karmai 'va tasmāt tvam
pūrvaiḥ purvataram kṛtam

Translation

Understanding this, the ancient seekers performed every action of life without attachment! Work like those who came before.

Metaphorical Interpretation

If you practice Kriya Yoga and the yoga of knowledge, you will not feel like you are inhaling: rather, you will experience the soul pulling the inhalation from within. When you perceive that the air rises through your nose and touches the pituitary—the soul—you will attain the divine calm with every breath. When you remain constantly alert in the soul, you will constantly merge with the divine, feeling divine joy. You will also be detached and you will have all-round success in your life.

Verse 16

kim karma kim akarme 'ti
kavayo 'py atra mohitāḥ
tat te karma pravakṣyāmi
yaj jñātvā mokṣyase 'śubhāt

Translation

To discriminate between *karma* and *akarma* requires knowledge; even many seers fail to come to the correct conclusion, O Arjuna! Therefore I will explain the truth about action. If you know Me, you will be free from its effects and you will attain liberation.

Metaphorical Interpretation

One must clearly understand what must be done and what must be avoided.

The Lord is saying that those who keep their awareness in the lower centers of the spine, all the way up to the five sense organs, remain immersed in the unreal *karma*. These people are always confused because they do not possess true knowledge. However, by practicing Kriya Yoga, the yoga of action and the yoga of knowledge, they can bring their awareness up into the pituitary. Then they will experience true *karma;* they will realize that they are not doing any work. Work seemingly performed by them is in fact done by the soul. The Lord is telling Arjuna that if he follows Him, he will never experience bondage. Without the proper attitude, all work is good work, which leads to liberation.

Verse 17

karmaṇo hy api boddhavyam
boddhavyam ca vikarmaṇaḥ
akarmaṇaś ca boddhavyam
gahanā karmaṇo gatiḥ

Translation

Even *karma* (enjoined by scriptures) is to be known. *Vikarma* and *akarma* must also be known because the nature of *karma* is mysterious (difficult to understand).

Metaphorical Interpretation

There are three kinds of *karma*. One is detached *karma*, the true *karma*. Another is *vikarma*, forbidden actions. The third kind is *akarma*, inaction.

The Lord is saying that by practicing the yoga of action, which is detached action, you can remain united with the soul while performing any activity. When you act, you will know the soul is acting, not the body. Detached action is the highest work.

Another class of people practice the *karma* of inaction. They go to the temple, church, or mosque and pray for material gain. They dance and sing songs of God. They chant the name of God loudly for their prosperity and for the betterment of their family. They read spiritual books and think of themselves as advanced; they are filled with ego, pride, and extreme worldly ambition. This is the second grade of religious people. Most people are ambitious and live in this middle stage. These people will not realize God, because God cannot be perceived by the five sense organs; the formless God will not easily grant their prayers until they attain the formless stage.

The third grade of people are busy with food and drink and remain immersed in worldly enjoyment. They think there is no God. Whatever they are doing seems good to them. Many are educated people, scientists, doctors, and engineers who think they are top officers and that their work is very important to a nation. They are the third grade of people. God is nothing to them. They do not realize that if the power of God does not inhale through their noses, they cannot do anything. Whatever we do is done by the soul, so we should seek the soul through our every work. But these people never do.

Moreover, some people earn money by unfair means, such as by killing human beings. For their own safety, they sometimes pray to God. These are also the third grade of people. They should renounce their negative habits, which are forbidden or unlawful actions.

The nature of action is mysterious. One should live and act intelligently in the world to be free from the play of *karma*, or action.

Verse 18

karmaṇy akarma yaḥ paśyed
akarmaṇi ca karma yaḥ
sa buddhimān manuṣyeṣu
sa yuktaḥ kṛtsnakarmakṛt

Translation

The one who comprehends non-action in action, and action in non-action, is wise among all human beings. That person is a yogi who has done everything that is to be done.

Metaphorical Interpretation

Those who have raised their divine power above the cranium always perceive that the power of God is functioning within them; they perceive the soul in every action. They can easily avoid bad *karma*. They know that only the soul can act. They always feel divine bliss and always remain detached. Even when they see, hear, eat, smell, taste, walk, work, and laugh, they feel that the soul is doing everything through their sense organs and work organs. They are steadfastly fixed in the transcendental state.

Verse 19

yasya sarve samārambhāḥ
kāmasamkalpavarjitāḥ
jñānāgnidagdhakarmāṇam
tam āhuḥ paṇḍitam budhāḥ

Translation

The person whose every action is free from attachment and desire, whose every action is consumed by the fire of wisdom, is a realized person, a true sage and wise.

Metaphorical Interpretation

When yogis of action or yogis of knowledge meditate deeply, they go above the pituitary, even above the fontanel. They are above their limited gross body sense and above their worldly sense. At that time, they are beyond their body nature, experiencing only the divine Mother

Nature. When they perceive that the soul pervades everything, they have entered the formless state. Here, they feel like they are remaining high above the sky; they are in the infinite, the state of cosmic consciousness. They feel the vacuum; they hear divine sound from the highest heaven down to the ground; they see light pervading the universe.

Jesus said: "If therefore thine eye be single, thy whole body shall be full of light." Yogis can feel that the limited body, and also the whole world, is full of light. In the Isha Upanishad (8), the same teaching is written: *Sa paryagāt chukram avranam asnāviram. Sa paryagat* means that yogis are omniscient. *Chhukram* means that light, illumination, fills the whole world. *Akayam* refers to the formless stage. *Avranam* means that there is no physical pain or existence. *Asnaviram* means yogis feel like they have no nerves, no veins, no tissues, no flesh, no bones. In this state, yogis hear divine sound filling the world and perceive vibration all over the universe. This is the single-minded meditation of yogis. They feel the nearness of God and have divine love for Him.

Sometimes yogis merge with God and have no separate existence. This is called *yoga nidra*, which does not mean sleep, but conscious *samadhi*. At that time yogis feel like a nonentity, experiencing divine joy, divine peace, and divine bliss. This is inexplicable. Only those who have attained this stage can understand it. Self-realized yogis call those who have reached this stage "people of meditation," who have almost reached the wisdom state.

Verse 20

tyaktvā karmaphalāsangam
nityatṛpto nirāśrayaḥ
karmaṇy abhipravṛtto 'pi
nai 'va kimcit karoti saḥ

Translation

Though fully engaged in action, those who are always content, independent, free from desire, always absorbed in meditation,

ever free from worldly action, feel that they are not doing anything, but that the soul is the doer.

Metaphorical Interpretation

Those who have attained conscious *samadhi* are truly free from worldly bondage. They are always absorbed in the soul that is Brahman. They are free from desire and from the bodily senses; they remain absorbed in Mother Nature. In this stage, when they work, eat, drink, or walk, they realize the soul is doing it all. They are not bound by any activity.

Ambitions and desires cause bondage. Those who meditate lead a life of detachment, even when they are active. They enjoy the nature of liberation through the experience of inner calm.

Verses 21–23

nirāsīr yatacittātmā
tyaktasarvaparigrahaḥ
śārīram kevalam karma
kurvan nā 'pnoti kilbiṣam

yadṛcchālābhasamtuṣṭo
dvandvātīto vimatsaraḥ
samaḥ siddhāv asiddhau ca
kṛtvā 'pi na nibadhyate

gatasangasya muktasya
jñānāvasthitacetasaḥ
yajñāyā 'carataḥ karma
samagram pravilīyate

Translation

For those with no desire, body and mind remain under thorough control, free from all cravings. Work is performed through the

body's actions only; such persons do not incur defilement or sin.

Those who are content with anything that comes automatically, who are free from the dualities of life (the pairs of opposites such as pleasure and pain), and from envy, who are steady in both success and failure, are never entangled in delusion while performing actions.

***Karma* resolves totally for one who is free from attachment, whose mind is fixed in the superconscious stage of Self knowledge, who performs deeds only for the sake of daily *yajña* (watching the soul during every inhalation.)**

Metaphorical Interpretation

These verses describe the rich life lived by spiritually advanced people, the life of inner tranquility and love.

When realized yogis seek God-realization, they remain in the astral body, in the divine. In that state, they do not have to watch their incoming and outgoing breath; these yogis are already constantly absorbed in the soul. This is called *kevala kumbhaka*, which means the body awareness has disappeared. Such people are detached and always satisfied with whatever comes to them. They do not ask anything from anyone. Any food they receive, they eat mechanically and are happy with it. They have no time to be envious because God has no envy. Filled with divine love and compassion, they remain unchanged in success and in failure.

In this stage, yogis always feel that everyone is Brahman, the soul is Brahman, every person is the power of God. These realized Kriya yogis who have penetrated beyond the veil of nature, who have thorough control of food and drink, who have penetrated behind the veil of all religions, reaching cosmic consciousness, are free from all bonds. They are not attached to anything. Merged in God, they can lead worldly people to God and salvation.

Verse 24

brahmā 'rpaṇam brahma havir
brahmāgnau brahmaṇā hutam
brahmai 'va tena gantavyam
brahmakarmasamādhinā

Translation

The means of offering is Brahman. The oblation is Brahman, offered by Brahman in the fire that is Brahman. Indeed, Brahman is to be reached by one who sees everything as Brahman.

Metaphorical Interpretation

When Kriya yogis fix their attention one hundred percent in the pituitary and fontanel, their divine power comes up from the lower centers to the upper center. They undergo absolute divine transformation as they are united with the soul, perceiving Brahman in everything. They cannot distinguish anything separate from Brahman. As melting ice merges into water, realized Kriya yogis merge into Brahman.

Verse 25

daivam evā 'pare yajñam
yoginaḥ paryupāsate
brahmāgnāv apare yajñam
yajñenai 'vo 'pajuhvati

Translation

Some yogis worship the deities in many ways, while other yogis offer only themselves, by themselves, in the fire of Brahman.

Metaphorical Interpretation

Lord Krishna relates the different kinds of *yajñas*, or worship. In our spinal canal there are five centers. In each center is a lotus. The first center, at the bottom of the spine, is the coccygeal, which has a four-petalled lotus. The seed syllable of this deity is *lam* (*long*), which means earth, and the deity is Ganesha, for success. In the second center, there is a six-petalled lotus, and the seed syllable is *vam* (*vong*), which means water. The deity is Durga, the deity of removing obstacles. In the third center is a ten-petalled lotus. The seed syllable is *ram* (*rong*), which means fire. The deity of this center is the sun for strength and vitality. In the fourth center, the heart center, there is a twelve-petalled lotus. The seed syllable is *yam* (*jong*), which means air. The deity of this center is Krishna or Vishnu (Krishna was the incarnation of Vishnu), for peace and harmony. In the fifth center, in the neck, there is a sixteen-petalled lotus. The seed syllable is *sam* (*song*), which means vacuum. The deity of this center is Shiva, for spiritual evolution.

When Hindus worship deities, they remain in the center associated with the deity. To fulfill a particular desire, they fix their attention on one deity. That is one part of devotion, but it is not complete meditation because their five sense organs are working. They are offering flowers, fruits, and sweets. They chant many mantras; therefore they remain in an extroverted state. Although deities can be worshipped with the five sense organs, God cannot be perceived by them.

Another class of devotees withdraws their divine power from the lower centers and raises it up into the upper center. They may even chant the five seed mantras of the five centers; however, they do not advance any further, because they are bound to the mind and the mantras, which is not single-minded meditation.

The highest devotees withdraw their divine power from the lower centers to the cranium, as instructed in the Upanishads and later by Jesus. The soul of every human being abides above, in the cranium, drawing every inhalation into every living body. The human nose is not in the bottom centers, meaning the first or second centers, or in any other center. The soul inhales the breath from above, and all worldly thoughts, mind, and intellect go from the lower centers to the upper center. Ultimately, the supreme power merges in the fontanel where the formless state is experienced. A dead person cannot inhale.

In the Isha Upanishad (17–18) it says, "Inhalation is the real oblation to the soul fire." Inhalation carries oxygen to the divine fire in the soul. Oxygen is the life of that fire. The soul, the divine fire, always abides in every human being. This inhalation is the true fire ceremony. In the yoga of action and yoga of knowledge, yogis are performing the true fire ceremony. Here, all mantras are burned. All past thoughts, restlessness, and human madness are burned. The body sense and worldly senses are burned. After the true fire ceremony, no remnant is left. There is only oneness with God.

Verses 26–27

śrotrādīnī 'ndriyāṇy anye
samyamāgniṣu junvati
śabdādīn viṣayān anya
indriyāgniṣu juhvati

sarvāṇī 'ndriyakarmāṇi
prāṇakarmāṇi cā 'pare
ātmasamyamayogāgnau
juhvati jñānadīpite

Translation

Some offer their organs of hearing and the other senses into the fire of self-discipline. Others offer sound and the other sense objects in the fire of the senses.

Others offer the activities of all sense organs and all bodily forces into the fire of self-control, kindled by wisdom.

Metaphorical Interpretation

The five sense organs and five organs of action need to be controlled; every activity related to the senses must be offered to the Lord with love. Lord Krishna is describing how to use the sense organs for spiritual evolution. Through the eyes one should see the beauty of God, through the mouth one should speak with love, and so on. This is possible only through meditation.

In conscious *samadhi*, the five sense organs and five work organs stop functioning. Even inhalation and exhalation become feeble. This is the true meaning of *pranayama*, which means the cessation of *prana*. Through this, longevity increases.

Superconsciousness and cosmic consciousness mean that the body and soul are perceived as one. This is the *so-ham*, or *hamsa*, stage, which means "I and He (the soul) are one"; in other words, the soul and the body nature are one. In this state yogis feel the human being in God and God in the human being. They continuously enjoy divine joy, bliss, and peace. They feel the soul functioning through their bodies. This is the real yoga of knowledge, which functions as a result of the yoga of action. For this reason the Lord narrated the yoga of knowledge after the yoga of action.

Verse 28

dravyayajñās tapoyajñā
yogayajñās tathā 'pare
svādhyāyajñānayajñāś ca
yatayaḥ samśitavratāḥ

Translation

Some people offer material things to the poor; some people follow prayerful discipline. Some people control their senses with austerity and remain in the knowledge of Brahman. Some people read various spiritual scriptures following the path of knowledge, with firm vows and efforts.

Metaphorical Interpretation

This verse is saying that there are four kinds of yogis: Those who practice (1) *dravya yajña*, (2) *tapa yajña*, (3) *yoga yajña*, and (4) *svadhyaya jñana yajña.*

The general meaning of *dravya yajña* is to offer food or grains to the poor, but metaphorically, *dravya yajña* has a deeper meaning. Many yogis roll up their tongues while practicing the yoga of action. The tongue penetrates the passage behind the uvula and goes up the passage near the pituitary. This is called *khechari mudra.* Then a liquid matter, called nectar, comes down from the fontanel. When that liquid matter rolls down and falls on the *vaishwanara agni*, the divine fire in the stomach, this is called *dravya yajña.*

The formal meaning of *tapa yajña* is to offer *ghee* into the fire for a long time, chanting a mantra with every oblation. But the metaphorical meaning of *tapa yajña* is that the soul is the divine fire in the cranium. (*See the Isha Upanishad 18.*) A fire cannot burn without fuel, such as *ghee*, and oxygen. In the same way, the spiritual fire burns in the soul because oxygen constantly rises with the breath and touches the soul fire. As a result, the soul fire is within us, and we are alive. A true yogi of detached action and knowledge constantly watches the soul, watching the soul draw in every inhalation, which then touches the invisible body of the soul. This is why the soul fire always remains in the yogi's body. This is the real fire ceremony, called *tapa yajña.*

Tapa means heat. Because of the heat always in the soul fire, all human beings are alive. If the soul does not inhale for us, we will die. So you see, our soul is very kind to us, constantly drawing oxygen in through our noses. Whenever a yogi of action and knowledge keeps constant awareness in the inhalation and watches the soul fire, it is *tapa yajña.*

Yoga yajña means using the power of the yoga of action and knowledge to withdraw all power from the lower centers to the upper center, remaining beyond the mind, thought, intellect, ego, and the body sense, entering into the formless state. These yogis find divine joy—*yoga yajshna.*

Svadhyaya jñana yajña. Usually, *svadhyaya* is interpreted as reading spiritual books, but the metaphorical meaning of *svadhyaya* comes from *sva* and *adhyaya. Sva* means the Self, who constantly inhales, and *adhyaya* means to read and study, so *svadhyaya* means our soul is the sole doer in us. The soul allows our eyes to see, our ears to hear, our mouth to eat and talk, and our hands and legs to work. All the organs of the body are conducted by the soul. So withdraw your divine power from the lower centers to the upper center and constantly watch the soul. Understand that He is very kind to us. If you study your soul in this way, that is *svadhyaya.* This study is *svadhyaya jñana,* the yoga of knowledge. In the Bible (Matthew 18:8–9) it says, "Wherefore if thy hand or thy foot offend thee, cut them off, and cast them from thee: it is better for thee to enter into life halt or maimed, rather than having two hands or two feet to be cast into everlasting fire. And if thine eye offend thee, pluck it out, and cast *it* from thee: it is better for thee to enter into life with one eye, rather than having two eyes to be cast into hell fire." The Bhagavad Gita, (5:8–9 and 4:42) says the same.

Verse 29

apāne juhvati prāṇam
prāṇe 'pānam tathā 'pare
prāṇāpānagatī ruddhvā
prāṇāyāmaparāyaṇāḥ

Translation

Others offer their exhalation (*prana*) as an oblation of the external air. Still others offer *apana* (inhalation) as an oblation to *prana*, and in this way they stop the flow of inhalation and exhalation. They practice *pranayama* (breath regulation).

Metaphorical Interpretation

Inhalation is *apana,* oxygen. *Apana* refers to the oxygen outside of the body, not yet inhaled (*a* means *na,* or not). The soul must inhale this oxygen into the body so it can be transformed into usable energy. So *apana* is the pure external air, oxygen, that is inhaled and offered as an oblation to the soul. This is why the soul remains in the body. *Sa* is inhalation, and *sa* is also the soul.

When *apana*, oxygen, is inhaled and offered to the soul, it is immediately burned, like oil that touches the flame in a lamp. As the pure soul flame burns the *apana*, it gives off life force, *prana*, to energize the body. We experience *prana* as body heat and as the ordinary consciousness of experiencing the world through the five senses. If the *ham* (body nature), constantly watches this normal breath and perceives the living power of God entering it in the form of oxygen, that body will experience God-realization. This is continuous oblation to God.

Prana is the outgoing breath of the soul, which provides the life force that animates the twenty-four gross elements of the body and mind. The soul's exhalation includes the carbon dioxide that is offered to the external air. When you do not watch your breath constantly, your spirituality, your godhood, is lost. Constant alertness produces continuous God-realization. Just by constantly watching your natural breathing, you can become a realized person.

In the Gheranda Samitha (5:84), it says, *hamkāreṇa bahiryāti saḥkāreṇa viśeta punaḥ*, which means that "the breath entering into every person makes the sound of *sa*, and when exiting (*bahiryati*) makes the sound *ham*." This is *ham-sa sadhana*, watching the inhalation and exhalation with *so-ham*. The outgoing breath is *prana, ham,* and the incoming breath, *apana*, is pulled by the soul, *sa*. Likewise, in the Shiva Svarodaya (51), it says, *hakāro nirgame proktaḥ sakāreṇa praveśanam,* which means, "the process of exhalation contains the letter *ham*, and the inhalation contains the letter *sa*."

Some advanced yogis take in very little breath. Their breath does not flow back out of the nostrils; instead, it remains inside the nostrils and enters the soul. This is the "rest of *prana*," the literal meaning of *pranayama*. The more feeble the breath, the more God-realization. These yogis keep their attention fixed in the atom point, in the soul, always watching the soul. They hear many sounds, like many instruments playing, and they see divine light constantly. These advanced yogis don't feel the world. They can live the family life. In ancient times, the *rishis* and *munis* all had families. In meditation, they stayed in a trance and did not breathe.

Some devotees practice another kind of *pranayama.* Keeping their attention completely on the soul, they do not watch their inhalation and exhalation. Their incoming breath and outgoing breath become very slow; the air moves only inside their nostrils. This kind of yogi does not place any importance on the breath. They watch the soul very calmly and feel as though their breath has completely stopped. But it has not stopped, it is simply very slow and subtle.

In Verse 28, the Lord said there are four types of yogis. In this verse the Lord mentions three more types. By practicing the yoga of action and the yoga of knowledge, they also can achieve the calmness of godliness. This is called *anta pranayama,* which means they watch only the power of God inside the pituitary and fontanel and reach extreme Self-realization.

Verse 30

apare niyatāhārāḥ
prānān prānesu juhvati
sarve 'py ete yajñavido
yajñakṣapitakalmasaḥ

Translation

Other yogis, who regulate their *prana*, (who inhale with a faint breath) achieve the breathless and pulseless stage. By knowing how to sacrifice the breath, the sins of these yogis are destroyed. Their life force is merged with the all-pervading soul.

Metaphorical Interpretation

Now the Lord is describing very advanced yogis who have thorough control of their breath. Very advanced yogis do not inhale or exhale when they meditate. They are in the breathless, pulseless stage, which is the deathless stage. This is *nirvikalpa samadhi.* Those who meditate in this state don't require anything. Whenever a thought arises, they will see the power of God in their minds. If they have a bad thought, they can remove it, and if it is good, they can work accordingly. In their practical life, they are constantly alert in the inner Self, free from everything, liberated. Remaining in the world, they are compassionately detached from it. They don't need to leave the family. They realize that God alone activates them and their whole family. This is *karma sannyasa.*

Verse 31

yajñaśiṣṭāmṛtabhujo
yānti brahma sanātanam
nā 'yam loko 'sty ayajñasya
kuto 'nyaḥ kurusattama

Translation

Those who eat the nectar that is the remnant of the sacrifice go to eternal Brahman. O Arjuna, the best of the Kuru warrior dynasty, without practicing this *yajña* (both the yoga of action and the yoga of knowledge), human beings can never live happily in this life. What then of the next life?

Metaphorical Interpretation

Those who know the Self, who attain the stage beyond thought, reach *samadhi.* At this time the divine nectar comes down from the fontanel. This is the true oblation to the soul. Devotees who drink this divine nectar attain the Brahman stage.

You can earn a lot of money and give it to charity. You can serve many people in many ways and save them from difficulty and danger. But these acts can create pride and vanity, and do not change your evil habits and lead you to divinity. To achieve purity and perfection, to become one with the divine, bring your awareness up into the cranium where your soul abides free from all evil. If by practicing *karma* and *jñana* you so ascend, you will perceive God in the human being and the human being in God. Otherwise, your life is useless. Your next life will be useless as well.

Begin practice now; your life will be more useful, and without doubt you will attain perfection.

Verse 32

evam bahuvidhā yajñā
vitatā brahmaṇo mukhe
karmajān viddhi tān sarvān
evam jñātvā vimokṣyase

Translation

Many and diverse disciplines are very elaborately described in the Vedas. All are born of karma. Understand them. Knowing this, you will be liberated.

Metaphorical Interpretation

You may hear a great deal of spiritual talk from many learned persons, but without taking action, you will never perceive the soul. One ounce of practice is far better than tons of theory. Knowing this, work practically, and you will be free from worldly bondage.

By merely hearing about spirituality you cannot perceive anything. As a pilot learns how to fly an airplane from the flight instructor, similarly you learn spirituality from a realized person who gives you the experience of Self-realization. Follow this guide and practice daily, and surely one day you will understand that you are not who you think you are. In truth, you are your indwelling Self. The marvelous power of God is within you, but it is covered by ignorance. Meditate and discover your Self.

There are many paths of spiritual practice. Follow the one that accelerates your spiritual evolution.

Verse 33

śreyān dravyamayād yajñāj
jñānayajñaḥ paramtapa
sarvam karmā 'khilam pārtha
jñāne parisamāpyate

Translation

O Paramtapa (destroyer of enemies), *jñana yajña*, discipline of knowledge, is better than *dravya yajña*, sacrifice of material objects. O son of Partha (Arjuna), after all, everything (all action) merges into the divine knowledge.

Metaphorical Interpretation

The path of knowledge, which comes from the self-effort applied to remain in the cave of the cranium, is superior. So long as you remain in the lower centers of the body and in the five sense organs, you will experience passion and attachment and find the world alluring. Even if you give many material objects to many people, you will still cherish some self-interest, pride, name, and fame, which are all worldly attachments.

In your body car there is a soul driver. The soul is your invisible body, which is not attached to the gross body. Even though the soul remains in the body, ten fingers above your eyebrows in the fontanel, it cannot be touched or cut. It guides you constantly in every step of your life. If, by breath control, you can bring your awareness up into the soul, all your world sense will disappear and you will attain the superconscious state, the formless. This is conscious *samadhi* and liberation. You will perceive that your soul is the real you. This state of knowledge brings the experience of liberation from all attachment.

Verse 34

tad viddhi praṇipātena
paripraśnena sevayā
upadekṣyanti te jñānam
jñāninas tattvadarśinaḥ

Translation

Understand that by bowing down, by asking the proper questions, and through service, you will be taught this knowledge by those who are wise, by those who have the vision of truth.

Metaphorical Interpretation

The disciple attains the state of wisdom by apprenticeship to an able master. You can learn about supreme consciousness if you become a favorite of your master. Follow the master deeply, serve the master humbly, remain indebted to your preceptor, and always ask how to achieve God-realization most quickly. If you do, the realized person will teach you the quickest means to success in God-realization.

In the beginning of the first chapter, Arjuna was in sorrow. In Chapter 2, Arjuna was not willing to fight, so he had no implicit faith and loyalty in the teachings of the Lord. In Chapter 3, the Lord gradually explained the yoga of action. Herein, Lord Krishna reveals the yoga of knowledge. Although He discusses the yoga of knowledge, He places more importance on the yoga of action. At this point, Arjuna feels love for the Lord.

Although, at first, the Bhagavad Gita seems to describe a fight between human armies, it is in fact a battle between knowledge and ignorance, conducted by the soul: the Lord. The Pandavas are the knowledge party. The Kauravas are the ignorance party, which remains below in every human being. The Lord is the soul, Who leads every human being from ignorance to knowledge. He is the sole doer, responsible for all your actions. If you do not maintain implicit faith, humbleness, and loyalty in Him and ask questions of Him, you fail to seek Him in your ignorance and evil. As a result, you cannot find peace, bliss, and joy—your birthright. The Lord is within everyone, so, if anyone asks his soul what is good and what is bad, the soul will certainly lead that person from darkness to light, from dishonesty to honesty, from mortality to immortality, from falsehood to truth, and from imperfection to perfection, and hence to God-realization.

Verse 35

yaj jñātvā na punar moham
evam yāsyasi pāṇḍava
yena bhutāny aśeṣeṇa
drakṣyasy ātmany atho mayi

Translation

O Pandava! If you know the superconscious stage, you will never again be deluded. In this state, you will see that you are in every being and in everything, and you will perceive all in Me.

Metaphorical Interpretation

Once one reaches enlightenment, one is free from delusion and illusion forever. To achieve this state, strive sincerely with meditation.

The Lord is the soul of every human being; He is all-pervading. There is nothing superior to Him in this world. Since there is nothing beyond the soul, the soul is everything in the universe. As many diamonds are strung on a thread in a necklace, so the whole world is connected with the all-pervading thread of Brahman. When the necklace thread breaks, all the diamonds are scattered. Likewise, if the soul does not inhale for human beings, no people will exist, nor plants, trees, and animals. If you can rise up and experience the Lord just once, by practicing the yoga of action, you will recognize His importance. In every activity you will feel Him working through every human being.

Verse 36

api ced asi pāpebhyaḥ
sarvebhyaḥ pāpakṛttamaḥ
sarvam jñānaplavenai 'va
vṛjinam santariṣyasi

Translation

Even if you are the most sinful person in the world of all sinners, by the boat of transcendental knowledge, you can cross the ocean of misery and sin.

Metaphorical Interpretation

The Lord assures us completely that every person, in spite of all their past deeds, can be free from all negative tendencies and can experience inner peace and love if they try.

"Arjuna! The Lord said all your sins and pitfalls remain below in your five sense organs. If you can withdraw your attention from your senses and bring it into the soul at any moment, you can be one with divinity."

Jesus said (John 3:5–8), "Verily, verily, I say unto thee, Except a man be born of water and of the Spirit, he cannot enter into the kingdom of God. That which is born of the flesh is flesh; and that which is born of the Spirit is spirit. Marvel not that I said unto thee, Ye must be born again." St. Paul, Matthew, and Peter were all living below, in the flesh nature. The moment they followed Jesus and were reborn, they became most spiritual. Similarly, in India, Ratnakara, Vilvamangal, Takshavill, Girish Ghose, Tulsidas, and many others were living their lives guided by the energy in the lower centers of the spine; they were sinful. But through the blessing of good company, they meditated and their negative qualities disappeared. They became very spiritual, realized, and respected people.

Verse 37

yathai 'dhāmsi samiddho 'gnir
bhasmasāt kurute 'rjuna
jñānāgniḥ sarvakarmāṇi
bhasmasāt kurute tathā

Translation

O Arjuna, as the little fire burns wood into ashes, so knowledge is the spiritual fire that burns all actions (calms all restlessness).

Metaphorical Interpretation

Knowledge is a fire that burns all ignorance and brings liberation. From the lower centers up to our five sense organs, the mind is engrossed in material objects. Our sense organs create extreme attachment to material objects. Our ignorance exists in this realm, but our knowledge is the fire of our soul inside the cranium. By withdrawing the senses into the soul, all material ambitions will be burned until no ashes remain. With the help of a realized master, this can be done. You can perceive divine illumination, divine vibration, divine sound constantly; you can feel the real love of God; you can be pure and perfect.

Verse 38

na hi jñānena sadṛśam
pavitram iha vidyate
tat svayam yogasamsiddhaḥ
kālenā 'tmani vindati

Translation

In this world there is no purifier equal to knowledge (superconsciousness). One who practices yoga and achieves perfection becomes Self-realized in time.

Metaphorical Interpretation

In this world nothing is as pure as cosmic consciousness. By practicing the yoga of action and the yoga of knowledge, people can enjoy all-round success in life. Self-realization can be achieved only in the soul, which remains above.

Nothing in this world is pure except Self-realization and soul culture. By the practice of the yoga of action and the yoga of knowledge, you can free your *ida* and *pingala* channels inside the spine. After this, your divine power can rise up and the restlessness caused by material objects will gradually disappear; then your awareness can enter the pituitary, the seat of the soul, and you can realize your true Self. When your gross self dies, you perceive your real Self. Our gross self is delusion, but our invisible Self, our soul, is real, pure, and perfect.

Verse 39

śraddhāvāml labhate jñānam
tatparaḥ samyatendriyaḥ
jñānam labdhvā parām śāntim
acireṇā 'dhigacchati

Translation

Those who have real love for the scriptures, the teacher, and God, who practice single-minded meditation, who have thoroughly withdrawn their senses from the lower centers to the pituitary, attain Self-realization. Having gained this knowledge, they find permanent peace and liberation.

Metaphorical Interpretation

When the minds of human beings leave the worldly nature and go above the pituitary and remain in the superconscious stage, that is Mother Nature; this leads to true love for God. The more these devotees reside in the soul, the more they will feel the oneness of Mother Nature and the worldly nature. In doing so, they can remain in the material world, keeping one eye on God and the other eye on the material world. They also experience divine joy, recognizing that without the soul, they are nothing but dead bodies. Only with the soul do we experience joy in the material world, which is really only the soul's joy.

Verse 40

ajñaś cā 'śraddadhānaś ca
samśayātmā vinaśyati
nā 'yam loko 'sti na paro
na sukham samśayātmanaḥ

Translation

There are those who have no knowledge of God and no faith in God, who always doubt Him; their desires are never fulfilled. A doubtful mind perishes. Those who have doubts have neither this world, nor the world beyond, nor any happiness.

Metaphorical Interpretation

In this world, virtually no one has any knowledge of God. Most believe that everything is physical matter. Even highly educated persons feel no need to seek God, living instead in pride and self-arrogance, passing their lives without soul culture. They are merely rational animals.

Human life is for Self-realization. God-realization is our birthright. Without the soul, humans cannot do anything. Those who don't understand this don't grow spiritually. Those who do not seek the soul deviate from the truth. They obtain neither peace nor liberation in this world. Rich professionals, business people, scientists, and all human beings should strive for God-realization. It is our duty to earn material wealth, but we must also earn spiritual wealth.

Those who are ignorant of the higher purpose of life and devoid of faith are always in trouble. They doubt everything, and a doubtful mind is always in trouble. These people are not able to live their lives in joy and happiness.

Verse 41

yogasamnyastakarmāṇam
jñānasamchinnasamśayam
ātmavantam na karmāṇi
nibadhnanti dhanamjaya

Translation

O Dhanamjaya (Arjuna), actions do not bind those who have renounced action through yoga; free from doubts through knowledge, they are Self-realized.

Metaphorical Interpretation

No work can be done by a dead body. All work is done by the soul. All human beings who withdraw their divine power up into the soul will achieve Self-realization. They will feel that any action they undertake is performed by the soul, and that any fruit that comes from any activity goes to the soul. They are just a motor car, and God is the driver. God is the driver of all body cars.

When you meditate and remain immersed in the soul, you can feel the soul's kindness. Even if you work all day and all night, you will know that, truly, only the soul is working, giving you divine bliss all the time. You are ever indebted to your soul.

Steadfastly practice the yogas of action and knowledge.

Verse 42

tasmād ajñānasambhūtam
hṛtstham jñānāsinā 'tmanaḥ

chittvai 'nam samśayam yogam
ātiṣṭho 'ttiṣṭha bhārata

Translation

O Arjuna! (Bharata) By the sword of knowledge cut out all the ignorance that remains in your heart. Be free from doubt and practice the yoga of action and yoga of knowledge. Don't be heartbroken. Stand up and fight your ignorance.

Metaphorical Interpretation

Impressions in the mind are formed from the five sense organs. Through these, human beings remain deluded. The mind, thought, intellect, ego, and body are always ignorant. This is why you do not have any peace.

"O Arjuna! Using the weapon of conscience, withdraw your senses from the lower centers to the upper center. Follow the yoga of action and the yoga of knowledge, and all your ignorance will be transformed into cosmic consciousness. You can keep your attention fixed in the cranium near the soul. Remaining there, you will feel that whenever you act from the lower centers, the divine energy does not stay below; rather, all the energy in the centers and in all the body parts rises to the soul. Without a soul, you have no body parts. Just as the trunk, branches, and leaves of a tree function from the roots; likewise, all your body parts, mind, and thoughts function from the soul.

In this verse the word *atishtha* means to remain in the north of your body focusing constantly on the soul. Give up your idleness and bad habits, rise up, and remain there. Right now. Witness every part of your body functioning from the soul. When you see that all your actions arise from the soul, you will surely feel indebted to it. You will love your soul. You will know that all pleasure is created there. If you are firmly established in this knowledge, you experience constant liberation.

The fourth chapter is titled "The Yoga of Knowledge." That knowledge comes from the yoga of action. This is why the Lord gives more importance to the yoga of action. In the next chapter, the Lord will discuss the yoga of renunciation, wherein you must work without feeling like you are working. In your family life and all worldly activity, if the soul does not inhale, you are dead, a mere body. As a vehicle, a house, you are not alive; only the soul driver, the soul occupant, makes it alive. In this sense, you are nothing but a lifeless body.

Feel your soul loving you. Feel that whatever you have, you really have nothing. Only the soul can function in the world, so everything belongs to the soul. When a nurse looks after a child and the child dies, the nurse does not feel the intense pain of losing his or her own child. Live in your family like the nurse; remain compassionately detached. This is the yoga of renunciation.

Summary

God has provided human beings with a head, two hands, and a heart, capable of knowledge, action, and love. These three capacities must be integrated and diligently practiced. To perceive the Self (*ya*) in every action (*kri*) is knowledge; every action must be offered to the Lord as worship (*kriya*). Freedom from the sense of doership and ego is love. Correct action, attitude, and outlook during every activity will lead to inner purity (*antakarana shuddha*), and thus to liberation. The oil and a wick together can create a beautiful flame in a lamp. Oil is the symbol of love, the wick is action, and the light is knowledge. United, this is the state of yoga.

This chapter consisting of forty-two verses can be summarized as follows:

Verses 1–3: A detailed narration of the yoga tradition as a lineage where the teacher instructs the student, and God is the real teacher.

Verse 4: Arjuna questions the plausibility of the lineage.

Verses 5–8: A detailed explanation of the doctrine of incarnation and the need for incarnation.

Verses 9–10: The significance of this knowledge: the unmanifest is made manifest, which leads to the ultimate truth.

Verses 11–12: Devotion and *prana karma* (Kriya) lead to liberation.

Verses 13–14: These verses explain the four castes and detached action, and describe the ancient sincere seekers.

Verses 16–20: The principles of action: action, inaction, and nonaction.

Verses 21–23: Through action (*kri* and *ya*), one can achieve the state of realization, which is glorious.

Verse 24: This verse describes *brahma yajña*, where every action is offering oblation to the absolute Brahman. (This verse is chanted before taking food).

Verse 25: This verse describes the *deva yajña* (divine sacrifice) performed by the yogis.

Verse 26: This verse explains the *yajña* of controlling of senses (*indriya samyama yajña*).

Verse 27: The *yajña* of self-control (*atma samyam*) leads to *samadhi.*

Verse 28: Four types of *yajñas* (sacrifices) are described: *drarya yajña* (the sacrifice of material things), *tapo yajña* (the sacrifice of breath), *yoga yajña* (the sacrifice of meditation), and *jñana yajña* (the sacrifice of self-study).

Verses 29–30: A detailed description of the very subtle technique of *pranayama,* called *prana yajña.*

Verses 31–32: Some concluding remarks on the principle of *karma,* action.

Verses 33–40: These verses explain what knowledge is, the means to achieve it, the qualifications of a seeker, and the result of gaining knowledge.

Verse 41: The Lord prescribes the practice of yoga for freedom from doubt.

Verse 42: The Lord advises facing the battle of the spiritual life, remaining awakened, and dwelling above in the fontanel, at the crown of the head.

Chapter 5

Karma Sannyasa Yoga

The Yoga of Renunciation of Action

Introduction

Living in the world is as difficult as crossing a vast ocean. Life is filled with obstacles as high as waves, and with the ferocious agnostic creatures: anger, ego, and vanity. To live in the world and pass through it safely, one must follow the path of action with knowledge. One must not be attached to the outcome of any activity; therefore, one must practice renunciation in action. Live in the world, but enjoy compassionate detachment. Most people don't know this art of living, and as a result, they are attached, acting and reacting to every vicissitude of life.

After having discussed the yoga of action and yoga of knowledge in detail, the Lord is now addressing the art of renunciation while living and working in the world. You cannot stop activity for even a moment. Breath, circulation, and digestion continue even when your physical and astral bodies rest completely during deep sleep.

A man of knowledge can easily lead a life of inner detachment. Renunciation of action is not to renounce the world, but rather to renounce the sense of doership.

Verse 1

arjuna uvāca
sannyāsam karmaṇām kṛṣṇa
punar yogam ca śamsasi
yac chreya etayor ekam
tan me brūhi suniścitam

Translation

Arjuna asked:
O, Krishna, you praised the yoga of renunciation, but then you spoke highly of the yoga of action. Please, tell me conclusively, which of the two is really better.

Metaphorical Interpretation

In the third chapter, the Lord praised *karma yoga*, telling the true seeker to meditate deeply and practice this technique for soul culture. The Lord also said to shun any *karma* (actions) that might hinder God-realization. Then for higher realization, the Lord revealed the yoga of knowledge in the fourth chapter. The Lord already spoke directly about the yoga of knowledge earlier (Bhagavad Gita 2:54–72), when He was describing the qualities of a true seeker who is firmly established in wisdom. These verses are very important. Every seeker should read these verses and commit them to memory to build a truly human life.

Now, in the beginning of the fifth chapter, Arjuna, whose name means "the true seeker of God," addresses Krishna, "O Krishna! I have listened closely to all your instructions about attaining the extreme superconscious state through the yoga of knowledge, as well as to your earlier instructions regarding the yoga of action. After hearing all this, I am confused. I request Thee, please tell me directly and conclusively, which of these two is better for my soul culture?"

The symbolic question asked here is whether meditating more and more deeply is enough for God-realization. Is the yoga of action better, or is the yoga of knowledge better? The devotee is in a dilemma and constantly wonders about the shortcut to God-realization. Should one shun work and remain in the state beyond thought or should one follow *karma yoga* as a technique for soul culture? The mental confusion must be presented to a spiritual teacher, who will help the student overcome it.

Verse 2

śrībhagavān uvāca
sannyāsaḥ karmayogaś ca
niḥśreyasakarāv ubhau
tayos tu karmasannyāsāt
karmayogo viśiṣyate

Translation

The Blessed Lord said:
Both renunciation and the performance of selfless action lead to the highest bliss and liberation, but of the two, the performance of selfless action is better than the renunciation of works.

Metaphorical Interpretation

The conscience of every human being knows that true understanding of the world or God cannot be obtained without the guidance of a teacher and without practical work. For example, a pilot cannot learn how to fly an airplane safely without a teacher. Practice and the guidance of the teacher are more important than reading books about flying. Lord Krishna is saying that even though He explained the yoga of knowledge in detail, He nonetheless prefers the yoga of action. You cannot reach Self-realization by the more theoretical yoga of knowledge alone, but what is the yoga of action?

First, you must cultivate your spinal field, the royal road to God, using *karma yoga*. If you only sow seeds in the jungle without preparing the field, you will not produce a harvest. Next, you must clear your mind of worldly thoughts and rise above the mind, thought, intellect, and ego by practicing Kriya Yoga, which is *karma yoga.* Then you will automatically become calm, which is godly. Through this, your *ida, pingala, vajra,* and *chitra nadis* will change their positions, and your *sushumna* canal will open. Then you can easily lift your awareness up and keep it fixed inside the cranium.

Verse 3

jñeyaḥ sa nityasamnyāsī
yo na dveṣṭi na kānkṣati
nirdvandvo hi mahābāho
sukham bandhāt pramucyate

Translation

The person who neither hates nor desires and who has balanced all the pairs of opposites should be recognized as the one who has the spirit of renunciation, O mighty-armed Arjuna. Such a person is free from duality; such a person is easily set free from bondage.

Metaphorical Interpretation

A karma yogi must practice the scientific techniques of *prana karma,* the art of breath control. The *karma* yogi takes slow and long deep breaths, and as a result, is free from all worldly thoughts and desires, knowing that the indwelling soul is the only doer. One who constantly knows the soul becomes the soul. The more a Kriya yogi meditates in this fashion, while fulfilling practical everyday duties, the more the yogi realizes that the soul is doing everything. Such yogis also feel the soul's freedom from hatred, and from ups and downs. They are aware of the divine sound and the divine vibration; they feel that they are one with God, and that they have been one with Him always. Perceiving the soul within every single action makes one *maha bahu,* the best seeker of God. By practicing Kriya Yoga, balance is maintained in life and the divine is present in every action.

The Kriya yogi may be a householder. The sincere seeker can have a family and do household chores, but must constantly be a *sannyasi* during all this practical work. *Karma sannyasis* constantly offer the fruit of their work to the soul, the true Self. Being unattached to the fruits of action and being free from the influences of the pairs of opposites, the yogi enjoys the blissful state of renunciation.

Verse 4

sāmkhyayogau pṛthag bālāḥ
pravadanti na paṇḍitāḥ
ekam apy āsthitaḥ samyag
ubhayor vindate phalam

Translation

Children (unrealized persons) say that there are differences between the yoga of action and the yoga of knowledge, but by following either properly, a person gains the result of both (the result of either yoga is liberation).

Metaphorical Interpretation

By practicing *karma yoga,* (Kriya Yoga), people can cross the six centers of the spine. They can bring their awareness from the lower centers to the higher center. While participating in the material world and earning money, they can feel God working through them, feeling divine vibration, sound, and light in the coccygeal center. When they are experiencing the sex sense in the second center, they are aware that if God doesn't inhale for them, they will have no sex mood. Similarly, while eating, they realize that a dead person cannot have an appetite, cannot eat food, cannot digest food, and cannot obtain energy from food. So without God, the third center is inactive. Without the power of God, the fourth, fifth, and sixth centers are also inactive. Through regular practice of Kriya, one will be free from temptation and will enjoy peace in every thought, word, and deed.

God is in the aspect of the soul, sitting in the fontanel of every human being. That is the kingdom of God. That is heaven. In the Bible (John 8:23), Jesus said, "Ye are from beneath, I am from above," and (John 3:5), "Except a man be born of water and spirit, he cannot enter into the kingdom of God." The Bhagavad Gita (14:18) says: *urdhvam gacchanti sattva-sthā.* This phrase means, "Until you go above into the soul, you cannot perceive the formless stage and divinity." When you bring your consciousness up into the soul, in the pituitary, and then into God consciousness in the fontanel, you will have knowledge of God, you will be compassionately detached, and you will perceive Him.

Karma and *jñana* are given by God. When you experience them, you are continuously liberated, even while living daily life. This was the method of the ancient *munis* and *rishis,* who had families. By working you can learn. This is *karma yoga.* What you learn is *jñana.* Here is a simple example: Before you learn how to swim, you require a lifejacket and an instructor; you must work at it. But the moment you gain the knowledge of swimming, you do not require the lifejacket or the swimming master. This is *jñana yoga.* By practicing *prana karma,* we learn to feel the *prana,* the life force within us that enables us to undertake all activity. We know that the soul is the sole driver of our body.

Many people believe that *karma yoga, jñana yoga,* and *bhakti yoga* are separate yogas, but that is incorrect. These yogas are all interrelated and causally connected. As in a sweet treat, many ingredients are used; similarly, to make life more loving and sweet, you must use all these techniques for self-unfolding. If you don't transform your mind, thought, intellect, and ego into knowledge consciousness using *prana karma* (Kriya Yoga), you cannot perform *karma yoga,* and you will not achieve *jñana* and *bhakti.*

Verse 5

yat sāmkhyaiḥ prāpyate sthānam
tad yogair api gamyate
ekam sāmkhyam ca yogam ca
yaḥ paśyati sa paśyati

Translation

The ultimate goal reached by the *sankhya* (or *jñana*) yogi is also attained by the *karma* yogi; therefore, the one who perceives *sankhya yoga* and *karma yoga* as one has the true perception.

Metaphorical Interpretation

The Lord reveals the unity and harmony of all spiritual practices. When householders practice Kriya Yoga, the yoga of action (*karma sannyasa*), they constantly focus on the soul—before, after, and while performing worldly actions. They feel the soul doing whatever they do, and they experience constant liberation. This is *karma yoga*, the yoga of action. When *jñana* yogis, having shunned everything, keep their attention constantly in the fontanel, perceiving divine sound, light, and vibration, they attain the same liberation.

True seekers discover same result for *karma* and *jñana yoga*. The methods of the two, however, are different. *Jñana yoga* is more a path of intellectual pursuit, which may appear very difficult. All day and all night, *jñana* yogis keep their eyes, ears, noses, and mouths shut, and they do not retain any worldly sensation. Their awareness is always introverted. They do not earn money. They do not have sexual relations. They fast for long periods. They take baths seven to eight times a day. Nobody may touch them. If anybody does touch them, they bathe again. Many *jñana* yogis take only special food that they cook with their own hands. They are vegetarian. They have too many restrictions.

In the Bhagavad Gita (2:59), it says that your five sense organs and the five organs of action seek enjoyment: Your eyes want to see the beauty of the world; your ears want to hear songs and sweet talk; your mouth wants to eat delicious food; your stomach wants food; your sex organs want sexual enjoyment. If you try to avoid these pleasures, the desire for them will become stronger. *Jñana* yogis try to suppress the desire for the sense pleasures, but desire may hide in the mind until the sense organs create more. That is why it is very difficult to achieve liberation by *jñana yoga*.

For the yoga of action (*karma sannyasa*), there are no restrictions. You can maintain a family life. You can eat food according to your own desires. You must only practice Kriya and rise up and remain in the soul. You ask your soul whether it is good to eat, to drink, or to enjoy. If the soul permits it (if it is not vicious or evil or wrong), you can work without feeling like you are the doer; rather, you realize that the soul is the doer. Then you cannot commit a mistake. You always remain in soul. You experience continuous liberation. The yoga of action is easier than the yoga of knowledge.

By practicing the yoga of knowledge with the fullest austerity, devotees can reach Self-realization the fastest, because the yoga of knowledge contains the yoga of action within it; thus, the true *jñana yogis* also practice the yoga of action. The yoga of knowledge provides more seclusion, through which devotees become free from worldly attachments. Free from the worldly sense, they can quickly introvert their attention and reach the abode of God in the pituitary. Once there, they receive knowledge, consciousness, superconsciousness, cosmic consciousness, and wisdom.

Wisdom means attaining the Brahman stage, *nirvikalpa samadhi.* Having attained this stage, one is free from darkness, ignorance, and delusion. Adept practitioners also experience *sarvam khalvidam brahma,* which means that whatever they are see or hear, they perceive only the indwelling Self. In the Bhagavad Gita (2:59) it says, *rasavarjam raso 'py asya param dṛṣṭvā nivartate:* "Those who perceive and realize the presence of the power of God within themselves attain liberation."

Human beings can be liberated using the yoga of knowledge, as described in the second chapter of the Bhagavad Gita, as well as by practicing the yoga of action.

Verse 6

samnyāsas tu mahābāho
duḥkham āptum ayogataḥ
yogayukto munir brahma
nacireṇā 'dhigacchati

Translation

O Arjuna, the mighty-armed (powerful seeker of God-realization), renunciation is difficult to attain without the union of knowledge and action. But with this union, the person of meditation can quickly attain God-realization, the stage of Brahman.

Metaphorical Interpretation

When every step in our life is associated with knowledge, our life is full of love. This is the path of yoga. To attain this, everyone should practice a technique such as Kriya Yoga to transcend mind, thought, and body sense—to go from the lower centers to the upper center in the pituitary, and then up to the fontanel. These seekers must also bring their awareness back down into the lower centers to purify them. Then, free from delusion, they will achieve a single-minded meditation, the superconscious stage. Even a yogi practicing the yoga of knowledge must open the passage of the spine; after this, the power of God can be perceived in each center of the spine, even in the whole body.

Sannyasa means to perceive God in the whole body and the power of God in each center. Without the soul, one cannot earn money, enjoy sex, or be hungry. Whatever you do is because the soul is in the body. The soul is inhaling every single breath from the top, so work can be done by the body machine. To realize Brahman, the *brahmins* (those who are aware of Brahman) always pay double attention. Some attention is kept on the soul, the rest is on the actions they are performing. This is *jñana karma samuchaya*, which means that the union of knowledge and action is concentrated in the soul, and simultaneously on the work being performed (*karma*). Thusly united with the soul, there is no work.

Anyone who practices the Kriya Yoga technique enjoys constant emancipation. Hence, everyone should be calmly active and actively calm; this divine calm is godliness, the Brahman stage of *karma sannyasa*.

Verse 7

yogayukto viśuddhātmā
vijitātmā jitendriyaḥ
sarvabhūtātmabhūtātmā
kurvann api na lipyate

Translation

The realized yogi's mind is pure (ever-fixed on God); this genuine seeker has mastered keeping the body and the sense organs under control and perceives the Self in all beings. This person of true devotion is free even though he constantly acts.

Metaphorical Interpretation

To understand this verse, one must understand the following qualities of the yogi:

1. *vishuddhatma*: inner purity. This comes through selfless action, practicing breath control, and leading a disciplined lifestyle.
2. *vijitatma*: control over mind.
3. *jitendriya*: the art of using the senses intelligently, in God consciousness.
4. *sarvabhutatma bhutatma*: one who perceives one's own Self in all.

A yogi endowed with these qualities is free from nature's play, free from all attachment and delusion. A realized *karma* yogi practicing Kriya sincerely is never attached to worldly persons or absorbed in worldly things. Finding God's presence in all men and women, and feeling the oneness of the soul, He is not be absorbed in anything, but seeks God constantly. Like a mirror reflects all that it sees, the yogi sees everything in the material world, but is not affected by it. While working, the yogi remains free, absorbed in the divine, like liquid mercury, which rolls on paper, but is not absorbed into it.

Verses 8–9

nai 'va kimcit karomī 'ti
yukto manyeta tattvavit
paśyañ śṛṇvan spṛśañ jighrann
aśnan gacchan svapañ śvasan

pralapan visṛjan gṛhṇann
unmiṣan nimiṣann api
indriyāṇī 'ndriyārtheṣu
vartanta iti dhārayan

Translation

The one who is established in yoga knows the truth and thinks, "I do not do anything at all," even while seeing, hearing, touching, smelling, eating, moving, sleeping, breathing...

... speaking, releasing, holding, opening and closing the eyes. The yogi remembers that the body organs function only in relation to the objects of those organs.

Metaphorical Interpretation

Even while they are engrossed in sensory activities, human beings fully charged with God consciousness know that only their senses are busy with their objects. This awareness frees them from ego and restlessness, allowing them to always remain in the state of yoga.

When the devotees' minds rise and remain above in the pituitary and fontanel, they become detached, watching everything with introspection. With their third eye they work in the world and feel God working through them. They are ever thankful to know that God is the doer, because in this state of awareness, they cannot commit mistakes. When they hear and when they feel, they are grateful that God is hearing and feeling for them. In this way devotees also touch, see, smell, taste, walk, dream, contemplate, inhale, gossip, laugh, and open and close their eyes. Soon they feel very fortunate, because they know God is functioning in them through His material objects. They are detached; they do nothing.

Verse 10

brahmaṇy ādhāya karmāṇi
sangam tyaktvā karoti yaḥ
lipyate na sa pāpena
padmapattram ivā 'mbhasā

Translation

Those who perform actions, giving up attachment and offering their actions into Brahman, are not affected by sin, just as a lotus leaf is not wet by water.

Metaphorical Interpretation

Those who merge with Brahman (soul) become Brahman. They don't feel like they are working; they feel Brahman working through the body machine. Anyone in this state is free from sin, just as the lotus leaf can rest on water without getting wet. Every action accomplished in God consciousness becomes worship. Inner joy manifests without a root of bondage or attachment.

Before a doctor operates on a patient, the patient receives an anesthetic so that there is no worldly sense and no pain. Similarly, when a person ascends from his lower centers and raises his awareness into the cranium, to the soul, he or she merges in Brahman and forgets the bodily existence. Remaining detached, the devotee feels that whatever is done by the twenty-four material elements is done by the soul. In this stage the devotee cannot commit a sin. Nothing is sin to this yogi.

Verse 11

kāyena manasā buddhyā
kevelair indriyair api
yoginaḥ karma kurvanti
saṅgam tyaktvā 'tmaśuddhaye

Translation

With the help of the body, mind, intellect, and sense organs, the karma yogi works in a detached way for self-purification.

Metaphorical Interpretation

The soul is the energy source for the body, mind, intellect, and ten organs of perception and action, making them active. Understanding this makes one inwardly pure.

By practicing the authentic Kriya Yoga, a true seeker can purify the mind, brain, and blood, and withdraw the awareness away from the mind's normal extroverted activity. While perceiving that the indwelling soul is doing everything, only divine joy is felt, and one always proceeds on the right path. This is divine *prana karma*, the yoga of action.

Verse 12

yuktaḥ karmaphalam tyaktvā
śāntim āpnoti naiṣṭhikīm
ayuktaḥ kāmakāreṇa
phale sakto nibadhyate

Translation

The one who is established in yoga, giving up expectation, gains eternal peace. On the other hand, one who is not committed to yoga, led by desires, is bound, attached to the results.

Metaphorical Interpretation

Yogis are ever fixed on the soul. They feel the soul working through them. Those who are absorbed in the material world are always caught up in desire for the fruits of their work, so they are always bound by those fruits. A yogi is truly free from the bondage of the fruits of action, enjoying inner freedom.

Worldly people are always absorbed in natural phenomena, so their biological forces lead them to commit mistake after mistake. Consequently, they have more worldly ambition, and their minds cannot go above the dorsal (heart) center. On the other hand, if they practice Kriya Yoga, they can learn to withdraw their sensory awareness from below and bring it above the heart center, and even above the cervical (vacuum) center, up to the medulla, the abode of soul. The divine kingdom is there, where divine thought automatically arises.

Without the union of knowledge and action, people are not aware of the soul. With this union, human beings perceive divinity in every action. The more devotees meditate, the more they perceive inexpressible divine bliss. With meditation, they become compassionately detached and feel joy, because they know the soul is constantly functioning through their bodies. In contrast, those who do not meditate remain absorbed in delusion, illusion, and error; they experience disease, dissatisfaction, and bondage.

Verse 13

sarvakarmāṇi manasā
saṁnyasyā 'ste sukham vaśī
navadvāre pure dehī
nai 'va kurvan na kārayan

Translation

A self-controlled yogi always remains happily in the physical body, the city with nine gates, performing no actions, and not causing others to act.

Metaphorical Interpretation

The mind of each human being has three levels. The first level is below the navel and includes the coccygeal, sacral, and lumbar centers. The second level is between the navel and the pituitary and includes the dorsal, cervical, and soul centers. The third level of mind is between the pituitary and the fontanel, at the top of the skull. The Lord is explaining to Arjuna that the minds of those who ascend above the third level are completely transformed into cosmic consciousness. Their minds merge in *brahmananda*, the divine bliss, and they are beyond pleasure and pain and bodily sensation.

The body has nine gates: two eyes, two ears, two nostrils, a mouth, a genital opening, and the anus. The five sense telephones and the nine gates of the body can be open, and the devotee can talk, hear, see, feel, and smell, and so forth. Through a self-controlled life, one has a clear sense of the world, and at the same time is free from pleasure and pain.

When a devotee enters the third level of his mind and enters the superconscious stage, only the soul is felt. No one can touch the soul, cut it, or burn it. In soul consciousness, the devotee can partake of any action, but remains detached from pleasure and pain. A realized person, who constantly remains in the third layer of mind, in the soul, feels the soul doing everything. In this state, the devotee is detached from everything and merges with the divine.

Just as mad people may wander out into the cold, without clothes, not knowing whether they have eaten or not, so extremely spiritual people remain in the thrall of the marvelous power of God. When obliged to eat, they sense the power of God eating through the gate of the mouth, while remaining deeply absorbed in the soul without interruption.

Verses 14–15

na kartṛtvam na karmāṇi
lokasya sṛjati prabhuḥ
na karmaphalasamyogam
svabhāvas tu pravartate

nā 'datte kasyacit pāpam
na cai 'va sukṛtam vibhuḥ
ajñānenā 'vṛtam jñānam
tena muhyanti jantavaḥ

Translation

The power of God (Ishwara or Prabhu) does not create the actions or reactions of any person. God does not act, nor does He make contact with the fruits of actions; rather one's own nature leads to action.

The omnipresent soul does not sin or perform pious actions. Knowledge is covered by ignorance; thereby people are deluded.

Metaphorical Interpretation

The Lord (soul) is saying: "O Arjuna, you are not doing anything. The tendencies of your previous *karma* are doing everything. Your knowledge is covered by ignorance. *Atma*, the soul, does everything." The soul is like divine electricity. No fan, no light, no song, and no theater exist in electric current. The air is in the fan. The light is in the bulb. Song is in the radio. Theater is in the television. However, when you plug your table lamp into the electric socket, you will see light from the current. When you plug in your table fan, you feel air from the electric current. When you plug your radio into the electric current, you hear song. When you plug your television into the electric current, you have theater. And the moment you unplug everything, you have nothing. Your soul functions through the five sense telephones and the nine gates of your body city just like electricity manifests through an appliance.

A human being is twofold, having a gross body, which is unreal, and having an invisible soul, the reality within the gross biological body. Your gross body is a delusion. Your invisible body, soul, is real, like the electricity. Without electricity, all electrical appliances are useless. Without your soul, you are a dead body; you are not a scientist, doctor, engineer, or anything. Everything you do is done by the soul. If you cultivate your soul and try to remain alert in the soul constantly, you will feel the soul as the sole doer behind every action, even while you live and work as a householder.

In this verse, the Lord emphasizes the destiny of every human being. Each human being has a different destiny. The soul cannot do anything without the preordained force of destiny. Accordingly, some people are doctors, some are engineers, some are scientists, some are administrative officers, and some are laborers—but without the soul current or energy or power of God, they are only lifeless bodies. In the fourteenth verse, the Lord tells Arjuna that "According to your destiny, you are a *kshatriya*, born into a warrior family; therefore, by destiny, you must fight in the war. It is ordained. I am not forcing you, but you must fight."

In this world, everyone acts according to destiny. In this way, they evolve. But without the soul, destiny cannot become manifest. That is why everyone should meditate and seek the soul. We are born only for soul culture.

In Verse 15, the Lord is explaining that the theory of evolution is based on heredity, environment, and culture. Since we work according to our destiny and by the power of soul, we cannot accomplish whatever our destiny is without the soul. Any human being, however educated or wealthy, can surely perceive the imperishable soul through deep meditation. If you can perceive the powerful, formless soul, you will evolve rapidly.

Verses 16–17

jñānena tu tad ajñānam
yeṣām nāśitam ātmanaḥ
teṣām ādityavaj jñānam
prakāśayati tat param

tadbuddhayas tadātmānas
tanniṣṭhās tatparāyaṇāḥ
gacchanty apunarāvṛttim
jñānanirdhūtakalmaṣāḥ

Translation

For those who attain knowledge (soul consciousness), ignorance disappears. Just as all things become visible when the sun rises in the sky, knowledge allows a person to perceive the all-pervading power of God (Brahman).

There are those whose minds and intellects are firmly absorbed in that (Brahman), those who are constantly centered in the soul for whom the ultimate end is that (Brahman); these people become free from sin by their constant soul consciousness. They need not go back into the delusion (of family bondage). They enjoy constant liberation.

Metaphorical Interpretation

Where there is light, there is no darkness. Darkness hinders clear perception. All human beings who overcome delusion, illusion, and error will perceive God and attain continuous liberation. They become completely free from mind, thought, intellect, ego and the worldly sense when they practice Kriya Yoga, which is *karma yoga*. Through this practice, they become completely free from all worldly thoughts and attain *paravastha*, or partial *samadhi*. From here, they go on to the formless stage and bliss. They may even reach *nirvikalpa samadhi*. After meditation, as these adepts gradually return to the human state, they recognize that the soul is the true sun illuminating the mundane theater. In this state, they feel the soul functioning in accord with their destiny while performing all material and worldly actions.

The seventeenth verse explains *samprajñata samadhi*, which is conscious *samadhi*. In this state, the devotee is always watching the soul functioning behind every action. Just as the knower of Brahman becomes Brahman, so the one who knows the soul in every action becomes the soul. These liberated persons feel spiritual enlightenment all the time, while still in the body, and after death they achieve *sayujya mukti*. They merge in God. Thus a person is free from all sins, which are soul forgetfulness.

Verse 18

vidyāvinasampanne
brāhmaṇe gavi hastini
śuni cai 'va śvapāke ca
paṇḍitāḥ samadarśinaḥ

Translation

Indeed, wise people see the Brahman in a Brahmin, a low-caste person, a cow, an elephant, or a dog. Nothing distinguishes them in the perception of a Self-realized person.

Metaphorical Interpretation

A yogi achieves equanimity and perceives the divine equally in everything. During deep Kriya Yoga meditation, dualities and differentiation vanish. Only pure consciousness, the soul, the all-pervading One, is perceived. To the God-realized person, in practical life, all the various forms and species of creation are superimposed on the all-pervading One, the power of God. Therefore, spiritually advanced people perceive the undifferentiated soul in everything, including the high-born Brahmin, the animals, the ignorant, and the sinners. They behave impartially, mercifully, lovingly, and kindly to every creature and treat them with respect. They perceive their own soul, the Self, in every creature.

Verse 19

ihai 'va tair jitaḥ sargo
yeṣām sāmye sthitam manaḥ
nirdoṣam hi samam brahma
tasmād brahmaṇi te sthitāḥ

Translation

The cycle of birth and death is defeated by those whose minds are in balance, who have conquered everything and are free from defects. Perceiving Brahman everywhere and achieving balance of mind amount to the same thing. Self-realized persons, due to their balance of mind, are in the stage of Brahman.

Metaphorical Interpretation

Everything is born, lives for a while, and then dies. In this way, the cycle of birth and death continues in this life. A self-controlled person, a yogi, is a liberated from this cycle.

Most human beings remain in the extroverted state, which results in much unpleasantness and frustration. Only by practicing Kriya Yoga will people find extreme calm and balance of mind, which can lead every human being to the gate of God. Remaining in this consciousness, bad things will not come to them and they will avoid mistakes. They will continue with their household duties, but they will also discover God-realization.

Verse 20

na prahṛṣyet priyam prāpya
no 'dvijet prāpya cā 'priyam
sthirabuddhir asammūḍho
brahmavid brahmaṇi sthitaḥ

Translation

Those who know Brahman, who are firmly established in the Brahman, are not delighted with gain or perturbed by loss, because they are steady in the superconscious state, free from delusion, and fixed upon Brahman.

Metaphorical Interpretation

Anyone who remains fixed in the pituitary and on the soul has the power and qualities of God. God is pure, perfect, kind, and loving. God is not jealous, boastful, irritable, or rude. God is carefree. We make many mistakes, but God does punish them. Mistakes are caused because of ignorance. Realized persons have entered the state of God. They are free from pleasure and pain.

Human beings are extremely restless and absorbed in worldly things. Kriya Yoga meditation can remove the distraction of worldly sensations within five minutes; it can focus your attention on God-realization in every facet of life.

Verse 21

bāhyasparśeṣv asaktātmā
vindaty ātmani yat sukham
sa brahmayogayuktātmā
sukham akṣayam aśnute

Translation

The yogi can introvert the mind, pulling it away from external (sense) objects, and can sit in the soul with the experience of fullness. By doing this, the yogi realizes divine bliss. Because yogis are engaged in the meditation of Brahman, they enjoy perennial bliss that is not dependent on anything.

Metaphorical Interpretation

Meditation brings balance and harmony in life, so sense objects cannot attract the mind. When human beings practice the higher and deepest Kriya Yoga techniques, they enter into the cranium, the divine kingdom, where they merge into the soul and divine joy. All human actions are conducted by the soul, and in every action, Kriya yogis can remain compassionately detached. They feel the body machine being driven by the indwelling Self. Brahman is bliss; one who realizes this remains in the blissful state. Yogis perceive nothing but imperishable divine bliss in the world.

Verse 22

ye hi samsparśajā bhogā
duḥkhayonaya eva te
ādyantavantaḥ kaunteya
na teṣu ramate budhaḥ

Translation

O son of Kunti (finest intellectual giant), Arjuna! Enjoyments born from contact with sense objects are indeed the source of unhappiness, for they have a beginning and an end. Wise persons do not find joy in them (they experience no joy from bondage).

Metaphorical Interpretation

The metaphorical meaning of this verse is very intricate. First, the Lord addresses Arjuna as Kaunteya, the son of Kunti. Arjuna is the third son of Kunti. Arjuna was not born by sexual pleasure; rather Kunti kept her attention fixed in the master gland, the pituitary, and then withdrew her inhalation from the navel (lumbar) center, and conceived. The navel center is very dangerous. The meditation Kunti achieved is called *ḍa-pha sadhana.* In the lumbar center there is a ten-petalled lotus, called *ḍa-pha,* after the seed letters of the Sanskrit alphabet on the petals of the lotus.

Food is digested from the navel center. After digestion, the food is transformed into a milky substance, and that milky substance gradually descends to the sex center where it becomes a condensed, milky substance. When one enjoys sexual activity, it comes out through the generative center. Then that condensed milky substance becomes more solidified into a protein-like substance and drops to the lowest center at the coccyx. Our entire energy, our divinity, is stored in the lowest center and is called *kundalini shakti.* This means that our whole body and brain are formed from food, and the food is transformed into *maya,* delusion. In the Guru Gita it says, *pindam kundalini shaktim,* which means your whole body is engrossed in delusion, illusion, and error. It also says, *hamsa iti udahritam,* which means that in our pituitary there is the *ham* (*bija*) seed, and *sa,* the soul, which is always covered in the three lower centers. So, food is the cause of all our delusion. Yet, food also causes illumination and emancipation. Our food must be spiritual and well-balanced *(as explained in the Bhagavad Gita 6:16).*

The derivative meaning of Kunti is *kun-dhatu* plus *ti.* The verb *kun* means to have the finest conception; Kunti had the finest concentration and conception of God. The place of Kunti is in the pituitary. Kunti thought that since food is the cause of all good and bad things, she would withdraw her inhalation from the food center into the pituitary center, the soul center. Kunti meditated, and within a short period the divine power came out from the food center into the pituitary. In this way she conceived a most powerful warrior child, who was given the name Arjuna.

If we do not eat, we won't have energy, strength, eyesight, or the finest of brains. If we do not have the finest brain, we cannot fight evil, delusion, and our bad tendencies. A mistake is not for the mistake, it is for correction. Because Arjuna ate food, he had many bad qualities in the beginning. In fact, at first, he was not willing to fight the Kauravas, who represent all the evil qualities in the human body.

The Lord knows all, so He thought that He could train Arjuna to come up from the lower centers to the upper center. Because Arjuna was born from the upper center of his mother, Kunti, the Lord believed He could easily convince him. First, the Lord told Arjuna to withdraw all his senses from the lower center, and then He taught Arjuna the Kriya Yoga technique.

The name "Arjuna" is derived from *a-rajju-na. A* means not, *rajju* means rope, and *na* is without bondage, although appearing to be in bondage. Therefore, the name "Arjuna" describes one who is not in bondage to the world, because he was born from the pituitary.

The Lord first told Arjuna to come up to the pituitary, so Arjuna could be freed from worldly bondage, so that he would realize that the soul (Krishna) was doing everything. In this way, the Lord (Krishna) became the driver of Arjuna's "chariot," and Arjuna sat behind Him. Arjuna fought with evils according to Krishna's (the soul's) instructions. The Lord instructed Arjuna: "Remain with Me, be merged in Me, and realize that you are not the doer in anything; I am the doer. You do not know My real existence. Before your birth, I was with you. After your birth, I constantly inhale for you and lead you to the truth. You should always feel that whatever you are doing is done by Me. Maintain implicit faith, love, and loyalty in Me. Then you will have true intellect and true liberation."

By this example the Lord is telling all human beings: "Come up to Me in the pituitary within your body chariots. I am the soul, the only driver of all human beings. If you follow Me, although you are in the world, you will be free. If I did not inhale in you, you would have no worldly experience."

Verse 23

śaknotī 'hai 'va yaḥ soḍhum
prāk śarīravimokṣaṇāt
kāmakrodhodbhavam vegam
sa yuktaḥ sa sukhī naraḥ

Translation

Those who can live in the world and control the forces of passion and anger before they die are yogis. They are indeed happy.

Metaphorical Interpretation

The Lord is symbolically explaining the divine qualities of human beings who can perfect their self-examination and introspection. The Lord is saying that from self-examination, human beings attain Self-knowledge, humility, steadfastness, the Brahman stage, and perennial joy. The Lord is also saying that when egoism and discrimination disappear, people perceive no distinctions of caste, color, race, creed, or country; they feel the presence of God in everything. Happiness and unhappiness, profit and loss, and good and bad are equal. Liberated devotees feel that their worldly duties are done by the soul alone. They know that all worldly things are perishable. Only the soul is imperishable.

This understanding can be attained by soul culture; therefore, always remain alert in the soul. As sleeping human beings feel nothing, so true devotees feel nothing. This is the *shambhavi* stage. But these devotees are not sleeping, they are in an extremely divine state. They don't become absorbed in pleasure or pain. They are not dead, but passion, anger, pride, and sorrow cannot bewilder them any longer. Working like machines, they feel only the divine in everything. They are free from evil, ups and downs, and pitfalls.

A concrete example of the *shambhavi* stage would be the death of a husband who leaves a youthful wife and two children. The grief-stricken wife hugs the dead body of her husband, and the children cry and throw themselves on his body. The dead husband does not experience sexual pleasure from his wife's hug or affection from his children. With this same kind of absolute dispassion, a highly realized person leading a family life will remain in divine bliss, completely detached from the worldly life about him. This is *karma sannyasa*. Those who achieve this stage do not leave their families; they are far more powerful than a monk.

Verse 24

yo 'ntaḥsukho 'ntarārāmas
tathā 'ntarjyotir eva yaḥ
sa yogī brahmanirvāṇam
brahmabhūto 'dhigacchati

Translation

The person who is fulfilled in the Self, who revels in the Self, and who is awakened in the inner light of the Self, that yogi alone, fixed in Brahman, merges in Brahman, and gains the freedom that is Brahman.

Metaphorical Interpretation

There are two bodies in each human being: One is the gross or physical body—the mind and senses—and the other is the soul body. The soul does everything, so a person who avoids acknowledging the soul cannot find peace of mind, and many troubles will follow. But every human being who feels that the soul is the real body, who believes that without the soul the body and mind cannot do anything, will feel divine joy in every action.

A person is a yogi if he or she fixes the mind on the soul during every breath. This continuous soul awareness leads to absorption in love, joy, happiness, and the ultimate experience of inner peace.

Verse 25

labhante brahmanirvāṇam
ṛṣayaḥ kṣīṇakalmaṣāḥ
chinnadvaidhā yatātmānaḥ
sarvabhūtahite ratāḥ

Translation

The *rishi* (a sage or person of right vision), who is free from impurities and has resolved all doubts, who is self-controlled, and who works for the welfare of all beings, is absorbed in *brahmanirvana* (gains liberation).

Metaphorical Interpretation

Meditation cleans the mind, the senses, and ultimately, your life. In a pure mind, there is no cloud of confusion and doubt. The life of a pure-minded person is saturated with love, and through an exemplary life, this person lives only for others.

Those who have attained *nirvikalpa samadhi* have the right vision for uplifting the masses. They teach Kriya Yoga practically. Perceiving the living soul in every human being makes them very humble towards everyone. They perceive that everyone is worthy of worship. They become very simple and liberal and try to serve any person who has difficulties and needs. They are pure like God, like a baby.

Verse 26

kāmakrodhaviyuktānām
yatīnām yatacetasām
abhito brahmanirvāṇam
vartate viditātmanām

Translation

The renunciates who are free from passion and anger, who have self-control and are Self-realized, attain liberation in Brahman both in this life and in the hereafter (they are always in Brahman consciousness).

Metaphorical Interpretation

Passion and anger are the doors to downfall. They bring unhappiness and misfortune. A yogi is free from such vices very easily.

The Lord is saying that by the practice of *karma yoga*, which is Kriya Yoga, a devotee can easily merge into all-pervading Brahman. Firm, pinpointed attention in soul consciousness produces constant liberation. Furthermore, when, through action, devotees are extremely absorbed in *samadhi*, they have eternal, inexpressible bliss and inexpressible effulgence within them. Absorbed in the formless all-pervading God, they enjoy constant emancipation. These *karma* yogis are in the state of *karma sannyasa*, freed from all worldly viciousness. After death they will be one with God.

Verses 27–28

sparśān kṛtvā bahir bāhyāmś
cakṣuś cai 'vā 'ntare bhruvoḥ
prāṇāpānau samau kṛtvā
nāsābhyantaracāriṇau

yatendriyamanobuddhir
munir mokṣaparāyaṇaḥ
vigatecchābhayakrodho
yaḥ sadā mukta eva saḥ

Translation

A person can be free and liberated while living in the body by shutting out all external sense objects, keeping the vision in between the eyebrows, and equalizing the outgoing and incoming breaths rhythmically through the nostrils.

Thus, the organs of action, senses, mind, and intellect become introverted, and thereby, the person is ever free from desire, fear, and anger, and attains the highest goal of life—liberation.

Metaphorical Interpretation

After a long introduction, the Lord describes the technique of Kriya Yoga. These beautiful verses teach the practical path of breath control.

Krishna is telling Arjuna how to cool down his mind to achieve God-realization. Krishna teaches that you must sit on a thick woolen carpet without thinking about anything. Then take a deep inhalation as you would during sleep, because during sleep you do not experience sound, touch, sight, taste, or smell; you have no passion, anger, pride, sorrow, anxiety, body sense, or worldly sense. Since the inhalation is not exactly the same as when you sleep, you must follow the instructions of your master.

Breath control is self-control. Breath mastery is thought mastery. With this mastery, you can be free from mind, thought, intellect, and ego, the main hindrances to meditation. When you sit for meditation many thoughts may enter your mind, but with Kriya Yoga practice you can quell the worldly sense within five minutes. Fix your mind between your two eyebrows. Take deep inhalations and exhalations.

If you practice in this manner for a short period and calmly seek the soul near the pituitary, you will feel a divine sensation. Your mind will remain absorbed in the soul, and you will perceive only divine light, sound, and vibration. Then, you need not watch your incoming and outgoing breaths. The breath will be very feeble, moving slowly inside the nostrils.

You must have the guidance of an experienced and realized teacher, who can help you to reach the introverted stage. Your mind will become completely transformed into knowledge and consciousness. Many other techniques are required for you to attain the formless stage, but gradually you can reach conscious *samadhi* and divine joy. There are seven levels of *samadhi*. Gradually, you will enter all these states.

With the guidance of a realized master you will ultimately achieve the *brahmanirvana* state. In this state the devotee is absorbed in the soul, feeling the soul doing everything, in every action, from within. The devotee feels divine vibration in the entire body, in every body part. The devotee may live in the material world, but perceives only perennial joy. All his addictions and worldliness disappear, and the devotee develops thorough control over food and drink. Food and drink will help lead the devotee to the state of divine being. (*See Bhagavad Gita 6:17.*) True devotees who follow all of the instructions of the Bhagavad Gita will have complete divine perception and God-realization.

Verse 29

bhoktāram yajñatapasām
sarvalokamaheśvaram
suhṛdam sarvabhūtānām
jñātvā mām śāntim ṛcchati

Translation

One who knows me as the Lord of all spiritual sacrifices (*yajña*) and disciplines (*tapas*), as great the Lord of the worlds, and as a friend of all beings attains peace (liberation).

Metaphorical Interpretation

The Lord is explaining the true cosmic, supreme nature of the Lord of the universe. He is also saying that any devotee who knows and realizes this nature will find supreme bliss and complete liberation.

In this chapter, the Lord places emphasis on *karma sannyasa*. *Karma* means work, but that work is done by the soul alone. Without a soul, a human being cannot inhale. The power of God inhales through every human being. Only the soul performs actions, not the human being. *San* means completely, and *nyasa* means watching the power of God. So a *san-nyasa* is someone who constantly observes that whatever is done is not done by the body, but by the power of God. *Sannyasa* means to be completely detached. A *sannyasi* is someone who has left everything, who has completed *karma* and *jñana,* who perceives the true love for God, *bhakti*, and who remains in the world in a completely detached way. *Karma sannyasa* is to be immersed only in God, perceiving that all actions are governed by the soul.

God is constantly performing actions through every human being, through animal beings, and through all His creation. Without the power of God, there would be nothing. Even knowledge (*jñana*) and love for God (*bhakti*) are not possible without *karma*. A God-realized teacher knows that evolution is not possible without destiny, environment, and culture.

In this verse, the Lord is indirectly saying that the power of God's action fills everything from top to bottom. This verse is about *yajña*, which means sacrifices, and *tapas*, which means austerities. But practically speaking, Krishna is not describing sacrifices and austerities such as the fire ceremony. Krishna is revealing that the soul is the real fire in every human being. The Isha Upanishad (18) says, *agne naya supatha*, which means: "O soul fire, remain in my cranium. Please lead me to the royal road to God." In the Bhagavad Gita (15:14) it says, *aham vaishvanaro bhutva*: "I am the *vaishvanara* (navel) fire in the stomach of each human being. I eat food through the mouth of every person, and I remain in the food." The power of God remains in the food because God is all-pervading. A dead person cannot eat. The real fire ceremony takes place when a realized devotee perceives that he gives oblation to the divine fire with every inhalation (symbolized by butter oil or *ghee* in the ceremony).

Similarly, *tapas* is not a question of austerities, it is a question of perception. One must perceive that the power of God eats through the mouth. This is true *karma sannyasa*, a living sacrifice to the living soul abiding within every human being. The soul is the enjoyer (*bhokta*), enjoying with relish through the mouth of every human being. Although soul is the non-doer, nothing can be done without the soul.

The power of God gives appetite to the body via the *vaishvanara* fire in the stomach. When a devotee perceives this karma (digestion) as *brahma karma* (God is digesting), this becomes *karma sannyasa*. This oblation of eating food is *brahma karma*. It is *karma sannyasa*.

In the Bhagavad Gita (4:24) it says that everything is an oblation to the divine fire inside the human being. The living fire of the living soul is constantly saying: "Please, in your every work watch Me, love Me, offer everything to Me. Please forget your human madness. Constantly watch Me within you." God is saying: "I am digesting your food. I am giving you energy and life. If you always watch Me, you will achieve a divine life."

The power of God is the enjoyer within you. He is enjoying everything. Watch His every action in you and in every human being. He is the well-wisher and intimate friend of every human being. Without Him, we have no existence. Feel and realize this and you will realize eternal joy, peace, and bliss. This is the real truth of *karma sannyasa yoga*.

This is the scientific and metaphorical interpretation of the Upanishads and yoga in the fifth chapter of the Bhagavad Gita.

Summary

This chapter is called as "The Yoga of Renunciation of Action." In both the historical and mythological context, both Shri Krishna and Arjuna are householders leading family lives. This chapter prepares the field for "The Yoga of Self-Mastery," the practice of yoga and meditation.

This chapter contains twenty-nine verses: The first verse is attributed to Arjuna, and the rest to the Lord. Those can be summed up as follows:

Verse 1: Arjuna asks about *samkhya* (knowledge) and yoga (path of self-control and meditation).

Verse 2: *Karma* (action) and renunciation (*sannyas*) are equally good for emancipation, but *karma yoga* is the superior path.

Verse 3: A *nitya sannyasi* (complete renunciate) enjoys constant liberation.

Verse 4–5: A description of the different aspects of intelligent and foolish personalities.

Verse 6: Yoga is superior to knowledge.

Verses 7–12: These verses explain beautifully how a yogi lives a life of detachment in spite of his actions through the sense organs.

Verse 13: The nine gates of the body.

Verses 14–15: These verses indicate who is the doer and how to renounce attachment.

Verses 16–17: These verses narrate how the inner experience dawns through destruction of ignorance and how to achieve liberation.

Verses 18–23: The result of self-knowledge is equal regard for all beings, firm establishment in God-consciousness, and indestructible bliss.

Verse 24–25: A description of a yogi's practice and experiences.

Verse 26: A description of the liberated state.

Verses 27–28: The path of meditation through breath-control (*pranayama*).

Verse 29: The concluding verse explains the state of liberation.

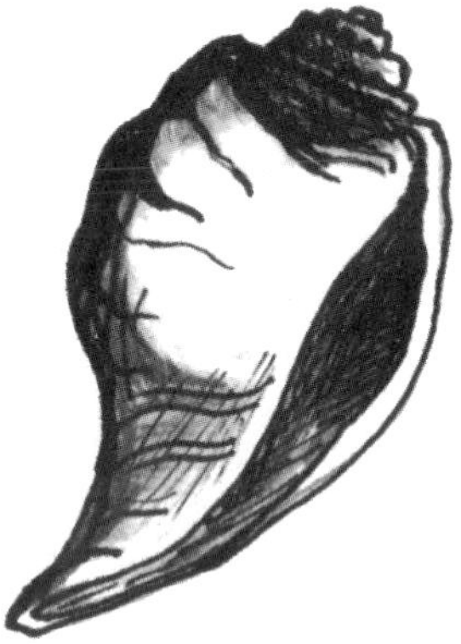

Chapter 6

Atma Samyama Yoga

The Yoga of Self-Mastery

Introduction

Being in the state of eternal union and imperishable bliss is the essence of spiritual life, and this is yoga. This chapter specifically emphasizes the significance of meditation, self-control, and the easy path to Self-realization.

Toward the end of the last chapter, the Lord described meditation through breath control (Verse 25 and 26), but did not completely describe this path. Also, wrong understanding and dogmatic ideas have caused many to think that yoga is a difficult path with many obstacles. However, in truth, it is simple and without hardship. It is a path of moderation and contentment.

In the previous chapter, the Lord said that one can attain the ultimate stage of liberation even while performing worldly activities. In this chapter, the Lord explains how to reach this state of inner detachment and renunciation.

Verse 1

śrībhagavān uvāca
anāśritaḥ karmaphalam
kāryam karma karoti yaḥ
sa samnyāsī ca yogī ca
na niragnir na cā 'kriyaḥ

Translation

The blessed Lord replied:
The one who performs inner duty (meditation) in a selfless way, not expecting the result of action, is a *sannyasi* and a yogi—not one who perfunctorily performs rituals or other actions.

Metaphorical Interpretation

When you read spiritual scriptures for clues to the truth, it is your soul (the Lord within, here called Krishna) that inspires you to search without, knowing that search will eventually lead you within to Him.

The Lord is describing the qualities of a yogi and a person of renunciation. He says that soul culture brings detachment from the results of all actions. A detached yogi does not think he is doing any work or even practicing Kriya. Instead, he knows that whatever is done is done by the soul. Even the fruits (results) of karma are avoided by those who are not attached, who know they are not the doer. One who is constantly watching the soul is free from all actions and is truly a *sannyasi* and a yogi.

Sincere meditation done by a yogi for Self-realization is the only truly selfless work, because meditative work is done by the Lord within, who remains selfless even though He has manifested as a human soul. Inhalation is the real oblation to the divine fire. If a yogi does not inhale oxygen, which is divine karma, then the soul fire, which is our real life, cannot exist in the body. Therefore, yogis always watch their inhalation. This is a yogi's real work. Every inhalation rises and touches the real fire, the spiritual fire, which is our whole life and our soul. Watching the inhaled breath is selfless spiritual work. There is no expectation of reward because the soul does the work, and therefore, the fruits of action easily go to the soul.

Yogic work is selfless in another way because your realizations are tested in the world. Even a monk must be very broadminded and must accept everyone as a child of God. This is not an easy task—it requires great selflessness, detachment, and concentration. If you are successful and achieve breath control and become Self-realized, it will inspire others to seek their birthright as well. Everyone is born for God-realization; every human body is made from Brahman.

Verse 2

yam samnyāsam iti prāhur
yogam tam viddhi pāṇḍava
na hy asamnyastasamkalpo
yogī bhavati kaścana

Translation

O Pandava (Arjuna), know that what is called renunciation (*sannyasa*) is also yoga. No one can be a yogi who has not shunned his own selfish desires.

Metaphorical Interpretation

The Lord calls Arjuna "Pandava." The word *pandava* comes from the word *panda*, which means the state of superconsciousness. The person who remains in superconsciousness is beyond body, mind, intellect, and soul. In Patañjali's Yoga Sutras, it says, *yoga-citta-vṛtti-nirodha*, which means that those who practice Kriya Yoga remain in the soul and are above mind, thought, and the worldly senses.

Both the yogi and the *sannyasi* remain in the state of cosmic consciousness. In that state they do not come down from constant absorption in the soul, which remains above. They remain free from the fruits of all actions, and they are free from all ambitions. A yogi is a real sannyasi, and a sannyasi is a true yogi; they have both renounced all attachment and are always absorbed in the bliss of the Self.

Verse 3

āruruksor muner yogam
karma kāraṇam ucyate
yogārūḍhasya tasyai 'va
śamaḥ kāraṇam ucyate

Translation

For the *muni* (person of meditation) wishing to attain yoga, work is said to be the means, but for the person who has attained yoga, total renunciation is said to be the means.

Metaphorical Interpretation

This chapter is explaining *dhyana yoga* as well as *abhyasa yoga. Dhyana* means meditation, and *abhyasa* means practice. Practice makes one perfect. Everyone should meditate and practice watching the power of God that is always functioning from within. By this they can attain God-realization.

Yogis who want to attain the supreme stage of God-realization must practice meditation such as Kriya Yoga very deeply. These yogis retain some worldly ambition, but they feel the power of God through these ambitions. The kingdom of nature, the body nature and the worldly senses, is below the pituitary, in the first through the fifth centers (chakras). These yogis remain in the body nature, but withdraw their sensory awareness from the five lower centers to the upper center.

If they meditate very deeply and transcend the five sense organs, they can achieve the superconscious stage and can even rise above the pituitary center to the fontanel. This is called *viraja.* For such yogis, there is no phenomenal existence. There is only noumenon: Mother Nature. The body nature creates delusion, but the Mother Nature dissolves illusion. When illusion disappears, yogis merge with God.

When you practice the yoga of action, you will automatically reach the superconscious stage. When you ascend above the pituitary and the fontanel, you will merge into the soul. If you remain in that state, you always will have balance of mind and divinity. Before that, you must keep your awareness in the pituitary. Descending below this center, you experience natural phenomena where you have some awareness of the material world, but above it, you are merged with the soul.

After attaining Self-realization, even when you are involved in worldly actions, you will always feel that soul is very kind to you. The soul is always working in your whole system, and you will have balance of mind and constant Self-realization. Any yogi who is a family person who obtains this stage is like Lahiri Mahasaya. Such a yogi will always remain in the soul and can have super power. Kriya Yoga meditation gives you power and peace. It augments all aspects of your life, both the mundane and the spiritual.

Verse 4

yadā hi ne 'ndriyārtheṣu
na karmasv anuṣajjate
sarvasamkalpasamnyāsī
yogārūḍhas tado 'cyate

Translation

One who is attached neither to sense objects nor to action, who has shunned all selfish thoughts and desires, is said to have attained yoga (liberation).

Metaphorical Interpretation

Realized yogis realize that the soul is the sole doer, that their bodies, minds, hands, and legs cannot work without the soul. In this state yogis feel a divine joy in everything. Yogis don't feel like they are doing anything; rather they feel the soul doing everything through their body machines.

For example, little children walk around without any clothes and don't feel embarrassed. They walk, eat, and move from one place to another while remaining carefree. Similarly, realized persons remain absorbed in the soul and are not affected by worldly influences, good or bad. They are free from all attachment and attraction.

Verse 5

uddhared ātmanā 'tmānam
nā 'tmānam avasādayet
ātmai 'va hy ātmano bandhur
ātmai 'va ripur ātmanaḥ

Translation

With the aid of your Self (soul consciousness), lift yourself up from delusion. Don't degrade yourself, for you are your own friend and you are your own enemy.

Metaphorical Interpretation

A realized master will purify your whole spine, which is covered with jungles of matter, as well as your five sense organs. With the help of this purification, soon you will feel divine sensation, divine light, divine sound, and love for God. A realized master will teach you, but you must practice daily, regularly, and sincerely, with love.

Self-effort is the key to success. The Lord stresses it. When you keep your attention on the soul and you control your mind, thought, intellect, ego, body sense, and worldly sense using breath control, you can easily elevate your awareness above the lower centers. As a result, you will know that you are not a limited, ordinary human being, but rather a limitless soul.

According to theory, evolution occurs partly as the result of environment and culture. If you don't learn from your environment, which is your teacher, and do not meditate deeply and sincerely, which is soul culture, you are your own enemy. On the other hand, if you follow your spiritual master sincerely and make your best effort, you will surely achieve Self-realization someday. Then you will feel the power of God within you in every moment of your daily life. Thus, you will be your own friend.

Verse 6

bandhur ātmā 'tmanas tasya
yenā 'tmai 'vā 'tmanā jitaḥ
anātmanas tu śatrutve
vartetā 'tmai 'va śatruvat

Translation

The person who has conquered his lower self becomes his own friend, but the person who does not subdue the lower self is his own enemy.

Metaphorical Interpretation

The lower mind pulls you down to the lower centers and ultimately brings difficulties, but the higher mind elevates you to the state of peace, joy, and happiness. Conquer the lower levels of your mind with your higher mind, which is knowledge and consciousness. Aided by self-knowledge, you must obey your master, follow your master's instructions, and subdue the lower levels of your mind with breath control. When you succeed, you will be able to move your consciousness from your lower centers to the highest center. You will be your own friend.

It all depends on one's choice and effort. If you don't conquer your mind, you will never find real peace, joy, and bliss. You will always be your own enemy.

Verse 7

jitātmanaḥ praśāntasya
paramātmā samāhitaḥ
śītoṣṇasukhaduḥkheṣu
tathā mānāpamānayoḥ

Translation

The one who has self-control and is always in a state of composure, whose mind is unaffected by pleasure and pain, heat and cold, honor and dishonor, is merged in the Supreme.

Metaphorical Interpretation

Those who meditate very deeply and regularly have no awareness of where they are sitting; they are in the formless state; they remain in infinity. They feel divine vibration from the high heaven to the ground, they hear divine sound all over the universe, and they see divine light everywhere. They are unaware of their bodies, so for them there is no question of pleasure and pain, heat and cold, honor and dishonor. They sense that the All is pervading everything while they experience continuous liberation and conscious *samadhi*. Even in day-to-day living they are not affected by any of the pairs of worldly experiences; their minds are perfectly balanced.

This is the reality of Mother Nature: God is in the form of human beings and human beings are in the form of God.

Verse 8

jñānavijñānatṛptātmā
kūṭastho vijitendriyaḥ
yukta ity ucyate yogī
samaloṣṭāśmakāñcanaḥ

Translation

The one who is content and established in the Self, resting unperturbed in *kutastha* (the soul center), who has mastered the organs of perception and action, for whom a clump of earth, a stone, and gold are the same, such a composed person is called a yogi. This state of equanimity is a blessing that is attained through meditation.

Metaphorical Interpretation

A yogi has three experiences in cosmic consciousness above the pituitary beyond the human stage. The first is *sarrapatti*, which means extreme effulgence. It is a light more powerful than sunlight, but this light is extremely soothing. Yogis who see this light are divinely charmed by it. Worldly gold is not as attractive as this light. The second is the *asamsakti* stage, when a divine nectar comes down from the fontanel. Tasting this nectar, yogis experience transcendent bliss and ineffable joy. The third is *padartha-bhabini.* A supernal power appears before the yogi that is so blissful that, with its help, yogis almost enter *nirvikalpa samadhi.* Yogis become spellbound when they perceive this power. Nothing is superior to a yogi in that stage.

Verse 9

suhṛnmitrāryudāsīna-
madhyasthadveṣyabandhuṣu
sādhuṣv api ca pāpeṣu
samabuddhir viśiṣyate

Translation

The one for whom everyone is equal, whether they are a benefactor, a friend, an enemy, an acquaintance, an arbitrator, a person who is deserving of dislike, a relative, one who is honest, or one who is sinful, who remains neutral and impartial in all things, is extremely exalted among the yogis.

Metaphorical Interpretation

When yogis rise to the highest states, they remain merged in God and achieve balance of mind. They become very simple and have childlike habits. They cannot discriminate; they do not judge who is good and who is bad; they feel that everyone is divine. Everyone is equal to them. Their love flows equally for all, free from all discrimination and dislike. These yogis experience God everywhere. They are respected by all.

Verse 10

yogī yuñjīta satatam
ātmānam rahasi sthitaḥ
ekākī yatacittātmā
nirāśīr aparigrahaḥ

Translation

A yogi, sitting alone in deep meditation in a solitary place with the body and mind relaxed, free from desire and greed, with self-control, constantly perceives oneness in everything and merges with the Absolute (Brahman).

Metaphorical Interpretation

The human mind is ordinarily turned to the outside world. Those who are true seekers of Self-realization will keep their attention inside the spine, which is the real solitary place. By controlling the breath, a yogi is free from mental disturbances; he does not have any greed or worldly desire. In deepest meditation, yogis gradually rise above the *ida, pingala,* and *vajra* channels inside the spine, coming up from the lower centers to the upper center, which is a very lonely place. Here, yogis perceive only the divine. Through deep meditation, they merge with the soul. The yogis who roam inside the mind and reach the fontanel are always free from all negative tendencies. They are self-controlled in every aspect of life. They perceive divinity everywhere, both within and without.

Verses 11–12

śucau deśe pratiṣṭhāpya
sthiram āsanam ātmanaḥ
nā 'tyucchritam nā 'tinīcam
cailājinakuśottaram

tatrai 'kāgram manaḥ kṛtvā
yatacittendriyakriyaḥ
upaviśyā 'sane yuñjyād
yogam ātmaviśuddhaye

Translation

In a clean spot that is not too high or too low, seated upon a piece of soft cloth (silk cloth), which is on a skin on a grass mat,

and making the mind one-pointed, the one who has mastered the mind and senses may practice meditation.

Metaphorical Interpretation

The Lord is telling Arjuna how a true seeker selects a place for meditation. If the spot is slanted, the devotee's body will be strained, which will cause pain in different parts of the body. The place for meditation must be clean, flat, and level. To enter inside the soul, human beings must sit for a long time. This is why the Lord gives specific instructions about what is needed for a good seat. While well seated, you must keep pinpointed attention on the soul and meditate deeply. This will cause purification, both inside and out.

In ancient times in India, many people did not have good houses. They lived in huts or thatched dwellings of straw and mud. At that time there was no cement, so the floors were made of mud and earth.

To avoid moisture, one needed to first place straw, which is non-conductive, on the floor. Over the straw, one would then place deerskin, which also is non-conductive, to further protect from moisture. Next, one would cover this with silk cloth, which also is non-conductive, and which, being very soft, enabled one to sit with pleasure and comfort for a long period.

With such a seat, people could meditate without getting damp. By staying dry, they would not acquire disease. Now, with the advances of this scientific age, there are many lofty, strong reinforced cement and concrete buildings and good houses in India. Most houses have cement floors, and some floors even have carpets. Many people use sofas or couches. So now, the Indian people do not use straw mats or silk cloth. A few people use deerskins, but that is also very rare. Most people use blankets folded four times, or wool or cotton prayer or meditation carpets.

In other countries, people are not accustomed to sitting on the ground with crossed legs. They generally sit on a sofa or a chair. For meditation a sofa is not at all good, because when you sit on it you cannot keep your spine, neck, and head straight. If you sit on a chair, you can sit erect for the first technique of Kriya Yoga (yoga of action). But for the other techniques, you should sit on something like a folded blanket. Then you can magnetize your spine and withdraw from the lower centers to the upper center. Then follow the techniques that are described in the Bhagavad Gita (6:13–16).

Verses 11 and 12 also have a metaphorical meaning: The real place of meditation is the cranium. This is also referred to in John (8:23), where Jesus says, "Ye are from beneath, I am from above." In the Prashna Upanishad the same thing is said, *atha-akshaya-urdhvam*, which means that you must sit in the north (top) of your body, inside the pituitary. In the Katha Upanishad (1:3:8) it says, *yas tu vijñana van bhavati sa mumuksha sada suchih,* which means that people who keep their attention inside the pituitary, in the soul, are pure. The cranium is the real place for meditation, the real place of solitude and purity.

Verses 13–14

samam kāyaśirogrīvam
dhārayann acalam sthiraḥ
samprekṣya nāsikāgram svam
diśaś cā 'navalokayan

praśāntātmā vigatabhīr
brahmacārivrate sthitaḥ
manaḥ samyamya maccitto
yukta āsīta matparaḥ

Translation

With body, head, and neck held firmly straight and still, and with the attention between the two eyebrows, not looking about in every direction,

the mind is tranquil, free from fear and anxiety (a *brahmachari*). May this yogi direct all thoughts to Me and seek Me deeply.

Metaphorical Interpretation

The Lord is teaching Arjuna, who represents any worldly person who wants peace and divinity, the correct posture for meditation, where to concentrate, and how to withdraw power from the lower centers to the uppermost center. When sitting for meditation, you must keep your spine erect by maintaining the body, head, and neck firmly straight. The midpoint of the eyebrows leads to the pituitary (the soul center). When awareness is withdrawn from without and from the lower centers, the yogi experiences inner peace and external relaxation, and can direct all thoughts toward the soul, the Lord, thereby attaining the thoughtless state, which is Self-realization.

The Lord is also saying that everyone who practices yoga according to these directions will become extremely broadminded, free from fear and emotion. They will also constantly remain absorbed in soul consciousness, Brahman. This consciousness is real liberation and Self-realization—even in the mundane world, day and night.

Verse 15

yuñjann evam sadā 'tmānam
yogī niyatamānasaḥ
śāntim nirvāṇaparamām
matsamsthām adhigacchati

Translation

Having mastered the mind in this manner, the yogi gains peace, emancipation, and absorption in Me.

Metaphorical Interpretation

The yogi constantly controls his breath and goes up to the pituitary; his mind, thought, and sensory awareness become fixed in the soul. These yogis attain the formless stage, emancipation, and extreme bliss. "Bliss is only possible for yogis who fix their attention in Me," says the Lord.

All human beings who practice the yoga of action, all day and all night, and in every step of their lives, will feel that they are merely a body car, and that the soul is the driver. They will feel the oneness of God and human beings. They will recognize that the Creator is always very kind to all beings.

The power of God comes down from the heavens to us. Every single moment the Lord is busy with every human being. He permeates our biological forces with divine peace, bliss, and joy. Although we all live in the material world, this world is not only material. It is also divine. Whatever we see, we see Him, because without Him, no one can see. Whatever we do, it is done by Him. The Creator always remains in His creation and in His creatures. When human beings perceive this by practicing the yoga of action, their lives become real, complete, divine.

But a spiritual life is not an inactive life. The yoga of action does not give rise to inactivity. Kriya Yoga meditation does not cause inaction; rather, it creates extreme alertness. From this kind of meditation human beings can recognize that they are fortunate: God is doing everything for them, continuously giving them renewed divine pleasure. Without Him, we are all dead bodies.

Verse 16

nā 'tyaśnatas tu yogo 'sti
na cai 'kāntam anaśnataḥ
na cā 'tisvapnaśīlasya
jāgrato nai 'va cā 'rjuna

Translation

O, Arjuna, the one who eats too much or fasts for too long, and the one who sleeps too much or doesn't sleep enough, cannot follow the path of yoga.

Metaphorical Interpretation

Those who eat too much or too little, or who sleep too much or too little, cannot attain yoga, which is oneness with the true Self. The yogi must have moderate food and moderate sleep.

Yogis who eat too much food will deposit extra fat and will have stomach and liver trouble. Constant sleepiness will overpower them so they cannot meditate. Those who eat too little for a long time will lose energy and brainpower and will develop gastric trouble, wrinkles in the face, and an emaciated, ugly, and unpleasant body. They will have lethargy and a dull brain. They, too, cannot meditate.

During sleep, people take long breaths for six or seven hours and get sufficient oxygen, the food of the brain. Also during sleep, the motor nerves and bodily tissues rest, creating fresh energy in the morning. The power of the body rejuvenates and regenerates, but those who sleep for long periods cannot meditate or grow in knowledge. Those who do not sleep enough will lose their brain power and bodily strength.

Those who take drugs or strong intoxicants will lose their mental powers. They don't contribute anything to their community and are dishonored by educated people. They only sleep; then they become poor, nasty, rude, fickle, and lack reasoning power; they cannot prosper or grow spiritually.

Eat only food that you can easily digest. In the scriptures it says that when you eat, one half of the stomach should be filled with food, one quarter of the stomach should be filled with water, and one quarter should remain empty for easy respiration. After eating, food should not be taken again for five hours. Everyone should work eight to ten hours, meditate two hours, and sleep for six or seven hours a night. Then they can meditate deeply. This is balance.

This verse also has a deeper, metaphorical meaning. Air is the vital, principal food of human beings. A yogi should take moderate breaths for his physical, spiritual, and intellectual growth. Yogis should not "eat," that is, inhale, a lot of air, as in *bhastrika pranayama*, which is a steady rapid inhalation and immediate exhalation. Yogis who repeat this breath very often get heart pain, enlarged heart, breath trouble, lung disease, or even nostril disease. Their vocal sounds are very harsh, they cannot sing sweet songs, and drowsiness and sleep overpower them. Those that teach these things suggest you should sit for meditation after this breathing, so you will feel that God is standing just behind your back. This perception is not achieved, however, because you will feel drowsy. People practice in this way at the suggestion of their teachers, but this practice does not help their spiritual growth.

Many also suggest that instead of inhaling more oxygen, the breath should be held by closing the nostrils with both fingers for a long period. This is also a very bad technique. Those who do this will develop heart disease and an enlarged heart. Many even teach that drugs and intoxicants should be used to help attain the thoughtless state, but this leads only to drugged sleep, where you cannot attain God-realization.

Still others claim that since the whole night is calm and quiet, you should meditate almost all night, sleeping for only two hours.

This practice is also very bad. Those who do it will surely become drowsy. During drowsiness, they will see many hallucinations, which are like half-dreams. In the morning they will say that they saw a huge Rama or Krishna or Jesus or Allah or Abraham in their meditation, but it is nothing but hallucination or imagination; it is not spirituality.

Moderate food, including the "food" of air, and moderate sleep, with meditation as directed by the Lord, are needed to perceive God.

Verse 17

yuktāhāravihārasya
yuktaceṣṭasya karmasu
yuktasvapnāvabodhasya
yogo bhavati duḥkhahā

Translation

The path of meditation requires a moderate, regulated life, avoiding too much or too little food, work, and sleep, or use of the senses. The attention must abide in the soul at all times. For such a person, yoga destroys all sorrows.

Metaphorical Interpretation

For soul culture, Lord Krishna not only teaches techniques for God-realization, but He also describes our true nature in detail, as well as the food, habits, manners, and qualities that are in accord with our true nature, which must be embraced. In addition, He describes the demonic habits that must be shunned.

The good qualities a spiritual aspirant must cultivate are described throughout the Bhagavad Gita. When devotees follow these teachings and apply them in their daily lives, they will learn moderation, loyalty, love, balance of mind, and that God is the sole doer. Ego, pride, and anger will disappear, and as they perform their duties in their households with their families, they will perceive God in every moment. In every action they will find peace, joy, bliss, and God-realization.

Soul culture can be compared to learning how to drive an automobile. A student driver must learn in detail about the brakes, how to start the engine, how to control the accelerator, when to change gears, and how to steer. The student driver must also develop a thorough awareness of traffic. Then through extensive practical knowledge and long practice, the student can use the car effectively to quickly reach a destination. Likewise for soul culture, people must have a thorough knowledge of all eighteen chapters of the Bhagavad Gita and must understand their practical application. Just as an automobile driver must constantly remain alert, true seekers of God must always keep their keenest attention on the soul. At the same time, they should apply the lessons of the Bhagavad Gita in their daily life.

Although the Lord is discussing moderation in diet, pleasure, work, sleep, and wakefulness, there is also a deeper meaning to everything said by the Lord.

For example, the instructions about food are more than just suggestions for eating. Without the soul, we cannot eat: A dead body cannot eat. The soul allows us to eat because food is required for life and hence for the practice of soul culture. The soul gives hunger or appetite, so yogis love the soul. The soul is in food. Food is spiritual, as explained in the Bhagavad Gita (17:8). Yogis must consider how much food they will offer to the indwelling Self, and whether they can easily digest it. *Annam brahma iti vyajanat*: "Food is Brahman and it is the first power of God" (Taittiriya Upanishad 3:6).

Near the end of the verse, the Lord says *yukta ahara*. *Yukta* means to fix one's attention, or to be constantly united with the divine in every step of life. When yogis keep their attention fixed on the soul, it is *yukta ahara*.

The last word in the verse, *avabodhasya*, means wakefulness. It means that true seekers of the soul always remain absorbed in God during every mental and emotional state. Thus, knowledge is thoroughly controlled in every respect.

Verse 18

yadā viniyatam cittam
ātmany evā 'vatiṣṭhate
niḥspṛhaḥ sarvakāmebhyo
yukta ity ucyate tadā

Translation

Withdrawing attention from the extroverted mind and establishing it in the soul, the seeker is said to be in harmony (in yoga).

Metaphorical Interpretation

Those who withdraw their minds from the external world, who are ever focusing on the soul and detached from everything, are called *yukta atma.* After devotees attain conscious *samadhi* and constant liberation, they become free from everything and merge with the all-pervading Brahman.

Generally, when people sit for meditation they have many thoughts and worldly sensations. By practicing Kriya Yoga however, they can reach the abode of God and can remain there. In this state they are completely free of the worldly sense and thoughts, and will find deep calm.

Verse 19

yathā dīpo nivātastho
ne 'ṅgate so 'pamā smṛtā
yogino yatacittasya
yuñjato yogam ātmanaḥ

Translation

As the lamplight and candlelight remain straight and steady and do not flicker when there is no wind, so the mind of the self-controlled devotee remains firm and absorbed in the soul.

Metaphorical Interpretation

When devotees withdraw their senses from the lower centers to the uppermost center in the soul, they are in *paravastha.* This is the stage of cosmic consciousness, which can also be called Mother Nature.

In this stage devotees experience *tasmin sati svāsa-praśvāsayor-gati vichhedaḥ prāṇāyāmaḥ* (Yoga Sutras of Patañjali 2:49), that is, "They do not watch their incoming breath and outgoing breath, and the air moves only within in the two nostrils, which is called *pranayama* (cessation of inhalation)." In this stage, devotees do not have any thoughts of past events, and they do not feel the madness of worldly human life. They merge in the formless, *avyakta*, and remain in divine bliss and love for God.

Verses 20–23

yatro 'paramate cittam
niruddham yogasevayā
yatra cai 'vā 'tmanā 'tmānam
paśyann ātmani tuṣyati

sukham ātyantikam yat tad
buddhigrāhyam atīndriyam
vetti yatra na cai 'vā 'yam
sthitaś calati tattvataḥ

yam labdhvā cā 'param lābham
manyate nā 'dhikam tataḥ
yasmin sthito na duḥkhena
guruṇā 'pi vicālyate

tam vidyād duḥkhasamyoga-
viyogam yogasamjñitam
sa niścayena yoktavyo
yogo 'nirviṇṇacetasā

Translation

When the mind has been mastered by the practice of meditation, it abides in the Self, perceives the Self, and rejoices in the Self.

Then, absolute happiness is experienced, which is recognized by the intellect, but is beyond sense perception. Being established in the Self, the mind never moves away from the truth,

and having realized the Self, it does not think there is any other greater gain. Such a mind is not affected even by great sorrow.

May one know yoga, the freedom from attachment and its sorrow. This yoga should be practiced with clarity of purpose, without the mind being discouraged.

Metaphorical Interpretation

Through the practice of breath control, the minds of devotees are stilled. With Self-realization, devotees gain inexplicable perennial joy and bliss. When devotees attain this heavenly peace, they feel that material peace is nothing in comparison with divine joy. In that stage, when the devotee has an experience that would ordinarily cause sorrow, there is no sorrow. By mastering the breath, the union of body and soul is perceived, which is yoga. Although it is a little challenging in the beginning, everyone should practice.

Using breath control, devotees can withdraw from their mind, thoughts, and body sense, gradually ascending to the seat of the soul. At that time devotees reach the kingdom of heaven, where there is no sense of worldliness. Divine sound, the divine movement sensation, and divine light cover the universe, and divine love is all around. From the fontanel, devotees receive the divine nectar and experience conscious *samadhi*, the formless stage, also experiencing continuous liberation, the ultimate goal of every human being. As long as these yogis remain in this divine state, they are free from pleasure and pain and great sorrow.

The human mind is extremely restless, but Kriya Yoga enables one to quickly calm it. When Kriya yogis start meditation, they magnetize the spine by bowing according to the directions of the realized guru. Then, within two to five minutes, these yogis become free from the worldly sense; their entire systems are invigorated with renewed divine circulation. All negativity, the power of the five lower centers, is transformed and rises up six-story building of human life, into the cranium, where every person's soul abides. This is the kingdom of heaven or *ku-ta-stha*: *kuta* means atom point, and *stha* means to remain still in that point.

When your awareness remains only in the soul center, at the top of the six-story building, you need not think of those persons who remain in the five lower levels. Remain in the heavenly abode and gradually seek Him in the seventh center; then your mind will be merged with God, Who is always hiding there in every human being (Shvetashvatara Upanishad 6:11).

The more you remain absorbed in the soul and God, the more you will be like a sleeping child. A sleeping child has no worldly sense and no urges, but only sleeps. Love God extremely in this way and He will give you the divine treasure. You will have all-round development, peace, bliss, and joy. There is no question of experiencing great sorrow, for a sleeping child has no sorrow.

The realized person absorbed in the power of God remains in wisdom. Wisdom is *prajñanam brahmam*, the pulseless state, *samadhi*. In this state people have no worldly urges and no worldly desires. They are absorbed in divine joy. Nothing is greater than this.

Since every human being is the living power of God, everyone is born to achieve this state. In this state one is truly educated; one knows one's own Self. These people are called *brahmacharya*, which means they constantly watch the soul to perceive how Brahman activates the whole body. People who attain this stage can remain in worldly life compassionately detached from pleasure and pain. God is in the human being and the human being is in God.

Verses 24–25

samkalpaprabhavān kāmāms
tyaktvā sarvān aśeṣataḥ

manasai 've 'ndriyagrāmam
viniyamya samantataḥ

śanaiḥ-śanair uparamed
buddhyā dhṛtigṛhītayā
ātmasamstham manaḥ kṛtvā
na kimcid api cintayet

Translation

Steadily, using self-restraint and discrimination, gradually rise from the lower centers to the upper center, withdraw knowledge into the soul, and do not allow the senses to go back down,

Having shunned all worldly desires and selfish moods born of thought, maintain thorough control of all your sense organs; then meditate and do not think of anything else.

Metaphorical Interpretation

In Verses 20 to 23, Lord Krishna said that all devotees who meditate can ascend into the cranium and reach the supreme spiritual result and power. In these verses, the Lord describes the process of meditation. Through sense control and steadiness, devotees can approach the soul. Using breath control, they can slowly, slowly withdraw their senses from the lower centers to the upper center.

There are four stages in bringing the power up from the lower centers to the upper center. The first can be accomplished in only three minutes with the preliminary technique. Using this technique, devotees will immediately reach *pratyahara*, where the mind becomes completely free from a sense of the body and the world, free from selfish desire, going inward to the abode of the divine.

In the second stage, devotees experience a new divine sensation in the whole body, *dharana*, which means the conception of the soul, where the mind becomes superconscious. In this state, devotees have super-perception throughout their bodies and even in each body part. In each center in their spine, and from head to toe, they feel only divine vibration. They also perceive divine sound and divine light and feel love for God.

The third stage is called *dhyana* (contemplation and meditation), and the ultimate stage is *samadhi* (inner experience and realization).

Verses 26–28

yato-yato niścarati
manaś cañcalam asthiram
tatas-tato niyamyai 'tad
ātmany eva vaśam nayet

praśāntamanasam hy enam
yoginam sukham uttamam
upaiti śāntarajasam
brahmabhūtam akalmaṣam

yuñjann evam sadā 'tmānam
yogī vigatakalmaṣaḥ
sukhena brahmasamsparśam
atyantam sukham aśnute

Translation

For whatever reason, the unsteady mind, always in a state of flux, escapes control, one must bring it back to the Self, and thus return it to tranquility.

Indeed the yogi (one who meditates) whose mind is tranquil, whose impurities have all dissolved, whose life is free from defects, becomes Brahman and reaches the supreme happiness.

The yogi, free from impurities, always being united with the divine, easily gains supreme happiness through oneness with Brahman.

Metaphorical Interpretation

By nature, the mind is restless, unsteady, and always turning outward. With self-restraint devotees should bring it back under control and introvert its awareness. The outgoing mind must look back in toward the atom point of meditation. In this way, one purifies the mind.

Devotees free from their worldly nature are broadminded and free from sin; they can attain Self-realization. Automatically, they perceive divine joy. This joy becomes perennial. Ever-harmonized and having relinquished sin, these devotees easily enjoy infinite bliss and merge with the power of God.

The higher that devotees rise in the stages of meditation, the more advancement and Self-realization they get. When true seekers practice the third technique of meditation, they get *dhyana*, where there is no sense of mind, thought, body, or the world. It is the formless stage, the all-pervading stage; the soul is perceived throughout heaven and earth. At this point, the aspirants perceive divine fire in the soul and divine light throughout the entire universe. Filled with divine love and divine joy, they sometimes merge into the Self, in the infinite. Sometimes they attain the fourth stage of meditation, *nirvikalpa samadhi*, merging with God.

Verse 29

sarvabhūtastham ātmānam
sarvabhūtāni cātmani
īkṣate yogayuktātmā
sarvatra samadarśanaḥ

Translation

By the power of meditation, Self-realized devotees perceive the Self abiding in everyone and everyone abiding in their Self. In everything, they see the oneness of the Self.

Metaphorical Interpretation

When the result of meditation dawns in the yogi, the soul is perceived everywhere. These adepts do not discriminate between rich and poor, good and bad, young or old, or anyone. They perceive the soul in everything, Brahman everywhere. They perceive all human life as one, because life is only the soul. Without the soul, no one is a human being.

Verses 30–31

yo mām paśyati sarvatra
sarvam ca mayi paśyati
tasyā 'ham na praṇaśyāmi
sa ca me na praṇaśyati

sarvabhūtasthitam yo mām
bhajaty ekatvam āsthitaḥ
sarvathā vartamāno 'pi
sa yogī mayi vartate

Translation

Devotees who perceive Me everywhere and perceive everything in Me are never lost to Me, nor am I ever lost to them.

Devotees with a balance of mind, who watch Me everywhere, who perceive Me in everything, and who don't judge anything, are the real yogis. In the world, in all circumstances, they always abide in Me.

Metaphorical Interpretation

When completely realized devotees come down to the human state of awareness, they maintain their experience of the soul as the sole doer. Completely realized devotees understand that the soul abiding in one human being abides in every human being. In this stage, devotees continuously perceive the seven lights in their seven centers. In any mood that comes to them, they feel that the soul is so kind, and that through Him they are enjoying everything. These devotees have balance of mind, they are free from anger and pride, and they can shun negative qualities.

Devotees who maintain conscious awareness in the center above the neck (in the pituitary) do not deviate from the soul, which abides there. When these devotees are working for money, they feel light in the lowest center and gain knowledge from that light. At the same time they feel the soul working from above. When these devotees eat food, they realize that without the soul they will have no appetite and cannot take food. When there is light in the food center, it means the knowledge is there, so the soul will tell them how much they should eat. The divine fire is there to digest the food. The realized soul does not deviate from the soul, maintaining constant alertness there.

Verse 32

ātmaupamyena sarvatra
samam paśyati yo 'rjuna
sukham vā yadi vā duḥkham
sa yogī paramo mataḥ

Translation

O Arjuna, those devotees who lovingly regard all beings equally, who maintain balance during pleasure and pain, are the best.

Metaphorical Interpretation

In this verse the Lord describes the outlook of the supreme yogis. Meditation leads to soul consciousness. A yogi is merged in the superconsciousness of love and harmony.

Those who are constantly alert in the soul know that the soul is not the body. The soul has no nerves, no veins, no flesh. No one can cut the soul, no one can touch it; the soul is beyond pleasure and pain. The soul always feels purity, perfection, love, and divine life, so those devotees who have realized their souls feel that everyone is pure, perfect, and divine. Every realized soul feels that the power of God remains equally in every human being, and they give love and regard to every human being.

Verses 33–34

arjuna uvāca
yo 'yam yogas tvayā proktaḥ
sāmyena madhusūdana
etasayā 'ham na paśyāmi
cañcalatvāt sthitim sthirām

cañcalam hi manaḥ kṛṣṇa
pramāthi balavad dṛḍham
tasyā 'ham nigraham manye
vāyor iva suduṣkaram

Translation

O Madhusudana, my Lord! Because of the restlessness of my own mind, I fail to understand the nature of equanimity and balance of mind, about which you have taught and advised.

O Lord, we all know the mind is constantly restless, deluded, turbulent, and wild. Just as no one can stop or control the wind, it is very difficult to subdue the mind.

Metaphorical Interpretation

In these two verses, Arjuna, a practical yogi, trying to follow his teacher, expresses the condition of the mind and its nature, which he feels is an obstacle to meditation. The minds of all human beings are engrossed in the material world, in the objects perceived with the senses; these people remain absorbed in the biological and psychological forces. Their minds are restless, full of delusion, very strong, and wild.

Arjuna represents all worldly people, who are continuously restless, because restlessness, stubbornness, and wild moods—all things—come from food. Without food and drink everyone would be inactive, a dead body. Arjuna is the food minister; only food will work and fight. This is why the Lord did not take all five Pandavas in the chariot. He took only Arjuna, the son of a warrior family, who will fight against the lower biological energy.

Without the Lord (the soul), human beings have no mind, no thought, no ego, no body sense or worldly sense. Here the Lord is called Krishna, which is derived from two roots: *krishi* and *na. Krishi* is the cultivated land of the human spine. The land of the spine is the jungle of matter. *Na* means the formless soul of every human being. If there is no *na* in the human body, there is no mind, and hence, no restlessness, no wildness, no stubbornness.

It is extremely difficult to control and subdue the mind, but all devotees must do so; the mind may be wild, but it can be tamed. The Lord has told us explicitly how to quiet the mind. He has described the postures and techniques of meditation for cultivating the spine, which is full of desire. He also has explained what food should be eaten, as well as emphasizing restraint of the senses, measured work, limited contemplation, and constant alertness in the soul.

It is the desire of every human being to remove the bad things from their house and keep the good things. Similarly, in our body house there are many bad qualities; however, it is very hard for us to remove them. Every human being is engrossed in mind and thought. After the Lord told Arjuna everything he needed to know about soul culture, Arjuna still said it was impossible for him to fight with his mind, thoughts, and ego, to climb up into the soul. Through His discourse with Arjuna, the Lord, the soul itself, is teaching soul culture to every human being in the world.

The Lord is asking you to please follow Him so that you can perceive that everything is done by Him, even while you are engrossed in the material world. This you should all perceive.

Verse 35

śrībhagavān uvāca
asamśayam mahābāho
mano durnigraham calam
abhyāsena tu kaunteya
vairāgyeṇa ca gṛhyate

Translation

The blessed Lord replied:
O powerful warrior, mighty-armed Arjuna! Undoubtedly, a restless mind is very difficult to control. O son of Kunti, it can indeed be controlled by constant practice and detachment.

Metaphorical Interpretation

The Lord is telling Arjuna two things. First, the constant practice of taking controlled breaths will change your life, because practice leads to perfection. Everything depends on practice. When you were young, you could not walk. Then gradually you practiced how to walk. Soon you were running effortlessly. In the beginning, you could not write your ABC's, but by constantly practicing reading and writing, you learned how to read and write quickly.

When we sleep, the Lord helps us control our breathing. By this control, we sleep and take long inhalations. Restlessness, anger, pride, sexual desire, and strong sorrow disappear. You may think that it is very difficult to control your restlessness, but every night you do it, when you are free from your worldly human nature.

Krishna's second advice is to constantly control the mind and be detached. You can easily do this if you keep good company. When you consort with bad company, you become a bad person. When you part with bad company and seek good company, stay with them, follow their advice, and practice what they teach, you will become a very good, divine person.

Here is an example from everyday life. People who do not smoke but who associate with smokers for several days will feel a strong desire to smoke. On the other hand, when they come in contact with those who are not addicted to smoking, and stay with them, they can more easily give up their habit. Or for some spiritual examples, consider Ratnakara and Takshavill, who were murderers who came into contact with good people, then completely changed. Similarly, Matthew, Peter, Paul, and Girish Ghosh were not good people, but when they came to receive the touch from Jesus or Ramakrishna Paramahamsa, respectively, all their bad habits disappeared. They all became extremely respected, well-known spiritual people. This can happen with the Lord's help.

"So Arjuna," says the Lord, "you are a son of Kunti, thus called Kaunteya, which means you have the finest intellect and talent. I tell you two things. One is that practice makes perfect. The other is that you must have firm determination and detachment. Follow Me, then, even though you once thought it very difficult to control your mind, someday you will say it is very easy to control your mind. Remember, in the beginning, all young children are not educated and respected. But in the company of their teacher they control their minds, and they become detached, with introverted senses. Then, in the future many of them become highly developed. If you follow Me, you will surely find success in your life."

By using breath control, those who practice withdrawing their minds from the lower centers to the upper center in the spine will automatically have their power ascend. They will surely attain extreme calm and detachment and will become one with the divine. From the very beginning, the Lord has exhorted you to remain in the upper center of your body, not in the lower centers. Please follow Him, Who is the soul of every human being. Practice His technique: Breath control is self-control. Please follow the teachings in this chapter, which is *abhyasa yoga,* the yoga of practice. If you follow this technique for liberation from restlessness, you will surely find success. By only hearing about these techniques, you cannot succeed. One ounce of practice is far better than tons of theories. Practice, then you will surely be free from extreme restlessness.

Verse 36

asamyatātmanā yogo
duṣprāpa iti me matih
vaśyātmanā tu yatatā
śakyo 'vāptum upāyataḥ

Translation

Those with minds not under control cannot attain Self-realization, but those whose minds are thoroughly controlled, who try their utmost for success, will surely attain Self-realization.

Metaphorical Interpretation

Anyone can evolve by controlling the mind. But those who do not try have no possibility of succeeding.

God is truth, peace, and bliss; therefore, these qualities are in all human beings. The power of God is behind the veil of nature's splendor. Human beings who remain below the cranium and are merged in delusion will never know truth, peace, bliss, or Self-realization.

Those who have the greatest desire for Self-realization must do three things: (1) they must find a realized master; (2) they must learn how to withdraw the divine power from the lower centers and bring it up near the soul by using breath control; (3) they need to practice Kriya regularly, which means practicing the yoga of action and detachment.

The cream is in every drop of milk, but if you do not churn the milk scientifically, the cream will not rise to the top. Similarly, by simple breath control, as taught by the realized master, all the divine qualities in the lower centers can scientifically be brought to the top. Jesus and all the scriptures say that you must withdraw your senses from the lower centers and bring your awareness up to the upper center.

Once the cream rises, it will not mix with the milk again. Once you reach Self-realization, you will feel that the soul is the sole doer in every moment of every action that arises from the functioning of the lower centers. In this way, devotees learn detachment and enjoy constant liberation; they truly perceive the all-pervading Brahman.

Verse 37

arjuna uvāca
ayatiḥ śraddhayo 'peto
yogāc calitamānasaḥ
aprāpya yogasamsiddhim
kām gatim kṛṣṇa gacchati

Translation

O Lord, if one has faith in the scriptures but makes inadequate effort and lets the mind wander, therefore not succeeding in yoga; to which end does one go?

Metaphorical Interpretation

It now appears as though Arjuna has been convinced by the advice the Lord gave him in the first six chapters. Arjuna is willing to fight with his evil qualities and wants Self-realization, but he still has some doubts: If he starts meditation and fails to continue it, what will the ultimate effect on his life's journey be? Will all his effort be futile?

Verses 38–39

kaccin no 'bhayavibhraṣṭaś
chinnābhram iva naśyati
apratiṣṭho mahābāho
vimūḍho brahmaṇaḥ pathi

etan me samśayam kṛṣṇa
chettum arhasy aśeṣataḥ

tvadanyaḥ samśayasyā 'sya
chettā na hy upapadyate

Translation

O most powerful Lord, those bewildered ones who have deviated from the path of Brahman, who do not seek the indwelling soul, will they not fall from both family life and spiritual life without support, like a torn cloud?

O Lord! Please remove completely my mind's doubts. Only You can resolve these doubts.

Metaphorical Interpretation

Human beings always want to enjoy the fruits of their actions, and they expect very big fruit. But Lord Krishna is a teacher of God-realization trying his utmost to teach Arjuna (all worldly people) the supreme method of Self-realization. Arjuna faithfully hears all this, but doubts whether he can achieve complete success. Arjuna perceives a great dilemma. He believes that since he is constantly restless, deluded, and extroverted, he might practice but fail to go beyond his body, mind, thought, and sense organs.

The Lord replies that all human life evolves only through constant practice and sense control. In the beginning no one knows their ABC's, but with practice, many become highly developed: even doctors, engineers, and scientists, for instance. Success depends on constant practice, extreme desire, and sense control.

As cream pervades every drop of milk, the soul abides in every drop of your body. You cannot perceive it, because you are deluded, fearful, and extroverted. When you churn milk for only a short period, a little cream will come up to the top, but nothing is lost. Likewise, if you meditate only a little, the result of this meditation will be small, but it will not be lost: The little bit of the cream that rises will surely remain on the top—the royal road to Brahman will not be destroyed. Your spinal canal is the royal road for going straight up into the kingdom of heaven where your soul constantly abides.

The Lord is pulling the vital air up from the lower centers. If you withdraw for a short period, your *sushumna* will open a little and some divine power will rise.

If a student does not progress to the next higher examination, what has already been achieved will not be wasted. Later, when there is a chance for further education, the student can continue and attain the best education. Similarly, if you cultivate the opening of your spinal canal, some success will occur, and it will not be lost. Those students who successfully complete the final examination, however, have passed for good.

When you meditate, the qualities of your spiritual education will remain within you; they will be preserved, not destroyed. If you practice yoga meditation even while living family life, you will undoubtedly evolve.

Verse 40

śrībhagavān uvāca
pārtha nai 've 'ha nā 'mutra
vināśas tasya vidyate
na hi kalyāṇakṛt kaścid
durgatim tāta gacchati

Translation

The Blessed Lord replied:
In this life and even in the hereafter, there is no destruction, my affectionate Arjuna, for those who remain in righteousness do not have ignorance, evil, or sorrow.

Metaphorical Interpretation

Practice Kriya Yoga with the deepest desire and detachment, and in this life you will find divinity and God-realization in the top center.

There are seven *lokas* in your spinal canal: (1) *bhuloka* is the money center; (2) *bhuvaloka* is the sex center; (3) *swaloka* is the food center; (4) *mahaloka* is the heart center; (5) *janaloka* is the vacuum center; (6) *tapaloka* is the soul center; and (7) *satyaloka* is in the fontanel, which is the center of the Almighty Father who created all the *lokas*. When you remain in *sapta loka* (*sapta* means seven, so this is the seventh center, *satya loka*) and descend into the other six centers, you will feel God doing everything in each center, and you will have constant liberation. The Lord gives divine joy to every person, even in the lower centers. Those who are righteous do not meet destruction or mortality. They perceive immortality in every moment.

The Lord has told Arjuna that without the soul, human beings have no existence. The soul constantly pulls the breath into every human being; therefore human beings are alive and enjoying and able to do many things.

The human body is like a motor car; the soul is the divine driver. Krishna is that soul, the divine driver of all human beings. Without a driver, a car cannot move. Furthermore, to drive a car, the driver needs both gasoline and air, and a rundown battery must be charged. If the battery is not charged and gasoline and air are not available, the driver cannot drive the car. In the same way, the battery of the human body is useless (will not give light) if you don't provide it with food, water, and air.

The driver must also know the technique for driving the car. In the body car, controlling the air intake is required. Food is the gasoline for the body car's energy and life. From this food, fire, energy, light, and life are generated, gifts from the Lord. The Lord has told Arjuna to control his breath, practice Kriya Yoga, and take a regulated diet. From that diet and air, the body battery will be charged. Then the battery will show you the royal road to the divine kingdom, which is in your cranium.

If you practice the yoga of action regularly, you will achieve God-realization in this life. You will also experience God-realization all day and all night during your everyday activities.

Now you know the techniques that will take the body car on the royal road to heaven. You can be in righteousness; you can avoid destruction and mortality.

Verse 41

prāpya puṇyakṛtām lokān
uṣitvā śāśvatīḥ samāḥ
śucīnām śrīmatām gehe
yogabhraṣṭo 'bhijāyate

Translation

After death, those who are not fully realized yogis remain for longer periods in the higher divine plane, enjoying divinity; then they are reborn into righteous and cultured families.

Metaphorical Interpretation

Arjuna asked whether those who are partially realized—but not fully realized and perceiving Brahman—will perish like a torn cloud? The Lord replies that these yogis do not meet complete destruction. The power of their meditation remains in their astral body (destiny). When they come back, that destiny continues to unfold.

In accounting, income and expenditures are shown on the first page and the totals of these accounts are brought forward to the second page. Similarly, whatever we have learned since our infancy is stored in our midbrain, and that knowledge does not disappear. Likewise, when human beings partially withdraw their divine power from the lower centers, that power remains up in the soul. With a little churning, a little cream rises to the top. The more you churn the milk, the more cream rises to the top and stays there. The power of meditation practice is never lost; it gradually increases from one life to the next.

In this verse, the phrase, *suchinam gehe*, literally means to be born in the house of a pure and spiritual family. But metaphorically, this phrase has a deeper meaning. Our pituitary, which is above our five sense organs, is the purest and most spiritual house. In the Katha Upanishad (1:3:8) it says, *yas tu vijñanavan bhavati sa mumukshah sada suchi:* "Those who remain above the five sense organs in the pituitary will attain real purity." The pituitary is our real spiritual home. Only by breath control can people ascend into the soul, where they can obtain purity and divinity.

A second important phrase is *shrimatam gehe. Shri* means divine light, divine spark, glory, and might. Symbolically this means that the soul is real beauty, glory, and the divine spark. The beautiful house of God is called *shrimatam gehe*. The beauty, might, and glory of all human beings is in their souls.

All people meditate will gain moderation and holiness. Automatically, they will see divine light everywhere. Jesus referred to this light. All people who practice Kriya Yoga will concentrate their power in the soul and discover the divine, lustrous power of God. Truly, this where all yogis are reborn.

Verses 42–43

athavā yogināṃ eva
kule bhavati dhīmatām
etad dhi durlabhataram
loke janma yad īdṛśam

tatra tam buddhisamyogam
labhate paurvadehikam
yatate ca tato bhūyaḥ
samsiddhau kurunandana

Translation

Or they might be born into the family of a learned yogi, but that birth is undoubtedly very rare in this world.

After taking such births, they regain the God consciousness they earned in previous lives, O joy of the Kuru family! Then they try their utmost to achieve complete liberation.

Metaphorical Interpretation

The Lord continues to explain how one who has not reached complete Self-realization proceeds to liberation.

Yogis should not remain in the astral plane; they should take birth again to continue their progress. They should always keep their attention fixed in the pituitary, that is, in the soul, or even above, in the fontanel.

From infancy, the soul constantly inhales and exhales through the nose of every human. Every inhalation is birth, and every exhalation is death. After exhalation, if the soul does not draw the inhalation into us, we are dead. The power of God, the soul, is very kind to all human beings and living beings. In every moment the Lord gives us birth and rebirth through inhalation and exhalation. As a result, we constantly grow; we constantly gain new experience, good education, bad education, and delusion. In this way, the Lord evolves us.

All our experiences are stored in the midbrain, including delusion and mistakes. But delusion is not for delusion; it is for illumination. A mistake is not for the sake of error; it provides an opportunity for correction. Ignorance is not for ignorance; it is simply the precursor of knowledge, consciousness, superconsciousness, and wisdom.

In the ancient ages, there was no advanced physical science. There were no technological achievements such as science has given us today. Similarly, during childhood and youth we had not yet attained our adult intellectual development, which required many corrections. The more we grow, the more we are corrected. Those corrections are also stored in our midbrain.

God is so kind to us. Through our inhalation and exhalation, through our continual birth and rebirth, we gain more experience and make lasting changes in our lives. This is why the Lord (the soul, Krishna) teaches Arjuna (all human beings): "You should all love Me, follow My techniques, and meditate. Then all your good and divine qualities will rise up and will be stored in the midbrain. That is the house of a yogi." Yoga means union of body and soul. That union is within every human being forever.

The Lord is telling us: "As the soul, I am doing everything. When you constantly watch every natural inhalation and perceive that I am doing everything, you will always be a yogi, one who truly knows the soul. In every moment, I give you a new birth and death. In every moment, I change the shape of your body, cells, atoms, muscles, tissues, head, brain, hands, legs, and bones, and I store every experience in your midbrain.

"Furthermore, when you practice meditation, all your good, divine qualities will also be deposited in your midbrain," continues the Lord. "Then you will realize that you are not the doer; rather, I am the sole doer. You will be able to love Me and you will always feel indebted to Me. You will experience My presence and perceive that this is your new spiritual birth. When you meditate deeply, you change completely. Then, in this state, you will feel that all your everyday duties are done by the soul. You will perceive unity in diversity, diversity in unity, the static in the dynamic, and the dynamic in the static. That is rebirth."

The Lord tells us that a human incarnation is rare in the universe. He advises us to watch Him during every natural inhalation so we realize that the soul is God in the human being and the human being in God. Then, in every moment we can be reborn. The more we ascend into the midbrain, the more quickly we proceed towards liberation.

Verse 44

pūrvābhyāsena tenai 'va
hriyate hy avaśo 'pi saḥ
jijñāsur api yogasya
śabdabrahmā 'tivartate

Translation

Bolstered by his practices in previous lives, the yogi continues to practice yogic techniques. With deep yoga meditation, the true seeker goes beyond ritual worship.

Metaphorical Interpretation

Practicing yoga in past births creates a strong wish to follow the path of yoga and meditation again. The Lord is teaching us that true seekers should meditate deeply, feel the presence of soul in the brain, and realize that the soul does everything from above. The soul even pulls our inhalations into us from above.

Advanced yogis rise above the allure of the five senses. They do not want ritual worship. The more they perceive the presence of the soul within themselves, the more they experience divine joy. They don't feel like they are eating; instead, they are feeding the soul. After meditation, these devotees know that the soul is hearing, eating, smelling, talking, walking, and laughing for them. In every action they perceive the soul and recognize its kindness. Without Him, there is no joy. The joy they perceive is not their joy, but the joy of the living soul within them.

Verse 45

prayatnād yatamānas tu
yogī samśuddhakilbiṣaḥ
anekajanmasamsiddhas
tato yāti parām gatim

Translation

The yogi who is a true seeker of the soul, who meditates deeply for long periods, birth after birth, gains purity of heart and reaches the supreme goal of liberation.

Metaphorical Interpretation

In this verse, the Lord explains that those who understand that the soul is responsible for drawing the breath into the nose of every human being are the true seekers of God. Those who feel Him, love Him, and watch Him all day and all night have no need for rituals;

instead, by breath control they will reach the introverted state and will attain divine calm, which is godliness.

If they remain immersed in the soul and do not descend again, they will be free from human madness, sin, impurity, and imperfection. They will not even feel their incoming and outgoing breaths; they will only feel God's all-pervasive presence. In every moment, they will spiritually evolve and advance quickly.

Human beings take about 15 inhalations in one minute, which is 15 births. Every exhalation is death. In an hour, there are 15 x 60, or 900, inhalations and exhalations. So in one hour, humans have 900 births and deaths. The soul inhales 21,600 times in one day. That is the number of births and rebirths in one day. But Babaji, Lahiri Mahasaya and Shriyukteshwarji said that if you can perceive that the soul is pulling one's inhalation 1,728 times in a day, which is 1,728 informal *kriyas* (breath awareness techniques), calmly watching the air touching the formless soul, within ten years you will attain continuous liberation.

Everything depends on practice and intense desire. By constantly watching the soul in each natural inhalation, even while you are performing every action of daily life, you will have dual consciousness, which is called the Brahmin stage, merging with Brahman. This is the true meaning of rebirth into a family of yogis or Brahmins. If you practice like this, you will remain compassionately detached even in family life. You will have continuous God-realization.

You cannot pay money, or purchase flowers, fruits, candles, or lamps to achieve Self-realization. Rather, understand that your heart is the one flower that you can offer to the soul.

The fruit of all actions comes from the soul. So the sincere devotee always thinks: "Lord, you are very kind to us. You give us many fruits. Without You, we could not work; we could not receive the fruits of actions; therefore we are offering the results of all our works and all our love to Thee."

It is not necessary to purchase a candle or a lamp when you offer your knowledge consciousness to God, the real light of the body. Practice more and more, as you have been instructed, and as you grow older you will surely attain constant liberation and the supreme goal.

Verse 46

tapasvibhyo 'dhiko yogī
jñānibhyo 'pi mato 'dhikaḥ
karmibhyaś cā 'dhiko yogī
tasmād yogī bhavā 'rjuna

Translation

O Arjuna, I tell you to become a yogi, because yogis are superior to those who lead a life of penance. They are greater than highly educated scholars of the scriptures, and they are more advanced than people who mechanically perform rites and rituals to ensure the fruit of their work.

Metaphorical Interpretation

In the first chapter, the Lord told Arjuna about the way of depression (dejection), which is essential for soul culture. Without sorrow, trouble, pain, and mental upsets, no one seeks God. In the second chapter, He taught Arjuna the way of rules and regulations, and the stages and qualities of God-realization. In the third chapter, the Lord described the process of karma, what work is good and what is bad. In the fourth chapter, He explained the process of acquiring knowledge, consciousness, wisdom, and God-realization. In the fifth chapter, the Lord discussed the processes and techniques for those who remain householders. He explained that they should perform all their duties, but realize that they are not doing anything—the soul alone is performing the actions. This is *karma sannyasa*, true renunciation.

The entire sixth chapter (as well as in 4:29 and 5: 27–28), the Lord teaches the methods, techniques, and processes of meditation. Following the Lord's instructions, human beings can meditate practically and can withdraw their *shakti* or vital energy from the lower centers and bring it up to the highest center.

The truth about soul culture is written in all scriptures. But simply reading the Bhagavad Gita, Bible, Yoga Sutras of Patañjali, Brahmasutras, Upanishads, Koran, Torah, and Vedas does not produce God-realization. The techniques in the scriptures must be read, but they must also be practiced in daily life. If you read a doctor's prescription one hundred times, your disease will not disappear. You must purchase the medicine and take it according to the doctor's advice; then your disease will be cured.

Moreover, human beings should not practice techniques only by reading about them in the scriptures. They should go to a genuine, realized master who can purify the spine and the five sense organs, who can transform the mind, thought, intellect, ego, and body sense into knowledge, consciousness, and wisdom, within a short period. Then they will attain the calm state within a short period.

In the scriptures it says, *madhu-lubdha yatha bhramra:* "Bees that do not get honey from one flower should go to another flower." When a doctor cannot cure a disease within ten or twelve days' time, the patient should go to another doctor. Likewise, true seekers of God who do not reach the divine, formless stage must go from one master to another. But their love for their previous teachers remains, and they must give deepest regard to their previous gurus.

Also, seekers must not retain dogmatic views or fanatical ideas, or hold on to emotions or speculations; this is not real spirituality. To explain this, the Lord describes several classifications of yoga for different kinds of yogis.

First, there are those who perform the fire ceremony. They must keep their eyes on the fuels, fire, butter oil, sesame seeds, wheat, leaves, herbal powders, and wooden spoon (with the spoon they lift the butter oil and offer it to the fire), and they must continuously chant many mantras. But they remain in lower states of awareness, using their sense organs and organs of action, even moving their bodies. Remaining in the lower centers of the body, they cannot attain the formless stage.

The Bible (Psalms 46:10) says: "Be still and know that I am God." In the peace invocation of the Upanishads it says, *sthirair angais tuṣṭuvāmsas tanūbhiḥ*: "In extreme calm you can know God. Only when the body does not move, will you feel the formless power of God in your body." So the real fire ceremony is not lit with butter: it is lit by remaining in the soul, the Lord, and watching each breath enter the body and touch the soul fire.

Second, there are intellectual scholars of religious books who are extremely learned in philosophy. They constantly argue and fight using their knowledge of the scriptures. They will say there is no God. They do not recognize that without the soul they are nothing but dead bodies. The soul pulls their inhalation from within, making it possible for them to be learned, but by intellect alone, you cannot attain the formless state. You are born for Self-realization; through soul culture you will achieve it—but only by seeking the soul in the cranium, which is the abode of God and the true life. Those with mere intellectual knowledge, such as philosophers, scientists, or doctors, cannot obtain the formless stage unless they practice the teachings in the Bhagavad Gita (4:29 and 5:27–28). Then they can attain the formless stage and God-realization. A yogi constantly remains in cosmic consciousness, so the yogi is higher than an intellectual giant. A yogi is anyone who watches his body and soul functioning harmoniously as one.

Third, some devotees never go beyond formal mechanical rites and rituals. They chant mantras, throw flowers, fruits, and sweets, show lights to God, sing religious songs, and constantly dance and sing, but they seek only the fruits of their actions, so they are in the lower stages of karma yoga.

The best karma yogis, by breath control, withdraw their *shakti* (vital energy) from the lower spinal centers into the upper center and perceive divine light, the divine touch sensation of God throughout the whole body, and love for God. They are the real karma yogis. These true seekers of God know what is best; they will follow a short-cut scientific technique that will give them a healthy body, sound mind, deep knowledge, extreme brain power, and *avyakta*, the formless stage.

Verse 47

yogināṁ api sarveṣām
madgatenā 'ntarātmanā
śraddhāvān bhajate yo mām
sa me yuktatamo mataḥ

Translation

The Blessed Lord said:
Among all the yogis, those whose minds are ever fixed in Me, who are extremely devoted to Me with unflinching love and loyalty, who maintain implicit faith, and who practice meditation with single-minded devotion, are My favorites.

Metaphorical Interpretation

The Lord is saying that all yogis—those who realize the soul, those who feel that the soul is their life, sight, and heart, and those who recognize the soul is in every body part—can develop true love for God.

The Lord has explained all there is to know in the first six chapters. Devotees who practice the teachings in these six chapters will be able to realize the meaning of the remaining chapters. In the first six chapters, the Lord explains that only selfless work (*karma*) combined with the superconscious stage (*jñana*, knowledge) can lead to true love (*bhakti*) for God. In the latter parts of the Bhagavad Gita, more details are given about these three yogas. The eighteenth chapter gives a detailed discussion of *moksha* yoga, which is complete immersion in God in every stage of life.

The first six chapters of the Bhagavad Gita are *karma-kanda*, which means pertaining to karma. Devotees cannot remove their restlessness if they do not control their breath to clear up their spinal canal, or *sushumna*, the royal road to God, Who resides above, in the cranium.

When we sleep, we have complete control of the breath, so sleeping people do not feel any human worldly passions. Sleeping human beings experience only calm, but they do not reach God-realization. Only by the yoga of action, or karma yoga, that is, by breath mastery, does the divine power come up so devotees can attain the real yoga of knowledge, *jñana yoga,* continuous cosmic consciousness inside the cranium. But these devotees are not sleeping; they are in the state of *yoga nidra*, which means they have no sense of the world. They do however have the fullest conception of God in the divine kingdom, in the soul, above, in the cranium. In this state yogis truly perceive God; they have a continuous sensation of His divine vibration, divine light, and divine sound, which deliver eternal bliss. These yogis are in *samprajñata samadhi*, or God consciousness, all the time. At times, these yogis even experience *nirvikalpa samadhi*, the pulseless stage. Through meditation they have continuous soul consciousness and constant liberation.

When these yogis come back down from the meditative state, they still feel the soul functioning from head to foot, continuously. These yogis are filled with divine joy. Wherever their minds, thoughts, and intellects run, they know the soul is acting through their bodies. During any work they perform, they realize the soul is very kind to them. This is called *bhakti*, true love for God.

Without *karma* (action), no one can reach *jñana* (knowledge), and without knowledge, no one can find *bhakti*, love for God. *Karma yoga*, *jñana yoga*, and *bhakti yoga* are correlated and causally connected. Yogis cannot experience attraction and love for God, if they don't perceive that there is no existence, no activity, and no knowledge without the power of God.

All human beings have trouble in their lives. This is the theme of the first chapter of the Bhagavad Gita; it describes dejection in the face of trouble. The Creator is very intelligent and perfect however; the troubles of this world have a purpose. When you are dejected, you will say, "O Lord, please save me." The troubles bring us to Him.

The second chapter of the Bhagavad Gita presents a detailed narration about the truth. The Lord also consoles Arjuna in this chapter. He teaches Arjuna about the nature of truth and falsehood.

In the third chapter, the Lord explains *karma yoga*. This karma is not the work of household duties. It is *prana karma*, the practice of withdrawing your sensory awareness from the lower centers to the upper center. The Lord reveals the dark side and the bright side of work and action. He also says that the five sense organs can lead you to trouble, but if you practice Kriya Yoga, you can discern the correct path. Then, even while you do your household duties, you will understand that soul is doing the work, doing everything.

In the fourth chapter, the Lord discusses *jñana yoga*. In this chapter the Lord says there are many types of karma, such as forbidden action, unlawful action, inaction, bad karma, and the true nature of action; however, if you meditate, you will develop knowledge. When you have knowledge, all your ignorance will disappear. Finally, the Lord tells Arjuna that if he keeps a long sword of knowledge at the forefront of his consciousness, he can remove all his doubts and can sit near the soul inside his cranium. This is how a yogi leads the true life.

In the fifth chapter of the Bhagavad Gita, the Lord explains *karma sannyasa.* This is the most important chapter. You should not be a monk and leave your family; rather, you should maintain the state of a monk and remain with your family. By practicing Kriya Yoga very deeply, you will always realize that you are not your body. You and He are one.

Without the soul, you cannot inhale; you are a dead body. A dead body cannot do anything—only by the instruction of the Lord, the soul, does the body machine work. The soul is pure, perfect, kind, and loving. This same nature is in you. When you practice Kriya Yoga, you can come up into the pituitary where the Lord sits. Sit near the soul and observe that the soul is the sole doer, and unchangeable, just as Arjuna sat in the chariot while the Lord drove and told Arjuna what to do.

If you practice Kriya Yoga, you will achieve *karma sannyasa. Sannyasa* means complete renunciation of the bodily sense and the material sense, as if your entire bodily existence has been burned, and only the soul remains. In this state, you will feel that you are nothing but the pure and perfect soul; you will be detached from the bodily sense; you will regard pleasure and pain as equal. Peace belongs to soul. Pain also belongs to soul. Practicing Kriya Yoga very deeply, you will remain absorbed in the soul. You will experience the extreme calm of godliness. When you remain in this stage, your ignorance disappears and you will enjoy cosmic consciousness. While living as a householder, you can experience continuous liberation.

In the sixth chapter, the Lord describes specific techniques for meditation: how to sit, where to sit, how to withdraw your senses from the lower centers to the upper center, what kind and quantity of food to take, and how to control your breath. In addition He explains how to be your own your friend and when you are your own enemy, how to remove evil, how to develop tolerance and balance of mind, where to fix your attention, how to transform your mind into wisdom, what type of yoga is best, who is a true worker, what is true oblation, which is the best kind of meditation, and how to truly love God.

If you follow the teachings in these six chapters and take instruction from a genuine Kriya Yoga teacher, you can have *karma sannyasa.* Like Arjuna, you can kill all the evil that exists in your body and mind; also, you can perceive God's all-pervasive presence, realizing that you are co-creating with the Lord.

The Upanishads and the Bhagavad Gita are like a milk cow, and Krishna is the milkman. Arjuna and every other human being are like the calves. After the calf sucks the nipples of the cow, the milkman can milk the cow. Arjuna asks Krishna many questions, and the Lord answers him. In this way, the true seekers of God drink the nectar of the Bhagavad Gita. All human beings should follow the Bhagavad Gita, and live the Bhagavad Gita.

Feel emancipation in every action. Feel that your life is complete. You and He are One and always have been One. This is the scientific interpretation of the Upanishads and the Yoga of Self-Mastery in the sixth chapter of the Bhagavad Gita.

Summary

The Bhagavad Gita is divided into three parts, each containing six chapters. Each part (*shataka*) highlights one aspect of spiritual discipline. The beginning of this first part explains the path of karma that leads to *jñana* (knowledge). *Karma* (action) does not merely mean physical activity; rather, it refers to the root of all activity, *prana karma*, the play of vital breath. This six-chapter section ends with "The Yoga of Self Mastery," which explains in detail the practical aspects of yoga and meditation.

This chapter has forty-seven verses. Five are attributed to Arjuna, and forty-two are the Lord's sermon about yoga and meditation as the means to Self mastery and realization.

Verses 1–2: A yogi becomes a true *sannyasi* (a person of renunciation) by renouncing attachment to the binding aspect of karma (action).

Verses 3–4: The means and qualities needed to be established in the path of yoga.

Verses 5–6: It is necessary for aspirants to make a sincere effort to eradicate vices and cultivate virtues.

Verses 7–9: The qualities of a perfected yogi.

Verses 10: Encourages meditation.

Verses 11–13: The correct sitting posture (*asana*) for meditation is explained, as well as where and how to sit.

Verses 14–16: Practical hints about practicing meditation.

Verses 17–26: The principles for achieving realization (*samadhi*) by avoiding extreme states and seeking moderation in every aspect of life are described.

Verses 27–28: The nature of the blissful state, free from impurities (*sattvika sukha*).

Verse 29: The experience of the Self within and without.

Verses 30–32: The results of meditation: seeing everything as equal, experiencing divinity in all.

Verses 33–34: Practical questions and concerns regarding the restless mind.

Verses 35–36: The need to control the restless mind and the techniques of *abhyasa* (practice) and *vairagya* (nonattachment).

Verses 37–39: What will happen to someone who is unable to attain the ultimate goal in this life through meditation?

Verses 40–45: Meditation develops gradually over time despite ups and downs.

Verse 46: The glory of the yogi and the Lord's direct instruction to Arjuna to be a yogi.

Verse 47: Concluding remarks on yoga, meditation, and Self mastery, describing how to be a yogi with devotion.

This chapter is practical, with clear and direct discussion about the restlessness of the mind and how to overcome it with a meditative practice and an attitude of nonattachment. It reveals that in meditation, one must always:

1. Concentrate
2. Live moderately
3. Maintain equanimity with equal regard for all

In this way, one may cultivate the divine qualities, preparing the way to divine knowledge and love.

Appendices

Glossary of Names

The Spiritual Meanings of the Sanskrit Names

Rulers of the Kingdom

Every human being must learn to rule the kingdom of the body, mind, ego, and intellect.

Blind King: Dhritarashtra (Mind, *manas*) "Container of all worldly desires" One who is blind to the indwelling Self and selfishly absorbed in matter.

King's Eldest Son: Duryodhana (Desires, *kama*) This ambitious, unwise king succumbs to bad advice and is unable to rule himself (his body kingdom). Every human mind is misled by bad ministers—the five senses—and remains trapped in the extroverted state of awareness.

King's Scribe (Minister): Samjaya "He who has controlled the five senses and conquered the extroverted state." He is absorbed in God and can foresee everything.

King's Preceptor: Dronacharya (Duality) This is the restlessness in every human being, the vacillating temperament that leads to death. Everyone knows the true soul is within, but their delusion is greater than their desire for truth.

Prime Minister: Matula (Shakuni) (Intelligence; *buddhi*) Duryodhana's maternal uncle is the superconscious stage of human development that can crush all evil within. Shakuni's whole family was crushed by Duryodhana. Shakuni vowed to destroy the entire family of Kauravas—all evil.

The Evil Warriors of the Kaurava Army

Kuru-kuru rava: *Those who are constantly engrossed in matter and memory, not in soul; Anything dark or ignorant that remains in the lower body centers. All negative mental tendencies trapped in the biological body are members of the Kaurava army.*

Commander-in-Chief: Bhishma (Apparent Awareness; *abhasa chaitanya*) Self-willed; firmly determined to remain in ego; extremely proud and rigid. Unwilling to marry.

Most Powerful General: Karna "Strong Ears." Engrossed in gossip; forgetful of the truth; easily swayed by flattery; the leading of others towards falsehood.

Ferocious General: Kripa Kindly, compassionate, but misled by attachment to diversity.

Son of Dronacharya: Ashvatthama Fickleness; new desires are eternally arising. Constant fluctuation of thoughts, moods, wants. Seeking ambition, glory, and fame.

Malicious General: Vikarna A disbeliever in God. Addicted to bad ideas and behavior.

Son of Somadatta: General Bhurishrava "Hears many things." Constantly extroverted; easily influenced; not absorbed in the soul.

Duryodhana's Brother-in law: Jayadratha Bluffs with his eloquence; having little learning but spreading dangerous falsehoods.

Vulgar General: Duhshasana (Anger; *krodha*) "Beyond control and extremely vulgar." Threatened to undress Mother Draupadi. She saved herself by calling on the soul, Krishna, Who wrapped her in endless cloth, so she was dressed no matter how much Duhshasana tore at her clothes.

The Five Pandava Brothers

Five kinds of light or knowledge hide in the spinal canal; these are the forces for spirituality.

Education Minister: Yudhishthira "Very calmly fights evil." This force rules the throat center (fifth center) and manifests wisdom. The vacuum element creates the power of detachment—"turning the other cheek."

Administration Minister: Bhima (Breath Control) "Directs breath from one thought to another." This force rules the heart center. The air element (fourth center) nourishes and controls all life.

Food Minister: Arjuna Krishna's disciple; "He who has no bondage, but appears to have bondage." Originally overpowered by the twenty-four gross elements, but with the soul's (Krishna's) help, there is the ability to acquire self-control. The fire element (third center) creates digestive power and appetite for life. The fire nourishes the brain and creates the power of the finest conception.

Irrigation Minister: Nakula *Na kula*: "No end to the desire for pleasure." This force rules the sacral center (second center). The sexual waters of life give birth to all physical life.

Agriculture Minister: Sahadeva *Devena-saha*: The "fallow land" that awaits cultivation. This force rules rules the coccygeal center (first center). All the material wealth and resources needed for survival are buried within the earth. He cultivates the earth to get its treasures of food and gold; likewise, we must activate the power of the soul (Krishna) within our earth center.

The Pandava Family

Father of the family: Pandu *Panda:* Knowledge, superconsciousness, cosmic consciousness, and wisdom.

Mother of Arjuna and Bhima: Kunti "Finest conception: pinpointed attention in the soul and bliss"; established in the pituitary. She also gave non-sexual birth to Yudhishthira. The power in the navel, heart, throat centers.

Mother of Nakula and Sahadeva: Madri The second wife of Pandu. An occasional lack of self-control.

Wife of the Five Pandava Brothers: Draupadi "Quickest means of success." In this sense, "wife" means the *shakti* power of the five Pandava brothers' elements; that which gives life to the seed. The five male brothers are impotent without the nourishing female life force.

Five Children of Draupadi: Draupadeya An essence of each of the five elements remains in the five centers in the spine. If we can control these elements, we can quickly perceive God.

Draupadi's Brother: Dhrishtadyumna The power to control the stubbornness and restlessness of five sons of Drupada: the five lower centers.

The Good Warriors of the Pandava Army

Panda: *The positive forces of Self-knowledge and inner light.*
Collectively, with the five Pandava brothers,
they comprise the knowledge body.

Greatest Pandava General: Drupada "Goes quickly and directly" from the coccyx to the top of the spine, and to God in the pituitary. Lives in the world doing everyday activities, but achieves God-realization by meditating constantly.

General: Yuyudhana Constantly fights evil; devoted; always goes toward God.

General: Virata *Vigata rat*: "Completely free from body and worldly senses." Liberation from thoughts and desires during meditation. Always realizes that the soul is the sole doer in the material world.

General: Dhrishtaketu *Dhrishtan-ketava-yah sah*: "Dragon's tail with no head." Always seeking the kingdom of God in the upper cranium.

General: Chekitana *Chekit tan*: "Hears the melodies of God." Constantly listens to inner sound: *aum*.

General: Kashiraja *Kashyate it kashi*: Illuminated He who is "illuminated with divine light." The spiritual king, constantly focused on the third eye.

King: Purujit *Puran jayati iti*: "One who conquers the body intellect sense" during meditation. Kunti's Brother. Uncle of Bhima. A well-balanced mind during everyday living.

General: Kuntibhoja When people fix their attention in the soul, they experience divine bliss.

General: Shaibya He who achieves the formless, pulseless power and transcends the human qualities is fully divine.

General: Yudhamanyu "Defends against evil qualities."

Arjuna's Son: Saubhadra (also known as Abhimanyu) "One who is merged in the soul." A nephew of Krishna. "Destroys vicious qualities in the heart." Kills many Kaurava warriors as he tunnels up the spine from the coccyx to the heart.

General: Uttamauja "Extreme power and strength." The power of the soul makes you forget the physical senses during meditation.

General: Satyaki *Sumati*: divine disposition.

General: Maheshwasa The extremely effective digestive power of human beings; the ability to obtain the strength and energy for removing all bad qualities.

General: Shikhandin The turbulent teacher in human beings, namely, *parashakti*, the power to crush one's own ego and bad traits. Bhishma was adamant in his beliefs, a zealotry that only Shikhandin could crush.

The Origin of Krishna's Name

Arjuna's Preceptor: Krishna "Body and soul are one." Krishna is the true king, the realized soul residing in the pituitary, which guides the mind and body.

Krishi: the cultivated land, the human body.

Na: the formless power of God that remains in the body as the soul.

Krishi bhuvachaka shabda: Every human being is a cultivated land (*ham*).

Nancha nirguna vachaka: The formless power is in the soul.

Tayoraikam parabrahma: If these two letters are added, the sum will be Krishna.

Krishna iti abhidiyate: It is said each human being has two qualities: one is body, and this body is cultivated (activated) by soul-Krishna.

Gam brahmandam gachhati iti ganga: Everything in the whole world exists in our entire body. The power of God pulls the breath into us. The 727, 210, 201 blood vessels through which pure blood is flowing are the Ganga river. Purity comes through the slow Kriya breath, inhaled by the soul, Krishna.

Alternate Names of Krishna

Traditionally, there are 1008 names for Krishna

Hrishikesha Conductor of the five senses and all the body parts.

Govinda *Go*: "the entire universe." *Vindah*: "gives." *Hridinam: ananda*. "He who gives peace, bliss, and joy to the entire universe."

Madhusudana One who can avoid all the demonic qualities. Krishna killed a demon called Madhu. All human bodies have two demons in them, Madhu and Kaitabha, that pull them into the extroverted state. Krishna can remain in the introverted state and overcome the extroverted state.

Madhava *Ma* is Mother Nature, the conductor of truth, the unlimited higher voltage of Krishna's energy. *Dhava* means master.

Janardana One who crushes demonic habits through the power of meditation.

Keshava *Ke* is the power of God, the soul, Krishna, that constantly hides inside all human beings. *Shava* is the lifeless body that is animated by the soul. Keshi is a demon with the body of a horse that ate people until Krishna choked him by the neck. This means that we must keep our focus above the neck to attain God-realization.

Shri Bhagavan *Bhaga* is the womb and divine creative organ of God, which gives birth to everything. Every human body is a womb that receives this power of God and gives birth to speech, sight, hearing, and so forth.

Names of Arjuna

Arjuna *A-rajju-na:* "He who is not tied by a rope to evil, but thinks he is tied." The five senses are so turbulent that only the warrior Arjuna can overcome them while remaining in cosmic consciousness, as a result of Krishna's teachings.

Gudakesha One who never sleeps and always remains alert. *Gudak* means *tandra*, or sleep, the forgetfulness of the inner Self. *Isha* is the formless power of God. If you meditate and perceive *Isha,* the soul, then you can wage war and remain in the superconscious stage, and can thus conquer all evil.

Partha One who has the strength to control the mind.

Bharata *Bha* is the superconscious stage; *rata* is one engrossed in that stage.

Paramtapa This is the extreme body heat that comes from the oxygen given to the soul fire by breath control. This vitalizes the food center, from which the warrior draws his valor, strength, and courage for fighting evil.

The Fields of Battle

Battlefield where the Kauravas and the Pandavas fight: Kurukshetra "Field of work." Every human body is battlefield where both positive and negative thoughts and actions arise nonstop during every moment of life.

Divine Field: Dharmakshetra "The place where the living soul resides." The spiritual body abides in the higher centers in the spinal canal. After realization, the navel center is also included. Also translated as, "The soul is the container of the body."

Chariot: Ratha "Coach." The symbol for the physical human body. The soul, Krishna, and the biological force, Arjuna, ride together in the body chariot while the battle for enlightenment is waged.

Miracles of Krishna's Childhood

Shri Krishna was the son of Vasudeva and Devaki. Devaki's brother was Kamsa, the king of Mathura. A few days after their marriage, Devaki and her husband, Vasudeva, were going home with her brother, King Kamsa, who was driving the chariot. When they reached the gate of the palace of King Kamsa, they heard a loud sound three times from heaven. The sound announced that the eighth child of Devaki would be a divine incarnation who would kill his maternal uncle Kamsa, because the king had no faith in God.

Upon hearing the voice from heaven, King Kamsa wanted to behead his sister, but Vasudeva, Devaki's husband, requested that the king spare her. He said they would give all their children to King Kamsa, so he could kill them. In this way, seven children were killed by Kamsa.

King Kamsa knew that the eighth child would be dangerous to him, so he decided to prevent Vasudeva and Devaki from enjoying sexually. The couple was bound by iron chains to two stone pillars on opposite sides of a room. The king also kept guards in the room to make sure they could not free themselves from the chains.

Many days passed. The husband and wife were able to see each other, and they meditated very deeply to become free. One night, while they were meditating, a divine light flashed in the room, which was the flash of God. The light gradually entered the body of Devaki, and by the power of God, without sexual union, she conceived.

King Kamsa had two wives. The elder wife was named Asti, which means "existence," meaning that the power of God is within. She was very devoted to God. She constantly prayed that Devaki would be liberated when she had her child. Asti was always in seclusion, and she told Kamsa that she was quite happy like that, so the king should spend his time with his young wife, Prapti.

Prapti, whose name means "one who has immense desire for worldly things," was always with the king, urging him to kill his sister. She said, "If your sister or her husband free themselves from the chains, they could enjoy sexually and conceive. If she does, the boy will kill you." The king said that is was not possible, because they were well chained, with four guards constantly in the room.

Eight months after the conception, baby Krishna was fully developed within his mother's womb. At this time, Devaki and Vasudeva were overwhelmed with anxiety, worrying that King Kamsa would learn about the child and immediately kill Devaki and the baby. During that time, Prapti said to her husband, Kamsa: "Go and look inside Devaki's and Vasudeva's room in the night to see what they are doing and saying."

King Kamsa went and he saw a divine, dazzling light in the darkness. Inside the brilliant light, Kamsa saw a healthy, divine male baby. King Kamsa was bewildered and terrified. He shouted to the guards to bring some light. When they did, the king saw that the divine light was coming from the body of Devaki and that the divine baby was in her womb. The king rebuked his sister and her husband, saying, "You have enjoyed sexually. How did you free yourselves from the chains?" He shouted insults at them. Then he gave blows to the guards and shouted, "You have been sleeping. How did they loosen the chains?" The guards replied that they had not been sleeping, that the chains had not been opened, and that the key had been in the king's possession.

King Kamsa was extremely afraid; his body was shaking and he was sweating. It was difficult for him to leave the room. He went to Prapti and told her that in the darkness he had seen a dazzling light in the body of Devaki, and that he had seen a divine baby in her womb. Prapti was extremely afraid that her husband would be killed by the baby, a divine incarnation. The queen said, "Please rest now and be quiet. Tomorrow, cut off your sister's head; then the baby will never be born."

Devaki and Vasudeva were frightened that the king would come and kill her, so they prayed to God to save the baby. In the dead of night, when all the guards were sleeping, Shri Krishna materialized in front of them in the form of Narayana (Vishnu) with four hands. He said to them, "Why are you so unhappy and in terror? I am the incarnation in your womb. I am the imperishable soul, the living power of God. Who can kill me? Please remain in a divine mood and don't be afraid. Neither of you will have any trouble." Then Vishnu disappeared.

At the same time, King Kamsa dreamed that Shri Krishna was coming to kill him. The king shouted loudly, "Prapti, please save me! Shri Krishna is coming to kill me." The queen said, "It is only a dream. Don't be frightened."

Krishna was born in the dark fortnight of the eighth moon in the month of August–September, during the rainy season. Vasudeva was miraculously freed from his chains, and he left the castle carrying Shri Krishna in a basket, heading to the bank of the Yamuna River. The way was lighted by the divine light emanating from Shri Krishna. The river was swollen and running heavily, but the current was completely stopped by the power of Shri Krishna so that Vasudeva could cross. He took Shri Krishna to the house of Yashoda in Gokulam, who was sleeping after having just given birth to a girl. Vasudeva exchanged Shri Krishna for the baby girl and returned to Kamsa's palace. He placed the baby with Devaki and put his chains back on.

Shortly thereafter, King Kamsa entered the room. He saw the divine baby girl lying at the side of Devaki. Kamsa picked up the baby and forcefully threw her to the ground to kill her. But the baby slipped away from his hands and flew into the sky, appearing as the younger sister of Vishnu, and saying, "He who will kill you is Shri Krishna. He is staying on the other bank of the Yamuna river in Gokulam, in the house of Yashoda." And the goddess disappeared.

The birth of Shri Krishna was attended by many miracles. The first was the divine light emanating from the divine baby while it was in the womb, which was seen by King Kamsa. The second was the manifestation by Krishna in the form of Vishnu in front of his parents, when he consoled them. The third occurred when Vasudeva was able to free himself from his chains and escape imprisonment in the palace to take Shri Krishna away. The fourth was the appearance of the divine light that lit the path. The fifth was the current stopping in the Yamuna river so that Vasudeva could cross. The sixth miracle was the appearance of the Divine Mother when King Kamsa tried to kill the baby girl.

A few days after Shri Krishna's birth, another miracle occurred when King Kamsa again tried to kill Krishna. Kamsa went to the house of his sister's daughter, Putana, who had just given birth. Kamsa gave her some poison and instructed her to rub it in the nipple of her breast and then go to Yashoda's house. Putana was to say that she would feed the baby with her milk. Then, while sucking on her poisoned nipple, the baby Krishna would surely die.

At Yashoda's house everyone was happy to see Putana, and she took the child in her lap. The divine baby Shri Krishna joyfully sucked her breast. Gradually, Shri Krishna took the whole breast in his mouth; then he took in all of her ribs. Then Shri Krishna took one half of her body in his mouth, pressed with his jaws and crushed her. Putana shouted, cried out, and then died.

Putana was an impure woman, a devil. The metaphorical meaning of her name comes from *puta*, which means purity, and *na*, which means no. The symbolic meaning of her name is one who has no purity. She had a son, but did not want the love of a son. So at the behest of King Kamsa, she went to kill a baby boy with poison. Shri Krishna, in his first days of babyhood, killed Putana because she was an impure woman.

When Shri Krishna was a boy of five months, there was a rice ceremony in which rice was placed in his mouth. Several hundred guests were invited, and there was to be a feast in the house. They had made a lot of yogurt, which was placed in an earthen pot with a huge quantity of milk. The baby Krishna was lying by the side of the pot. Krishna gave one kick to the earthen pot with his heel and turned it over. He then turned around and placed his mouth over the opening of the jar and sucked and swallowed all the yogurt.

When Shri Krishna was several months older, he was crawling and licking clay off the earthen floor with his tongue. A lot of dirt got on his tongue. Yashoda came over to clean his tongue, but when she opened Shri Krishna's mouth, she saw the whole world and all of creation inside of his mouth, throat, belly, and intestines. In this way, Yashoda discovered that Shri Krishna was a divine child.

When Shri Krishna was a boy of eight to nine months, he was constantly crawling everywhere. His mother Yashoda was very busy with her household duties, so she decided to tie the baby with a cord around his waist so that he couldn't go far. She brought a rope, but when she tried to encircle Shri Krishna's waist, she saw that the rope was not long enough. Each time she got a longer rope, Krishna materialized a bigger waist. Yashoda could not to encircle his belly. She was astonished and believed that Shri Krishna was undoubtedly the incarnation of God. She gave him the name Damodara, which means "very big belly."

In Vrindavan there was a pond named Kalandi that contained many venomous snakes. Everyone who passed by this pond on the road was bitten by a snake and killed. When he was two years old, Shri Krishna jumped into the water. Immediately many snakes came up to bite him, but Shri Krishna stood on the hood of the serpent king and killed them all.

When Shri Krishna was only three, there was a very large bird named Bakasura that would swallow boys aged two, three, or four. Shri Krishna was walking on the street one day when the bird appeared and took him into his big bill. Shri Krishna suddenly took a huge form with a heavy body. With his feet, he pushed down on the lower bill, and with his hands he pulled up the upper bill. With his power, he tore off the two bills and killed Bakasura.

There was also a demon named Mendhasura that ate young boys and girls around the age of five. When Shri Krishna was five, the people of Vrindavan came to Him and asked him to kill Mendhasura. Shri Krishna said, "Mendhasura is a powerful demon, and if a drop of his blood falls on the ground, immediately the same Mendhasura will appear there. It is very dangerous to try to kill him."

Shri Krishna instructed everyone, "Prepare a vast place and cover it with sand two feet deep. Then cover the sand with two feet of barley powder. Any blood that falls will be absorbed by the barley powder. Above the powder set many logs in a square a few feet high. Then many people should hide themselves nearby and when the demon comes, set fire to the stack of wood."

Shri Krishna then said, "When Mendhasura comes, he will take me into his mouth and swallow me. Immediately I will make my body huge, so he will suffocate. The moment he suffocates, I will jump from the ground over the fire and hold him over the fire. When his body has started burning, I will tear out his heart, and blood will pour out. I will rub this blood all over my body. Then from below, you all throw barley powder over me."

Mendhasura came and swallowed Shri Krishna, who assumed a very large body, larger than Mendhasura. Mendhasura died and his body was burned in the fire, held by Shri Krishna. Since Shri Krishna is a divine incarnation, He is a divine fire. Fire cannot burn fire, so Shri Krishna was not burned. As everyone constantly threw barley powder on Krishna, Mendhasura was burned to ashes.

This incident occurred in March, one day before the full moon. In India, there is a festival called *dola purnima* (*purnima* means full moon). It is also the occasion of *holi*, the color festival. During this festival immediately after Mendhasura's demise, the overjoyed people of Vrindavan threw colored barley powder to celebrate. In India today, colored powder is put on everyone, both male and female, every year at this time. Everyone meditates on that day because Mendhasura, the demonic power, still abides in every human being. On most days, people quarrel with each other; they do not have amity and friendship with each other, but on this unique, balanced day, everyone removes their enmity, anger, and cruelty. Everyone meditates all day and meets one another as friends. They rub colored powder over their bodies, just as the power of Shri Krishna exists in the entire body, just as the spirit of God pervades us. On this day, people perceive this spirit and mingle and play divinely—it is almost a spiritual enjoyment. This is one of the greatest spiritual ceremonies in the world.

Another special spiritual celebration in India, called *rasapurnima*, occurs on the full moon day in the month of August–September. This festival also celebrates events from Shri Krishna's childhood.

From his birth until the age of seven, Shri Krishna gave his extreme love to all the people of Vrindavan. He was always playing his flute. It was so melodious and touching that even the animal beings—cows, deer, goats, and dogs—were charmed by the sound of Shri Krishna's flute. They would all gather and silently stand to listen when he played. They were absorbed in this divine power, listening to the divine music. He was so kind, loving, and generous that he conquered the minds of all the people in Vrindavan, Mathura, and other nearby localities.

Shri Krishna had one great devotee who was deeply absorbed in spirituality. Her name was Radha. She remained with Krishna all the time and served Him. Much older than Krishna, Radha was the wife of Krishna's maternal uncle. Shri Krishna and Radha are often pictured together, clasping each other, side by side. Radha symbolizes the gross body of every human being and Krishna symbolizes the soul.

Many people have the misconception that Radha and other ladies made physical love with Shri Krishna. But this is a misinterpretation, because at that time Shri Krishna was only six years old. At the age of ten years and eight months, he left Vrindavan. Shri Krishna was the life of all the inhabitants of Vrindavan. *Vri* comes from *vrajadham*, which means to perceive Krishna in the whole body and to merge with divinity. Every human being has a physical nature, the body. In Hindu terminology and Sanskrit, the feminine gender is used for the body. Our body nature is feminine. In the body nature, there is cosmic nature—the power of Shri Krishna. Those who do not perceive Shri Krishna in their whole body live in delusion and error; they are engrossed in their body nature, which is the lower nature.

At the age of seven, Shri Krishna left Vrindavan because of Radha. Radha had a misconception that Shri Krishna loved only her deeply, that He could not give His love to any other person. This was her ego. She told Krishna, "You love me very much. You can't give this love to any other person in the universe."

Shri Krishna said, "I know you have implicit faith, love, and loyalty to Me. You are My greatest devotee. But due to your ego, you have lost all your power. I love everyone equally. As the sun shines and gives its rays to all equally, similarly I shine as the incarnation, more powerful than the sun. This is your misconception."

Radha said, "If this be so, then go to Kubja who is very ugly and not so devoted. (Kubja was a hunchback.) Can You give the same love to Kubja that You give to me or others in Vrindavan? Can you give the same love to Kubja?"

Krishna answered: "You think that you are your body—this is your downfall from spirituality. In every human being in the universe, I am the soul, the spirit; that is why all gross bodies are alive. Your beauty is not your beauty; your spirituality is your beauty. Because of your spirituality, I gave you extreme affection. But due to your human state of mind, you do not realize that I am the sole doer. Your beauty is not yours, it is My beauty. Without Me, your body is dead. I have given you much affection, but because of your ego you have become like a monkey—an animal being."

Radha, the greatest devotee, had ego. Out of pride she said, "Thank you very much! You can leave me and leave Vrindavan and go to Dwaraka and stay with Kubja."

And Shri Krishna said, "Thank you very much. I am happy. I will go."

Then Radha said, "The whole of Vrindavan, all the inhabitants, have given you so much love—even I who am your greatest devotee. You cannot leave Vrindavan and go to Mathura."

Shri Krishna answered, "I am not a body, I am the incarnation. To Me, everything is equal. I have no attachment to Vrindavan. I have no attachment to anything because I am the detached, marvelous power of God. So I am leaving this place." Radha thought, "Surely He will come back within five minutes and talk with everyone, even with me." But He did not return.

Radha sat down under a tree. She felt that Shri Krishna would come back at any moment. An hour passed. Days passed. Months passed. Summer rains became the dews of autumn. Still Radha sat calmly thinking that Shri Krishna would return. She didn't know how long she sat. Constantly she thought of Shri Krishna, expecting Him to return. She was continuously in the mood of Krishna.

All the inhabitants of Vrindavan were also extremely unhappy, so they too constantly thought of Krishna. In this way, they were all transformed. They were no longer in the worldly mood. They merged into Shri Krishna and began to think, "We are Krishna." Quietly, they all went to Radha. They did not want to disturb her. Radha was transformed because she was so deeply engrossed in the living power of Krishna, the incarnation.

The villagers brought cotton and placed it under her nose and found that the cotton didn't move. They thought she would die immediately. So they sent a lady to Mathura to tell Shri Krishna that Radha was dying. She said, "We placed cotton under her nose and the cotton did not move."

Shri Krishna laughed and said, "Radha won't die. Radha is now completely transformed into Krishna. If you go to her and chant "Krishna, Krishna, Krishna," you will see Radha stand like Krishna.

As I am accustomed to take up my flute in my hand just so, you will see Radha do the same. Radha has achieved complete transformation."

The name of the girl who took the message to Krishna was Vrinda, which means the inhabitants of Vrindavan. When she returned, she told the inhabitants of Vrindavan what Krishna said. Those who were completely absorbed in the mood of Krishna went and chanted "Krishna" in Radha's ear. Slowly, slowly, Radha stood up and bent her hand in the position Krishna used to hold the flute, and bent her leg just like He did. She stood like that and felt the living power of Krishna in her.

This story reveals the value of dejection. Until there is dejection, vanity will not disappear. While she was dejected, Radha achieved pinpointed attention on Krishna, the soul; then she merged in that soul and found the truth. Afterwards, she had no more desire for Krishna, because she was transformed into Him. Upon seeing this, everyone began dressing and moving like Krishna. They circled around Radha, rotating and dancing around her. Radha symbolized Krishna, the transformation into Krishna. This is *rasapurnima.*

Metaphorically, the story explains that when human beings fix their attention on the indwelling Self in the Christ center, the Krishna center, within the pituitary, they will surely achieve transformation. Until a person is totally merged in the pituitary, the breathless state cannot be attained; on the contrary, there will be restlessness. When one attains the breathless state, God is perceived in the whole system.

In the entire Bhagavad Gita, Krishna teaches Arjuna to bring his awareness up from the lower centers to the upper center. As Shri Krishna said, "I abide in the body chariot inside the pituitary. I am the soul and you are My most loyal disciple, so sit behind Me and follow Me absolutely. Then surely you will discover peace and godliness."

This is the real meaning of *rasapurnima. Rasa* refers to the transformation of the inhabitants of Vrindavan into Krishna, and *purnima* means the full moon day.

The symbolic meaning of the name "Krishna" comes from *krishi* and *na. Krishi* means cultivated land; every human body is a cultivated land. Everything in the whole world exists in every human body. There are many kinds of cultivation. From mental cultivation, we develop medicine, science, engineering, law, and business. When we cultivate the land, things grow, such as fruits, flowers, and wheat. Coal, diamonds, gold, iron, manganese, and petroleum can also be cultivated from the land. Everything in the earth is also in the human body. However, a well-cultivated body land is nothing if the *na*, the formless invisible body, does not remain within it. Our gross body is *krishi*, and our invisible body is *na*. Our gross body is nothing. It is lifeless if the *na* (formless body) does not inhale.

Our body cannot cultivate anything without the invisible body. You cannot cultivate any food grains or earn any money. You cannot create your sex mood in your body without the soul, or *na*. You cannot feel hunger in the *krishi* body without *na*, the formless body. A dead person cannot eat, cannot enjoy, and cannot move without the formless body. We have five sense organs in our gross body, but without the formless body, the ear cannot hear and give pleasure, the eyes, skin, nose, and tongue cannot function or experience unlimited forms of pleasure.

Our body form is *krishi* land and our formless body, the soul, is the cultivator of the *krishi* land. "Krishna" is the soul and body together: form and the formless united.

Every human being is a Krishna. If you cultivate your body nature, you will perceive the formless nature. Krishna will lead you from dishonesty to honesty, from illiteracy to literacy, from poverty to wealth, from delusion to disillusion, from impurity to purity, from unhappiness to happiness, and from bondage to liberation.

In each drop of milk there is cream, but people cannot perceive it. If a large quantity of milk is churned, from every single drop of milk the cream will rise to the top. The cream separates from the milk body. This is why Shri Krishna constantly tells Arjuna to rise above his body nature and churn it. In the Bhagavad Gita (6:25), it says, "Gradually come up from the lower centers to the pituitary, where I am sitting. I will be the driver and you follow Me. I will drive you nicely."

The same thing is said in the Bible in John (3:3–5). Jesus said that you are born of flesh, but you are to be born again, from above, of water and spirit. The life of Jesus in the universe was only for purity, perfection, love, and kindness. Similarly, Shri Krishna was the incarnation of purity, perfection, love, and kindness.

Life of the Author

Paramahamsa Hariharananda, the greatest living realized master of Kriya Yoga, is a legend among the spiritual seekers. He has attained *nirvikalpa samadhi*, the state of no pulse and no breath, where all activities of the body, mind, thought, intellect, and ego cease. He is merged and absorbed in God. *Nirvikalpa samadhi* is the long-cherished goal of all aspirants in the spiritual path. In the Kriya Yoga tradition, he is in the lineage of the realized masters Shri Babaji Maharaj, Shri Lahiri Mahasaya, and Swami Shriyukteshwarji.

Paramahamsa Hariharananda was born on the twenty-seventh of May, 1907, in the hamlet of Habibpur on the bank of the sacred river Ganga, in the Nadia district of Bengal, just a few kilometers away from the birthplace of Shri Chaitanya Mahaprabhu—a God-intoxicated divine incarnation of the fifteenth century. The village of Habibpur was sanctified by the birth of this holy child, whose childhood name was Rabindranath. His father, Haripada Bhattacharya, was a disciplined, dedicated, devout, and determined Brahmin, well-versed in all Hindu scriptures. His mother Nabinkali, was also extremely divine—a pious, generous, and loving lady par excellence.

Endowed with uncommon and marvelous brainpower, this divine child memorized all the intricate mantras, hymns, and prayers in Sanskrit, surprising everyone. At the age of eleven, he took the vow of *brahmacharya*, also known as the *upanayana* ceremony of the Brahmins. His desire for spiritual upliftment was growing, so he went to Shri Vijay Krishna Chattopadhyaya, a householder realized master living in the outskirts of Calcutta, and took initiation into the path of *jñana yoga* at the age of twelve. He excelled in sacred and secular education and was eventually well placed in society as a technocrat.

His thirst for spiritual enlightenment could not be quenched by material achievement. As a result, he was inspired by his family preceptor, Vijay Krishna, to meet Shriyukteshwarji, the most befitting disciple of the great master of Kriya Yoga, Shri Lahiri Mahasaya. As advised, he called on Shriyukteshwarji at his Serampore Ashram in 1932 and received initiation into Kriya Yoga, the sacred and scientific meditation technique.

Under Shriyukteshwarji's holy guidance, Rabindranath learned much more of astronomy, astrology, and palmistry along with strict spiritual discipline and meditation. Later, in 1935, when Paramahamsa Yogananda returned to India from the U.S., on the advice of Shriyukteshwarji, Rabindranath was blessed to witness Yoganandaji's *samadhi* and was initiated into the second Kriya.

Shriyukteshwarji had the wish that this young, celibate Rabindranath should renounce the material life and take charge of his ashram in Puri. However, by God's will, it took several years for the fulfillment of his noble wish. In 1938, he moved to the land of Lord Jagannath, a seaside city near Puri in eastern India. Later, he lived permanently in Karar Ashram, accepting the ascetic life with the new name of Brahmachari Ravinarayan.

He started the strict spiritual practice of sincere meditation, observing silence for several years. Within a short time, he attained perfection in three yogic *mudras*: the *khechari, bhramari,* and s*hambhavi mudras.* After this attainment, a supernatural divine light (aura) was emanating from his body.

In the early 1940s, the head of Shriyukteshwarji's Karar Ashram, Shrimat Swami Satyananda Giri, initiated him into the third Kriya. Subsequently, he learned all the other higher kriyas from Shrimat Bhupendranath Sanyal Deva Sharman, a householder and realized yogi, the youngest disciple of the great guru Yogiraj Lahiri Mahasaya.

In the mid-1940s, the most secret technique of *samadhi* was revealed to him by a young, anonymous, and mysterious yogi who appeared in Karar ashram. During this period he attained six stages of *samadhi.* Finally in 1948, he was blessed to achieve the highest spiritual attainment, the state of *nirvikalpa samadhi* (breathless state with no pulse), and the *paramahamsa* stage.

During this period of spiritual practice and attainment of perfection, he not only engaged himself fully into meditation and God communion, but he also looked after the construction and beautification of the holy Karar ashram, including the Samadhi Temple of Shriyukteshwarji.

In the late 1940s, the divine master, the great incarnation Mahavatar Babaji, miraculously appeared first in his closed living room, then again in his personal meditation room on the premises of Karar Ashram. He blessed him twice and expressed his satisfaction with his spiritual practice and attainment. He also predicted that Brahmachari Ravinarayan would be his divine instrument, propagating Kriya Yoga in the East and West. In the 1960s he visited Ranikhet in the Himalayas and meditated in the holy cave where Babaji initiated Lahiri Mahasaya. While there, he and heard the divine voice of Babaji saying, "This time you cannot see me. Go and spread my work everywhere."

As a symbol of divine love and service, and in spite of his busy schedule, he kept many helpless orphan children in the ashram, who with his loving care and guidance, over the course of time, not only became well educated, but also well placed in society.

In 1951, Paramahamsa Yoganandaji requested and authorized him to initiate sincere seekers into Kriya Yoga. Immediately, he started initiating and teaching the divine technique of Kriya Yoga to thousands of people, leading them on the spiritual path.

He made his life a symbol of the synthesis of *karma* (action), *jñana* (knowledge), *bhakti* (devotion), and, above all, an ideal symbol of the practice of Kriya Yoga. Most of the time he meditated through the night before his presiding deity Mother Kali, a form of the formless divine mother. On September 27, 1957, the divine mother appeared before him with Her divine effulgence, graced him with blessings, and directed him to spread his divine mission for the spiritual upliftment of the world.

In the Indian tradition, a *brahmachari* ultimately becomes a swami, a monk. With some rites and rituals, the Shankaracharya of Puri Gobardhan Pitha, Jagadguru, Shrimat Swami Bharati Krishna Tirthaji Maharaj, initiated him into the life of *sannyas*, or complete renunciation. White-clad Brahmachari Ravinarayan became saffron-clothed

Swami Hariharananda Giri. Hariharananda means the divine bliss coming from the absolute formless God. It happened incidentally on his birthday: May 27, 1959.

During his long residence in Puri, he was loved by almost all monks living there. Many came to him for discussion or explanation of scripture or for clarification of their doubts.

He was blessed by many God-intoxicated divine masters like Anandamayi Ma and Nanga Baba Digambara Paramahamsa, a naked and realized master living at one end of Puri near Lokanath temple.

Soon he dedicated most of his time to teaching and preaching Kriya Yoga. People of all castes, creeds, and social strata gathered around him to hear his sweet, divine interpretation of the scriptures, in new metaphorical terms. He started touring through India and widening the Kriya Yoga network throughout the country.

In the early 1970s, the Conference of Religions of the World took place under the auspices of the Divine Life Society, a leading spiritual organization, at Cuttack Barabati Stadium. The venue was packed with thousands of people from different parts of the world—a very spiritual audience. There Swamiji delivered two talks in English: "The Essence of All Religions" and "The Message of Spiritual Life." All the monks and renowned intellectuals were amazed with his brilliant, convincing, and influential talk. After that, many spiritual organizations invited him to their ashrams and conferences to bless and grace the devotees with his divine utterances.

The smell of the flower cannot be hidden. Hundreds of people from all over the world started gathering in Shriyukteshwarji's Puri Ashram, accepting Swamiji as their divine guide, the master. His message spread to the Western world by word of mouth through those who came to receive his touch. Many sincerely requested that Swamiji travel to the West to help make the extroverted and restless minds of Western people introverted and tranquil, helping them to spiritually advance by perceiving the inner calm through breath control.

Ultimately, in 1974, he had no choice but to accept these requests and invitations to come to the West, to carry out the divine will of Babaji, Lahiri Mahasaya, and Shriyukteshwar—to give people a taste of original Kriya practice. He went first to Switzerland, then later to Germany, France, Holland, Belgium, England, and many other

European countries. In 1975, Swami Hariharananda traveled to the U.S., Canada, South America, and many other countries. Thousands of people in the West were transformed by his holy touch. After receiving his divine touch, students can perceive the triple divine perception, seeing divine light, hearing divine sound, and feeling a divine sensation in the whole body. Ever since, he has toured the world, carrying out the divine work.

Swamiji is well versed in the Vedas, the Upanishads, the Bhagavad Gita, the Brahmasutras, Smritishastras, Karmakanda, other holy Indian scriptures, and he has a thorough knowledge of the Torah, the Holy Bible, the Koran, the Buddhist scriptures, and the ethical and metaphysical teachings of all the religions of the world. A master of different systems of yoga, Swami Hariharanandaji is a unique spiritual preceptor, who through his simple lifestyle and love teaches the scientific technique of Kriya Yoga in theory and practice.

Saffron-clad, blessed with a body of unique divine aura, with a red vermilion mark on his forehead like a rising sun, with a beard and long hair, his divine physical appearance attracts the mind to the divine state. At this publication he is 93 years young. In spite of the pressures of age, he marches forward, with God in himself, spending every moment and every breath for the betterment and spiritual upliftment of mankind.

A master of many languages, Swamiji touches the heart of his disciples with his sweet divine voice, like that of a singing bird. His simple smile is enough to perceive divine bliss. He is a child to the children, young to the youth, and old to the adults. He is so loving, caring, and affectionate, that everyone who comes into his divine company remembers the sweet memory. He is not dry or silent like a stone statute as some other monks are; rather, he is an incarnation of love, compassion, and service. His life is an ideal life of sacrifice and God consciousness. He is teaching at every moment in time, and in many different ways, how to progress along the spiritual path.

The author of many books in India and in Western languages, Swamiji also spends some time writing and sending his message to different parts of the world. His books contain scientific, yogic, and metaphorical interpretations, and have been translated into many languages. Due to his proficiency in many languages, his teachings are widely accessible to even an illiterate person. Sincere seekers around the world gather and flock around him to realize their own Self.

Paramahamsaji's commentary on the Bhagavad Gita is based on the divine wisdom revealed to him during deep meditation. He has also benefited from studying the teachings of Lahiri Mahasaya and Shriyukteshwarji regarding the Bhagavad Gita, as well as by studying the Suradhuni Gita, the Jagadisa Gita, the Arya Mission Gita, and the Pranava Gita.

Paramahamsaji's purpose is to present the metaphorical meaning of the Bhagavad Gita in this translation and commentary. Attention is paid to those aspects of the Bhagavad Gita that are most helpful for practical meditation and for spiritual awareness in daily life. The psychological aspects of spiritual growth are discussed along with specific spiritual practices. This work is offered to people of both the East and West. Following the teachings of the Bhagavad Gita, as revealed here, can lead each person to the truth.

Paramahamsa Hariharanandaji, lovingly addressed as Baba, the divine father, the unique world teacher, free from religious dogma and sectarian belief, is a godlike personality. He may be described as having the heart of Jesus, the head of Shankara, the love of Shri Chaitanya, and the compassion of Buddha. Come to him and realize his spiritual stature and love. Sit face to face with this God-intoxicated and God-realized master, listen to his lilting and sweet voice declare the key of the authentic Kriya Yoga in a nutshell:

Breath control is self-control.
Breath mastery is self-mastery.
The breathless state is the deathless state.

About the Editor

Swami Prajñanananda Giri

Born in 1960 in Cuttack, district of Orissa, India, Triloki Dash was a sincere seeker of truth since childhood. After completing his postgraduate degree in economics, he left for the Himalayas and met many saints and visited many ashrams. But his spiritual hunger remained unsatiated. Returning to Orissa, he became a professor of economics who not only taught his subject, but also guided and inspired his students spiritually.

While he was a student, he met his master, Paramahamsa Hariharanandaji, at the Karar Ashram in Puri and learned the marvelous technique of Kriya Yoga under his guidance. The divine master guided, shaped, and transformed his life so he became a sincere follower of the Kriya Yoga path.

An accomplished orator, philosopher, scholar of scriptures, author, and editor of many books, proficient in many languages, highly advanced in Kriya Yoga practice, and a truly young reflection of his master, Swami Prajñanananda is currently teaching and propagating the authentic and original Kriya Yoga in the East and West. His brainpower is remarkable, and he is deeply versed in all of the world's scriptures—Vedas, Upanishads, Patañjali Sutras, Brahmasutras, Bible, Koran, and so forth. He is Paramahamsa Hariharananda's designated spiritual successor.

About Kriya Yoga

Kriya Yoga is a direct gift from God. The modern revival of Kriya Yoga began in 1861 with Mahavatar Babaji and has been handed down to this day from master to disciple.

Most of us live with a conception of God as almighty, omnipotent, and omnipresent, but few are searching for God within ourselves. Moreover, we do not feel the living presence of God within us during our daily chores and duties. Kriya Yoga can make us feel the living presence of God through breath control and meditation. All work, *kri,* is done by *ya*, the indwelling soul.

This mission has brought ancient secret teachings within the reach of householders and families who are searching for eternal peace and happiness, and who are hungry to know God. It provides information about initiation into the original Kriya techniques and explains how this meditation can enhance one's religious and spiritual practice.

Other Books on Kriya Yoga

Kriya Yoga: The Scientific Process of Soul Culture and Essence of All Religions, 5th revised edition, by Paramahamsa Hariharananda.

Isha Upanishad: The Ever New Metaphorical Interpretation for Soul Culture, by Paramahamsa Hariharananda.

Bhagavad Gita in the Light of Kriya Yoga—Three Volumes, by Paramahamsa Hariharananda.

The Bible, The Torah and Kriya Yoga: Metaphorical Explanation of the Torah and the New Testament in the Light of Kriya Yoga, by Swami Prajñanananda Giri in consultation with Paramahamsa Hariharananda.

Words of Wisdom: Stories and Parables of Paramahamsa Hariharananda, compiled by Swami Prajñanananda Giri.

Nectar Drops: Sayings of Paramahamsa Hariharananda, compiled by Swami Prajñanananda Giri.

Babaji: The Eternal Light of God, by Swami Prajñanananda Giri.

Lahiri Mahasaya: Fountainhead of Kriya Yoga, by Paramahamsa Prajñanananda.

Swami Shriyukteshwar Giri: Incarnation of Wisdom, by Paramahamsa Prajñanananda.

Paramahamsa Hariharananda: River of Compassion, by Paramahamsa Prajñanananda.

Yoga: Pathway to the Divine—Two Volumes, by Paramahamsa Prajñanananda.

Discourses on the Bhagavad Gita—Two Volumes, by Paramahamsa Prajñanananda.

To be Released at a Later Date:

Jñana Shankalini Tantra in the Light of Kriya Yoga (working title), by Paramahamsa Prajñanananda.

The Yoga Sutras of Patañjali in the Light of Kriya Yoga (working title), by Paramahamsa Prajñanananda.

Kriya Yoga Contacts

Web Site: http://www.kriya.org

For more information please contact the following centers:

U.S.A.

Kriya Yoga Institute
P.O. Box 924615
Homestead, FL 33092-4615
Tel: +1 305-247-1960
Fax: +1 305-248-1951
Email: institute@kriya.org

India

Kriya Yoga Ashram
Nimpur, P.O. Jagatpur
Cuttack 754021, Orissa
Tel/Fax: +91 671-682724
Email: ssgiri@cal3.vsnl.net.in

Europe

Kriya Yoga Centrum
Heezerweg 7
PP Sterksel 6029, The Netherlands
Tel: +31 40-2265576
Fax: +31 40-2265612
Email: kriya.yoga@worldonline.nl

Kriya Yoga Zentrum
Pottendorferstrasse 69
2523 Tattendorf Austria
Tel: +43 2253-81491
Fax: +43 2253-80462
Email: kriya.yoga.centre@aon.at